The Star

Sheffield Folk

there's nowt like 'em

Author
Bob Horton

Published
youbooks.co.uk

Printed by
Pickards.org.uk

ISBN 9781905278275

Printed in 2009 by Pickards.org.uk

Published by youbooks.com

11 Riverside Park, Sheaf Gardens, Sheffield S2 4BB

Telephone 0114 275 7222

www.youbooks.com

Printed by

Pickards.org.uk

Contents

Acknowledgements

Research for this book has taken about three years to complete and has involved me finding and speaking to many people who in some way are, or have been, associated with the characters about whom I have written. Such people include relatives of the characters, members of the public who knew them, directors and other management of some of the companies referred to in the stories, and teachers and administrators in two schools.

In addition, I have used the facilities of the Central Library on many occasions where many fruitful hours have been spent either reading through old newspapers held on microfilm or searching through dozens of reference books.

To all the people involved in the above I give my sincere thanks for their kindness, patience and help, without which I could not have undertaken my project.

Although it is not possible to identify by name all those who have helped me, I would like to mention the following who have willingly given me much of their time and effort with a smile. These include JULIE MASON from Cadbury Trebor Bassett, ROGER and CHRIS PITCHFORK from Maxons Ltd, MAUREEN and PETER GRANT regarding the Warsop story, Constance Grant's daughter JUDITH SILVESTOR, RICHARD and NORMA for lending me their shop for a day or two, Don Brookes' wife DORA and son MICHAEL for agreeing that I write about Don, ninety two year old RON COWEN for telling me his life story, LES and DOLLY WATTAM for their help regarding the Pond Street Nora story, and DAVID MOWATT for his help on the same subject. A very kind, elderly couple, whose names and contact number I have sadly misplaced, gave me considerable help with the Thomas Ward story. I am very grateful for their contribution and I must apologize for being unable to put their names in print

I would also like to mention that although most of the photographs which appear throughout each story have been taken by myself, there are quite a few old images which I have reproduced with the kind permission of The Star newspaper to whom I am most grateful. There are also a few images I have reproduced from very old publications which are out of copyright and a few anonymously produced images which I found in charity shops. I trust that none of these have slipped through the net where permission is required.

Finally,I would also like to thank IAN NETTLETON for his support and editing advice, EDNA JESSOP for her support and proof reading, KEITH STUBLEY for his support and advice and PHILIPPA NETTLETON for her excellent typing which she carried out with cheerful dedication. Last but not least, I would like to thank my very dear wife for her patience and support, without which I would not have succeeded.

If I have inadvertently missed any one out, I trust that you will forgive me.

Introduction

This book on Sheffield folk follows on from my first book entitled 'Living in Sheffield-1000 Years of Change' which describes the birth of the city and its exciting years of change to the year 2000.

I have chosen to write this book, my second, around the times and lives of twenty or so Sheffield characters who represent a cross section of those who live or have lived in our city in order that the intriguing history of their very diverse lives can live on in the minds of this and future generations for ever. The final Section departs slightly from the individual character format and encompasses the lives of young schoolchildren living in Victorian times. Some interesting comparisons with today's schoolchildren are also made.

The stories of our subjects' lives are set in the time-scale in which they lived and are brought to life by photographs, maps and detailed descriptions of the areas in which they worked and lived.

The information upon which the stories are based has been obtained from detailed research and person to person verbal accounts. As far as I am aware it is all factually correct, although experience tells me that some facts and figures may occasionally get accidentally changed as time passes by and memories become a little fuzzy. I trust you will bear with me if this has occurred anywhere in the text.

Where I have expressed my views on any subject in this book, which I have done on quite a few occasions, I would like to point out that they do not necessarily represent the views of the publisher.

Finally, I hope that you enjoy reading the stories that follow. You may perhaps be able to relate your own lives to some of the characters who appear in them. Who knows?

1 *Shop Folk*

Have you ever thought what it would be like to run a small, general-provisions shop which sells everything from sweets to sausages, teacakes to toilet rolls, and tobacco to toys, as well as being the local news-agent? Wouldn't it, in fact, be a relaxing, yet fairly exciting, adventure for someone approaching retirement age who enjoyed the challenge of change? Such a challenge had been offered to a local photographer-cum-writer by the name of Bob who was in his early sixties. R & N News, on the western side of the city, was the name of the shop in question.

It was on a bright summer's morning that the willing, but naively optimistic, sixty-odd-year-old had been asked to report for duty.

"Morning folks," Bob chimed as he breezed into the shop's compact but well laid out interior which was as bright and cheerful as he was. "I hope I'm not late."

Richard and Norma, the hard-working owners of this typically popular, sell-what-you-can establishment which struggled to compete with local supermarkets, had known Bob as a customer for several years. It had been during one of his shopping visits that he had offered to run the shop for them for a day while they and their young son had a well deserved break.

"Good morning, Bob, it's nice to see you," responded Norma. "Are you sure you can manage while we're away?"

Norma's kindly face was gently creased with etchings of concern as her big, brown eyes peered out questioningly from under a shock of dark, curly hair.

"He'll be alright. Don't worry yourself lass," boomed Richard, puffing out his barrel-like chest whilst fondly stroking the slightly thinning hair on his head. "If he makes a mess of it, I'll dock him half his wages."

Bob's rueful smile and slight hitch of his shoulders was enough to tell Norma that it was pointless her trying to say anything further.

"Look, you two", interjected the new caretaker, shopkeeper, "just go and collect Jaimie and take him to the coast for the day. You've not had a break for the last few years, and a ten year old lad needs the chance to bury his dad in the sand and throw sea-water over his mum once in a while."

Ten minutes and what seemed like five hundred instructions later, Bob found himself alone in the shop at last. It was only 7.30am and he let his early morning gaze wander round the bewildering shelves of multi-coloured tins, toys, boxes, bottles, sweets, cards, magazines and papers which seemed to be taunting him.

"He doesn't know what I cost," they all seemed to whisper. "He hasn't got a clue…he'll never sell me…just wait until he gets a long queue…I bet he can't even use the till properly."

"STOP!"

The sound of his own voice caused the bewildered, new entrepreneur to spin round in shock, only to be confronted by a wall full of white packets clothed in stripes of blue, green, red and gold which all screamed out messages of doom.

"SMOKING KILLS . . . CIGARETTES CAN KILL YOU . . . HARMFUL TO HEALTH . . . "

"Bloody 'ell. I feel more like an executioner than a shop-keeper," Bob muttered to himself as he gazed in

amazement at the seemingly endless varieties of the deadly weed which came 'with-tips', 'without-tips', 'normal size', 'king size', 'roll-your-own', and anything else you might want to include in a modern, tobacco suicide-kit.

"MORNING."

Bob hadn't heard the smartly dressed gentleman in his 50's enter the shop and choose several magazines from the top shelf of the adjacent display.

"I'll take these please. How much are they?"

A quick glance at the glossy covers lying innocently on the counter in front of him convinced Bob that today was going to be more of a challenge than he had bargained for. Trying to find the prices of the magazines, which had been printed in the smallest type and cleverly hidden amongst an array of bare bottoms and boobs, was like trying to find a needle in a haystack. The degree of difficulty was also compounded by the sudden influx of young delivery boys and girls who were impatiently waiting to be given bags, newspapers and details of their morning paper-rounds.

"Come on, mister, Richard doesn't keep us waiting," piped up a spiky haired youth.

"Me mum says I've not got to be late this morning," squeaked a bossy looking young girl thrusting her pale, almost white, face onto the counter to see what the hold-up was.

"Are you going to tell me how much these are or not?" retorted the smartly dressed 'early bird', now clearly rattled.

"Ooh, I say mister, are these all yours?"

As if by magic, a chorus of further comments deluged the gentleman's ears.

"Just look at them, they're abnormal…can I have a look mister?...they're disgusting they are…me mam says only perverts look at them…why do you want so many, mister?"

It was only quarter to eight, yet Bob felt as though he'd landed in the middle of a battlefield and had been fighting for at least two hours. He decided that it was about time he took control.

"Right you lot," he exclaimed with new-found enthusiasm, "I'll be with you in a minute. Excuse me sir, can you please point out the prices of these publications so I can serve you. Thank you."

Now, with the authority of an army general, Bob put the magazines into a well used Tesco bag and ushered the embarrassed customer out of the shop whilst wondering where to put the £15 that had been hastily thrust into his hand as correct payment. He was not yet ready to face the till, which appeared to be built to the same design and specification as the one owned by the well-known Mr. Arkwright of 'Open All Hours' fame, so he delayed this important aspect of his job until things calmed down a little.

By 8 o'clock, largely due to the efforts and knowledge of the young, impatient workers, the newspaper deliveries were all underway and, to a novice shop keeper, that was very good progress.

Now you might think that such a devastating start could only herald in a calmer, more dignified period of customer relations. After all, serving in a shop is not that difficult, is it? Let us see.

Bob glanced up from looking at the long price list he was trying to memorize as the shop door slowly creaked open. A frail, elderly lady, who was probably 80 but looked about 130, hobbled with difficulty towards him, leaning very dependently on her old, gnarled walking stick.

"You'll have to do something about them steps," she gasped. "It's taken me five minutes or more to get into your shop this morning. And another thing, I'll not have them young savages covered in bags full of newspapers trying to knock me down the steps when I'm only half way up. And that's not all…who are you? What are you doing here? Where's Richard and Norma? I don't like strangers, and..."

"Excuse me madam," interjected Bob as politely as he could, "I've just taken over for the day whilst…"

"TAKEN OVER? You mean you've bought the shop? Oh, I don't like that at all."

"No, no, it's only for the day while they take their young son to the sea-side."

"Well, they didn't tell me about it, but I can't stand here chatting all day. I'll just take my usual."

"Actually, I'm not sure what your usual is Madam."

"Well, that's a fine start, isn't it? I come in here every morning for my usual and you've gone and forgotten what it is. I'll have to speak to Richard when he gets back. He'll soon sort you out."

Bob let out a gentle sigh as he tried to keep calm and patient.

"Perhaps you could tell me what it is, and I'll get it for you madam."

"Richard doesn't keep on calling me madam either. He calls me by my proper name. I'm Mrs. Wright, and proud of it."

"Well it's lovely to meet you, Mrs. Wright, but I still don't know what your usual is."

"It's the Sun newspaper, lad," bellowed the elderly and obviously impatient customer who had shuffled in halfway through the conversation. He seemed about as agile as Mrs. Wright, and just about as tolerant.

"It's more like a geriatric ward in here," Bob whispered to himself, recalling that the shop was located directly opposite a large complex of elderly persons' flats.

"There we are, Mrs. Wright. Your Sun newspaper. That will be thirty pence please."

"I'm not paying twice, if that's what you think! Richard lets me pay at the end of the week like other sensible folk."

"Of course, of course. I'm sorry about that. I forgot," grovelled our harassed hero. "Have a good day Mrs. Wright …. and mind the steps."

As the elderly, but rather intimidating, lady made her way slowly to the exit, the relieved temporary shopkeeper closed his eyes for a moment and reassured himself that things could only get better from now on.

"Oi! Are you going to serve me or not?"

This retort was from the elderly gentleman who'd 'kindly' helped Mrs. Wright to obtain her newspaper as he still hadn't been served, and he continued to grumble until he was firmly grasping the two packets of strong mints he'd come in for.

Bob, however, was now convinced that he was probably just having a typical day in the shop after all, and that little was likely to change. Take the till, for example. Unlike modern machines, which calculate how much change a customer should receive after keying in the prices and the amount tendered, this one almost demanded university-level mental arithmetic from the person using it. It also required the pre-entry of different coded keys for food, tobacco, cards, stationery and 'Uncle Tom Cobley and all' before the cash drawer would open.

"It's a wonder I don't have to enter my shoe size and what I had for breakfast on this chuffin' machine," he chuntered to himself as he tried in vain to gently close the cash drawer after serving a rather fussy young mother who'd just popped in and bought a loaf of bread, two toilet rolls, three lots of sweets and a green ice-lollipop for 'dearie', her mithering little daughter who was doing her best to destroy the transparent cover on the fridge.

"Are you sure that's the right change you've given me," she retorted rather sharply. "I gave you a £10 note you know."

Bob was tempted to say that he wasn't sure of anything this morning as 'dearie' suddenly found out that the fridge cover would slide open with a loud crash if you tried hard enough.

"I'm very sorry madam. I must have been distracted for some reason. Here's the other £5 I owe you."

With a final flourish, Bob managed to close the drawer out of which he taken the customer's missing five pounds, realising as he did so that the till appeared to move forward a little due to the firm push which was required for this operation each time. Little did he know that the consequences of this fractional movement would be dramatically apparent later on in the day.

Fortunately, things did begin to improve a little, and after an hour or two, Bob was feeling proud of himself as he got the hang of selling most things with reasonable confidence and accuracy. However, the huge variety and cost of cigarettes and other tobacco products still presented quite a challenge. This was evidenced when old Mr. Jones came in later in the morning.

"Morning Sir," chirped our much happier shopkeeper. "What can I get you?"

With much gasping and heavy breathing, which led Bob to wonder whether or not Mr. Jones would actually live long enough to say what he wanted, he blurted out, "Twenty Forres."

"Forres?" murmured Bob as he turned to study the jam-packed wall of cigarettes behind him. "I don't remember seeing those on the shelves."

After several minutes of fruitless searching, Mr. Jones began to chunter impatiently, pausing only to choke and stop breathing for frighteningly long periods.

"Perhaps you could point them out sir? Just show me where they are on the shelf."

A long, bony finger waving about like a twig in a force 10 gale tested Bob's powers of observation to the limit as he tried to focus his eyes in the direction that the elderly gentlemen was trying to point.

"Ah! The bottom shelf?"

"Ney, ney, ney. Twenty Forres."

To say that Mr. Jones' command of the English language left something to be desired was the understatement of the year, and Bob felt that the possession of psychic powers topped-up with a degree in psychology wouldn't go amiss in this job also.

The long bony finger, which even the mythical film alien ET would have been proud of, was now getting more active and was banging on the counter top with obvious agitation. Its owner's face was becoming rather flushed, and Bob wondered whether he should continue pursuing the gentleman's request or dial 999 for an ambulance.

"Under...counter."

This supreme effort of communication by Mr. Jones to indicate where the 'twenty Forres' were located was a revelation, and the surprised but relieved would-be shopkeeper quickly bent down to survey the contents of the shelves under the counter. Two, large, well-thumbed books stared out from the semi-darkness, one entitled A-J and the other K-Z. A few seconds later, A-J was resting on the counter to the obvious delight and relief of Mr. Jones, whose life-threatening breathing difficulties calmed down to a more respectable rasping, bronchial-pneumonia type of sound, which encouraged Bob to believe that the poor man might at least eventually make it out of the shop in due course.

"Ah! Twenty Forres," the old gentleman spluttered with delight.

Wiping away the remnants of the shower which had attacked both his face and the counter top during Mr. Jones' excited outburst, the remarkably patient Richard and Norma stand-in carefully turned the pages of the large, intriguing book. As the truth suddenly dawned on him, he turned to page F and, thumbing down the neatly written entries which he saw in front of him, he found one which said it all:

20 FORRES ROAD: Mr. Jones: Amount due for papers £7.90.

It was now Bob's turn to breathe rather heavily as he turned to the long-suffering customer with an apology.

"I'm really very sorry, Mr. Jones. I thought it was cigarettes you were after. Never mind, we got there in the end didn't we? That will be £7.90 please."

Not surprisingly, there was little conversation between the two of them as payment was duly made, and as Mr. Jones eventually made his way to the shop exit amidst a crescendo of racking coughs, there was little Bob could say other than:

"Bye, Mr. Jones. I hope we'll see you again."

By now, it was rapidly approaching midday and, in-between trying to serve customers and charge them the correct prices (which was nigh on impossible when queues built up), the shell-shocked shopkeeper had, from time to time, managed to gulp down a few quick sips of coffee from the flask he kept on the shelf behind him.

"I'm bursting," he muttered to himself. "I'll have to shut up the shop for a few minutes while I go to the loo."

However, as if by magic, the shop suddenly became the busiest it had been all morning, and all thoughts of popping out for a 'quickie' had to be postponed.

"Allo, allo! Are you new here?"

A gleaming set of ultra-white teeth suddenly appeared round the little shop door, closely followed by a large and rather intimidating face from which two gleaming eyes sent darts of expectancy flashing round the shop. By the time the whole body had appeared, which was quite considerable in size, it was obvious that Mr. Fullofhimself meant business as he began to speak.

"I can see you've sold out. I'm not surprised because mine are definitely the best in the trade. I'll leave you a good selection made fresh this morning."

As yet, the stunned shop minder had been unable to do anything but chase disturbing thoughts around his mind.

"Who the bloody 'ell is he? Oops. I must stop swearing every time a crisis arises. He's not on Richard's list, I'm sure of that. I don't even know what he's got in that strange bag he's carrying. I hope he's not a nutcase…"

The penetratingly loud voice suddenly continued and interrupted his thoughts.

"I've got BLT, chicken with, chicken without, cheese and chutney, cheese and pickle, ham with, ham without and some SCRUMPTIOUS cream cakes for afters."

"Good grief. He's a chuffin' sandwich- man," Bob muttered to himself. "I thought he was at least the Prime Minister's personal secretary."

"I'll leave you six of each and four bottles of orange," continued the larger than life salesman. "Just sign here."

As if on automatic pilot, Bob signed the itemized receipt and bade a mumbled farewell to the gleaming teeth which took their owner out of the shop as rapidly as they had come in.

"So. I'm managing a take-away as well now, am I?" sighed Bob in bewilderment as he turned once again to fix a 'back in 2 minutes' notice to the glass face of the shop door.

"Just a minute luv. You're not shutting are you?"

The frail, white-haired figure on the doorstep carrying her bulging Woolworths plastic bag just couldn't be resisted.

"Of course not madam. Come in. What can I get you?"

"I've brought me 'usband's trousers, luv. I've got his grey pair, his working pair and his Sunday-best. Do you know, luv, he's had these grey ones for about forty seven years and they're still going strong. In fact, luv, you'll never guess, but he even got married in them. Just look at the quality of these."

'Luv' carefully felt the thin, frayed fabric of the crumpled, baggy, wide-bottomed flannels and wondered what on earth a pile of old trousers was doing on the sweet counter.

"They're very nice madam, but…"

"Oh, you can call me Vera, luv. Everybody else does. When will they be ready?"

A fresh set of jumbled thoughts attacked the weary mind standing behind the counter.

"Ready? What the 'eck do I do with these? Surely I'm not looking after a blinkin' laundry as well. Perhaps I'm dreaming?..."

"Are you alright, luv? You're looking a bit pale. Why don't you sit down a bit? I've not seen you in here before have I luv? Can't you find the dry-cleaning tickets? They're in that top drawer over there. When did you say they'd be ready?"

If Bob's mind hadn't been scrambled before, it certainly was by now.

"Oh, I'm not sure madam, I mean Vera. I didn't know Norma took in dry cleaning, but I'll have a look in that drawer and see what I can find."

Luck was on his side in this instance, as not only were the dry-cleaning tickets in there, a list of collection and return dates, together with costs, was also to hand.

"Next Wednesday, Vera. You can collect them next Wednesday and pay for them when you come in."

"Thank you, luv. That wasn't too difficult was it? You'll soon get the 'ang of it with a bit more practice. I'll see you again luv."

As fragile little Vera left the shop, she met another customer coming in, and couldn't help giving her views on the service she'd received.

"He's a luvly lad, that new one behind the counter. He's ever so 'elpful he is. Very polite. You don't get many like him these days you know. You mustn't keep him long 'cos I think he wants his lunch. 'Bye luv."

Whilst Vera Talkalot's comments were very kind, Bob couldn't help but think that shopkeeping wasn't quite the job for him as it became more complex and stressful. Even finding time for a comfort break or a spot of lunch was nigh on impossible. The next customer, who had met Vera going out, was no better.

"I've not got long lad 'cos me lunch is nearly ready. The missus is gettin' me some fish'n'chips in and I can't be late or she'll 'av me."

Looking at the unshaven, tousled-haired, elderly man in front of him, Bob thought that his missus was welcome to him.

"Listen lad. I want today's lucky number, a check on whether I've won 'owt on yesterday's number, and one of them there lottery ticket things for Wednesday and Saturday."

As Bob stood there in amazement at this latest request, he found himself having more and more uncharacteristic, unfriendly thoughts:

'I feel more like strangling him than serving him. Why can't he just buy a newspaper or a tin of beans like normal people? No, he wants to complicate my life by asking for things I haven't got a clue about. It must be a disease that affects everyone around here.'

However, not wishing to be defeated, the figure of frustrated, but calm, politeness standing behind the counter responded accordingly.

"Did you say lucky number, sir? What might that be?"

"Don't be daft lad. I get one every day. You just press them buttons on that there machine, and out pops a ticket. Norma knows 'ow to do it, and she's only a young lass."

Bob had acknowledged that taking on this job meant accepting that the customer was always right and that he may have to bite his tongue a little. What he hadn't realised was that he would almost have to chew his tongue off to be polite. In addition, no-one had mentioned to him that the average age of the shop's customers would be about 91, and that half of them would be either at death's door or totally incoherent. Of the rest, a significant proportion of them thought that being cantankerous was the norm and that patience was a dirty word. Strangely enough, Bob knew a lot of people in the area where the shop was located, all of whom were kind, polite and friendly. It was just his luck that very few of them frequented this shop on the day that he chose to temporarily take it over.

"It looks complicated to me, sir, but let's give it a try."

Five minutes later, after entering all the information that the machine asked for, it had chewed-up Tousled Head's lucky-number ticket for today, refused to print one for tomorrow, and swallowed up the payment inserted. Further attempts had simply resulted in 'helpful' print-outs stating FAULTY ENTRY – TRY AGAIN. Needless to say, Tousled Head was not impressed.

"What the 'ell 'av you done there, lad? Tha's made a reight mess o' things. I've lost me money and I 'avn't won nowt. Me missus'l be goin' mad and me fish'n chips'l be goin' cold."

"I'm very sorry sir. I can't imagine what happened. Here, take this refund from the till, and Norma will sort you out tomorrow when she gets back."

With that, now totally stressed-out and cross-legged, Bob ushered the irate customer out and briefly shut up shop.

The pleasure of having a few minutes to himself without the pressure of know-it-all customers giving him constant hassle was almost beyond belief. A brief stroll round the back kitchen also revealed that Norma had prepared him a small buffet-lunch which he gratefully ate whilst sitting on an old, but comfortable settee next to the fridge. Perhaps looking after a shop wasn't so bad after all?

'Back in 2 minutes', said the sign hung on the shop door, but it really should have said 10 minutes, as by the time Bob returned from his short break, a small queue of fairly irate customers had formed outside.

"I've been waiting nearly half-an-hour," retorted Mrs. Bright-Red-Lipstick as she bustled in swinging her posh Marks and Spencer food bag. Behind her, Mr. Struggle managed three steps forward and two steps back, and was soon overtaken by a couple of local shop workers who had heard about Mr. Gleamy-Teeth's wonderful sandwiches and buns.

However, our Bob was now refreshed and had decided to adopt a new 'take it as it comes' approach, which proved fairly successful when serving the two red lips which were poised menacingly in front of him.

"I've ordered a Mirror, young man, and I've called to collect it."

"Certainly madam. Is it a small one or a large one?"

"Look here, young man, I've just ordered a normal size one."

"Actually madam, I don't recall seeing one on the shelf. Does it have a coloured frame? Silver? Gold, maybe?"

"What are you talking about? Richard saves me one every day and puts it on that pile behind you."

Turning round, Bob stared down at the pile of reserved newspapers which sat mockingly on the bottom shelf of the display rack. The large distinct lettering of the Daily Mirror seemed to be screaming at him as his flushed face did its best to match its bright red colour.

"I'm very sorry madam. I thought you meant…never mind, I'll just get you one of these."

This experience was fairly typical of that which persisted throughout the day, although 'young man' was now taking things more in his stride. In fact, he almost enjoyed the humorous incident which occurred when Mr. Leaning-Tower-of-Pisa entered the shop. At about 6'-5" tall, with a generous lean forwards and sideways and with the build of a stick insect, an air of expectancy awaited his arrival at the counter.

"Pie pipers."

The high pitched, squeaky voice which emanated from the lofty, albeit leaning, figure was quite a surprise.

"Beg your pardon, sir."

"Eh?"

"I couldn't quite catch what you said, sir."

"Eh? You'll have to speak up, I'm a bit deaf."

"I COULDN'T QUITE HEAR WHAT YOU SAID SIR."

"Pie pipers!"

The fact that Mr. Leaning-Tower-of-Pisa's voice was almost a true replica of a Willow Warbler's mating call, only succeeded in adding to Bob's confusion.

"I wonder if he wants some of those 'roll it yourself' papers for making his own cigarettes," he mused. "Surely he doesn't expect me to have a book on the Pied Piper, does he?"

Suddenly, help was on hand. A kindly customer standing behind the tall, leaning gentlemen offered his advice in a somewhat less-than delicate manner.

"'E wants to pay his chuffin' papers!"

The vigorous nodding of a lofty head, which threatened to fall off at any moment, followed by another extra squeaky, "Pie pipers," convinced the genuinely stunned not- very-with-it shopkeeper that he had failed to interpret a simple, local request once again. It was particularly concerning on this occasion as the request was rather similar to the earlier 'twenty Forres' which he had misunderstood. We can only presume that he had thought that lightening couldn't possibly strike twice.

"I do apologise, sir. It's not been one of my best days today."

It was obvious that things would not change in this paper-cum sweets–cum groceries–cum hardware–cum toy –cum laundry–cum sandwich shop, no matter how long Bob served there. He would just have to ride it out and hope that Richard, Norma and their young son Jaimie had encountered driving rain at the sea-side which would force them to return early. No such luck! It was not until just after 6 o'clock and several incidents later that the sun-tanned trio made their entrance through the shop doorway.

"How's it gone then?"

Richard's cheerful, booming voice irritated Bob's now ultra-sensitive ears.

"I knew you'd find it a doddle. I said so to you, didn't I Norma?"

Norma nodded, knowing that Bob's hollow-eyed, expressionless face said otherwise.

"I tell you what," she said quietly, "you just pop into the back and have a nice cuppa-tea and I'll serve the rest of the customers."

It was a grateful, totally exhausted, not-very-successful shopkeeper who shuffled into the back room with Richard.

"Piece o' cake," Bob muttered with difficulty to himself. "No problem. Just you go anytime and I'll pop in and look after things for you."

"Hey," the irritating voice boomed out again. "You didn't eat the chocolate cake that Norma left for you. Didn't you like it? Here Jamie, you'd better eat it."

Bob didn't like to admit that he hadn't actually had time to eat it and was saving it for later.

"Oh, I was a bit full Richard. Good idea. Give it to Jamie. He must be hungry after that long drive from the coast."

Suddenly, an almighty crash followed by a shrill scream cut through the meaningless conversation like a sharp piece of ice. Both men looked at each other in alarm for a split second, then dashed into the shop to see what had happened. There, they were met by a colourful sea of mints, chewies, chocolates and winegums which had rolled with difficulty through a maze of Kit Kats, Mars Bars, Liquorice Allsorts, toffees and every other item of confectionery you could imagine.

"Chuffin' 'eck Norma. What have you done?" asked Richard in a less than delicate manner.

Poor Norma, looking shocked and shaken, had done nothing at all really. She had simply taken the last customer's payment and put it in the till as normal. However, this was the straw which broke the camel's back, as the till had been moving forward a fraction of an inch all day every time the drawer had been opened then closed. It just so happened that luck was on Bob's side for the first time that day, as that last fateful payment had been put in by Norma. The last minuscule movement had then dislodged the large confectionery display in front of it which had exploded with glee onto the shop floor.

"I can't believe it," Bob said quietly. "Just one customer more and it would have been my fault and, indeed, a fitting climax to my day. Perhaps someone's looking out for me after all."

At this point, Jaimie strolled in, having finished off 'his' chocolate cake.

"Wow. They look good. Can I have one of these, mam?

His calm, relaxed approach to the disaster was of benefit to everyone, and the whole episode concluded with laughter as they all helped to clear up the very attractive looking 'display' on the shop floor.

As Bob finally relaxed with a cup of tea half an hour later, he recounted just a few of the incidents that had taken place in order to put Richard and Norma in the picture. As he did so, he realised what a wealth of Sheffield characters he'd encountered that day, and what a truly valuable experience it had been. It made him realise just how down to earth Sheffield folk really are and, whether by design or accident, how hilariously funny they can be. It was an experience to savour and never be forgotten, and one which Bob is proud to share with this book's readers. He hopes you enjoyed it.

As for the sweet-counter catastrophe, the sight of all those multi-coloured delicacies on the shop floor made him wonder just who made the huge variety of sweets that gazed back at him. Perhaps many, if not most, were made in Sheffield by Sheffield folk? Perhaps there was an interesting history to unearth? Bob thought it was worth looking into. Let's see what he found out.

The Sweet Makers

2

Although the story of sweet-making in Sheffield involves a large number of manufacturers of varying size and type, I have chosen three companies who, between them, introduced to Sheffield, and the world, the majority of sweets with which Sheffield folk are familiar.

The characters behind these sweet-making establishments are different, yet interesting, in their own, individual ways. Furthermore, the companies which they spawned are equally interesting and, in fact, rather complex as they encompass several families en-route to the names we know them by today.

If I mention the names Bassett, Johnson, Warsop, Dixon, Macdonald, Butler and Pitchfork, there are probably only two or three of these which immediately spring to mind when you think of sweet-making. Nevertheless, in their own right, they all made a significant contribution to the sweet, sticky favourites which we and our parents have enjoyed over the years. Let us have a look at how it all happened, beginning with the Warsop family.

The Warsop Story

Just close your eyes and imagine the scene. You are standing in a small room about the size of a dining kitchen with its white-washed walls reflecting the searching rays of the early morning sun. The small front window, which had kindly opened its old wooden shutters to let in the welcome, yet impatient, warm orange light, was glancing down enviously at rows of shiny grey cobbles on the street outside as if to say "It's all right for you out there in the fresh air. It's like a blinkin' oven in here. I'm sweating cobs."

In the corner of the room, a stained, well-worn copper, not dissimilar to a small version of grandma's old, round wash-tub, was sitting proudly in a recessed hole carefully formed in the top of a purpose-built stone oven attached to the outer wall. Yellow and red flames from the hot coal fire below were licking hungrily around its base as the rising heat caused its contents to bubble and plop with delight as they gave off gentle clouds of 'to die for' aromas which drifted tantalizingly around the room.

The year is 1948, and you are standing in 38 year old Jack Warsop's small, sweet-making workshop in Rockingham Street, experiencing the wonders of his craft. In the room above, which is accessed by a flight of narrow wooden stairs, a cutler is patiently finishing-off knives which have been produced in one of Sheffield's rapidly dwindling number of forges down-town, where other self employed Little Mesters still operate.

This area of Rockingham Street could reasonably be classed as an interface between the old and the new as the city continued its almost breathless progress into automation and expansion. As we can see, Jack and his

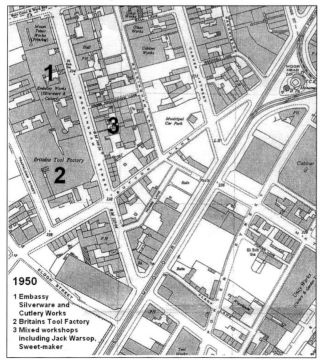

1950

1 Embassy Silverware and Cutlery Works
2 Britains Tool Factory
3 Mixed workshops including Jack Warsop, Sweet-maker

neighbours are part of the old Sheffield, and are still working on a very small scale using skills acquired and handed down over a century or more.

However, perhaps we'd better go back to the beginning and find out how the Warsop sweet-making story began.

THE FIRST MARK WARSOP

To give you a complete picture, we ought to pop back a further 130 years to 1818 when the first Mark Warsop was born. King George III was still on the throne, and stage-coaches were the normal mode of public transport. The canal between Sheffield and Tinsley was still being constructed by navvies and out of work cutlery workers using picks, shovels and wheelbarrows, and was due to open the following year.

Although Mark was born in the little village of Werrington, now a suburb of Peterborough, his father decided that he should be christened in Boston, which was a thirty- three mile stagecoach ride away. His mother, however, felt that going all that way was rather unnecessary and would be rather tiring for both herself and her tiny baby. She decided, therefore, to raise her concerns with her husband.

"You know, Mr. Warsop, I don't know why we have to travel all the way to Boston when there's a lovely little Abbey only seven miles up the road at Crowland we could go to. After all, it is only a christening."

"Only a christening, Mrs. Warsop? Only a christening! You know as well as I do that if our Mark isn't churched properly, he'll not be allowed in any of our friends' and neighbours' houses. No my dear, a tiny little Abbey is not my idea of being churched properly. Boston Parish Church was good enough for me and my father before me, so our Mark is going to follow suit."

There was little else that a humble wife could say in those days, when important decisions were nearly always taken by the men-folk. So, on the 4th October 1819, a jolting two and a half hour coach ride to Boston and a two and a half hour return ride to Werrington introduced the eleven month old Mark Warsop to travelling, a tendency which would influence future generations of this enterprising family.

Mark enjoyed his early life in and around the pleasant Lincolnshire countryside and married a local lass in his early twenties before moving to Spalding to run a small bakery shop. Whilst there, his wife gave birth to two sons, Mark Warell and Joseph William, who were destined to build on their father's determination and success, as we shall see shortly.

MARK AND JOSEPH –
THE YOUNG WARSOP BROTHERS

By the time the two brothers were seven and five respectively, their father Mark had moved south with his young family to the village of Crowland where, now as a 43 year old Master Baker, he ran a successful bakery and grocery shop in Church Street. Business flourished over the following years, and whilst young Mark chose to stay and eventually work for his father, Joseph moved up to the village of Barnetby le Wold in north Lincolnshire in his

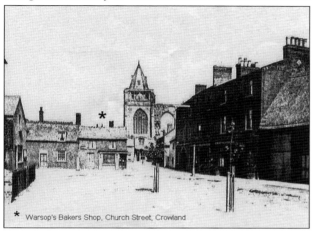

* Warsop's Bakers Shop, Church Street, Crowland

late teens to work in a small shop similar to his dad's. His more independent nature had prompted this move which, within two or three years, proved to be successful in another way. He met and fell in love with a pretty young lass from Market Rasen by the name of Mary Alice Hand, to whom he successfully offered his own hand in marriage at the age of 22.

This marriage seemed to be the catalyst which further spurred Joseph on.

"You know what Mary," he said one day, "I know we both like it up here, but now that we're married, I'd like to get a better job, particularly as we both want children. I've a mind to ask my father if I can join brother Mark in his business."

"Well, it's all right with me, Joseph, but you know how independent you are. Do you think it's wise?"

Joseph recognised and accepted Mary's concern, but decided, with his father's agreement, to give it a go.

Business was booming at the Warsop Grocery and Bakery Store, probably because it was the largest store of its kind in the busy little village of Crowland which sat on the main road from Peterborough to Spalding. Mark Senior, now 60 years old, was pleased to have his second son back, and for the next two years they all prospered. In particular, Joseph noticed how popular their confectionary items were with the local residents.

"I've been thinking, Mary."

"Oh, not again, Joseph. I'm eight months pregnant and you've had another thought? Well, I hope it doesn't affect me having our first baby."

"Of course not my dear. I've only been thinking of our future again. It's just that I've noticed that our best seller at the shop is sweets, many of which come from that big town up north called Sheffield."

"Sheffield, Joseph? I thought they were famous for knives, cutlery and silverware and stuff, not sweets."

"Well, that's true my little poppit, but a couple of firms up there have started making sweets, and they're doing very well. I reckon there's a big opportunity for the right man to set up business in such a thriving place. What do you think?"

Poor Mary knew, of course, that there was really no use arguing, although she did insist that she was able to give birth to her baby before any thought of moving was finalized. And, of course, so she did, as little Mary Alice duly arrived a month later.

JOSEPH AND MARY
MOVE TO SHEFFIELD

It wasn't long, however, before the new father started looking for both employment and a house in Sheffield, and before the year was out the new little family had moved to 55 Cross Bedford Street, just round the corner from the large, Portland Street factory of sweet-maker, George Bassett. Whether it was by coincidence or design that Joseph chose this location near to a sweet factory for his home is uncertain. It was, however, convenient for him, as although his new place of work was a grocery business nearby, it is quite possible that he chose to become one of many part-time workers (probably evenings or weekends) at this factory, which would have enabled him to learn a lot more about the sweet-making process. Support for this assumption is given by the fact that over the next few years Joseph not only obtained a post with a successful confectionery business in Gibraltar Street, a little nearer to the town centre, but he was soon appointed as its manager by its owner who was nearing retirement age.

Joseph's new-found position, and the wealth that came with it, allowed him to move to a larger house at 61 Melrose Road in Burngreave, where his wife Mary gave birth to two sons, Willie and Walter, and another daughter Jessica. Such was Joseph's success by the time his second daughter was born in 1889, that he was even able to afford the services of a live-in domestic servant. Not bad for a 32 year old baker's son, was it?

However, Joseph Warsop knew that he would soon have to make an important decision, as the imminent retirement of his employer meant that the business would be put up for sale.

"You know Mary," he said one evening whilst trying with difficulty to eat his tea with Jessica perched precariously on his left knee. "I've been thinking."

"The day you stop thinking, Joseph Warsop", his wife retorted with a little frustration, "will be a miracle. What is it now?"

"Well, there are two things really, my absolute precious. Firstly, I'd like to buy the confectionery business where I work from old Fred Jones, and secondly, I'd like my brother Mark to come in with me as a partner."

Now Mary knew her husband like the back of her hand, and the thought of him sharing his business success with anyone else, even his brother, didn't quite ring true.

"What you mean dear, is that you're desperate to own the company, but can't afford to buy it without some financial support from Mark. I don't disagree with your idea, but we may as well be honest with each other, don't you think?"

Joseph gave his wife a rueful smile as he nodded his agreement. It was in fact an ideal marriage that they had in many ways, with the ambitious husband having good ideas, and the shrewd wife keeping him on the straight and narrow. They also loved children of course, although Joseph was pleased that his wife had the 'pleasure' of giving birth to them, rather than himself.

As Joseph's ambitious ideas involved both his brother and his father, for whom Mark Junior still worked in Lincolnshire, perhaps we'd better have a quick look at how the two Marks were getting on. Their bakery and grocery business was thriving, but with Mark Warsop senior now being 73, he had virtually retired and left the running of the business to his 36 year old son. Not surprisingly, when Joseph announced that he was going to take Mary and the children on a surprise visit by rail to see their grandad, everyone was delighted.

"Can we see Uncle Mark and Aunty Laura as well as Grandad?" questioned Mary Alice, who always looked forward to one of these family visits.

"Of course we can, Mary. I'll write to them straight away."

Mixing business with pleasure was a rare occurrence for Joseph, but this was a key moment in his career and he felt that all the family deserved a holiday. Mary Alice, now 11 years old, had only travelled on the huge, noisy steam trains on two occasions, and was excited beyond belief at going on them for a third time. Willie, Walter and Jessica, aged six, five, and twoyears old respectively, had only heard about the wondrous smoking machines, and obviously had a wonderful surprise awaiting them.

THE TRAIN JOURNEY

You couldn't have wished for a better morning for a train ride as the Warsop family's day of departure down to Peterborough arrived. Alice had been telling her little brothers Willie and Walter what it was like to travel on a train, and they were almost beside themselves with anticipation. The beaming sun in the clear blue sky was as happy as the children were as it allowed the prancing horses pulling their taxi-cab to clip-clop through ever changing shadows which it playfully painted on the cobbled streets.

Their arrival at the steep approach road leading up to the Victoria Station was almost as magical as the trains would prove to be.

"Mummy, is that a palace up there? Is that where the Queen lives, asked Willie exitedly.

Willie's mother had told her young sons about Queen Victoria, who had been on the throne of England for over fifty years by this time, and six year old Willie's sharp mind must have made the association with the Victoria Station. In particular, the magnificent hotel which stood proudly at the top of the station approach, shimmering magically in the sunlight, must have looked just like a palace to an impressionable young lad's eyes.

Victoria Station Hotel

"No, Willie dear. That's a very posh hotel where rich people stay overnight if they're visiting the town. Mind you, it is named after the Queen, and I think she'll probably stay there when she visits Sheffield."

By this time, the snorting horses had finally pulled their chattering passengers up the last few yards to the station entrance, and were ready for a rest. Several other pairs of horses looked on with interest, and men in funny uniforms and black caps were scurrying around collecting luggage and cases in little wooden barrows and taking them onto the station platform. One of them made a beeline for the Warsop taxi cab.

"Carry your bags, sir?"

It was with relief that Joseph handed over his family's luggage to the red faced, willing porter who'd arrived to guide the excited family to the gleaming metal monster which was waiting expectantly for them within the station.

"Ah, you've arrived," hissed the engine excitedly as it sent clouds of steam spiralling into the air which almost scared the living daylights out of the two boys. "Look sharp and get aboard and we'll be off."

The sight of the Manchester, Sheffield and Lincolnshire (MS&L) train standing there in all its glory reminded the open-mouthed Willie and Walter of a giant chocolate log, similar to those which their mother sometimes baked. The main difference, of course, was its size and the fact that this chocolate log was supported on wheels. The cake decorations were also different, as this one had a tall chimney stuck on top at its front end and half a monster Easter egg stuck upside down a little further along at its mid point. This 'egg', which was actually the engine's steam dome, did in fact look rather peculiar as it didn't really seem to do anything. However, the same couldn't be said for the two smallish metal tubes which projected upwards at the rear of the engine. Whilst these looked rather innocuous, they were in fact the steam release valves

and had been the cause of the unexpected noise which had made the children jump so much a few minutes earlier.

Suddenly, another short impatient hiss interrupted Willie's thoughts.

"Let's get inside quickly, daddy. It's a bit scary out here."

With four little anxious faces now pressed against the glass windows of the first carriage, the mighty engine huffed, puffed and coughed into activity, belching clouds of thick black smoke skywards to the annoyance of the sun. A sudden lurch, accompanied by the clanking of steel couplings, signified the first movement of the train to the delight of the now smiling faces. They were on their way at last, on a journey of a lifetime.

As the train slowly left the busy, thriving surroundings of Sheffield, the seemingly ever present industrial noise and smoke gave way to the clear, relaxing innocence of the countryside. Acres of rolling green landscape formed a magical backdrop to the wonderful scenic adventure which played out before the excited children. Hundreds of lumbering dairy cows and flocks of white woolly sheep grazed lazily in the lush fields, whilst brightly coloured pheasants paraded brazenly adjacent to the many wooded copses which popped up with regular delight. Even the swathes of golden wheat and barley waiting patiently to be harvested looked up and waved their tall heads in friendly greetings as the long, panting giant chuntered noisily by.

After a while, the train began to slow down and a large sign saying 'Platform 1' drifted passed the window as the booming voice of the train's guard shattered the hitherto exciting but relatively calm atmosphere in the gently swaying carriage.

"Change 'ere for Peterborough. Don't forget yer luggage."

Joseph had forgotten to tell the children that they had to change trains at Retford, and the upheaval was rather unwelcome.

"We're not here yet are we, daddy? You said it would take ages and ages to get there and we've only been travelling a few minutes."

Their journey to Retford had probably taken nearer to half an hour than the few minutes Willie had calculated in his young mind, but Joseph could understand the children being a bit confused and he had to quickly think of what to say to placate them.

"Now then boys, and you too Mary Alice, I've got a lovely surprise for you. The train we're going to go on in a few minutes has got the largest wheels in the world. Just wait 'till you see them.

Clever Joseph had now created excitement out of disappointment, and as the children tumbled out of their carriage onto the station platform, their eyes darted around looking for this special engine.

"There it is, daddy. Just look at it. The wheels are nearly as big as our house!"

Willie was, of course, a little prone to exaggerating things, but the two, eight-foot diameter drive wheels on the engine which stood proudly on the adjacent platform did look enormous.

It wasn't long, however, before the excited family were sitting on their very special new train, and although the ride was a little noisier than the first part of their journey due to the huge wheels mercilessly pounding the metal track beneath them, no one really seemed to notice. It was just a joy for them all to marvel at the ever changing scenery which drifted lazily by, painting untold pictures of beauty and drama which the children in particular would hold in their memories for ever.

To say that the whole family enjoyed their 100 mile trip down to Peterborough would be the understatement of the year. Even the normally exciting journey by horse-drawn carriage from the station to Uncle Mark's home was rather tame compared to the ever changing kaleidoscope of colour and adventure which they had experienced.

WARSOP BROTHERS, SWEET-MAKERS – THE BEGINNING

However, let us not forget the purpose of this memorable holiday. The gathering of the Warsop family itself was a momentous occasion which everyone enjoyed, but it was Joseph's future that was the main topic of discussion. This was dependent on his brother Mark's response to his proposal for them both to take over Fred Jones' successful confectionery business. I don't suppose it takes a genius to work out that Mark agreed with the idea, as this is a story about the success of the Warsops as sweet-makers. The proposal did, in fact, suit everyone, as their father was now able to take a proper retirement and spend quality time with his loving wife. Mark agreed that Joseph should be Managing Director of their new company primarily because his brother had the knowledge and expertise to make it a success, and Warsop Bros., Manufacturing and Wholesale Confectioners was born, with its first factory-cum-shop being located at 195 Gibraltar Street in Sheffield.

With the new joint business being located in this town, it was, of course, necessary for Mark and his wife Laura to move house. With his brother's help, they found a nice home at 16 Westmoreland Street, which was not far from

* Warsop Brothers' first shop/factory at 195 Gibraltar Street

the factory. In addition, probably to make life easier for both families, Joseph and Mary also moved back into the area and bought a house at 109 Upperthorpe Road for themselves and their four children.

It is interesting to note at this stage that Joseph was never afraid to travel or move house to progress in life. Whilst in Lincolnshire, he had moved from Spalding to Crowland when young, and then from Crowland to Barnetby le Wold when in his teens. His subsequent move back to Crowland to join his father was then followed by a move north to Sheffield where, up to the present date, he had lived at three different addresses. He was destined to move nine more times in this town he loved, before finally moving to Caister upon his retirement. Although moving houses is common in today's fast-living life, to have sixteen different houses during a lifetime, as Joseph did, was particularly exceptional during the difficult years of the reign of Queen Victoria, King Edward VII and King

George V. Perhaps it indicates a restless mind or, more likely, one which was prepared to accept and respond to change to get the best out of life? However, we seem to be getting ahead of ourselves, so let's get back to where we left off.

Joseph and Mark, the Warsop brothers, still in their mid thirties, were an instant success with their new confectionery business and within two years had bought and occupied a large factory in Bowling Green Street just a stone's throw from their Gibraltar Street building, which they now used as both a warehouse and a shop. Having

Warsop Brothers' Bowling Green Street Factory

moved to these new premises, production was able to be increased and they were now able to employ 80 girls making many varieties of delicious sweets for which the company was subsequently famous. These included specialities such as Lime fruit Drops, Flu-Flu-Drops, Marry-Me-Quick, Lemon Kali, Rum Toffee, Lemonade Crystals and Mintoes. In addition, medicinal sweets such as anti-septic cough drops and cough candy were also very popular.

As business prospered, however, Joseph felt that the time was right for them to expand further into the retail area, and that owning another local shop wouldn't go amiss.

"I've noticed a vacant shop unit just round the corner on Moorfields," remarked Mark when his brother told him of his idea. "It's quite a decent size and it would be ideal now that we're producing so many different products."

This shop unit proved to be a perfect spot, being on a busy road with housing all around, and was soon doing a roaring trade. This wasn't really surprising as Sheffield was rapidly expanding due to the continued growth of steel production in the city, and with an ever increasing population, now at 330,000, no-one was able to stand still and let things happen around them.

The next two or three years, in fact, brought significant changes to Sheffield as it moved into the 20th Century. The new Town Hall, the construction of which began adjacent to St. Paul's Church in 1894, was now complete. Electric trams had begun to run on the city's streets and competition from motor cars was just beginning. In 1901 the country mourned the passing of their beloved Queen Victoria and welcomed in her son as King Edward VII. Sadly, poverty and sickness was still rife, but, of course, life carried on.

The Sheffield General Infirmary about 1800

On a brighter note, it was during the early years of the new century that the Warsop brothers decided to expand their retail operations even further by opening a confectionery stall in the prestigious Norfolk Market Hall.

WILLIE WARSOP JOINS THE COMPANY

However, let's not forget Joseph and Mary's children who were also growing up. In particular, we ought to see what their older son Willie had been up to, as he was the one who had always wanted to follow in his father's footsteps. Joseph often recalled with amusement and pride the brief conversation he had held with his son on numerous occasions each year since the lad was able to talk:

"Can I be a sweet-maker when I grow up, daddy?"

"Of course you can, son. As soon as you're old enough you can come and help me in the factory."

Willie had now reached the working age of 14 and, as promised by his father, eagerly went to work at Bowling Green Street factory where his sweet-making career began in earnest. He was still living with his parents at this time in Upperthorpe Road, which ran along the southern boundary of the Royal Infirmary. However within a few months, the Warsop family moved to Albert Terrace Road on the western boundary of the Infirmary where they managed to settle down for a few years before moving yet again, this time to Montgomery Terrace Road bordering the eastern side of this large hospital.

You might wonder what the attraction was of living on roads which ran along three sides of this huge stone-built complex which provided medical care for most of the residents of Sheffield. These roads obviously had the advantage of being within easy reach of such care should any injury or serious illness befall the family. They were also within walking distance of the Warsop

Brothers' factory and shops. However, unlike a hundred years earlier, when, in 1792, the brand new General Infirmary nestled comfortably in pleasant rural surroundings known as Upperthorpe Meadows, the year 1900 painted a completely different picture. The site was now surrounded by thousands of acres of dense housing, much of it terraced and back-to back, which formed the wards of Walkley, Crookesmoor, St. Philips and Neepsend.

However, as we've observed earlier, Joseph Warsop was no fool, and a careful look at the property which existed on these three roads surrounding the hospital shows that they contained several very nice detached and semi-detached residences most suitable for a man of his means. Indeed, they were probably the three poshest streets in the area.

A HISTORICAL STROLL

At this stage of our story, I think it's worth taking an interesting look at how things have changed in and around the site of the General Infirmary (which changed to the Royal Infirmary in 1897) since Joseph and Mary and their four children moved there.

If we take a look at the family's first home in Sheffield in 1881, for example, we can see that 55 Cross Bedford Street was one of many small terraced houses which ran along most of its length. Of the dozens of houses which did exist, only one now remains, this being a large detached property at number 62. This part of the street, along with the short length of Portland Street adjacent to it, now encompasses a large complex of buildings, open space and

The General Infirmary about the mid to late 1800s

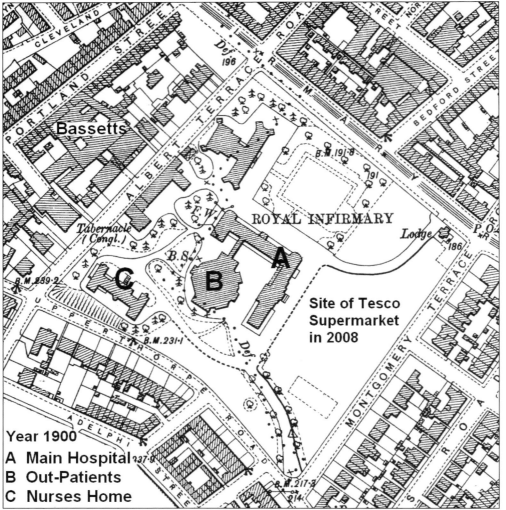

Year 1900
A **Main Hospital**
B **Out-Patients**
C **Nurses Home**

Site of Tesco Supermarket in 2008

Philadelphia Church occupy the site which once housed the Warsop's home at number 109. Strangely enough, once again the house belonging to their old, next door but one neighbour at number 113 still exists, once more in the form of a grand detached house.

To complete our mini exploration of the area, we'll turn right into Albert Terrace Road where Joseph and his family once lived at number 54. This area has changed most of all in this last century or more, with the existing properties, including Bassetts' large sweet factory, being demolished and replaced by the huge, innovative Kelvin flats complex in the late 1960s. This complex, which contained 947 dwellings housing 3,165 residents, sadly became an area blighted by vandalism, insecurity and fear, and was itself demolished in 1995 and replaced by 200 single storey and two storey dwellings in a more relaxing and pleasant setting. The photographs and accompanying text displayed on this and subsequent pages give an interesting look at the impact that Kelvin and its eventual demolition had on the area.

parking areas used by St. Thomas' Church at Philadelphia. These buildings are used as teaching, training and conference centres by the church, whose use of the name Philadelphia relates to the fact that the area itself was known by that name when the Warsops lived there. In addition, it also reflects the existence at that time of the adjacent, huge Philadelphia Steel Works on the site bounded by Penistone Road, Rutland Road and the River Don.

A quick pop across Infirmary Road to the bottom entrance of the hospital finds us strolling up Montgomery Terrace Road where all the old houses up to number 49 have been demolished and replaced by offices and medical related organizations. You will recall that Joseph and his family lived at number 47, and it is interesting to note that the property which is still standing at number 51, which would have been their next door but one neighbour, is a large detached house. It is very likely, therefore, that Mum, Dad, Mary, Willie, Walter and Jessica Warsop had a similar size house, which gives us a flavour of how they had progressed by 1902, twenty one years after their move to the city.

If we nip round the corner to Upperthorpe Road on the top side of the hospital, we can see that a large, landscaped green area has replaced the mass of terraced houses which once existed. Tower-blocks now line the route of Martin Street, and the Philadelphian Club and the adjacent

The Philadelphia Church in 2007 occupies the site of the large house in which the Warsop family lived in 1905

Main Kelvin flats complex

View of demolition from the Infirmary/Safeway Supermarket site

View over site of demolished Kelvin flats - 1997

Well, that's the tour around the area complete; or is it? Let's not forget the Royal Infirmary itself which, nearly 200 years after it was opened, was closed in 1980 as part of the Health Authority's rationalization of hospitals in the city. Whilst the main hospital building together with its attached octagonal outpatients department and the large nurses' home have been retained as a Heritage park, part of the site was let to Safeway as a supermarket, this itself being taken over by Tesco in later years. The old nurses' home is now called Centenary House and is shared by the North and West Child and Family Therapy Teams and other Sheffield Children's NHS Trust services. The Norwich Union Insurance Company now occupies the remaining buildings which consist of Heritage House (the main old hospital block) the Round House (the old outpatients department) and Victoria House, a new block built in 1990.

The old Nurses Home- now Centenary House

Heritage House
Main Hospital Block

The Round House
Out-Patients Dept.

Victoria House-Built 1990

WILLIE WARSOP MARRIES – SON JACK IS BORN

So, to get back to our story, we can see that during the ten year period which followed 14 year old Willie joining his father's business at Bowling Green Street, he appeared to gain nearly as much experience moving houses as he did learning about confectionery. Fortunately, the young lad was able to progress from trainee to General Manager over that period, as well as finding time to regularly visit his grandparents in Market Rasen. It was during these visits that he met and courted a lovely Lincolnshire lass by the name of Ada Wilson who he married just after his 24th birthday. Willie's parents had since moved to St. Philips Road, and the newly-weds were happy to live there with them for a year or two, knowing full well that it wouldn't be long before they would be alone, as 'gypsy' mum and dad would almost certainly take flight and move once again. This prediction proved to be true, as within a couple of years Joseph and Mary flitted to Park View Road in Owlerton, leaving their other home to Willie and Ada.

It was about this time that the young couple had their first child, a beautiful baby boy to whom they gave the name Jack. It was now the year 1910, and the newest addition to the Warsop family had arrived at a highly competitive time in the confectionery manufacturing industry. Competitor G. Bassett and Co. had already opened a second large factory in Owlerton, whilst Henry Dixon had taken the sweet market by storm with his acclaimed Dixon's Mint Rock. Willie, however, was unperturbed by these events, as life for him couldn't have been better. Business at the factory was booming, he had a beautiful wife and now he had a son to carry on the family name. Little did he realize, however, how important a part Jack would play in the future progress of Warsops the sweet-makers.

As you might have expected, it wasn't long before the proud father decided to introduce young Jack to the delights of confectionery production methods. Mind you, Ada thought that her husband was going a bit over the top when he first mentioned the idea.

"William! You can't take our Jack on a tour of that noisy factory of yours. The little mite's not even two years old yet. Just what are you thinking of?"

It's not really worth recounting the discussion which took place as Willie had made his mind up, and, as the man of the house, got his way as usual.

The following day was rather cold when father and son arrived at the main factory door and made their way to the toffee-making section. The little white face which peered out from under the fur-lined, hooded coat firmly grasped in Willie's arms looked rather puzzled.

"Now look at these, Jack," explained his proud dad. "This is where grandad makes all his lovely toffee. We've got Cream toffee, Rum toffee, Bank-quick toffee and Everton toffee. I don't know where he got some of the names from, but they all taste good."

Little Jack didn't seem too impressed with his dad's knowledge of toffee types, but he was interested in the bubbling pans of toffee mixture which gurgled their greetings to him in a language only he could understand.

"If you're a good little boy, grandad might let you have one of his special chocolate- coconut bars which those ladies are making over in the corner. Don't they smell lovely?"

Willie took Jack's squeaky response as a 'thank you' and proceeded to blind his young son with more science.

"Do you know, Jack, all that sugar, glucose and condensed milk in that pan has to be boiled at 235 degrees Fahrenheit and …"

"WILLIE! I don't think that little son of yours really wants to know all the technical details of sweet-making at his age," exclaimed Joseph as he strolled over to see how the pair of them were getting on. "I think giving him a small piece of marshmellow or marzipan would suit him better at 18 months old, don't you?"

Willie's father was right of course, but every dad wants to show off his new son and try and impress him. As it happens, this early experience Jack obtained must have whet his appetite, because he spent all his spare time in later years, from the age of 9 or 10, helping out and observing everything that went on in the factory.

By the time Jack had reached the age of 10, he had acquired a sister Joan and two brothers, Ken and Fred, none of whom ever expressed any real interest in the family business. His great uncle Mark had also reached the age of 65 and had decided to retire from the business, this leaving an opening for Jack's father, Willie, who was still only 35, to take over as Marketing Director. Joseph, meantime, was still feeling young at 63 and led the company into even more success until, in 1926, he also decided to retire at the age of 70.

WILLIE WARSOP IN CHARGE

Willie Johnson Warsop

Now, at the age of 42, Willie became the new Managing Director of Warsop Bros. He had followed in his father's foot-steps and reached the top of his chosen career, and the future looked bright with his own teenage son, Jack, showing a very keen interest and flair in this most magical of careers.

However, we never really know what is just around the corner, do we? Within a couple of years of Willie taking over the company, he began to feel unwell.

"You know, Ada," muttered Willie to his wife one morning before leaving for work, " I've been feeling off-colour for a few weeks now, and I keep getting a bit short of breath. I think I'll pay the doctor a visit."

Willie and Ada Warsop had moved to a new house in Millmount Road in Meersbrook a year or two earlier, just across the valley from their parents' home in Rupert Road in Nether Edge, a very well-to-do area in those days with large, expensive houses lining many of the streets. His father Joseph had obviously chosen this district as a suitable location in which to retire. The doctor's practice there was highly recommended, and Joseph had encouraged his son to have a private consultation there.

It was with some trepidation, however, that a few days later Willie found himself sitting patiently in the large, rather unwelcoming waiting room of his doctor's surgery. He didn't have long to wait to be seen, although his examination took longer than he had expected and the rather concerned expression on his doctor's face did nothing to relieve his anxiety.

"It appears, Mr. Warsop, that you may have contracted consumption. I'm going to have to refer you to a specialist at the Royal Infirmary."

These words from the stern looking, yet kindly, doctor came as an absolute shock to Willie. He was, after all, only 44 years old, and consumption was something you only got when you were older. Illness, however, has never been a respecter of age, and the subsequent consultation with the specialist at the hospital around which he had spent so much of his early life, confirmed the worst. Willie had indeed got consumption, an illness which we now know as tuberculosis. There was no known cure for this illness in those days, and despite receiving the best medical attention

available, his condition worsened over the next few years, during which his confectionery business fell into decline.

THE DEMISE OF THE WARSOP BROTHERS – SWEET-MAKERS

Eventually, Willie was unable to work at all and Warsop Bros., now effectively leaderless, was on the verge of bankruptcy. There was little or nothing that the relatively young Jack Warsop could do about the situation, particularly as his retired grandfather, Joseph, was also in very poor health and was unable to offer any assistance. The end came a year later in 1932 when his father, at the age of 49 and his grandfather, at the age of 75, both tragically lost their fights to live, leaving Jack to care for his remaining, grieving family.

For father and son to die in the same year was an absolute tragedy, and the implications on their families were devastating. Wives, sons, daughters and grand-children were all grieving, and their livelihoods had gone with their loved ones. The final demise of this great confectionery firm appears to have been unrecorded, and we can only speculate that its premises and equipment were sold to pay off debts which may have arisen over its last few years.

So. Was that the end of Warsop's wonderful sweets? Let's see shall we?

Jack Warsop was only 22 when his dad and grandad both died. As we know, he had gained a wealth of experience and knowledge in the sweet-making processes, although there was no money or property left from the former company for him to use to try and kick-start his own business. Times were also very hard in those early years of the 1930s, and even established companies struggled to survive. Unemployment had risen to dramatic proportions, and finding alternative work was like looking for a needle in a haystack.

This, therefore, was the position that Jack found himself in. Should he forget the idea of a career in confectionery? Should he accept the total demise of the name Warsop in quality sweet-making? Should he take the easy way out and just tell himself that it was not possible to start again? His answer to all these questions was an emphatic NO.

The 1930s, however did nothing to encourage him to keep up his belief in pursuing his early dream. He struggled at first to find a permanent post, although he did manage to move between different jobs as they arose in order to build up desperately needed savings. But, of course, being the oldest of Willie Warsop's four children, his mother Ada depended on him for financial support following her husband's premature death. This put enormous pressure on Jack, whose ambition to move back into confectionery was somewhat compromised by the need to look after his family.

JACK WARSOP MARRIES

It was during these troubled times that Jack fell in love with Nellie Biggin, a lovely Sheffield lass he'd met down at the Labour Exchange whilst job-hunting. This 'ray of sunshine' was just what he needed to brighten up the dark days, and it re-kindled that same determination and drive that had made his father, grandfather and great-grandfather so successful in years gone by.

"You know, Nellie lass, I'm a new man again since I met you. You've given me a new lease of life and I'm more determined than ever to succeed."

The old Woodside Brick Works site - Now the Homebase Superstore

Whether it was Divine Intervention or just good luck I'm not sure, but following the emergence of this new, invigorated Jack, a permanent job opportunity cropped up at the large Woodside Brick Works on Chesterfield Road on the town side of Woodseats. This site, which is now occupied by a huge Do-It-All complex, was surrounded by the towering trees of Smithy Wood, and overlooked the meandering Sheaf Valley in which nestled the quaint hamlet of Norton Hammer. It was certainly an attractive location in which to find employment, but the type of work on offer was tough with long hours, and as Jack turned up for interview in his Sunday Best, he knew that if he were to be successful, it would be a life-changing event.

It was with some surprise to him that the venue for his interview on that windy April morning was in a rather scruffy site hut, and as he made his way across the brick strewn yard, trying with difficulty to shield his eyes from

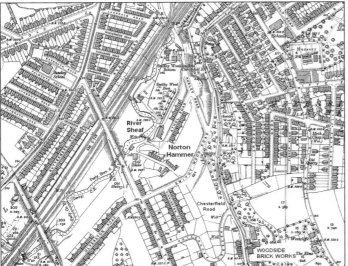

the whipped up brick dust trying to engulf him, he wondered what he had let himself in for. But, work was work, and by the time he found himself sitting in front of the yard-foreman's paper-and dust-covered desk, he was ready to do his best.

"I tell you something lad. Wi' wearing posh clothes like that, anyone'd think that tha'd come for 'manager's job", laughed the rough-looking but kindly man who faced him. "I'm impressed, mind you, and tha looks strong enough, so the job's yours if tha wants it."

Although completely taken aback by his brief but successful interview, Jack was overjoyed and, extending his strong hand, shook the foreman's offered hand in appreciation.

"I'll not let you down sir, you'll see."

As he left the large imposing brickworks and sprinted across the road to catch the tramcar rattling down towards him, he knew that this could be his big chance in life.

Nellie was, understandably, delighted when Jack returned with the good news, and the two of them began talking of marriage in the not too distant future. His mother's reaction to her son's success was greeted with equal delight, although her observations thereafter were a little disturbing to Jack's ears.

"I'm very proud of you Jack. I knew you wouldn't let us down. A regular wage coming in will help us all and give us the security that I and your brothers and sister need."

"Well, I was going to mention, mam", replied her son a little nervously, "that me and Nellie were considering getting married soon."

"Getting married, Jack! Absolutely not. Don't even think of it. You're needed here in this house young man. You can't go wasting good money by going off and getting married. We all depend on you."

His mother's words hit Jack Warsop like a sledge-hammer, and, for a few minutes he felt that his world was falling apart. But, of course, his mother's life had fallen apart already, and with only one full-time wage coming in from her four children, Jack knew she had a point.

"It's alright, mam. We'll wait until Ken and Fred are earning properly before we name the day."

Despite the continuing lack of employment opportunities over the next few years, brothers Ken and Fred Warsop did manage to get jobs, and it was with great delight and relief that Jack and Nellie were able to be married on the 8th May, 1937. With their modest savings, they were also able to buy a few essential items to furnish a cosy little terraced house at 23 Nettleham Road in Woodseats which they had managed to find at quite a cheap rent and which, helpfully, was within walking distance of Jack's work-place. Buying a house had never been an option for the young couple, as with them both wanting a family and Jack's take-home pay from the brickworks being only nineteen shillings and eleven pence a week, paying a typical £1 a week mortgage was impossible. The icing on the cake, however, was the birth of their beautiful daughter Maureen on August 29th of the following year, an event which seemed to signal that good times were ahead.

Nettleham Road, Woodseats, in which newly married Jack Warsop set up home at no. 23 with his bride Nellie.

However, as history (and long memories of some of us) can recall, another event was destined to intervene. World War Two was declared. Jack, along with thousands of other young men, was called-up to serve his country and, for the next six years or so, all thoughts of moving back into sweet-making were put on ice. As for Nellie, she, like many others, had to struggle to bring up little Maureen over those dreadful war years. Jack did manage occasional home-on-leave visits during this time, and towards the end of hostilities the couple were blessed with a baby son, John, to complete the happy family unit.

Nevertheless, the war did end in due course, albeit leaving death and destruction in its wake. The re-building of their great city and the lives of many of the families who lived there was a huge task for Sheffield folk. Nellie was one of the lucky ones as her husband Jack returned home in one piece, a privilege sadly not afforded to many of her friends. A new beginning was the main objective of almost everyone, and Jack, now in his mid thirties, was still keen to pursue his dream.

WARSOPS THE SWEET-MAKER RISES FROM THE ASHES

It was Jack's first weekend at home following his eventual return from the forces. Maureen was upstairs looking after her little brother John, and Jack's younger brother Fred had promised to pop in for a cup of tea on his way home from Church. The main thoughts in Jack Warsop's mind, however, were trying to get a job and eventually becoming a sweet-maker.

"You know Nellie, love, if they'll have me back at the brickworks, we can save up for a couple of years or so until I've got enough to start my own business. What do you think?"

"Well, it's not going to be easy Jack," his understanding wife replied gently, "but if that's what you want to do, I'm behind you all the way."

Scrimping and saving had been second nature to this determined man since his father died, although paying the rent and feeding a wife and two children seriously reduced his ability to save very much.

Suddenly, a knock on the front door interrupted the couple's thoughts. It was a rather cheerful Fred Warsop who was let in by his sister-in law Nellie, and after much hugging and shaking of hands, Fred announced that he had something important to tell them.

"Well, Jack, you probably know that I've done well for myself recently and I'd like to do something in appreciation of your kindness and generosity in providing for our mam and us kids before the war."

With bated breath, Jack and Nellie wondered what was coming next.

"I'd like to provide the finance for you to set yourself up in the sweet-making business, although I wouldn't want any involvement in it myself. I'd be more like a sleeping partner, if you like, and if you eventually make enough for the two of us, so be it. Mind you," he added with a chuckle, "I could do with a cuppa' cha if that's all right. I'm parched."

Amidst tears of laughter and gratitude, Fred, Jack and Nellie toasted the future with three mugs of Brook-Bond Dividend tea in the small front room of no. 23, whilst eight year old Maureen and two year old John gratefully accepted two small bars of chocolate which Uncle Fred had managed to get hold of, despite severe food and sweet rationing being in force everywhere. It was, in fact, this rationing which restricted Jack to opting for a small beginning to his sweet-making aspirations, as not only was there a significant shortage of sugar, but ration coupons limited the amount of sweets able to be bought.

Nevertheless, in 1948 and now approaching his 49th birthday, J. Warsop, Confectioner was established in a small room in Rockingham Street which Jack had been able to rent. One hundred and thirty years had passed since his great-grandad Mark Warsop had been born and subsequently introduced the family into the bakery and grocery business which itself had subsequently developed into confectionery. Twenty-six years had passed since the demise of the successful Warsop Bros. business, and Jack was now feeling proud that, although only in a small way, he had been able to resurrect it.

Jack Warsop in his garden

A TRAM RIDE TO WORK

It was now the beginning of the six weeks summer break from school which every child in the country eagerly looked forward to. Jack's young daughter, Maureen, was no exception as she had something particularly exciting to look forward to. Her father had promised that she could help him in his new sweet-making venture.

"Come on Maureen. Let's go and make some sweets."

Maureen Warsop about 11 years old

Holding her father's hand, the little auburn-haired girl skipped out of the front door of their home in Nettleham Road and set off on their journey to the new sweet factory on the outskirts of the city centre. They were just in time to catch a Sheffield Lane Top tram that had left Meadowhead terminus five minutes earlier and was now clanking to a stop outside Woodseats School almost opposite the bottom of their road.

"Let's go upstairs daddy. I like sitting in the front bay."

Jack smiled at his daughter and climbed the winding staircase behind her to ensure that she didn't fall as the tram slightly lurched and swayed its way forward. The view from the front bay was magnificent through the huge, curved glass windows which wrapped themselves around two pairs of reversible seats. It was as if you owned the world up there, especially when you had all the bay to yourself. As the tram moved on and the sun peeked through yellow and red striped clouds which lit up the early morning sky, Jack spotted his old work-place on the right hand side of the road.

"Look Maureen, that's where I used to work, at those brickworks. I can hardly believe that we're being driven past it and I don't have to go in."

Maureen, however, was more interested in looking to her left where the ground suddenly dropped steeply down to the valley bottom below.

"It's like being on a cliff top up here, daddy. I hope the tram doesn't fall in."

There was no doubt that sitting on a swaying tram 150 feet above the burbling River Sheaf which was trying to race the London train puffing its way along the Midland Railway line, was rather daunting. It was, nevertheless, rather exciting, particularly for Maureen, who couldn't help but marvel at the vista of buildings, both large and small, which dominated her view for as far as the eye could see. It was definitely better than going to school, and as this was the beginning of her summer holidays, she was looking forward to a regular dose of this excitement for the next few weeks.

In what seemed like no time at all, the lurching tram had reached the edge of town and was travelling up The Moor. On the right hand side of the road, just beyond Ellin Street, Arthur Davy & Sons' famous bakery and grocery shop was producing its wonderful mixed aromas of baking bread and hot meats, whilst just a few yards further up at the corner of Hereford Street, the National Provincial Bank was opening its doors for its usual early customers.

The Moor at this time, however, was still looking a bit sorry for itself following the devastating damage caused by the Sheffield blitz about eighteen years earlier, although rebuilding work was still proceeding at quite a pace. As the tram slowly rattled past the site where the once proud Atkinsons Department Store had stood, it was good to see that the construction of its new store was now taking shape. John Atkinson had not of, course, given in to the wave of

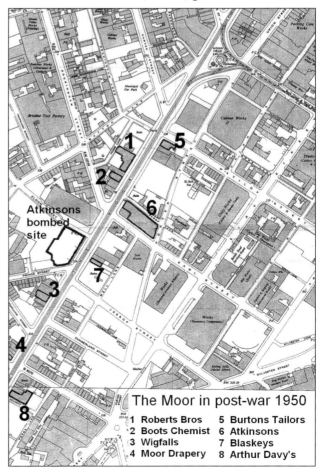

The Moor in post-war 1950

1 Roberts Bros	5 Burtons Tailors
2 Boots Chemist	6 Atkinsons
3 Wigfalls	7 Blaskeys
4 Moor Drapery	8 Arthur Davy's

bombings that had taken place on those never to be forgotten nights of the 12th and 13th December in 1940. Although his store had been rendered to a mass of twisted steelwork, his large temporary store opposite the end of Rockingham Street had soon risen out of the ashes of despair to stand defiantly on Sheffield's most famous street, more determined than ever to serve the residents of our great city.

Atkinsons after the Blitz

It was here that Jack and Maureen's tram journey ended, and as they strolled hand in hand up Rockingham Street to Jack's new works past the many cutlery and tool manufacturers which still lined this street, they were looking forward with optimism to a new, bright future.

MAKING SWEETS WITH JACK AND MAUREEN

It only took a few minutes to walk from the tram-stop to Jack Warsop's little room where we began our story. The sugary solution in the copper pan on the old stone oven was now well over 200 degrees Fahrenheit and was bubbling and plopping even more frantically as if to let Jack know that it was ready for pouring. Adjacent to the oven, a firm wooden table on which a steel slab had been securely fixed awaited the next move with apprehension. A small upstand around the four edges of the slab seemed to almost stand to attention in anticipation of a battle that was just about to begin.

"Move back, Maureen, love. I'm just about to pour."

Wearing thick leather gloves and a protective leather apron, Jack carefully lifted the boiling hot copper by its short, sturdy handles, being careful to keep it upright until it was hovering over the centre of the 'anxious' steel slab. A gentle tilt of the hand allowed the first of its bubbling contents to begin their journey to fame, some of the sizzling sugars being happy to finish up as Pear Drops or Sugar Fish, whilst others aspired to reach the heights of Aniseed Rock, Humbugs, or even Marry-Me-Quick, Jack's speciality.

Amidst an explosion of hisses and gasps, a race to reach the edge of the slab began as hot, squirming rivelets formed in all directions. The solemn, cold steel had other ideas, however, and was totally unforgiving as it rapidly cooled down the underside of its attackers and caused them to curl up and fall over each other in their blind pursuit of victory. As the sweet-maker turned the copper further over to complete the pour, the final wave of blistering hot sugars began their final assault, cascading down in a sea of steamy defiance which raced to all corners of the now struggling steel slab, climbing over their suffering comrades which had gallantly fallen in the first wave.

This time, however, help was at hand for the brave steel, which was now beginning to warm up as the battle raged. Jack's strong, gloved hand appeared, manipulating a wooden spatula which scraped the advancing sugars up and tossed them back into the still sizzling inferno which was awaiting their return in the centre of the slab. Scrape and toss, turn and scrape, push and lift; the continuous motion continued for what must have seemed an age to the angry sugars which had earlier also been subjected to squirts of flavourings and colouring for their sins.

Suddenly, everything stopped. The cooler air of the room and the defiance of the thick steel had won. Although still quite hot, the treated sugars had transformed into a large, brown-coloured, jelly-like mass which sat defeated in the centre of the slab.

"That'll do for now Maureen, love. I've got to split this jelly in two now and stretch one half before it cools down too much."

The wide-eyed little nine-year old had been standing in the far corner of the room, totally intoxicated by the sweet aroma which circulated everywhere, and spell-bound by the 'battle' which she had witnessed with excitement and some trepidation. Even bonfire night was never as spectacular as this, she thought. But how can that big, brownish blob on the table turn into sweets?

"I'm making Marry-Me-Quick today, love. Come over here and watch me, then you can give me a hand if you like."

This delicious sweet was simply a brown and cream striped coil of rock made from a secret recipe combined with a simple yet clever technique to produce the two-tone stripe effect. The process started with Jack rolling half of the blob into a long, thick sausage which he expertly threw up and over a large metal hook in the wall behind the rapidly cooling slab.

"Maureen, I want you to roll this other half into a long sausage just like I've done while I work on this piece."

So, here we have it. Father and young daughter were making sweets together, a far cry from the eighty-strong workforce at the Bowling Green Street factory where Jack had learnt his craft. But, this was a new and exciting beginning for the Warsop name, and size didn't matter.

Jack grabbed the two ends of the long, pale-brown sausage dangling over the hook and began the simple but skilful procedure of pull-stretch-remove-fold together-over the hook again, which was repeated many times until its consistency and colour changed to a light creamy, sausage-shaped dough. This change was produced by air which was entrapped in the sweet mixture whilst being stretched and folded for just the right amount of time to create the required effect without cooling off too much.

Speed was the essence of the next process as both Maureen and her father rolled their respective brown and cream rock sausages into long thin strips and placed them closely side by side before further cooling could prevent a bonding-stage taking place. This stage of the procedure was ideally suited to Maureen's smaller hands which eagerly but gently pressed measured lengths of the two rock strips together and rolled them into tea-plate sized 'catherine-wheels'.

This successful marriage of cream and brown rock strips and their formation into a circular striped delicacy was only possible if critical temperatures and consistency of materials were just right. In fact, if you listened carefully, you could almost hear Mrs. Cream whispering to Mr. Brown as they clung together side by side on the warm steel slab: "Marry me quick, and we'll be alright."

This wasn't the only sweet-making process in which Maureen helped her dad, as on subsequent visits she helped to feed similar sausages of warm, processed sugars through the toffee-mangle (just like grandma used to have on wash-days), which produced a thick flat carpet of various flavoured toffee which could then be chopped up into chunks. Even sweets such as Pear Drops, Humbugs and Sugar Fish could be formed through the mangle, which used metal rollers incorporating shaped moulds as necessary.

Jack spent four years at his small factory in Rockingham Street making a large variety of sweets which he personally delivered to various shops in the area. Eventually, however, he needed more space and time to meet demand. He couldn't really afford to employ anyone else to help him, and larger, suitable accommodation for his sweet-making process was difficult to come by. He was aware, however, that a new general-store by the name of Kitchenalities had been opened at the bottom of Aisthorpe Road in Woodseats. This road was, in fact, adjacent to the

one in which he lived, and the store was, therefore, only a couple of minutes walk from his home.

Old Kitchenalities Shop in Aisthorpe Road Now called Woodseats Sowing Machines

"I must pop in," he mused as he strolled past the brightly lit windows one evening admiring the unending variety of goods displayed. "Perhaps they'll sell my sweets."

It was Mr. Cooper, the proprietor, who was standing behind the long counter when Jack entered the shop a day or two later.

"Morning, Mr. Warsop. What can I do for you?"

The surprised sweet-maker was taken aback when Mr. Cooper addressed him by his name for, as far as he could remember, they had never met.

"You've made a bit of a name for yourself around here, Mr. Warsop, with all those wonderful sweets and toffees that you're making. I half expected you popping in actually."

The two men were obviously on the same wavelength, and Jack was delighted when the shopkeeper put in a very large order for his sweet products. The only problem was that such a large order would over-stretch Jack's ability to produce what Mr. Cooper asked for, a problem which the two of them began to discuss.

"I tell you what, Jack, I've got a nice little place in Olivet Road just a couple of streets away from here which would suit you down to the ground. You could make as many sweets as you want, and I'd take them all off your hands. In effect, you'd be working for me and I'd deliver them to wherever they need to go."

This wasn't, of course, what Jack really had in mind, although it was tempting. According to the shopkeeper, the new little sweet factory in Olivet Road would have 'Coopers' name above the door, despite producing Warsops sweets, and Jack would be an employee of Mr. Cooper, rather than retaining his preferred independence. He would, however, be under less pressure and, providing the public's insatiable desire for his confectionery continued, he would be more financially secure. This was decision time.

Following long chats with his wife Nellie, during which the pair of them almost sent themselves dizzy weighing up the options, Jack agreed to Mr. Cooper's proposal and spent the next eight years producing his famous Warsop delicacies which were sold not only in the Kitchenalities shop, but in many more shops around the city also. Most Woodseats residents of a more mature age will fondly remember going into Kitchenalities and buying a bag of Lemonade Crystals, Tom Thumb Drops, Cough Drops, Fruit Rock, Sugar Fishes and many more, having only popped in originally for a bundle of fire-lighters. The children in particular loved to ask for 2oz of Marry-Me-Quick, and they always loved it when the large saucer-size pieces of this special rock had to be broken up into small pieces using a miniature steel hammer. Those were the days.

THE END OF AN ERA

Sadly, however, due to no fault of his own, Jack Warsop's bubble was about to burst. Confectionery was big business in Sheffield, and the large manufacturers were busy trying to expand and take-over the smaller companies. To Jack's dismay, Mr. Cooper decided to sell-out to one such large manufacturer and, all of a sudden, in 1960, he found himself without a job. He was still only 50 years old, but fortunately his 22 year old daughter Maureen and his 16 year old son John were both working. Life had dealt the dedicated sweet-maker another hard blow which was decidedly below the belt.

But, as we sometimes hear said: 'You can't keep a good man down for long', and within a month or two Jack had secured himself a job as a postman. The change, of course, was dramatic, as hours of working in isolation making sweets was replaced by meeting and chatting to hundreds of householders to whom he delivered letters and small parcels on a daily basis. He enjoyed the change and remained with the GPO for the next fifteen years until his retirement in 1975. Thereafter, Jack Warsop relaxed with his memories for another nineteen years until he passed away at the age of 84.

We have, of course, been privileged to share most of Jack's memories already in this story of Warsops, the sweet-makers. There is, however, one little box of memories which we have not yet unlocked. Fortunately, I have found the key, so, with your permission, we'll have a look inside.

It was a typical Easter-time in the Warsop household at 23 Nettleham Road. A large pile of chocolate bars was stacked on the kitchen table, and the Yorkshire Range had been stoked up to a cosy, orange glow. Jack was about to make Easter eggs for neighbours' and friends' children, as well as for Maureen and John of course, and an air of expectancy hovered above the sweet-maker's family. The chocolate had been arriving at their door over the last few weeks, delivered either by the children themselves or their parents, and, not by coincidence, they were all Fry's Sandwich Bars. Many of you will remember these scrumptious bars which were made with layers of milk and plain chocolate, a perfect combination for melting as well as eating.

"Right kids. I want a few bars breaking up and putting in this big basin. Be careful not to drop them on the carpet, mind you, or your mam'll tell us off."

Nellie laughed at her husband's remark and helped her children to take off the wrappers to speed up the process. Within a few minutes, the basin was proudly sitting on the cast iron shelf above the fire in the Yorkshire Range, and the incredible, mouth-watering aroma of melting chocolate filled the whole room. At the other end of the kitchen table, several pairs of different size Easter-egg moulds, together with a few chicken-sat-on-a-basket moulds, waited expectantly, their shiny silver surfaces glinting in the room lighting.

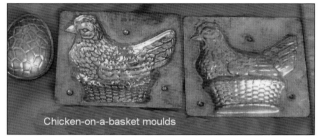
Chicken-on-a-basket moulds

"Ok. It's ready. Pass me a mould please, Maureen."

Jack's daughter always delighted at watching her dad pour a little hot chocolate into the half-egg shaped mould which he skilfully rotated round until an even coating of chocolate had solidified on its surface. Carefully putting this down on a large sturdy tray, Jack repeated the process many times until the whole tray was full of chocolate coated inverted moulds of varying shapes and sizes. To young children who adored chocolate, there could be no better sight than this, and their excited, expectant eyes followed the tray full of goodies to the pantry door, behind which the cold cellar steps awaited their arrival for cooling.

"Are they cool enough yet, daddy?"

Five year old John's innocent question after only ten minutes had elapsed since the tray of chocolate moulds had been placed in the 'cooler' made everyone smile, but within an hour the selection of eggs and chickens were ready for a second coating using the same process adopted for the first coat. This second layer of chocolate would give the final  Easter-egg the strength to withstand handling and, most importantly for the children, would give them more chocolate to chew on.

Easter egg moulds

However, another hour in the 'cooler' was necessary, after which came the big moment.

"Daddy, what are you doing? Won't it come out?"

"Patience, John. Patience. You can't rush these things."

There's nothing worse, is there, when you've lined a

tray full of Easter-egg moulds with mouth watering chocolate and the resulting delicious brown shell sticks when you're trying to remove it? A despairing glance towards his wife didn't help either.

"Don't look at me, love. You're the expert."

Comments like that from his wife didn't really encourage Jack in his endeavours as he applied a gentle pressure to the lip of the chocolate shell to loosen it. Nor, in fact, did the constant barrage of questions from his impatient young son help him to remain calm and relaxed during this delicate operation. In theory, of course, this part of the process should be simple, as the solidifying chocolate should contract on cooling, allowing it to slip out of its mould with relative ease. However, varying conditions could contribute to the chocolate sticking, particularly dampness in the air which often affected the moulds.

"YES, YOU'VE DONE IT!"

Maureen's shout of glee almost made her father drop the first chocolate shell, which had decided, with reluctance, to gently slide out. Jack, understandably, was relieved, as the release of the first shell usually meant that all of them would come out quite easily. Indeed, within ten minutes, the large tray now proudly displayed a host of the delicious chocolate shapes, with the brown 'clucking' chickens looking particularly attractive.

"Now what's the matter John?"

Jack thought everyone would be smiling and happy following his success, but the look of concern on his son's face was somewhat puzzling.

"I didn't want you to make half an egg, daddy, I wanted whole ones."

It was, of course, the first time that the young lad had stayed up to watch Easter-egg making, and the sight of a tray full of chocolate halves rather than full egg shapes had confused him. This situation was soon resolved, however, as his father picked up two chocolate halves and pressed them gently onto a warm oven plate for a second or two before placing the slightly melted edges together to form a single egg. Little John was happy at last.

Not all of Jack's neighbours and friends wanted empty, hollow eggs, however, and many had sent smarties and small gifts with their Fry's chocolate which the obliging sweet- maker would place inside before fusing the two halves of the egg together. It was Nellie's job to put the finishing touches to these lovely chocolate Easter creations, which usually involved icing an edging around the egg joint and writing the children's names in icing on the front. The resulting products were quite a work of art, and all the children who received them were absolutely delighted.

This activity, along with similar kind acts such as making and handing out bonfire toffee on Guy Fawkes night and making chocolate Santas and sugar pigs at Christmas, was what Jack liked doing most of all. He loved his family and he loved children, and there was no better

Chocolate Santa moulds

reward for him than to see their happy smiling faces and wide-eyed amazement upon receiving his magical gifts made out of chocolate and sugar at a time, in the late 1940s and early 1950s, when sweet products of any type were an absolute luxury to the not so well-off.

So, there we have it. The story of the Warsops has come to an end. No longer can we buy their wonderful products in the shops, although many sweets of the same type (but not the same recipe) are still available. Nearly two hundred years of this family have appeared in our confectionery adventure, all of them dedicated to what they believed in. For the last hundred and twenty years they all lived in Sheffield and can all rightly be regarded as Sheffield folk. Jack personified a characteristic trait which ran through the whole family over these two centuries; one of dedication, determination and kindness. This still exits in his two

Maureen and her husband Peter in 2007

children, Maureen and John, living today. And, of course, the Warsop name is still alive and kicking with John and his son Paul proudly wearing the mantle. Perhaps we will see yet another resurgence into Warsop sweet-making in future years. You never know do you? In the meantime, we will bask in the glory of what has gone before us, and acknowledge that, as Sheffield folk, there's really nowt like 'em, is there?

The George Bassett - Samuel Johnson Story

George Bassett - Early Days

It was almost 200 years ago that a young wool–comber by the name of John Bassett lived happily with his wife in the attractive little village of Ashover in Derbyshire. They had two children, a boy and a girl, and Mrs Bassett was expecting her third. Trade, however, was poor and as her husband was struggling to make a reasonable living, an extra mouth to feed was not really what they wanted at this time.

However, on a rather hot April day in the year 1818, with a beaming sun adding to the expectant mother's normal difficulties in child birth in the rear bedroom of their modest, stone roofed little cottage, a gusty, unusually loud cry heralded the arrival of baby George Bassett.

"By gum lass, he's a bonny 'un. I don't know how we've managed to have one that big. He must weigh nine pounds or more."

"WE!" the worn out mother exclaimed. "I don't recall you taking any part in giving birth to this one, John Bassett. From what I hear, you were outside suppin' ale while I was pushing 'till I almost burst!"

And so began the life of George Bassett, third born of eight children, five of whom were boys and three of whom were girls. With the gradual arrival of the additional five children however, life for the Bassett family became more and more difficult. This situation was compounded by a deepening depression in the wool-trade, which led to John Bassett leaving his trained job as a wool-comber and turning to farming. By working extremely long hours, he was just able to afford to educate his children by sending them to the local village school at a cost of 3d (1¼ pence) a week for the younger children and 4d (2 pence) a week for the older ones.

Sadly, when George was only 12 years old, his father died at the age of 58, following several years of declining health, leaving poor mum to bring up her eight children. Income from the small holding which her husband had built up was only modest, but, with many helping hands and hearts, mum and her eight little helpers struggled on.

Now George's father had known for many years that his failing health would not enable him to live to any great age, and, when he was 50 years old, he had written a letter to his children in which he left them invaluable advice based on half a century of experience of living. This advice was worth far more than money or property, and would form the basis of young George Bassett's future outlook and philosophy on life, which was to stand him in good stead forever. Because of the importance that this letter had on George's life, it is reproduced on the next page in full, for your interest.

George Bassett

My dear children I think it probable that I may be taken from you while you are young; and as your welfare lies near my heart, I feel desirous of leaving you some advice, which I entreat you to observe. A little consideration will convince you that I have no end in view but your good. I have lived long enough to know something of human life, (being now fifty years of age) and to form a judgement of what is best to be pursued, and what ought to be avoided in the journey of life.

The first, and most important duty of life, and to which every other thing should be subservient, is the care of your immortal souls; for if you lose your souls you lose your all. Let me entreat you, my dear children, above all things, to be truly religious; and then, whether you be in prosperous or adverse circumstances; whether you be caressed or scorned in this world, you will have God for your friend, and all shall be well. But beware of taking a round of duties for religion; such as going regularly to church or meeting, saying your prayers morning and evening, and refraining from gross sins.

These things, it is true, must not be omitted, but they will not do of themselves. A change must take place in your hearts; your affections must be set on things above, and not on things below. The scriptures inform us, that, "except ye be converted, and become as little children, ye shall not enter into the kingdom of heaven".

Be not afraid of being singular in this respect: what signify the jeers and scoffs of poor mortals, who, as well as you, are hastening to the grave? Remember, that in the prospect of death nothing will be of any consequence but a consciousness that God is reconciled to you, and that you enjoy his favour.

The second, (I believe,) is to be careful of your health. To this end, it is good to avoid all intemperance, to avoid running into danger, and to use exercise in the open air. Let no one cause you to run into danger by daring you to it. Carefully avoid running into perilous situations, except absolutely necessary.

The third thing I advise you to, is to be prudent and careful in the management of the little property I leave you. With care, it may help to put you in a way to live comfortably; but if you are wild and extravagant, it will soon be spent, and you will be forced to labour hard for a scanty subsistence. I do not wish you to be covetous; but I wish you to be industrious and frugal, especially when you begin to manage for yourselves.

Be obedient to you mother. Be kind to one another. Be strictly honest. Never tell a lie. Make it a rule to attend some place of worship regularly. Always keep in your minds that God sees you.

GEORGE, THE APPRENTICE

Within two years of his father's death, young George reached the magic age of 14, when young men were expected to start work, and, on the last day in April 1832, he became apprenticed to William Haslam of Chesterfield, a confectioner and fruiterer, where he was to learn his trade. The cost of this apprenticeship, which was for seven full years, would normally have fallen on George's hard-pressed mother. However, a kindly family friend put-up the sum of £25 which William Haslam had requested, and George Bassett was now 'on his way'.

During those next, formative, seven years, the young apprentice worked hard and learnt his trade thoroughly. He not only became skilled in the art of sweet-making, he also gained valuable experience by learning how the business was managed. Despite regularly sending his mother a small amount of much needed cash each week, he still managed to save enough to build up a small nest egg by the time he was a young business man at the age of 21. Having worked for Mr. Haslam for those long years, he was, understandably, wanting to make progress in the business he had chosen and clearly enjoyed. However, his nest egg was still too small to enable him to consider setting up on his own, so, now being able to command a 'proper' wage from his employer, he stayed with him for another three years and saved every penny he could.

BASSETTS: THE BEGINNING

It was now April 1842, and George was celebrating his 24th birthday morning in Haslam's shop on the Low Pavement in Chesterfield. His sturdy figure with his cheerful ruddy face and white apron had almost been a landmark there for ten years. It was no surprise, therefore, that he had been 'keeping his ear to the ground', searching for news of any opportunities which might be available in his line of business. The local travellers (now called sales representatives) were always a good source of gossip, and the one from the nearby town of Sheffield who popped into Haslam's that morning was no exception.

"I've 'eard a whisper that 'enry Brooks wants to sell 'is confectionery business in Sheffield, mester Bassett. 'E's not been well lately, and as 'es gettin' on a bit, 'e wants to put 'is feet up and enjoy life. It's not a bad little business either, up there in the Park district on Broad Street."

The wrinkled forehead and winking left eye of the helpful traveller who leaned knowingly over the neat shop counter to quietly pass on his secret knowledge made George smile. He was, nevertheless, pleased to receive the information which earned his informant the reward of a bag of freshly picked apples. Despite knowing nothing about Henry Brooks, Confectioner and Wine Retailer, at number 30 Broad Street, George instinctively knew that this could be his golden opportunity and, with his nest egg now much fatter, he successfully bought the business a month or so later.

This move to Sheffield in 1842 to run his own confectionery business was the real beginning of the Bassett Empire. The shrewd, hardworking assistant had now become an entrepreneur, with upwards being the only direction he had in mind.

However, there was one more delight for George in this 24th year of his colourful life. He had begun courting a Sheffield lass by the name of Sarah Hodgson and, shortly after securing his independence by buying Henry Brooks' business, he married her. The wedding took place on December 7th of that year in the Sheffield Parish Church (now the Sheffield Cathedral), where the 20 year old bride took pride of place in her stunning, but simple, white wedding dress.

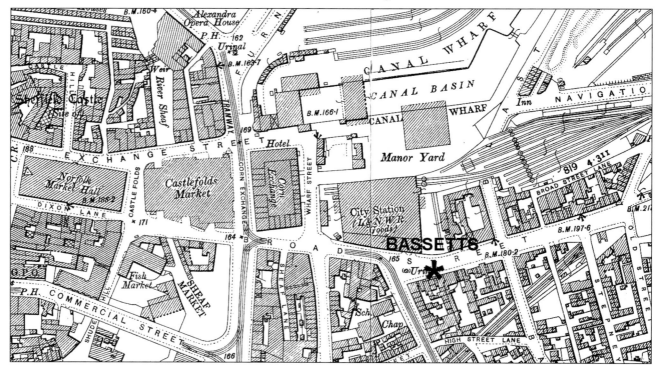

What a new beginning this was for the young man of promise. He had a new business, a beautiful young wife, a vision for the future inspired by his father and the determination to succeed. What more could he ask for?

Within the next three years, George's business grew from strength to strength and, by 1845, "George Bassett, Wholesale Confectioners, Lozenge Makers and British Wine dealer" was ready to further expand. In that year, he opened a shop in the Fitzalan Market Hall and another in West Bar, following which, by 1847, still at the tender age of 29, he opened very large premises in New Haymarket. Not content with simply dealing in confectionery and wine however, this enterprising young man decided to provide a 'package service', evidenced by a notice placed in the 'memories' column of the local newspapers at this time, stating:

FUNERALS FURNISHED WITH

HOODS, SCARFS, BUSCUITS

AND WINE,

On the shortest notice, by

G.BASSETT, CONFECTIONER,

New Haymarket, Sheffield.

As George's business interests grew, and having now reached the grand 'old' age of 33, he felt that it would be useful to take on an apprentice himself, recalling how he had benefited from such an opportunity nineteen years earlier. The applicant for this post, 12 year old Samuel Johnson, had, by coincidence, been born in 1839, the year that George's apprenticeship had been completed.

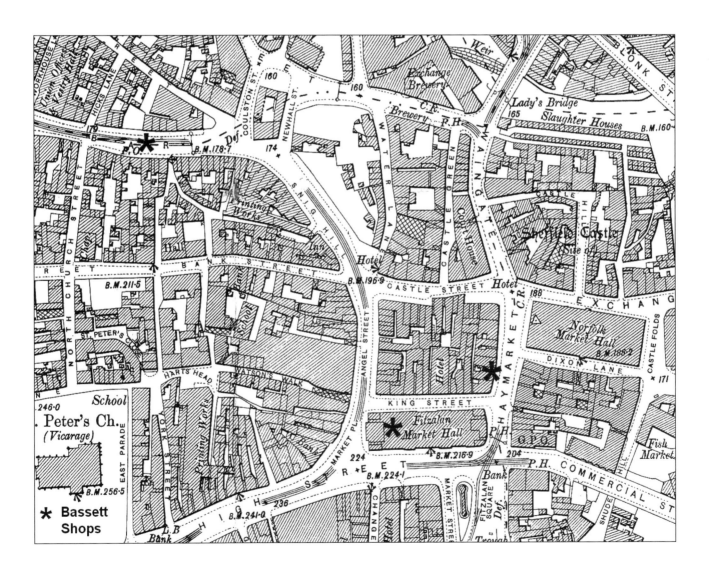

Samuel Johnson arrives

Samuel Johnson

It was early afternoon in the rather sombre, oak-panelled office tucked away at the rear of the New Haymarket premises. A gentle tap on the door heralded the arrival of Samuel for his interview, and an intimidating "ENTER" from within indicated to the young applicant that he might be in for a rough ride.

"Why, you're nothing but a young sprat, me lad," boomed George.

The slight, pale-faced Samuel glanced across at the burly figure which was leaning forward over a large, oak desk in a rather intimidating fashion.

"I know I'm not very big yet, sir, but I can work very hard. Just ask my dad."

The plaintive, yet optimistic, response from Samuel struck a chord with George who, knowing that the youngster's mother had died and that his father had recently remarried, offered him not only the post, but the opportunity to live at his own house in Endcliffe Crescent.

This decision to take on young Samuel Johnson was probably the next most important one George Bassett ever made, (the most important, of course, being his decision to enter the confectionery business himself), and was to shape the future of G. Bassett, Confectioner to the present day.

Samuel settled in well during what was a busy time for the business, which continued to grow. It was during the fifth year of his apprenticeship that a very famous Sheffield showman, Thomas Youdan, the owner of Sheffield's well known Surrey Theatre and Alexandra Opera House, approached George Bassett and his assistant with a most unusual request. It was New Year's day, 1856, when he dropped his bombshell!

"George, I'd like you to make me a cake to celebrate the end of that awful war with Russia. I want it to be a big 'un mind; say between four and five tons in weight."

"FOUR OF FIVE TONS! What are you doing, feeding the whole army?"

"Don't be daft George. I want to pay you eleven pence a pound to make it so that I can sell it for a shilling and make a penny a pound profit. With a cake weighing several thousand pounds, this should make a tidy sum to help our brave lads, or their families, who fought in the war, shouldn't it?"

The flabbergasted confectioner couldn't really argue with the sentiment behind the idea, but felt a little overwhelmed at the prospect of actually making it.

"I'll leave all the details to you George. Just make sure that it's ready by the end of the month, if you don't mind."

"Bloomin' 'eck, Mr. Bassett," blurted out Samuel, who had been present during the discussion. "How on earth can we manage to make a cake that size in such a short time?"

But, of course, George Bassett was no ordinary mortal, and he was never one to dodge a challenge, despite the seemingly impossible odds.

"No trouble, Mr. Youdan. Just leave everything to Samuel and myself and you'll have your cake on time."

Poor Samuel was lost for words, but if his boss said it could be done, then it could be done! Who was he to question the great man? George, of course, had now got the bit between his teeth and, having bade farewell to the showman, set about sorting out the recipe for such a monstrous feat of bakery in order that its ingredients could be ordered and delivered without delay.

"Right, me lad. I've spent all night sorting out this list of ingredients and costs, and I want everything delivered within the week. Get to it, and don't take no for an answer from anyone, or they'll have me to deal with."

Samuel read down the list with almost disbelief, whilst at the same time feeling proud that George Bassett had mastered this stage of the seemingly impossible so quickly. Perhaps we could all have a look at his 'work of art'.

CELEBRATION CAKE FOR MR. THOMAS YOUDAN
Ingredients, weights and costs

1,364lbs of raw sugar	*at 50/- per cwt*	*£30.9.0d*
1,364lbs of butter	*at 102/- per cwt*	*£62.2.6d*
1,705lbs of currants	*at 92/- per cwt*	*£70.0.0d*
1,705lbs of raisins	*at 62/- per cwt*	*£47.7.0d*
2,046lbs of flour	*at 3/- per stone*	*£21.18.0d*
1,024lbs of Candied lemon	*at 74/8d per cwt*	*£34.3.0d*
10,208 eggs	*at 9/6 d per 100*	*£48.9.0d*
412½lbs of icing	*at 9d per 1b*	*£15.9.4½d*
12lbs of coloured icing	*at 9d per 1b*	*£0.9.0d*
Total weight: 9,767lbs	**total cost of ingredients £330.6.10½d**	

In his calculations, which resulted in a cake weight of just under 4½ tons, George would be paid a sum of £447.13.1d, which represented 9,767lbs at 11 pence a pound. This would leave him with £117.6.2½ over and above the cost of ingredients to cover his and Samuel's time spent over the next month, his working overheads, and the difficult task of transporting such a mammoth cake. Any remaining balance would be his profit.

As far as Mr. Youdan was concerned, he would be able to recover £488.7.0 selling the cake at one shilling a pound, which would leave him with £40.13.11 to give to his chosen charity after deducting the £447.13.1 he'd paid George Bassett to make it. It doesn't seem a lot does it? However, of you take inflation into account over the last 150 years or so, it probably represents somewhere between £4000 and £5000 at today's prices.

But, of course, the confectioner-cum-baker had yet to make the cake, and the next few days saw cart-loads of ingredients arriving at his New Haymarket premises. Not unsurprisingly, the coke & coal ovens there were limited in size, so George chose to bake the cake in one hundred and seventy sections of just under 58 1bs each. Then, with sweat, toil, dedication and undoubted skill, the determined duo worked relentlessly until, on Thursday, January 31st 1856, exactly 30 days after receiving the order, the huge cake, complete with icing and ornaments, was finished.

Unfortunately, there is no record of the physical dimensions of what was recognised at the time as "the largest cake ever seen in Sheffield, if not in the country".

However some indication of its size is given by an article which appeared in the Yorkshire Weekly Post of March 18th 1861, which stated that "It took three trolleys abreast to convey it through the town, and those who knew Sheffield streets sixty years ago, know it would take a good pilot to navigate". Sheffield streets in the 1850's were, in fact, no more than 16 or 17 feet wide, and you can well imagine the difficulties encountered in making this delivery to Mr. Youdan and the comments it received from the public en-route.

"Mam, why are those horses pulling that great big birthday cake up the street?"

"Well, it's not a birthday cake dearie; it's called a celebration cake. Clever Mr Bassett's made the biggest cake in the world because we're not at war any more."

"Yes, but Mam, it's much too big. It can't get round that corner."

It seemed as if the whole town had turned out to watch the amazing spectacle. The three-horse team pulling the trolleys seemed to be snorting both with pride and frustration as they endeavoured to negotiate the tight corner into the street running along-side the Shambles known as Fruit Market. Many children were waving flags and cheering wildly which, combined with the almost incessant yelping and barking of several excited dogs, did nothing to help the situation. But, this was the way things were. A challenge was designed to be met and conquered, and success was achieved with pride on this occasion.

We must not, of course, forget Mr. Youdan and his quest to sell the cake at one shilling a pound. Despite communications being nothing like the efficient and speedy systems of today, news of the cake spread like wild-fire, and requests came pouring in. As the Yorkshire Weekly Post succinctly put it in their March 18th article 60 years later, "The cake was distributed in the districts between the North and South Pole wherever there was a Sheffield blade to cut it". It appears that the whole venture was a great success all around.

SAMUEL JOHNSON LEAVES

The next two years of Samuel's apprenticeship seemed to fly, and the raw, 12 year old recruit had now become a very competent and experienced confectioner. This had been helped by the fact that during the later part of the apprenticeship, George had given him more and more responsibility whilst he, himself, had broadened his horizons by becoming a town councillor.

So, on the seventh anniversary of the arrival of the slight, timid youngster at George Bassett's desk, a strapping, confident young man now stood in his place. The time had arrived for both men to make a decision about the future, and a meeting in George's office was taking place almost seven years to the day after Samuel's first nervous interview.

"Well Samuel. You've done me proud, I must say. I'm very pleased with your work and progress, and I'd like you to stay with me. I'm prepared to give you the going rate now that you've finished your apprenticeship, and I'll throw in an annual bonus based on our profits. How does that sound?"

Unfortunately, despite George's obvious desire to keep such a 'star pupil', Samuel was unhappy with the offer made to him that day, wishing to have more responsibility than that already given to him in his capacity as an excellent, practical confectioner. He wanted more of a say in running and managing the business, just as George did, sixteen years earlier. The two could not, however, agree, so, rather regretfully, Samuel decided to leave Bassetts and go and work for his father who had a high class furnishing business in Leopold street by the name of Johnson and Appleyard.

You could be forgiven for thinking that this was the end of Samuel Johnson's involvement in the famous company. Indeed, following Samuel's departure, George decided to broaden his business portfolio by greatly increasing his manufacturing capacity and consolidating his activities at one location. This resulted in the acquisition of much larger premises in Portland Street, a stone's throw from the General Infirmary, where he fitted up a factory with a steam engine and boiler to stream line the sweet-manufacturing processes.

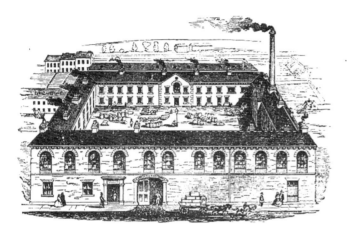

However despite his desire to move with the times technically, he was also keen to keep abreast of his other interests, particularly those relating to local government. So at the age of 40, the busy man decided that it would be of benefit to himself and his business to have a partner.

Perhaps because of the relatively recent departure of Samuel Johnson, George did not choose to ask him if he would be interested in re-joining the company. Perhaps he thought Samuel was too young, or that he would be unable to invest an adequate amount of money into the business, as would be expected of a partner. Whatever the reasons, he chose instead to invite a local grocer by the name of William Lodge to be an equal partner, and he subsequently signed a ten year deed of partnership with him. Although Mr. Lodge brought £1500 capital with him, the rather risky agreement relieved George Bassett of active participation in the day to day management of his new works, this being left to his partner.

This decision proved to be a disaster, and within two years, Bassett and Lodge, as the business was now called, was hardly able to survive, with no profit at all being recorded for the year 1860

But, how could this have happened? What had gone wrong? The answer is simple. Although William Lodge had brought with him some cash and modest experience in

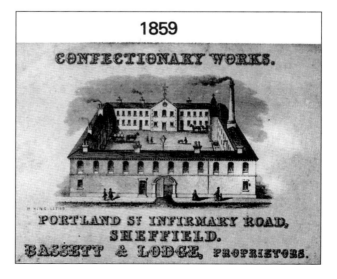

running a grocery shop, he had no real vision and was unable to cope with a large business such as Bassetts. To compound matters, the company had effectively been neglected by George who had chosen to withdraw his initiative, flair and direction from his company in favour of his other outside interests. The end was, therefore, inevitable, and the partnership was thus dissolved by mutual agreement, leaving George searchingly for a miracle.

However, miracles do not grow on trees, do they? Who, for example, would want to come into a failing business? Who would be prepared to work for 'next to nothing' to try and get the business back on its feet? In particular, who had the experience, knowledge and drive which the company now needed? There was only one answer, Samuel Johnson.

SAMUEL JOHNSON RETURNS

It had only been two years since Samuel and George had parted company, so it was now George's turn to go cap-in-hand to a meeting with his former apprentice. The meeting at Johnson and Appleyard's furnishing company took place in a bright, exquisitely designed office overlooking Leopold Street. No expense had been spared to create an atmosphere of calmness and relaxation, and George was somewhat taken aback by the obvious luxury of the surroundings as he entered the room to greet his former assistant.

"It's nice to see you Samuel."

"The pleasure's mine, Mr Bassett."

Several niceties later, the pair of them got down to business, and George asked Samuel to return.

"I would be happy to return, Mr Bassett, but I could only do so as a true partner in the business, with an interest in the profits."

It was at this stage that Samuel Johnson was advised that there were, indeed, no profits available and that the business was in a bad way. He was, however, assured that, when the time was right, a partnership would be offered to him. Upon this promise, the 42 year old former master and his 21 year old former apprentice shook hands and joined forces. The dynamic duo were back together, and they set about restoring Bassetts to its former glory.

With such talent, drive and knowledge steering the company, Bassetts went from strength to strength. Within two years it was successfully employing 150 people at its Portland Street factory, where it made its popular lozenges, liquorice comfits, pastilles, ju-jubes, acid drops, candied peel and marmalade. It is also interesting to note that the Geo. Bassett & Co. advertisement which the company put out at this time refers, surprisingly, to another Bassett outlet at 5 Jewin Crescent, Cripplegate in London, a fact which most history records seem to be unaware of.

Sadly, just as the business was doing well, George suffered the tragic loss of his wife. Poor Sarah, who had given birth to eight children in eighteen years, had become weak and ill. Large families were common place in these days as contraception was non-existent. Unfortunately, many babies died at birth due to the lack of medical knowledge and facilities and, for the same reason, many

also died within the first few years of their delicate lives. Of Sarah and George's eight children, six were girls and all these survived. Sadly the two boys who were born died in infancy. Although no details of Sarah's death at the young age of 39 appear to be available, there is little doubt that the trauma of bearing and bringing up such a large family, as well as losing two sons, had taken its toll on her health. Sadly, such was life for women in those days.

Life, nevertheless, had to carry on, and in an attempt to cope with his grief, George poured every ounce of effort into his successful business. He also felt that it was now an appropriate time to offer his young assistant a share in the company profits. Samuel was still only 24, but three years had elapsed since his return to the company at George's request. However, whilst a share in the profit was attractive to him, it was still not what Samuel really wanted. A partnership had always been his aim and, having considered this latest offer, he wrote a letter to George to try and make him understand what his true ambition was in life. This letter sets out, far better then I could, the feelings and aspirations of this genuinely talented young entrepreneur, and gives us all an insight into the character, foresight and honesty of this man I have, therefore, reproduced the original letter for your perusal:

Private

Mr. Geo. Bassett,

Dear Sir,

More than four years have elapsed since the term of my apprenticeship expired, and I now feel that the time has come when I should seriously look at my prospects for the future. The proposal which you kindly made to me last week has occupied much of my thoughts but before I can give expression to my wishes, I feel it is my duty to tender to you my very warmest thanks for the many acts of kindness I have received at your hands during the time that I lived under your roof and since, and whether the proposal which I am about to make meets with your approval or not I feel that wherever I may be found, memory will recall to me many acts of courtesy and forbearance which I have received both from you and your family and for which I trust I shall ever feel grateful. I would especially remember that gratuity you gave me twelve months ago and also the one you gave me last week and for the proposal referred to above I feel in duty bound to thank you.

As you will be aware the granting of a percentage gives me no real standing in the commercial world; that whether the benefits I derive from it be much or little I can only look upon myself in the light of a servant and as such I am liable (in common with others) to the chances of holding a situation; now what I want to feel is (simply what you and thousands more have felt when at my age) that I am settled in business, that I am acting on my own account; in short, I want to feel myself as a master even if it be but a small business, rather than a servant even if it be under a large business; and in order to effect this purpose I wish most respectfully to ask you that instead of carrying out the proposal made last week, you will devise some scheme by which I shall become a partner in your business. If you ask me on what grounds I make such a request I would briefly state the following.

1st. It is the fulfilment of your own promise made in a letter to my father dated March 1860, and also of promises made to me. It was with the distinct understanding that I should become a partner in your business that I left my father's situation, and you will no doubt remember that when we were discussing the terms of my entering your situation you arranged that this should be the time when I might look for a partnership.

2nd. I pledge my competency. After having been in your service more than nine years it is not necessary that I should attempt to speak of my abilities; you know me and know me thoroughly and are therefore well able to judge. I think I can look back upon the past and say that to the best of my abilities I have faithfully laboured to secure your interests; I mention this not as any ground of merit, because in doing what I have done I have only performed my duty, but I mention the past as a pledge for the future.

3rd. Although but in a humble station in life myself – my connections and associations are both numerous and respectable; certain gentlemen (whose names I do not feel at liberty to mention) have kindly undertaken for me, and at the present time I have an offer to this effect, viz. that if I think well to commence business on my own account they will find me the necessary means for carrying on a trade of a respectable magnitude, so that in justice to myself as a man, and as a Christian, it behoves me to make the best of my position.

I do not wish to dictate to you on what terms I desire a partnership; I want not one penny more than I am fairly, justly and honourably entitled to; the one thing I feel bent upon is to change my position from a servant to a master. In making this request I am not actuated by any vindictive feeling. I do not wish to put myself in opposition to you. I desire that these friendly relations, which have so long existed between us, will continue; my sole object is to make the best of my position as far as I can consistently and conscientiously do so. I have carefully weighed the casualties and probabilities of both sides and would put before you one, out of many reasons, why I seek a change: - suppose that in a few years you retire from commercial life, or death should call you away (which latter change I hope may be far distant) your business would, in justice to your own interests, doubtless be sold, and would probably fall into hands to whom I am a perfect stranger, and whom in all human probability would not require my services; hence instead of me having nursed and cherished a business for myself, I should be cast upon the world having in reality, the battle of life to commence afresh.

In conclusion I would say that if in this letter I have expressed my thoughts in any irreverent or dictatorial manner you will excuse it and praying that we may each be guided by "the spirit of Truth"

I am, dear sir

Yours faithfully,

Samuel Meggitt Johnson

GEORGE BASSETT AND SAMUEL JOHNSON PARTNERS IN BASSETTS

No-one could fail to be moved by the sincerity of this letter, and from that time, January 1893, the two men became genuine partners in confectionery works which were described at the time by his contemporaries as "the largest and most complete of their kind in this or any other country".

George, however was a man who liked people, and they, in return, liked him. Within a year of the death of his dear wife Sarah, he had met and fallen in love with another Sheffield lass of the same name. Whether or not it was something about the name he liked, or whether it was just coincidence, we don't really know, but in late 1863, at the age of 45, the energetic confectioner married Sarah Ann Hague. Following the early death of his two young sons born to his first wife, George had almost given up the idea of having anyone to carry on the family name. It was with great joy and relief therefore, that he was able to celebrate the birth of two healthy sons by his new wife over the next two years.

Not to be outdone by his partner, however, Samuel, now 25, started courting George's eldest daughter who, by this time, had reached the golden age of 21. George was quite approving of courtship, although it was not until four years later, in 1868, that the happy couple actually got married. Tragically for both men, the new family bride died in childbirth about eighteen months later, another victim of those difficult Victorian times of relative medical ignorance. The only saving grace in this very sad situation was that Sarah Ann left behind a beautiful baby daughter as a constant reminder of herself, which helped both her husband and her father to better cope with their grief.

GEORGE BECOMES A TOWN COUNCILLOR

Samuel was still only 31, and decided, like George before him, to throw himself into the business to work off his sorrow and despair. George, meantime, was nearing 50, and turned even more to local politics, looking after the welfare of the people of Sheffield who he represented as a local councillor. Within three years he was invited by the Town Council to became an Alderman, an honorary position second only to the Mayor, which was bestowed on him for his long, loyal service to the town. However, the pinnacle of his involvement with local government and his deep concern for the well-being of the citizens of Sheffield occurred in 1876 when, at the age of 58, he was appointed to the position of Mayor. This was undoubtedly one of the proudest moments of his life.

However, whilst George was a rising star on the local political scene, Samuel had virtually taken over the running of the company, and extended the Portland Street premises by the building of a new factory. Of even more importance, during this eventful year of 1876, he fell in love again and married the daughter of the reverend John Harvard, the headmaster of Wesley College, later to become King Edward V11 School.

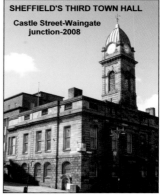
SHEFFIELD'S THIRD TOWN HALL
Castle Street-Waingate junction-2008

Now, George Bassett was a man who enjoyed celebrations, particularly on occasions such as this. He had achieved the exalted position of Mayor, his partner had got married again, and he had a new factory which increased his workforce to over 200. So, what could he do to celebrate? He decided to invite his entire workforce to tea in the Mayor's parlour. It was a sight to behold as sweet makers and sorters, machine operators, supervisors, accountants, administrators and management all arrived in their 'Sunday best'. The parlour was full to bursting as two hundred excited people (mostly women) sipped tea and munched sandwiches and buns in the most prestigious room in town. What a tale they had to tell their families and friends for years to come!

Sheffield's third Town Hall
Early 1800s

However, it wasn't just local people that the new Mayor entertained. He was delighted to receive into his home in Endcliffe Crescent, none other than General Ulysses S. Grant, the President of the United States of America from 1868 -76, who was visiting the town on completion of his eight years in office. As well as staying with George Bassett at his home, the President was honoured by a banquet given by the Mayor at the Cutler's hall on September 27th, 1877, during which both host and guest devoured a wonderful eight course meal.

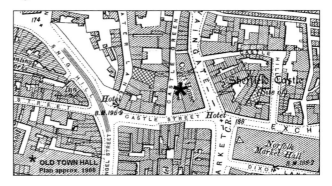

GEORGE BASSETT
SAYS GOODBYE

From all appearances, life for the extraordinary sweet-maker was going quite well, though the stress of the recent loss of his daughter and the pressure of his fairly hectic life-style must have taken their toll. But, of course, we never know what it is just around the corner, do we? Unfortunately, within a year of his successful year in office as mayor, he suffered a stroke at the age of 60. He was unable to continue with any business duties and, following several more attacks over the next five years, he became a virtual invalid. Sadly, on May 1st, 1886, he suffered a further stroke and died at the age of 68.

Sheffield had lost a real character, a man who had made his mark on life, and who was probably one of the best known people in town. Although he was born in Derbyshire and spent ten years in Chesterfield, the major part of his life, forty four years, was spent in Sheffield, the place he loved. His entitlement to be classed as one of Sheffield's 'folk' is thus undisputed. In his obituary notices, George Bassett was described as "the foremost confectionery manufacturer in England", a fact which no-one could deny. At his funeral, his good friend and partner Samuel Johnson spoke of him with great fondness and respect:

> "One feature that was specially prominent in Mr Bassett, was his promptness and decision of action; even when a boy this was notably conspicuous; he no sooner formed an idea or conceived a desire upon a certain course of action, then, without wavering or hesitation, he promptly began to execute it; some of his family would often express: "with our George, it is a word and a blow", and so it was; not only things temporal, but in things spiritual also."

Is this, then, the end of the story? Was the great man's death the end of the Bassett era? In a way it was, although, in another way, it was also the beginning, as G. Bassett and Co. rose to even greater heights under the guidance and control of an equally great man, Samuel Meggitt Johnson.

Before we move on to see how Samuel Johnson influenced Bassetts future, it is just worth diversifying for a few moments to have a brief look at another famous name which has links today with Bassetts sweets. That name is Granelli, the maker of a very well known Italian ice cream.

This traditional ice cream was introduced into England by Louis Granelli about the same time that George Bassett died and today its business is still run from a small shop at 66-68 Broad Street, just a short distance above Bassetts' first shop at number 30. Rosita Granelli (now Rosita Hunt) is the proprieter of this intriguing shop which not only sells its own ice cream, but also most of the old fashioned sweets which were around a hundred years or more ago. Bassetts' sweets are prominent among the rows of multi-coloured glass jars which adorn the shop's shelves and a visit to this very old property, which sits on the periphery of Sheffield's 21st century Supertram interchange, is really worth a visit if you like stepping back into the past. I wonder if George Bassett could ever have imagined his sweets being sold a few yards up the road one hundred and sixty six years after he moved in at number 30?

Charles Granelli with his first horse-pulled ice cream cart

Peter Granelli in his posh new ice cream van

Today's streamlined van

GRANELLI'S ICE CREAM

Granelli's Broad Street shop in 2008

Inside Granelli's shop with Rosita

SAMUEL JOHNSON IN CHARGE AND DISASTER STRIKES

Although George Bassett was survived by his widow Sarah Ann and their two sons, none of them had taken an active interest in the family business. Barely out of their early teenage years, and possibly with little or only modest knowledge of the confectionery business, the boys agreed with Samuel that they wouldn't join the family firm (even though they and their mother owned half of it) as long as he was able to establish a new company for them to manage. Thus, the Don Confectionery Company on Bridge Street was set up by Samuel, with himself as senior partner with little practical control, and the two sons managing it. This arrangement, with Samuel also retaining his position of managing director of Bassetts, seemed to suit all parties.

For the next six years, every-thing went well for all concerned until tragedy struck.

It was getting on for midnight on a cold February day in 1892, when a pounding on Samuel's door at home awoke him from a troubled sleep. It had been a long day for him at Portland Street, with some problems with the manufacturing process needing to be sorted out. He had been unable to resolve one specific problem by knocking-off time, so he had decided to sleep on it.

"Mester Johnson. Come quickly. The factory's on fire!"

Those words, which forced their way through his stout front door amidst a constant hammering of fists, cut through Samuel's semi-conscious mind like a sharp knife. Struggling to throw on some clothes, he staggered downstairs and opened the door to confront his distraught night-watchman who was nearly in tears.

"I don't know 'ow it started Mester Johnson. One minute everything was fine, and the next minute the whole place had gone up in flames."

"All right William. Try and relax. Just take me there as fast as you can."

The horse taxi which William had commandeered clattered frantically over the dark, cobbled streets as the two silent men sat grim-faced with their private thoughts in the wildly swaying buggy which did its best to shake its occupants out. As they reached Infirmary Road, the glistening steel rails, which carried the daily horse trams, also did their best to upturn the hard-wheeled carriage, whilst the sweating, powerful mare careering them along snorted in protest through clouds of angry, hot breath which swirled around its head. It was as though everything was on fire that night.

Suddenly, Samuel saw it. An orange glow in the distance gradually changed to a noisy, fiery red cloud which exploded into huge flames engulfed in billowing black smoke as they turned into Portland Street. A horse-drawn fire engine with fire fighters had arrived from Rockingham Street, but the magnitude and ferocity of the fire rendered their efforts almost totally ineffective. The whole factory seemed to be ablaze, with the hungry flames determined to have their taste of the huge stock of delicious sweets which were stored there.

This was the largest fire Sheffield had ever known at that time, and the factory suffered such severe damage that only a small part was able to be saved to enable some confectionery production to continue there. The lack of adequate fire-fighting appliances for such a large blaze was obviously a contributory factor to the extent of damage caused, and it wasn't until the year 1900, eight years later, that much improved facilities were provided at modern premises built at West Bar.

This fire was a devastating blow to poor Samuel, who was as gutted as his factory. Although the building carried some insurance, it was totally inadequate to cater for the extensive damage caused. Years of hard work and effort had gone up in smoke, and Samuel Johnson, now 53 years old, felt total despair. As he stood there, gazing with disbelief at the crumbling building, the wild, uncompromising flames almost seemed to taunt him as they crackled with laughter at the tears which had begun slowly rolling down his cheeks. Time seemed to stop on that dreadful night, and when it became clear over the next few days that the building insurance was totally inadequate to cover the extensive damage caused, Samuel sank into a deep depression and suffered a nervous breakdown. At the insistence of both his wife and of his doctor, he took a complete rest abroad for six months which necessitated his three teenage sons taking over the running of the business in his absence.

The following months proved to be very difficult for the Johnson boys who, without their father's guidance, struggled to cope. In addition, due to the lack of adequate facilities at Portland Street following the fire, most of the confectionery production was transferred to the Don factory in Bridge Street under the watchful eyes of George Bassett's two sons, thereby taking much of the control away from the caretaker brothers.

SAMUEL JOHNSON
OWNS BASSETTS

It was, however, a much changed Samuel Johnson who arrived home after his enforced rest. His resolve and determination had returned, and he was ready to move forward with optimism. However, he was unhappy with the way that many of Bassetts' most lucrative products appeared to have been 'taken over' by Don Confectionery. This situation led to a permanent breakdown in his relationship with his old partner's sons, resulting in an agreement between them that he would take over the total Bassett family business (of which he was already managing Director) in exchange for his financial interest in the Don business. I wonder how George Bassett would have felt about this sad state of affairs. Despite having had two sons to carry on his name within the business, neither had chosen to do so. I suspect that he would have been very disappointed.

However, the Bassett name was in good hands as Samuel, now the sole proprietor of the company, rose out of the ashes of the Portland Street like a 'phoenix' to grasp the nettle of opportunity and endeavour to restore Bassetts to its former glory. This, however, was no easy task, as the dreadful fire had created a significant financial problem for the company, which struggled to survive for several years. Samuel didn't have to face this struggle alone, however, for although his older son did not wish to stay in the confectionery business, his two younger sons, William, aged 15 and Percy, aged 13, were not only keen to do so, but showed the same ambition and flair as their father.

Over the next few years, William and Percy gradually took over more management responsibility from Samuel as all three slowly turned the business round. As I've already mentioned, none of us really know what is round the corner of life. Unfortunately, several of those corners had been rather dark to date, but a flash of brightness was about to appear.

The Birth of
Bassetts Liquorice Allsorts

The year was 1899, probably the most important date in Bassetts' history, and the fortunes of the company were destined to change forever. Up to this time, Bassetts had, with reasonable success, been happily making a range of liquorice creams, solid liquorice chunks and liquorice military buttons. All these lines were packed and sold separately. George Bassett had, in fact, introduced and specialized in liquorice sweets early in his business career, and perhaps now is an appropriate time to digress once more and take a quick look at how liquorice had become so popular. Let us go back a hundred years or so to Pontefract (a small town about 12 miles north of Doncaster) where a local chemist, by the name of George Dunhill, had produced

the first liquorice Pomfret cakes (Pomfret being the old name for Pontefract). These sweets, made by the incorporation of liquorice root in a confection consisting of flour, sugar and molasses, were known locally as Yorkshire Pennies because of their origin and shape. These were the precursor to other liquorice sweets such as Catherine

Wheels, Bootlaces and Pipes, all of which continue to be popular to the present day. It is also interesting to note that it was during the 11th century that liquorice first made its presence known in Pontefract. Liquorice plants were brought to this famous town by a group of monks from France who established a monastery in the town and grew their plants there. Evidence suggests that liquorice was extracted from the roots of the plant at that time for use in the preparation of medicines. Following this, the local farmers continued to grow liquorice, and a lucrative local industry developed making liquorice lozenges "to ease stomach disorders".

However, let's come back to that eventful year of 1899, and find out exactly why it was so special. To do this, we will have to join Charlie Thompson in Samuel Johnson's office one fine morning in June of that year. Charlie was one of Bassett's four full-time travellers and had worked for the company for many years gaining a wealth of knowledge and experience. He was a very down to earth sort of person who always carried out his duties with a cheerful smile and total dedication. Today was destined to be the pinnacle of what was to be a 61 year career with Bassetts.

"I'm off to see Mester Walker in Leicester today, Mester Johnson. I fancy he'll like our Liquorice creams now that you've added a few new 'uns in. I'll take a sample tray of 'em all so that he can choose which ones he likes best. Wish me luck guv."

Walker's Wholesale Co. in Leicester was a good customer, but was always on the lookout for something different with which to tempt his retail customers. Today, the cheerful traveller was taking the full range of liquorice sweets which he had neatly arranged in order of shape and design in his purpose- made sample case.

It took a couple of hours or so to travel down to Leicester, and Charlie always looked forward to catching the gleaming steam train which took him to within a short horse-taxi ride from his customer's warehouse. He loved the journey which took him through open fields and rolling countryside, and always marvelled at the streaming clouds of smoke which belched out of the powerful engine as it proudly pulled its train of swaying carriages.

"My, this is the life," he mused as he glanced out of his window, feeling rather like royalty as he acknowledged a crowd of excited children who were frantically waving at the metal monster which thundered by.

The journey was almost too quick for our Charlie, but all good things come to an end sometime he thought, as the train pulled in at its destination. As the train clanked to a grinding halt, he jumped down onto the station platform amidst the deafening hiss of escaping steam which seemed to engulf the whole station. Within ten to fifteen minutes, he was standing outside the warehouse gates, having caught one of several horse-taxies which always waited patiently outside the station gates. Having entered the familiar reception area, he was shown to an office where the director's shiny oak table and chairs occupied their usual place.

"Morning Charlie," boomed the smiling wholesaler as he bustled into the office, offering his hand in friendship. "What have you brought me today?"

"Mornin', Mester Walker. It's nice to see you again."

Charlie opened his precious case and proudly placed it on the table, displaying several rows of Bassetts finest liquorice-based sweets which looked like coloured soldiers standing smartly to attention.

"Well, Mester Walker. They look delicious, don't they?"

"I tell you what, Charlie. Put them on that chair over there while we have a chat over a cup of tea."

Bassetts' slightly over-eager traveller couldn't help but notice the wholesaler's slight disappointment with his display as he carefully moved it to make way for some morning refreshments.

"Ah, there you are. Thank you, Miss Jones. Just bring the tray over here if you would."

Amidst a gentle rattle of cups, saucers and spoons, 'elevenses' appeared on the table, and the kindly secretary backed away and turned to leave the office.

"Oops! Oh my goodness, I'm so sorry Mr Walker. I didn't see that case on the chair."

Charlie looked in horror as his carefully assembled selection of sweets tumbled to the floor, scattering in all directions. Miss Jones was sobbing, Mr. Walker was trying to comfort her, and the white-faced Charlie was frantically trying to scoop his precious samples together.

As traveller, customer and secretary gazed in disbelief at the multi-coloured sweets which adorned the office carpet, Mr Walker's eyes suddenly lit up.

"Just a minute, Charlie. I rather like the look of that assortment on the floor. There's something about all those colours mixed together that's rather attractive."

Miss Jones suddenly stopped crying, the bewildered salesmen stopped trying to rescue some red and blue sugary buttons which had rolled under the chair, and a deafening silence descended upon the room.

"You know Miss Jones, you've done us all a favour," boomed the now smiling wholesaler. He now realised that he might just have got a new and different product to sell as a result of this accident.

"I tell you what Charlie. See if you can let me have fifty boxes of all sorts of your liquorice sweets mixed up together. I reckon they'll sell like hot cakes in the shops."

It was a thoughtful Bassetts traveller who arrived back at Portland Street later that afternoon. He'd popped in to see Samuel Johnson to tell him about the morning's events, but both men were a little sceptical about the idea of mixing their liquorice sweets together.

"Even if we provide what Mr. Walker wants, what do you think we should call such a selection Charlie? It will need a good name for it to sell you know."

"I've been thinking about that, Mester Johnson. As we've been asked to supply all sorts of sweets, why not simply call them Allsorts or, better still Bassett's Liquorice Allsorts?"

So, this was the birth of what were to be, and still are, the most famous and well known sweets in the country. Although the following few weeks were a little worrying, with little or no reaction to the new line filtering through, an amazing order suddenly arrived on Samuel's desk for an unprecedented 5 TONS of liquorice Allsorts! This was the beginning of the 'Allsorts phenomenon' as huge demands for the selection spread around the country. Bassetts was back in business again with a vengeance.

BASSETTS FACTORY BUILT AT OWLERTON

So large was the success brought about by this new confectionery innovation that shortage of factory space at Portland Street was now becoming a problem. Realising this, Samuel decided to buy a site at Owlerton where, in 1900, he built his new factory. Confectionery production traded here under the business name of S.M.Johnson and Sons, and was managed by Samuel's youngest son Percy, who by now had reached the age of 21. Initially, the factory was responsible only for Bassetts considerable candied peel output, but, when its production was isolated from all the other confectionery lines, it became obvious that the product rarely made a profit. As a result, it was decided to

reduce the quantity of candied peel produced, and to introduce instead new confectionery lines such as gums, pastilles, toffees and caramels.

The Owlerton factory now took off, and by 1912 demand was so great that a new, large, four storey production block was built on the same site.

Up to this time, Liquorice Allsorts had continued to be made in vast quantities only at Portland Street. However, with the erection of the new Owlerton block, part of its production was moved there. Several new products were also added to the range, most notably glace cherries, and the candied peel business also slowly improved. It is worth mentioning, however, that the peel and cherry business only lasted just over twenty years, and was wound up in 1934 due to lack of demand. Such is the 'fickle' nature of the buying public.

SAMUEL HAND OVER THE COMPANY TO HIS SONS

1914 brought the outbreak of the First World War. As a consequence of this, sugar supplies for confectionery were reduced by 75%, and Owlerton began making Jam for the armed services instead. This range of 'S.M. Johnson and Sons' jam proved very popular at this difficult time, and helped to keep the factory going.

By this time, however, Samuel Johnson had reached the incredible age of 76 and was still working full-time. During the four war years, therefore, he delegated much of his responsibilities to his two sons, with William Johnson managing Portland Street and Percy continuing to fully manage Owlerton. Following this, in 1919, the business

which Samuel had joined in 1860 at the age of 21, and of which he became sole proprietor in 1886 at the age of 47, was converted to a private, limited company, Geo. Bassett & Co. Ltd, with himself, now 80, as Chairman and his two sons as directors.

It is worthwhile digressing for a few moments here, to look at what other interests Samuel M. Johnson had pursued

Percy Johnson

William Johnson

during his remarkable business life. They had, in fact, stretched way beyond his confectionery activities, and included directorships of several public companies including the Ebbw Vale Coal and Iron Company of South Wales and the Sheffield Forge and Rolling mills, a company of which he was chairman for many years. He was also chairman of the Sheffield Union Banking Company, and held several directorships of shipping companies. The busy man was also a staunch Methodist, and was a local preacher for more than half a century. I wonder what he did in his spare time?

Unlike his predecessor George Bassett, this great man chose not to take part in public life, having more of a reserved temperament than his former partner. His total dedication to his work, as well as to his faith, was evidenced by the fact that he still retained his active position as chairman of Bassetts until his death on the 29th November 1925 at the age of 86. Hard work and dedication had certainly suited Samuel Johnson. At his funeral, his grandson Gordon, who was himself destined to be chairman one day, described him as "a man of outstanding ability, with a very acute business brain, a great capacity for work, and a high sense of justice".

The passing of Samuel Johnson was as significant in the history of Bassetts as was the passing of its founder, George Bassett, almost forty years earlier. Between them, the two remarkable men had overcome significant business and personal adversities to develop Bassetts from its small beginnings to probably the most successful confectionery business in the country. Although advances in sugar confectionery production had been considerable during this period, which spanned eighty three years between 1842 and 1925, much more was still to come. Who better, therefore, could there be to guide Bassetts into an entirely new dimension of sweet making than William and Percy Johnson, Samuel's two sons?

BERTIE BASSETT CREATED

The year following their father's death, the brothers decided to float the business on the Stock Market, with William, now 49 and Percy 47, occupying the positions of chairman and vice-chairman respectively in the public company. They also decided that it was time to look for a 'Bassetts' trademark, a task which they gave to Greenlys Advertising Agency. This company, inspired by the huge success of the Michelin Man trademark of Michelin tyres, decided to create the similar, and now nationally and internationally well known, figure of Bertie Bassett.

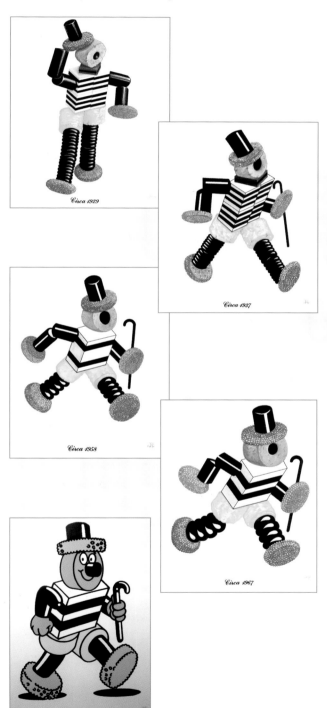

Circa 1929

Circa 1937

Circa 1958

Circa 1967

Bertie was a colourful character created from pieces of liquorice confectionery and, following his first appearance in 1929 complete with a top hat, he acquired a cane in 1937,

changed shape slightly in 1958 and 1967, and eventually acquired a smiling face in 1982. Not content with just being a trademark, he manifested himself, with the aid of a kindly volunteer wearing a multi-coloured costume, as a live Bertie, who visited people in hospitals, appeared at important events and even starred on children's television. Just about everyone in the country was familiar with Bertie Bassett (and, indeed, still are), and you could say that he was the David Beckham of the sweet world!

Bertie's introduction into the Bassetts scene was obviously a resounding success and, with William and Percy at the helm, the business expanded rapidly. A confectionery laboratory was also opened at Owlerton which, together with the appointment of the company's first chemist, took the pioneering business to the forefront of development and food safety. Indeed, one of the first products to come out of the laboratory was a new, low priced speciality called Silky Toffee, sales of which went 'right through the roof'.

However, despite the success, William and Percy were not destined to have an easy ride at the top. Even Bertie didn't foresee the serious trade depression and rising unemployment which hit the country in the early 1930's and resulted in a world slump. During this time, the 'little man' had to work extra hard to encourage the public to spend as much of their income as they could afford on Liquorice Allsorts, in order that Bassetts could just keep its head above water. This emphasis on these multi-shaped, multi-coloured sweets was, in fact, the company's saviour during this difficult period.

It was also during this time that Bassetts high flying sales manager, Mr E.M. Mott, hit upon an idea to capture the low end of the popular market to help keep the company's head above water. All Bassetts lines, and almost all those of other manufacturers also, were selling at 3d (1¼ pence today) per quarter.

Mr Mott was well aware that the public was having to tighten its belt, and thought that it would be a good idea for all concerned if a more affordable line at 2d (3/4 pence) per quarter could be made available. In order to produce this cheaper product, which Bassetts did not wish to have directly associated with their name for fear of it having a detrimental effect on the 'high quality' reputation it had built up, he hit upon a solution that is common practice today, but which at the time was innovative. He suggested to William and Percy that they buy an old, established business in Dewsbury by the name of Slade and Bullock, and use this as the outlet for the cheaper 2d per quarter sweets which would, nevertheless, be manufactured by Bassetts in Sheffield. Although Slade and Bullock Ltd became a subsidiary of Bassetts, this fact was not made public for ten years or so, and the cheaper confectionery was gratefully brought by the sweet-eating public in large quantities without any link being made with the Sheffield Company.

GEORGE BASSETT'S SONS

It is probably an appropriate time in our Bassetts story to have a brief look at the fortunes or otherwise of George Bassett's two sons who ended up with the Don Confectionery Company on Bridge Street in 1892. Sadly, his younger son died within eight years of the split with Samuel Johnson, leaving older brother John to run the business on his own. This he did with reasonable success for the next three years until his company ran into financial difficulties, like many others, during the 1930's depression. John was 69 by this time, and gratefully sold out to William and Percy in order that he could take some well earned retirement.

Don Confectionery had, therefore, gone full circle, and was once again under the ownership of Bassetts. This time, however, the transaction was friendly and amicable, and the staff and workforce retained their jobs, working at the Bridge Street factory for a year or more before all being absorbed into Bassetts' Owlerton and Portland Street works, to which production was transferred. It is, however, a little sad to note that the last Bassett family member had left the confectionery business for good, and although George Bassett's proud name remains to this day, he would, no doubt, have been a little upset at the demise of his family's involvement in the trade.

However, it was 1933, and as one well-known name retired from the confectionery business, anther began. Douglas Gordon Johnson, who preferred to be called Gordon, joined his father Percy in the family business, having spent several years in training. Times were changing at Bassetts, and plans were afoot to consolidate all production at Owlerton and close the Portland Street factory. Percy Johnson, now 55, was in poor health, and his brother William, Company Chairman and Managing Director, was also feeling the strain. Mr Mott was accordingly appointed as joint managing director to alleviate the situation.

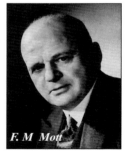

F. M Mott

CHANGES AT THE TOP

To accommodate the proposed move to Owlerton, an additional large, new factory block was proposed to enable the entire production of Liquorice Allsorts to be more efficiently carried out in one location. The building of these new premises took place over the next few years, and during this time Percy Johnson's health deteriorated and, sadly, he died in 1936 at the age of 57. This was a major blow, not only to the Johnson family, but to Bassetts the company, which he had served with dedication, flair and enthusiasm from the young age of 13. Gordon, his son, had only been with the company for three years and had insufficient experience to expect promotion to any senior post, although he did become a member of the board of directors a year

later. The obvious choice to succeed Percy as Vice Chairman was the Joint Managing Director, E.M. Mott, whose extensive knowledge of confectionery and the company was unquestionable.

Following this personal tragedy, William Johnson, now ably assisted by Mr. Mott, pushed for the rapid completion of the new 'Allsorts' production block at Owlerton, and within a year of his brother's death, production began to be transferred there.

OWLERTON ON FIRE

However, who said that lightening never strikes twice? Before the whole transfer was complete, it happened again.

"Excuse me Mr. Johnson, sir. Isn't that a fire we can see in the distance? The sky's very red, but it doesn't look like a sunset to me."

The production manager was in William's office going through the latest trading figures and had casually glanced out of the north-facing window which overlooked the Don Valley way up to Hillsborough. Although it was difficult to judge distances on that late spring evening, both men showed deep concern as impossible thoughts raced through their minds. The sun had long since disappeared over the horizon, but the slowly spreading orange glow caused a numbing chill to strike through William's pounding heart.

"Are you all right, Mr Johnson, sir? You've gone real pale, you have!"

William had been away at boarding school in Lytham at the time of the fire which nearly destroyed the Portland Street works. As a 15 year old lad, he'd been both upset and just a little bit excited that Sheffield's biggest ever fire should occur at his father's factory.

Today, however, his emotion was one of extreme concern. Surely it couldn't happen again?"

"Harry, get the car and take me over to Owlerton. I just want to make sure everything's alright."

The journey, short though it was, seemed to take an age, and as the clanging bells of fire engines converging on the area grew louder, William knew to expect the worst.

"Just look at that Mr. Johnson, sir. The four-storey block's completely ablaze. It's like a bloody bonfire out of control!"

Harry knew he'd overstepped the mark with his coarse language, as the chairman was a stickler for protocol, but with tears welling up in his eyes, his emotions had got the better of him.

With bowed head, William stood by the side of his posh, new ford motor car, which Harry had parked at the Penistone Road end of Beulah Road, knowing now how his father Samuel had felt forty six years previously. As the huge flames caused dark shadows which danced playfully over the orange glow which illuminated his pale, anguished face, the tired confectioner seemed too stunned to respond. Little did he know as he stood there, that this fire would also be identified as 'Sheffield's biggest', and that Bassetts would hold the unwanted 'honour' of being the victim of both of Sheffield's worst ever fires, these being in 1892 and now in 1938.

Samuel Johnson had been 53 at the time of the first fire, after which he had suffered a nervous breakdown due mainly to the lack of adequate insurance taken out on his

factory. William was now 61, older but wiser than his father before him, and had gained valuable experience from the earlier incident. Terrible though it was, the fire completely destroying the four storey extension built twenty six years earlier, its impact on production was only temporary. Good fire-insurance cover was in place this time, and with the Portland Street factory still being available, it continued to be used for several years longer than had been planned, to make up for the one which had burnt to the ground at Owlerton.

It is worth pausing for a few seconds at this stage to consider the incidents, problems and tragedies which we have encountered so far in our Bassetts story. These, you will no doubt realize, are typical of those which affect most of us throughout our life. We all, from time to time, ask ourselves "Why is this happening to me?" thinking that our problems are greater than anyone else's. Of course, when these problems or tragedies occur, they are indeed completely personal to us, and we are entitled to ask such a question. However, in the grand scheme of things, most of us realise that everyone has to endure most of the experiences encountered by the generations of people we have met so far in the Bassetts story. Indeed, but for the setting and the subject matter, we could in fact be reading about ourselves. That, perhaps, is why we find much of it so interesting.

WORLD WAR TWO ARRIVES

With these thoughts in mind, let's go back to William Johnson after his disastrous fire. He was quite philosophical about the event, which he endeavoured to take in his stride without creating excess self-imposed stress. It was just as well that he did, as yet another blow was to hit this and all other companies in the country. World War Two was declared in 1939. At this time, Bassetts was employing about nine hundred girls in its confectionery manufacturing processes. However, following drastic reductions in the sugar allocation imposed by the government, Bassett's had no option but to release three hundred of them as production plummeted. Although most of the girls were able to be transferred to work of national importance, the future of many of the remaining six hundred was still in the balance. Desperate measures were now needed by William and his team to cope with the crisis which, of course, was affecting all food manufacturers in the country. Diversity was the idea they came up with.

The first decision made was to install a plant for dehydrating vegetables such as carrots, cabbage and potatoes for the Ministry of Food. Whilst these lightweight, packaged vegetables may not have tasted as good as the real thing, the ability to distribute them cheaply and efficiently without them perishing was a considerable advantage at this difficult time. An even more diverse activity which they introduced was the packing of surgical requisites for Johnson and Johnson, a well known American firm. This unusual, but very necessary, task benefited about one hundred and fifty of the older women at Bassetts who were unable to be employed on war work, and who might otherwise have lost their jobs. In addition, due to the large availability of space at the Owlerton factory, part of it was used for the assembly of trimmer boxes for the Wellington bomber, whilst a Home Guard Battalion and a Home Guard Anti-Aircraft Battery set up their head-quarters in another part of the factory.

It must be said, William Johnson and his board of directors cannot be criticised for showing any lack of ideas in this war crisis. Indeed, due to their initiative, Bassetts not only survived, they made a significant contribution to the war effort also.

Although sugar controls and food rationing (including sweets) continued for many years after hostilities had ceased, the ugly cloud of war did, nevertheless, have its 'silver lining' for those who were able to see it. Bassetts was one such organisation with the foresight to build on the government's exports ban, which continued in Europe for some years after. William made the decision, therefore, to look further afield and focus his export business on Canada and America instead. This proved to be a very sound strategy as, by the time the home market was freed in 1953, Bassetts had increased its pre-war exports of 5% of its production to a staggering 25%. This was initiative-taking at its best.

After 1953, as would probably be expected at the end of the dreaded ration book era, the whole of the confectionery business boomed in response to the public's immediate demand for sweets. Bassetts was no exception as its home sales increased to more than double its normal pre-war level, this being the highest increase by a long way in the highly competitive confectionery trade. Life for the Allsorts company was rosy again.

But, of course, time had also been marching on in the boardroom, and William Johnson, who was now 71, decided to retire as Company Chairman. It was 1954, and he had guided Bassetts through the ups and downs of peace and war with great success. His father Samuel would have been very proud of him. His natural successor at that time was Mr. E. M, Mott, the current Vice-Chairman, whose skill, integrity and dedication to the company made him a worthy Bassetts leader. Tragically, Mr. Mott died suddenly at the age of 68 after only seven years in the post, and so, in 1955, Percy Johnson's son Gordon, still only 44, took over the reins of his grandfather's famous company. Bassetts had a Johnson in charge once more.

BASSETTS FACTORY IN THE 1950S BEHIND THE SCENES

Before moving on to the last remarkable chapter in the story of Bassetts and the Sheffield folk who were responsible for its success, let's pop into the 1950's factory at Owlerton and have a peep behind the scenes. At that time, Bassetts was still the largest employer of women in South Yorkshire, a fact which reflected the role of women in those days who, for a very modest wage, were employed en-mass to do what today has been mainly taken over by computers and machines.

It was break-time on that 1950s morning, and the early-shift ladies had gathered together in the large canteen area for a bit of snap, a cup of tea and a good chat. They were a cheerful bunch, with their smiles nearly as bright as their white head-scarves and smocks as they splish–splashed their way to the tables with their generously full cups.

"Eeh! I'm ready for this cuppa', aren't you Dorothy?"

"Not 'alf Mary," her good friend replied before stuffing half a cream bun into her mouth with a sigh of extreme pleasure.

"You know, standing there for two hours or so counting sweets and dropping them into those irritating plastic boxes which never stop moving makes me feel a bit dizzy sometimes. Does it get you like that, Dorothy?"

"Well, it's funny that you should mention that, Mary. I find that my eyes get glazed over after a time and my body

sways with that moving belt contraption. We are funny buggers aren't we?"

Both women broke into fits of laughter, Dorothy trying hard not to spit the remainder of her cream bun into her colleague's half drunk cup of tea.

"It's alright for you two," piped up Elsie, swiftly wiping away the moustache of coffee froth which had suddenly decided to adorn her round, bespectacled face. "I'm at the end of the line and it's not fair when you rely on me to get the right weight of sweets in your boxes when you keep putting the wrong amount in. I don't know whether I'm coming or going sometimes."

Elsie's concerned expression, combined with her cappuccino adornment, set the two women off laughing again, which created a ripple effect amongst the ladies sitting at adjacent tables, who all joined in the hilarity.

A slightly more raucous laugh from Mavis two or three tables away indicated that she and her colleagues were involved in women's talk, which we don't really want to go into here do we? Let's move on then.

The factory floor itself was the next port of call. A large machine had just extruded a four foot length of rolled paste, approximately one and a half feet in width, which was to be used as the base and top of some single-sandwich Liquorice Allsorts Nuggets. This paste, which looked rather like pastry, was made basically from flour, glucose, sugar, flavourings and colourings, and was quickly and accurately overlaid with a pre-rolled two foot layer of black liquorice by two Bassett ladies. These two production workers, once again wearing head-scarves and white smocks, quickly folded the remaining two foot length of paste neatly over the liquorice to form a two foot by one and a half foot 'sandwich'.

"Right, lets have it girls. I'm ready."

A few feet away, holding her rotary 'pizza-cutter' over her head, was Agnes. This lovely lady had worked for Bassetts for many years, and was probably the best Allsorts-

Nuggets-cutter in the business. A gentle press on a red button by one of the two paste- folders sent the unsuspecting, sweet smelling 'sandwich' gently forward, to stop directly under the raised blade. With neither guilt nor hesitation, Agnes attacked with firm, skilful movements, and before you could say 'Jack Robinson', the once proud sandwich had become a heap of square, Allsorts Nuggets.

"Next one," she cried, almost impatiently.

"Just a minute, Agnes. We're not super-girls you know."

The regular banter which flowed between the sweet production ladies was typical of the fairly relaxed and always friendly atmosphere which exists within Bassetts, this being a culture which its management have always encouraged.

Not too far away from our Nugget makers, the popular coconut-covered Liquorice-Allsorts production was in full swing. Two rows of four ladies stood attentively at each side of a fairly rapidly moving conveyor belt which was continuously collecting these delicious sweets being churned out of a hungry chopping machine. This, in fact, was the more modern area of the factory where a bit more automation had been introduced. The ladies' job was to

Bassetts Ladies inspecting and checking

keep a careful eye out for mis-shapes and any foreign objects which might inadvertently have joined the army of round black eyed delicacies which passed in front of them before rolling off at the end of their journey into shallow boxes.

A casual glance around the huge, factory floor revealed many stacks of such trays, which were then transported to the mixing- area in the centre of the room. Here, each stack of trays contained a different variety of Allsorts sweets, and had been placed adjacent to a long, steel-sided mixing bed into which the correct amount of each variety had to be tipped by two more hard-working ladies. This process involved the building-up of several layers of Allsorts, which actually necessitates the sweets being thrown out of their trays and spread evenly by hand.

"We need a tray of coconut chips, Phyllis. They're in that stack behind you."

June and Phyllis worked on this mixing

Mixing the Allsorts

bed together, and had to make sure that all the Allsorts varieties were correctly and evenly layered before they slowly and continuously moved on before tumbling off the end into a vibrator. It was a back-aching job, but by and large, they enjoyed it.

"Come on June, luv, we'll soon have finished our shift and then you can put your feet up for a bit."

"I tell you what Phyllis. I wouldn't mind a quick lie down in that bed for a minute or two to get rid of my aches and pains. I could get up to all-sorts in there, couldn't I?

Poor Phyllis absolutely creased up at June's corny but intentional pun, and had to stop to wipe her cheek with her smock sleeve to stem the tears of laughter streaming down her face.

Once again, it was good to see the laughter and friendship which was inherent in this factory. It was just the medicine that all these sweet-makers needed to cure their ailments, eliminate potential boredom, and keep them going. The maxim that a happy workforce is an efficient workforce certainly seems to apply here, doesn't it?

We couldn't, of course, leave our whistle-stop tour of the factory without catching a glimpse of the jelly baby production area, could we? These delicious, chewy sweets, which come in five different flavours and colours, are nearly as popular as Bassett's main line of Liquorice Allsorts. This is not simply because they taste so good, but

Bassetts' happy workforce

because they are also something of a novelty. How many times, for example, have you heard a mother saying to her child "Now then Emma, which little head shall we bite off first? Yellow? Red? Green? Or, what about the orange one?"

So, as we carefully entered the gums and jellies area, we were met by an invisible cloud of sweet aromas which circulated tantalizing all around us like soft, fruit flavoured snowflakes. Large, steel jelly-making drums hummed with pleasure, and pressure cookers hissed with delight as sugar and glucose syrup were first boiled together with water, before gelatine, colour flavouring and citric acid were added to the

```
THE ASSORTMENT
There are five different colours of Jelly Babies:-

        Red    - Strawberry flavour
        Orange - Jaffa orange flavour
        Green  - Lime flavour
        Yellow - Lemon flavour
        Black  - Blackcurrant flavour
```
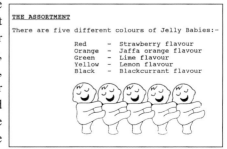

bubbling mixture. The end result of this process is known as the 'Finished Jelly Baby Boiling', a mixture which is now ready to be made into the famous sweets.

A large machine called a Mogul, which you imagine could easily have been part of a 'Doctor Who' setting, was sitting patiently nearby, waiting to receive this mixture. Within it, shallow trays filled corn starch had been stamped out with mouldings which had left impressions in the starch in the shape of Jelly Babies. A gentle shudder suddenly signified the entry of the liquid jelly, which then filled the moulds to produce correct size 'Babies'. Whirring gears and mechanical moans then gave way to movement as the filled trays of moulds were stacked automatically within the Mogul and placed in hot stoves for a final heating. A short time afterwards, they were then allowed to cool and set before the relieved 'little people' were tipped out onto sieves which separated them from the starch in which they had made their epic journey.

As the soft jellies, dusted with flour, emerged from the machine in their hundreds and began their now relaxing ride to the mixing and packaging area, it was really quite a sight to behold, particularly when they all gathered together in a tumbling mix of happy, rainbow-coloured babies.

It's strange, isn't it, how magical a sweet factory can be? Despite the obvious monotony of some of the production lines, the whole sweet-production 'show' is full of colour, shapes, aromas and sounds which feed both the imagination of those who work there and of those who would like to do so. Whilst it is not quite a 'Willy Wonka' setting with its weird and wonderful machines, it is, nevertheless, very similar. If we were to create a picture of Bassetts, we would see that those who work there in their varying coloured smocks and head gear are the real back-cloth upon which the wonders of production can be painted. Multi-coloured pavements of sweets meander at varying levels, linking bubbling, rumbling and chattering machines of all shapes and sizes, whilst glistening silver and shiny black pipes criss-cross the space above, delivering a host of different ingredients to just about everywhere. Around the edges, a host of figures in varying attire give their full support to the 'show' in the guise of marketing, sales, administration, training finance and distribution. It is in fact just one, big, magical scene in which all sorts of people, machinery and processes are interdependent, and upon which a soft, aromatic glaze is finally applied to give it its long lasting finish. Such is the wonder of Bassetts. However, we can't stay there all day, can we? Let's pop back and see what the new boss is doing.

Gordon Johnson now Chairman and Managing Director

It was a strange, nostalgic moment for Gordon Johnson as he sat at the large, polished desk in the boardroom at Bassetts on that hazy, autumn morning in 1955. It wasn't just that he was sitting there alone that made it feel rather unreal. It was also the fact that he was sitting in the large, padded chair at the head of the table, the one always reserved for the Company Chairman. He was the third Johnson to hold the post of Chairman and Managing Director at this famous company, and he had the distinction of being the youngest. His grandfather Samuel had become Managing Director at the age of 47, albeit not sole proprieter, whilst his uncle William was 48 when he took over the Chairman's role from Samuel, thirty nine years later. Another thirty years had passed, and the burden of success now rested on Gordon's shoulders. Now, at the age of 44, he was engulfed with feelings of both pride and

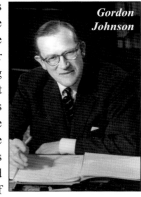

Gordon Johnson

trepidation as his gaze wandered slowly over the empty chairs in front of him which would soon be filled by his expectant board of directors looking to him for leadership, guidance and success. This was indeed a momentous occasion for the latest, and destined to be the last, Johnson to take Bassetts forward to an even better future.

Over the next half a century, which more or less brings us up to the present date, challenges and changes would arise which not even a super-optimistic Gordon would have anticipated. It would not be appropriate for us to go into the fine detail of change over this period, as our story is really about Sheffield folk. However, for completeness, significant events need to be mentioned which I'm sure you will find interesting.

At the time Gordon Johnson took over the Chairmanship of Bassetts, competition within the confectionery industry was very fierce. He and his board decided, therefore, to identify four important objectives. Firstly, the company should introduce modern, more efficient methods of confectionery production. Secondly, they should aim to expand the company's overseas markets. Thirdly, the company should build up a group of manufacturing units to both consolidate Bassetts' control of the liquorice market and broaden its manufacturing base. Last, but not least, it should move into the wholesale market.

Let us have a brief look at each of these decisions to see how successful they were.

PRODUCTION

With regard to the introduction of improved methods of production, Gordon started off by visiting modern, hi-tech confectionery plants in America during his first year in office. Having viewed these with great interest and admiration, he set up a research department at Owlerton to explore the application of his findings to the production of Liquorice Allsorts. Changes began to be introduced to Bassetts' production methods within a year or thereabouts, and, by 1961, the first, highly efficient continuous production line was introduced. By 1966, further radical improvements had taken place, and the Sheffield factory was now described by Bassetts' contemporaries as "one of the most efficient and highly mechanised in the county, if not in the world". It is interesting, isn't it, to recall similar wording used to describe Bassetts Portland Street factory buildings a century or more earlier in 1862, which stated that they were "the largest and most complete of their kind in this or any other country". Bassetts was back on top of the world once again.

OVERSEAS MARKETS

Expansion into overseas markets was something that Bassetts had begun in earnest just after the second world war. Now, the company had the services of Gerald de Pinna, a director with outstanding knowledge and experience in this field. Under his guidance, expansion in this area grew rapidly, and very strong marketing positions were built up in Norway, Finland, Denmark, Holland and West Germany. Indeed, so successful were Bassetts in this field that, in 1961, the President of the Board of Trade, Reginald Maudling, sent them a special letter of commendation.

Gerald de Pinna was such a valuable asset to Bassetts, that by 1963 he had risen to the position of Vice Chairman of the company. He also became a member of the Common Market Committee, as well as becoming Chairman of the Alliance Export Committee and, later, Chairman of the newly formed British Food Export Council.

The culmination of all this effort and success in Bassetts' export drive came in 1967, when the Prime Minister, Harold Wilson, recommended Her Majesty the Queen to confer Her Award to Industry on Geo. Bassett Holdings Ltd, in respect of the export achievements of Bassetts and Wilkinsons, an honour which Gordon and his board of directors were thrilled to receive.

The board's last two objectives were probably their most ambitious, and contained a significant element of risk, as they necessitated considerable expenditure in the acquisition of other confectionery-based companies.

GROUP DEVELOPMENT AND EXPANSION

Gordon's first acquisition was that of Voile and Wortley, a long established, London based, liquorice manufacturing company which was, at that time in 1955, the market leader in liquorice novelties. This was a welcome new line for Bassetts, who had never really dealt in this area to any significant extent. Although production continued in London until 1962, it was transferred to the Owlerton factory in Sheffield thereafter.

It wasn't until 1961 that the next acquisition materialised. This time, the first move was made by the Marshall family, the owners of Bassetts leading liquorice competitor, W.R. Wilkinson and Co. of Pontefract, about 15 miles north of Doncaster. The family wanted to sell the business, which was famous for its Pontefract Cakes, and, following the usual negotiations, became a member of the Bassett Group in May 1961, remaining in Pontefract where they still exist today.

Bassetts manufacturing base had now expanded considerably, but more was still to come. In May 1961, the leading Dutch liquorice manufacturer N.V. De Faam was looking for a buyer. This company was about the same size as Wilkinsons, and specialised in the production of salted liquorice gums, which were very popular in Holland. In addition, it also produced a range of other products such as boiled sweets and peppermint lozenges which were sold in roll packs. With the opportunity offering itself for Bassetts to get a foothold in the European community, Gordon took

the plunge and commenced negotiations. Despite many financial and taxation problems, which delayed the eventual acquisition, N.V. De Faam became the first overseas member of the Bassett Group in March 1964.

It was during this expansion programme that Gordon Johnson and his Board decided to consolidate the creation of the Bassett Group by changing the name of the parent company from Geo. Bassett and Co. Ltd, to Geo. Bassett Holdings Ltd. The existing Sheffield Company thus became one of several subsidiary companies of the new parent company in 1964.

Although the Bassett Group now included Voile and Wortley (now absorbed into the Sheffield works), Wilkinsons of Pontefract and N.V. De Faam of Holland, as well as its original Sheffield based company Geo. Bassett & Co. Ltd, the 'icing on the cake' had yet to be negotiated. Gordon's desire to broaden the manufacturing base, rather than simply expanding it, had not yet materialised. Most of his eggs were still in one liquorice basket, and he was eager to move into other sugar confectionery areas. He decided, therefore, to look at the children's 'self-purchase market' which had become very lucrative by this time. The acknowledged leader in this area was Barratts of London, one of the largest sugar confectionery manufactures in the country.

The popularity and subsequent expansion of this market had arisen as more and more children were given weekly spending money with which to buy sweets, and, as the name suggests, were able to purchase their favourite inexpensive delicacies themselves. Sherbet Fountains are a good example of these products, and have been available from Barratts since 1925. You won't be surprised to hear,

Barratts of London-Early method of transport

therefore, that Gordon Johnson had his eye on this large, successful company and subsequently began negotiations with its chairman, George Walsh. A satisfactory deal was subsequently thrashed out to the mutual satisfaction of both chairmen and their shareholders, and in November 1966, Barratts also became a member of the Bassett Group, with Barratts' Chairman and his Managing Director becoming members of the Group Board.

So, Bassetts had now acquired a company, not only whose name is second to none in the children's market, but one which boasted a large range of production facilities and expertise, with a workforce in London in excess of thirteen hundred. Because of a growing shortage of labour there, Gordon further extended his Sheffield factory, phased out the one in London, and rebuilt and greatly enlarged a small overflow factory in Uddingston, south-east of Glasgow, which Barratts had previously acquired. Bassetts had now reached its manufacturing objective, with the Group's U.K. production vastly increased and consolidated in three factories at Sheffield, Pontefract and Uddingston. As for the overseas market, N.V. De Faam in Holland, and a small factory in Australia, previously owned by Barratts, served to gently spread Bassetts sweet, sticky fingers around the world!.

WHOLESALE MARKET DEVELOPMENT

However, the last phase of Gordon Johnson's plan involved, not the production side, but the ever growing Wholesale Distribution side of the confectionery business. In particular, he was concerned that without a foothold in the wholesale trade, the company would find it progressively more difficult to compete with the large chocolate manufacturers who, by using their own wholesale distributors, were beginning to control what confectionery appeared in the main high street shops.

In pursuit of this concern, Bassetts proceeded to move into the wholesale market by acquiring the large Goodman Group of wholesale confectionery and tobacco companies which operated in Devon, Somerset and Cornwall. Following this, new groups were built up around wholesale firms in Bradford, Grimsby, Cambridge, Bristol and Belfast, and these were integrated into a single company which Gordon named Drakes Sweets Marketing. This wholly owned subsidiary of Bassetts became one of the largest wholesale confectionery and tobacco groups in the country.

Not content with this major advance into wholesale distribution, Bassetts extended its operations into South Wales in 1972 by the acquisition of a leading wholesaler in Cardiff, and then moved into Scotland in 1974, where it acquired the leading Scottish wholesaler and small manufacturer J.E. Esslemont of Aberdeen, a company with a proud history stretching back to 1864.

Bassett's wholesale distribution network now embraced England, Scotland, South Wales and Northern Ireland, and even served territories such as the Shetland Isles in the far north and the Scilly Isles in the far South. This, then, was Gordon Johnson's idea of having a foothold in the wholesale trade. It's a good job he wasn't more serious about the idea, wasn't it? Goodness knows what he would have bought next.

GORDON JOHNSON RETIRES

Well, it looks as though we're nearly at the end of our story as far as our two main family characters, the Bassetts and the Johnsons are concerned. It was now 1978, and Gordon, the last of the Johnsons to preside over Bassetts, was 67 years old and ready for retirement. His forty five years with the company, twenty three years of which were as Chairman, had seen it develop and prosper into one of Britain's top confectionery groups, with profits in excess of one million pounds annually.

Apart from this dramatic success with Bassetts, Gordon was also very highly respected within the confectionery trade. He held the post of President of the Cocoa, Chocolate and Confectionery Alliance (the trade association of confectionery manufacturers), and was later a member of the Food Manufacturing Economic Development Committee. On this committee, he and Adrian Cadbury, Chairman of Cadburys, were the only two people allotted seats to represent the chocolate and confectionery industry.

Before we say goodbye and happy retirement to Douglas Gordon Johnson, it is worth reproducing the text of some words of wisdom which he produced in 1974 at a time when Bassetts were then employing 4500 people. His words encapsulate his philosophy as the 'guiding light' of such a great company, and are a fitting tribute to a very sincere and dedicated man:

It is a far cry from the present day Bassett group, with its four and a half thousand employees, to that day in 1832 when our story began with the signing of George Bassett's indenture of apprenticeship. Yet the same basic principles that animated George Bassett animate his successors to-day. Central to those principles is recognition of the company's simultaneous obligations to its consumers, customers, employees, shareholders and the communities in which it works. Implicit in such recognition is the concept of management not as the employer – that is the role of the customer- but as an agent whose function it is to serve the interests of all these parties and to weld them into a harmony that provides pleasure for all. For in a competitive economy those who live to please must please to live.

During the past century and a quarter the world around us has changed more than during any similar period in history. Yet throughout all the changes Bassett's has presented a continuous tradition of enterprise and endeavour, an oasis of stability in an unstable world. Its achievements have been the work, not of a few people alone, but of many devoted lives in many different fields. However varied their talents and occupations, they have all possessed one indispensable asset in common – an abiding pride in the firm and its products. Their loyalty has generated a tradition which it is our privilege in this generation to enrich before we in turn hand it on to our successors. Let us therefore
salute the past heritage it has bequeathed us as we scan the horizon of the future to seize the opportunity it holds in store.

LATER CHANGES TO BASSETTS

As we've covered the Bassett-Johnson story over a period of one hundred and sixty years, from George Bassett's birth in 1818 to Gordon Johnson's retirement in 1978, it would only be fitting to have a very brief look at how the company has fared over the remaining quarter of a century to the present day.

The immediate successor to Gordon Johnson was Bill Mills, the existing Group Managing Director, who had joined the company from the tobacco and hand-tools industries. The company turnover at that time was a healthy thirty one and a half million pounds (1978/9), and the future looked promising. However, the following year saw a devastating UK inflation rate of 20 % which, when compared to that of only 4% prevailing in Bassetts' important export markets, resulted in serious losses in their export business. This resulted in the worst performance in the whole one hundred and forty year's history of the business, with a loss of over one million pounds being declared for the year ending 31st March 1980.

Despite this very difficult period, Bassetts, as always, recovered well and went on to buy three other confectionery companies, namely Anglo Bellamy in 1986, Jacksons in 1987 and Jamesons in 1989.

However, just as Bassett's had eyed-up and then taken over many famous-named companies in the past, a very famous name indeed had been eyeing-up Bassetts. Cadburys, the country's largest chocolate manufacturer, had already bought Pascall's fruit-sweets business in 1964 and was as keen to expand further into the sugar confectionery market following their recent merger with Schweppes. Bassetts was their main target, along with the Chesterfield-based Trebor Company which enjoyed a 52% share of the UK mint market, this being aided, no doubt, by the cleverly marketed TV jingle "Trebor mints are a minty bit stronger", which helped it become a household name.

CADBURYS TAKE OVER

Thus, following the acquisition of Bassetts and Trebor by Cadbury Schweppes in 1989, the Trebor Bassett Company was established one year later in 1990. Trebor, which itself had bought Sharps in 1981, and Maynards in 1985, was founded in 1907 as Robertson and Woodcock. It acquired its later name from the house used initially as the company's offices in Forest Gate, London, which was called Trebor House. In addition, its name also spelt Robert Robertson's Christian name backwards, making the name Trebor particularly appropriate for the new company.

So, it happened. The glorious star of our story has been taken over by an even bigger organisation. The Bassetts Company at Owlerton now sports the name Cadbury Trebor

Bassett instead of Geo. Bassett and company. Could this be the end of our hero? Absolutely not. The huge, three storey brick built factory building still has BASSETTS LIQUORICE ALLSORTS emblazoned in eight foot letters at the top of its main frontage, and production inside is

continuing as before. The link with a group as powerful as Cadbury Schweppes ensures that research can continue into the production of new and improved confectionery, modernization can continue as appropriate, and doors can be opened to many new exciting markets overseas. In effect, Bassetts can continue to keep at the cutting edge of the confectionery business and be more than ready to accept the challenge of fierce competition which is always present. Changes will, of course, continue to take place. This is inevitable in our ever progressing world. However, thanks to the efforts of the Sheffield folk who have guided Bassetts to its present position as one of the jewels in the Cadbury Schweppes crown, I'm sure that we can all feel reassured for the future.

A STROLL AROUND BASSETTS IN 2006

Let's finish off our story, therefore, by taking a last stroll through Sheffield's Owlerton factory towards the end of the year 2006.

It was a bright, sunny day with a shimmering blue sky as I drove up the drive from Livesey Street to sign-on at the gated reception. Although security was exceptionally tight,

the uniformed officer was both helpful and friendly, and directed me to a secure visitors' car park within the company grounds. Due to Bassetts' equally stringent requirements regarding safety, I was obliged to walk from my car to the internal reception office via a pedestrian route identified by yellow painted lines. I felt almost like 'Dorothy' following the yellow brick road in the 'Wizard of Oz' as I progressed to the huge, sweet-making complex, where I signed-on again at the request of a pleasant lady dressed in a smart, navy-blue suit.

"If you'd like to take a seat sir, she'll be along to see you in a few minutes."

My appointment that morning was with Julie Mason, Bassetts' very helpful Training and Development Co-ordinator. Despite her posh title, she was very friendly and down to earth, and nothing was really too much trouble for her. I had met her on two previous occasions, and I was here today to have a look round, and take one or two photographs where confidentiality and security allowed.

As I sat there in the bright, cheerful reception area, my eyes were instinctively drawn to the opposite wall showing an aerial view of the complete layout of the Bassetts factory and offices complex in which I was now sitting. In front of

Owlerton Site

me, and equally tempting to look at, were two bowls of multi-coloured sweets on an elegant coffee table. These delicacies, covering much of the Cadbury Trebor Bassetts range, were made available for visitors such as myself, and almost begged to be picked up and tasted.

"Good morning Bob, I'm sorry I've kept you waiting."

As Julie breezed in through the reception doorway, I had to concede that she was in fact about twelve seconds late, albeit not late enough for me to have time to select one or two sweets of my choice.

After a brief, friendly greeting, we made our way to her office, being careful to follow the yellow brick road and cause no conflict with any vehicular traffic. En route we passed the huge gleaming sugar and flour silos, beyond which a Tate and Lyle container lorry waited patiently to service the treacle, caramel or glucose inlets set in the wall of the adjacent building. Two cheerful ladies, on their way to a well-earned tea-break,

Sugar and flour silos

gave us a welcome wave, as they strode between rows of majestic green topped trees which also rustled their Bassett's greeting in the light, warm breeze.

Upon eventually reaching our destination and entering the clean, brick-built building, we were met by a large, double door which better resembled a colourful firework display than the entrance to a busy, administration block.

'Rockets' of Crunchie Bar, Trebor mints, Dairy Milk Chocolate, Softmints and Caramel Bars formed a spectacular photographic montage on the doors' surface, a

feature which Willy Wonka would have given his back teeth to have in his chocolate factory. Venturing through this magical door, we found that Julie's office was quite normal, although the corridor beyond led to yet more spectacular visual delights. Bassetts' playfully Jelly Babies adorned the first entrance we encountered, whilst the door at one at the

end of the corridor hosted a colourful Bertie Bassett surrounded by his delicious Liquorice Allsorts, looking very pleased with himself.

Today, I had entered into the home of a modern confectionery giant, where the welcome, the surroundings, the sights and the people were as bright as the late summer son which blazed down.

"It's time for our walk-about, Bob."

Julie's voice cut through my private thoughts, and reminded me why I had come to Bassetts today. We began our brief tour in the main Allsorts factory which was brimming with modern, highly mechanised production equipment. Complex looking machines were churning out endless lengths of flat, white and coloured paste which were then being automatically covered by equally endless lengths of flat, black liquorice. Further down this continuous production line, yet another endless length of paste was being lowered carefully onto the liquorice layer to complete the endless 'sandwich' which finally emerged.

You'll remember, of course, how we watched these liquorice sandwiches being made by hand, fifty or so years ago, in small, two foot lengths, with Agnes the dreaded nugget- maker wielding her sharp pizza cutter to devastating effect. Now, everything was automatic, as the conveyer belt began winding its precious cargo upwards to the floor above. Here, it passed through a refrigeration unit which hardened the giant, flat Allsort in preparation for its encounter with the hungry jaws of the cutting grill which, without pity, sliced the cold flat sandwich into continuous, thin strips. Not content with this, the same machine's chopping blade then fell mercilessly down onto the long suffering strips with regular monotony, resulting in the once proud endless layers of paste and liquorice ending as a sea of tiny squares. These shivering, shaking nuggets then tumbled protestingly off the end of the conveyor belt into large plastic trays, in readiness for mixing with all their multi-coloured friends before being packaged and boxed. What a way to start life as a famous Liquorice Allsort.

It was interesting to see that, during this end-process of cutting and chopping, the the irregular edges of the long wide sandwich were automatically sliced off and collected in scrap buckets. These scraps were then re-cycled and used as essential ingredients in the liquorice-production tanks to improve the consistency and flavour of the end product. Thus, waste was eliminated, and product quality was improved as a result, a good sign of positive application to the production process used by Bassetts.

Despite the wonders of automation, I was struck by one aspect of production which caused, in me, a tinge of regret. Conspicuous by their absence were the hundreds of Bassett Ladies, whose skill, dedication and enthusiasm had been the back-bone of the company. In their place on the factory floor are wonderful machines whose operations are supported by relatively few operatives, inspectors and engineers. To compensate, however, a small army of marketing, sales, and administrative staff are employed in large offices amidst a sea of desks, telephones and computers. This, of course, is progress, as without such changes, demand couldn't be met, and Bassetts wouldn't exist. In addition, although we have lost this wealth of fun-loving, down to earth ladies, better paid operatives and staff have taken their place, and I suspect some of the children and grandchildren of characters such as Dorothy, Mary, June and Agnes are working here now, with rates of pay and working conditions which would make the four ladies gasp with envy.

Bassett Ladies of yesteryear

Bassett Ladies of yesteryear making Comfits

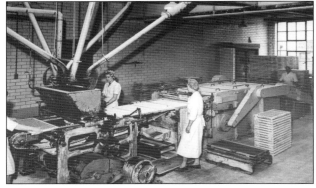

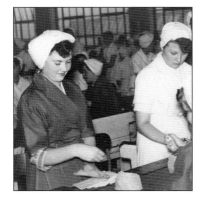

A series of photographs showing Bassetts ladies of yesteryear

Having said all this, the last part of the giant factory complex which Julie took me to made me think that, perhaps, all may not be lost after all. I was now about to enter the LIQUORICE NOVELTIES PRODUCTION AREA.

Liquorice-making boiler and operative

As I carefully opened the door and gazed into the large expanse before me, the view was like a blast from the past. In this area, which produces the well-known and much-liked liquorice Catherine Wheels, large, sophisticated tanks and boilers connected by an array of gleaming pipes occupy the space at the far end of the room, busily producing a continuous supply of hot, delicious liquorice. This in turn was piped into large hoppers supported over clever machines which managed to extrude the liquorice in long

Extruded liquorice strips

thin strips which, believe it or not, were chopped into measured lengths by an Agnes look-alike wielding a pizza-cutter.

Cutting liquorice strips

However, the real sight for sore eyes was in the centre of the room, adjacent to huge stacks of cream-coloured trays. Here, twenty or more little machines were occupied by two rows of opposite-facing ladies looking like something from outer space in their white coats over blue trousers and their hair covered by white, semi-transparent caps. This was a typical old fashioned assembly line, with an assortment of Bassett-Babes of varying age, size and nationality who all gelled together as a happy, cheerful and efficient unit producing their famous product.

This was one area where I was allowed to take my camera and see production at close hand, albeit without disturbing the lovely ladies present. Their job was, unfortunately, a little monotonous, entailing the gathering of strips of liquorice from large metal trays placed in front of them, and attaching these to foot-operated spindles and spools which gleefully spun the liquorice around blue, red or orange sugar coated buttons which form the centre of the wheel. The operation is, nevertheless, one which demands skill and timing, as the continuously moving conveyor belt, set between the two rows of workers, carries small transparent plastic moulds, each of which has to be filled with six completed Catherine Wheels in the correct order, at the correct time.

Packaging, at the end of the production line, is assisted by two more ladies who top-up missing 'wheels', or change-over wrongly positioned ones, before passing them on to the automatic cling-film-covering machine, which in turn sends them on to the final lady for boxing,

As I smiled to myself, watching this hive of activity in an environment which combines old and modern procedures, I recalled that my Grandma used to wear a 'rain mate' similar to the head gear now worn by these ladies. However, upon reflection, I suddenly realised that I must have looked the weirdest person of all. Bassetts have the most stringent health, hygiene and safety rules that I have

Completing Catherine Wheels

ever come across, and before I was given permission to enter this, or any other working area, I was obliged to gear myself up accordingly. The hair-net given to me looked positively ridiculous pulled well down over my head. This embarrassing situation was compounded by the need to wear a whispy, blue moustache- net which extended under

Final sorting

Today's Bassett Ladies

my chin and over my ears to complete my facial fiasco. Together with a white translucent coat, a pair of chunky safety shoes, and an un-stylish pair of ear-plugs to completely shatter my image, I looked more like the head space- man than a visiting author simply wanting to learn more about Bassetts.

However, it was worth any degree of discomfort to observe this delightful mixture of old and new, whose ingredients of skill, dedication, friendliness and teamwork combined magically with the intoxicating aroma of freshly prepared liquorice to produce an experience I shall never forget. I, like thousands of other Sheffield folk, will remain ever grateful to George Bassett and Samuel Johnson, and their respective families, for creating the never-never land of Bassetts which has given so much to so many for so long.

Today's Bassett Ladies

To complete our story, let us have a whistle-stop photographic tour around some of the interesting people and events that have punctuated the firm of Bassetts over the years.

The Special Novelties ladies. A selection from the last of the few.

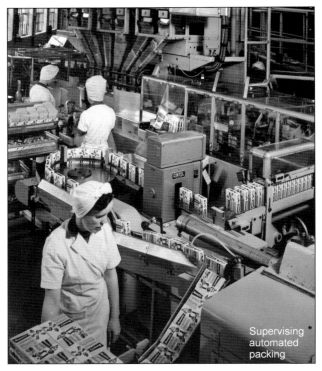

Supervising automated packing

Fork-lift truck driver

Selecting Allsorts mixtures

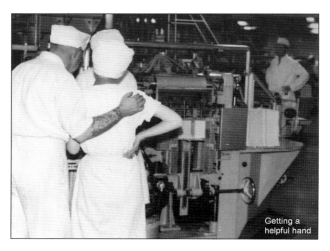

Getting a helpful hand

Bassetts host Chinese Delegations.

Bassetts hold an Open-Day.

Chinese Deleg.

Local footballers
chat up the ladies

Bassetts' new canteen with
HRH Queen Elizabeth (look-alike) waiting to be served.

THE SWEET SIDE OF SHEFFIELD

BASSETT'S
CAPITAL CITY
SINCE 1842

Happy visitors and workers

Bassetts Ladies at work through the years.

Loading the Allsorts conveyor

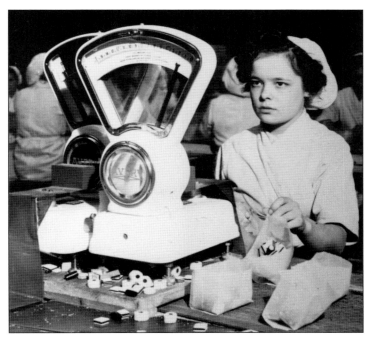

Bassetts' early and later transport.

Traveller's horse and trap

Princess Margaret's visit to the factory.

Elsie Tanner (Pat Phoenix) from Coronation Street pops in.

A glimpse behind the scenes at Bassetts' dedicated kitchen staff.

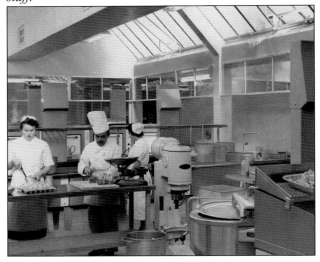

No jewelry allowed on the shop floor!

Thank you for the memories, Bassetts. Long may you continue.

The Dixon-Maxons-Pitchfork Story

Although the Dixons–Maxons–Pitchfork story is about one of Sheffield's best known groups of sweet-making families spanning nearly 150 years, it is interesting to firstly look back at the ancestry of the oldest family in this group; the Dixons.

PHASE ONE: HENRY DIXON AND FAMILY

Henry Dixon, whose confectionery company was famously known for its Dixons Mint Rock, was born in Arundel Street in Sheffield town centre in 1860. His father, Fanshaw Dixon, was a silversmith at the Cornish Works of James Dixon and Sons Ltd., which was founded by his great uncle James. His mother, Sarah Ann, on the other hand, was a butcher's daughter whose brother Henry Hides became the largest butcher in town, with Hides' Abattoir being recognised as the most up-to-date of its kind in the Shambles. The Shambles became known later as the Fitzalan Market Hall which opened on this site in 1786 before the Hole in the Road flanked by C&A Modes later occupied the site.

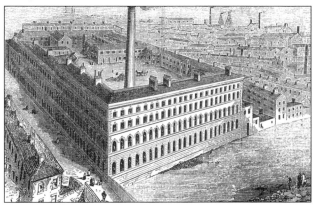

Moving back in time, Henry's great-grandfather was the Reverend Francis Dixon of Lee Croft Chapel, whilst William Dixon, Henry's great- great- great- great grandfather, who died in 1734, was the first Dixon born with the current spelling of the family surname. However, it was two generations before William Dixon that William DYKENSON, the first of the known family line, was born in the year 1540, being registered as a 'burgess (inhabitant) of Sheffield'.

So, we can trace Henry Dixon's ancestry back three hundred and twenty years before his own birth, with not a

Henry Dixon Senior

sweet-maker amongst the seven Dixons and two Dykensons that formed this eminent, historical Sheffield family. What, then, made our Henry follow this difficult but very interesting career in the sugar confectionery business? Let's start at the beginning and find out.

HENRY'S EARLY DAYS

Although Henry's father had been working in the family silversmith business when his son was born, he was keen to go-it-alone and be more independent. As a result of this desire to move on, Fanshaw Dixon left the Cornish Works when Henry was four years old, and set up as a self-employed silversmith with a small workshop at the back of his Arundel Street home.

However, a year later it was here that young Henry experienced something that was to affect his life forever.

It was late morning in the rear, steamy kitchen of the Dixon family's small but cosy terraced house. A pan of potatoes was bubbling merrily on the hot-plate of the black fire range which took pride of place in the centre of the room's longest wall, and the aroma of well-stewed lamb and onions drifted out from the oven heated by the range's hot fire. Henry's mother was washing the bowls they had all used for their breakfast of porridge earlier that morning, but he was feeling bored.

"I'm just going to see what dad's doing, mam."

The tiny five-year-old had decided to climb the rather steep stone steps which led up to the workshop in order that he could help his father working there. He loved to watch this kindly silversmith shaping varying-sized flat sheets of shiny silver by hammering them on his anvil, and was particularly thrilled when he was allowed to have a go himself on some small off-cuts which his dad usually saved for him.

Best of all, however, was the fusing together of the delicate pieces of silverplate by his father using a glowing soldering iron which he heated up in a small coke fire which always burned merrily in the farthest corner of the room. During this process the sizzling solder always dashed excitedly around the joints being fused before finally forming a piece of tableware such as a jug or a teapot. Young Henry would always clap his hands with amazement and delight whilst watching his father create such magic. However, today was not destined to be such an occasion.

"Well, don't be long Henry," his mother called out. "Dinner's nearly ready."

Now, if there's one thing that the little lad liked even more than watching his father work, it was eating his mother's home-made food.

"Coming mam."

Having reached the top of the steps, Henry decided to respond to the temptation of food rather than continue on into his father's den, and, with a quick about-turn, began a rapid descent.

"Mam, mam, mam!"

Henry's desperate cries cut through the peace of the mid-day lunch time with a suddenness that brought both his parents rushing out to see what had happened. There, at the bottom of the steps, lay a crumpled, limp figure, his white face staring up in anguish.

"It's my eye, mam. I can't see out of it properly."

Young Henry Dixon had, unfortunately, broken a blood vessel at the back of his right eye. Despite the rapid attendance of the family doctor and a spell in the Moorfields Eye Hospital in London, his sight in that eye was unable to be saved.

EARLY SCHOOLDAYS

Being blind in one eye at the age of five was a real blow to the youngster, and another year would pass before he was able to attend school. By this time, the family had gone to live at Norton, and Henry went to the local Woodseats Infants School at the bottom of Bolehill Lane where, for the

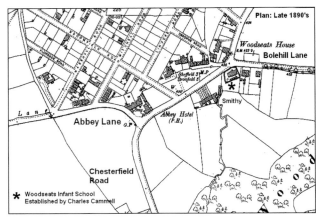

Plan: Late 1890's

Woodseats House
Bolehill Lane

Smithy

Abbey Hotel (P.H.)

Abbey Lane

Chesterfield Road

★ Woodseats Infant School
  Established by Charles Cammell

next year, his attendance was somewhat intermittent. Within a year, nevertheless, the headmistress decided that even though he was only seven years old, Henry should start teaching some of the infants in the school. This not only meant giving them tuition in the very basics of the three R's (reading, writing and arithmetic), it also placed the burden of class-control on the youngster at such a tender age. Unfortunately, when she returned to the classroom one day to find the infants laughing and talking, Henry got his ears boxed so severely that the memory of the undeserved assault stayed with him for the rest of his life.

Woodseats Infants School

You would think, wouldn't you, that this unusual action by the lady responsible for running the school was probably an isolated incident. However, this was not so. Take, for instance, another of young Henry's regular duties with which he was less than pleased.

It was lunchtime and, as usual, he left the safety of the school, scurried across Chesterfield Road and made his way along the hundred yards or so to the Big Tree public house, which he nervously entered.

The Big Tree-early 1900s

"Excuse me Sir," the young lad muttered as he made his way to the long bar at the back of the rather gloomy room. "I'd like a gill of porter for my teacher's lunch if that's all right."

The surly barman who moved forward to serve him could barely see the little hand that reached over the edge of the counter, tightly clutching the coin the teacher had given him. Serving seven year old schoolboys with a quarter of a pint of ale was not strictly done, even in those days, but there was obviously a standing arrangement between the pub and the school that hadn't to be questioned.

"Well, don't drop it lad, else you'll be in dead trouble, believe me."

Teaching and controlling young infants under threat of punishment and collecting alcoholic drink from pubs for his teacher was not what Henry's parents really had in mind when they sent their son to Woodseats School. Nevertheless, the young pupil was gaining experience that probably helped him to formulate his own views on life at a later date. We will see as we continue our story.

There were, of course, other important influences which guided Henry through life at this time. The most important of these was the kindness, honesty and love shown to him by his parents who, like many in those days, raised their children as good Christians and encouraged them to regularly attend church. Indeed, Henry's own views, reflected in his 84th year, are a good example of how successful the influence of his parents had been in his formative years. Perhaps you'd like to read what he said:

"The vital seeds of love and hate, honesty and humility are sown during those first seven years. Harmony in home life, the habits of parents, is a great forerunner of years to come."

He continued:

"From my earliest days, my Mother used to read a passage of scripture and offer a prayer every morning, her family around her. As soon as I could read, she offered me two pence to learn the twenty-third psalm. It was not long before I was able to claim the reward. In after years, it was my pleasure to tell her that it was the best investment she ever made. I have never forgotten it and it has been a great help to me during my life's experience."

It was with this early guidance to support him that the seven year old was thus able to cope with the problems he encountered at school. On Sundays, he enjoyed the family visits to Norton Church as well as the Sunday School at Woodseats. Also, like all other children, he enjoyed playing in Graves Park, watching the new railway being laid to Chesterfield, and cheering on the horse-bus which rattled its way from Sheffield to Meadowhead at regular two-hourly intervals.

SAD TIMES

Henry was not an only child, mind you. He was one of four children, his mother having sadly lost two other children in infancy. One of these was a little brother, whose loss he remembered vividly.

It was early morning, and the sun was only just beginning to rise. His father was strapping a small wooden coffin onto the back of his horse, and everything was silent except for the friendly greetings of a few birds and the occasional snort from the patient chestnut-coloured mare. Two sad, white faces were peering through the partly drawn curtains of a front window which looked out from their little family home.

"Where's Daddy going, mam?"

"He's just going to Castleton Church, Henry my dear. He'll be home by tea-time. Don't worry now."

At seven years old, it's difficult, sometimes, to know how a child is thinking in a situation like this. A tear rolled down Henry's pale cheek, and a tiny voice whispered "Goodbye". As the front door to the house gently closed, the silhouetted horse and rider slowly disappeared into the morning mist on its long and lonely journey to the family grave. A little life had come and gone. Sadly, it wasn't unusual in those days.

As we can see, life in the Dixon family was not easy. Henry had certainly experienced a lot in his first seven and a half years, and his mother Sarah was, not surprisingly, rather worn out. The stress of losing her second child was affecting her and her children rather badly, and they were all in a general state of poor health. By the time Henry was eight years old, the family's doctor had advised that mum and her four children should move to a coastal location for some time to gain the benefit of clear, sea air which, he suggested, was essential for their health. Thus, in 1868, the poorly little group moved to Morecambe where they rented a house and took in boarders to make ends meet. Sarah's husband had to stay in Sheffield, of course, as his silversmith business was the main source of income for the family.

LIVING IN MORECAMBE

Despite the health trip to Morecambe being planned only as a rest from smokey Sheffield for a few months, it turned out to be much longer than that. Sarah's venture into the boarding-house business, which proved to be the first such activity in that part of Morecambe where they were living, lasted for about four years, after which she returned home to Sheffield to be with her husband, whose business was now quite successful.

Meanwhile Henry, being a very ambitious and determined eight year old when he arrived, had begun to enjoy life at the seaside resort and actually stayed there for five and a half years. Initially, he began earning pocket money by carting luggage from the station to nearby boarding houses in an old wooden barrow his mother had bought for him. Later, he managed to get a job as organ-blower at the Clark Street Congregational Church, where he also regularly attended its Sunday School and, later, its Young Men's class.

It was not, however, all work and no play for the active youngster. He loved to stroll around the developing town and its shore-line where he watched many houses being built and the promenade being extended. Many an exciting hour was also spent on the rolling sands which were regularly washed by mischievous, white capped waves which threw debris and driftwood into his path as he skipped along. Occasionally, a ship would get wrecked, or have to throw some of its cargo overboard, and it was with great delight that Henry would gather up the spoils and proudly take them home to his mam. Indeed, the driftwood he retrieved from the beach was able to keep their home warm and the cooking pots bubbling for the whole of their time in Morecambe.

However, as young Henry Dixon had a very active brain which demanded stimulation, his father decided to send him to a good school. Fortunately, with his silversmith business doing well, he was able to let his son attend the East View Boarding School in Morecombe, where he was a star pupil. As he approached his 14th birthday, the usual school-leaving age in those days, his headmaster suggested to him and his parents that, because of his obvious ability, he should stay on and do further study.

Now in Victorian times (it was now 1873), a true test of academic excellence and potential was acknowledged as being able to be assessed by a Phrenologist, a specialist in the study of the shape and size of a person's head. Such a person professed to be able to judge the character and mental facilities of an individual by careful measurement and analysis of that part of the skull which enclosed the brain. As it happened, Professor Fowling, a well known London Phrenologist, was visiting Morecambe at the time, and Henry's mother popped over from Sheffield and took her son for a consultation with him. The outcome of this visit was that the professor advised that Henry should pursue a profession in medicine, a suggestion which appealed to the gifted young lad.

So, what went wrong? Why didn't the King of Candy become a doctor or surgeon instead? There were three factors which influenced the overall decision, the most significant of these being that his parents couldn't really afford the expense of such protracted study and training. In addition, Henry felt that having only one eye was a real disadvantage, and that having, as he described it, 'an over active brain' was an added problem. This 'problem', however, was to influence his life for ever, as his urge to be involved in a host of activities at all times gave him the variation and challenges which he thrived on. Despite this, Henry did admit in later life that he always regretted not being able to pursue the medical profession.

BACK TO SHEFFIELD TO FIND WORK

As a result of these influencing factors, we now see our young man leaving school at the age of 14 and returning to Sheffield where his family had moved to their new home in Crosspool. For a short while he worked for his father but he soon became bored. He then tried his hand with a wire-manufacturing company for a wage of six shillings (30p) a week, although this work didn't really interest him either. However, within six months Henry had successfully applied to work for Messrs. Wilson and Son, a well known firm of toy merchants on Snig Hill. This time, the 15 year old hit the jackpot.

Crosspool about 1900

Working for Wilsons was just what Henry needed, although the hours were very long, being twelve hours a day from 8.00am to 8.00pm on Monday to Friday and fourteen hours from 8.00am to 10.00pm on Saturday. With only three and a half days holiday a year, which embraced Christmas Day, Good Friday, Whit Monday and half of New Year's Day, he was eager to make the best use of his precious Sundays on which he attended Queen Street Chapel. It was here that he joined the Band of Hope, of which he was elected secretary when he was still only 15, and also began teaching his faith at the age of 18. Indeed, Henry continued teaching at Queen Street for the next fifty years, a record he was proud to hold and one which gave him a sense of achievement.

But let's get back to the young man's job as an assistant at Wilsons. Over the next few years there, he obtained a good grounding in business methods which included experience in buying from and selling to companies both in this country and in many others overseas. An important part of Wilsons' business was also with fairground people. Fairs, in those later Victorian times, played a very important part in the community life of Sheffield folk, and to many it was their only treat. The huge fairground between the canal and the Victoria station was Sheffield's main attraction, and apart from the usual roundabouts, it included attractions such as boxing booths, wrestling booths, freak shows, a circus and a zoo.

However, it was the dozens of stalls which sprang up like daisies in and around the site which were the target of Wilsons, who supplied toys, novelties and trinkets by the hundred to tempt the excited customers. It was Henry's job to walk around the fairground collecting money from the stallholders, although with no bank notes being used in such transactions, his bulging pockets of heavy coins often made it difficult for him to walk. It is also interesting to note that there were never any records made of these transactions with the fairground people. I wonder if the tax-man ever knew?

This wasn't the only entertainment offered to the eager, yet mostly poor, population of this rapidly developing steel town. Sanger's Circus would pay a visit and parade its whole entourage through the town's narrow streets, and thus provide a free show for all the kids who couldn't afford a proper visit to the big top. Barnham and Bailey's Circus also visited the town occasionally and set up their tents on land adjacent to the Barracks on Langsett Road - yet another big event in the townfolk's calendar.

Unfortunately, Henry could only enjoy the delights of such entertainment if it didn't interfere with his long working hours or his visits to church on Sundays. Occasionally, he would stare wistfully out of the window

Snig Hill about 1900

full of Wilsons' toys and wonder what it would be like to be a shopper rather than a shop assistant. On a Saturday, for example, there were so many people forcing their way up and down the shop-lined, narrow cobbled lane of Snig Hill, that they more resembled a football crowd than eager shoppers anxious to get the best bargains and freshest food.

But, of course, Henry was still enjoying life at the age of 21. His job was interesting and varied, and his passion for the church involved many activities and opportunities to meet many different people. One such person he met

2008-New office block on the site of the old Queen Street Chapel

whilst attending Queen Street Chapel was a young lady by the name of Elizabeth Challenger. She was the love of his life who he courted for four and a half years before marrying her at the age of 24. They were together for sixty-two years, and married for fifty eight of them, a relationship which proved to be the rock upon which Henry's continued success and happiness in life was firmly built.

However, let's not rush ahead too quickly. Following Henry's engagement to Elizabeth at the age of 22, he was becoming a little restless for change and improvement. During the year that followed, the long shop hours and little proper exercise were also beginning to affect his health. If we add to these personal difficulties the fact that Wilsons was beginning to lose a few customers, we arrive at a pivotal point in this young man's life, and one which was to shape his ultimate career in the confectionery business.

Henry had been with the toy merchants for about eight years by now, and during that time their retail customers had always come into the store to choose and pay for their goods before having them dispatched to their own shops where they would be sold. However, times were changing, and several merchants were employing sales representatives (then called 'travellers') to visit their customers with samples and details from which choices were made and orders given. Henry was aware of this customer-based trend, and felt that his firm should adopt it. One morning, when business was quiet, therefore, he decided to raise his concerns with his employer.

"You know, Mr. Wilson, I've been thinking. Instead of us putting the responsibility on customers coming to us to choose their goods, what do you think of us going to them instead to make sure we get their orders?"

"Us go to them Henry? It's a preposterous idea. I wouldn't dream of doing such a thing."

"But Mr. Wilson, we're losing customers, and other merchants have started doing it. If you let me be your traveller, I can guarantee an increase in sales."

"Nonsense young man. I've been in this business longer than I care to think of, and I certainly don't intend to be pushed into following some crackpot modern idea."

Mr. Wilson's decision was a real blow to his bright young assistant, who not only wanted to ensure success for his employer, but also needed to get out and about more for health reasons. His employer's words were still on his mind the next morning as he trundled down to the Pack Horse Inn at the bottom of Snig Hill with a cart-load of parcels and packages for dispatch to customers. He was doing his weekly round of the 'carriers', today's equivalent of the parcel post, whose headquarters were well known public houses in the town centre. The next port of call for the willing piebald horse and his important luggage was the Yellow Lion in Haymarket, followed by the Bull and Mouth in Waingate and the Royal in Exchange Street. From these locations, the carriers ensured delivery far and wide, either by horse-power or the now popular train services which steamed regularly out of the Midland Station, the Victoria Station and the City Station (at Broad Street), as well as those stations wholly dedicated to goods at the Wicker and the Canal Wharf.

"It's no good," he muttered to himself as he arrived back at the shop. "I can't stay here and suffocate just because Mr. Wilson won't move with the times. I'll have to leave."

HENRY CHANGES JOBS AND GETS MARRIED

And leave he did. With the small savings which he had built up over the last few years, Henry joined a small Baker and Confectioner who was looking for a partner to help him with his growing business. He had made the move into the confectionery business at last, more by default than by design. He was still only 23 and, with his usual enthusiasm, bought a horse and dog-cart with which he was able to travel round his customers, selling goods and taking orders. His partner, who was more of a hands-on person, was responsible for the manufacture of the pastries and sweets, and, for a year or so, everything went well.

It was at this time, now that he was settled in his new job, that he and Elizabeth decided to get married and move into a small house near to the bakery and confectionery factory. Whether or not it was tempting fate, I'm not really sure, but within a few months of their marriage and the setting up of a home convenient for his work, his partner took to drink, being unable to cope with the pressure of the business' success. His inability to fulfil the orders which his partner brought in made him drink more, resulting in an inevitable downward spiral which was destined to ruin the company. Once again, Henry had little choice but to move on.

Having now learnt that working for and being dependent on others for future success was not very reliable, the small man with the big heart and big ideas decided to go-it-alone. A small wholesale shop from which he could supply retailers with confectionery was in his sights. He wasn't moving into making sweets himself at this stage, but his knowledge of both the manufacturing and retail aspects of production enabled him to buy and sell those sweets which he knew his customers wanted.

His new venture as a confectionery wholesaler, called a 'factor' in those days, was now up and running, although the location of his first little shop is unknown. Within a year, helped and encouraged significantly by his wife, Henry's business progressed to such an extent that not only was he able to move it to much larger premises at 87 and 89 West Bar, but he was also able to buy a house for Elizabeth and himself in St. Philips Road. Real success had now been achieved by the 25 year old, and with the birth of a son Henry and a daughter Alice over the next two years, life for Mr. and Mrs. Henry Dixon was very good indeed.

As the wholesale business continued to grow, Henry decided to diversify and employ workers to make children's sweet novelties with cheap toys which he then sold on to shops for public sale. Such was the extent of his success at this stage that he needed help to run his factory, particularly when he was travelling round the country securing orders, or in London buying stock. He decided, therefore, to approach his closest friend, William Sudbury, who he had known since their very early schooldays.

"You know, William," he said as they chatted over lunch one day. "I need to find someone I can really trust to help me to run my business. It's becoming a real problem, particularly when I'm away."

Henry and William had a great deal of respect for each other, and William knew that his friend was very independent and had never been keen to share the responsibility of his business with anybody. It was with surprise, therefore, that he listened to Henry's proposition.

"How about you coming in with me William? We're both only 29 and the world's our oyster. What do you think?"

"Well Henry," responded his friend, clearly taken aback by the suggestion. "I don't know what to say. I've got no experience of confectionery, although I am good with figures."

After much discussion, William Sudbury joined Henry Dixon and stayed with him as an invaluable and loyal manager of his business for many years, although he was not destined to reach the old age which would be achieved by his friend and employer.

INTEREST AND OPPORTUNITY FROM THE SKIES

It was at the time that William joined the firm that an American, by the name of Professor Baldwin, came over to Sheffield to give parachute-jumping demonstrations. He was well-known for his daring activities and, on a warm, summer's afternoon in August, hundreds of children and nearly as many adults waited patiently in Hillsborough Park with heads tilted backwards and eyes fixed sharply on a huge air balloon hovering way above them in the clear, blue sky.

"Look at that balloon right up there, mam. It won't burst will it?" said a small lad standing among the large crowd.

Hillsborough Park in 2007

"Dad, dad, there's a man leaning over the edge of that tiny basket. He's not going to fall is he?" exclaimed an even smaller young girl standing next to the anxious lad.

Alice and Henry Junior were only three and four years old respectively, and mum and dad Dixon had taken time out to watch this truly amazing spectacle about to take place high above them. The year was 1890, and the delights of aviation had not yet filled our skies with the magic of aeroplanes. It would be another thirteen years before Orville and Wilbur Wright achieved powered, controlled and sustained manned flight in a heavier-than-air craft on December 17th, 1903. On this historic day, Wilbur Wright managed to fly his craft 852 feet in 59 seconds, and by 1908 the two brothers had managed to stay airborne with complete control of their craft for over an hour. The sight of a manned balloon floating above one of Sheffield's main parks on this August afternoon was, therefore, something to behold, whatever your age was.

A loud gasp from the anxious crowd signalled the presence of a small, lonely figure standing perilously on the edge of the balloon basket. A further, even louder gasp, accompanied by several screams, heralded the figure's sudden leap into nothingness, before it began a somersaulting plummet down to earth. A hushed silence descended on the area until, as if by a miracle, the billowing white form of a parachute burst forth from a small insignificant pack which was attached to the figure's shoulders. At this point, apprehension turned to relief, and the spectacle was greeted by tumultuous cheers from the large gathering below. The small figure of Professor Baldwin dangling beneath the parachute grew larger and larger before landing safely in the centre of the grassed area reserved for his escapade. Sheffield folk had seen something unusual and daring, and they liked it.

What, if anything, you might ask, is the connection between this remarkable event and our Henry? Well, he and his family obviously enjoyed the show, which would be a talking point amongst them for many months to come. However, of significant importance to him was that his ever agile business brain had immediately hit upon an idea which could be a money-spinner. Why not, he thought, make a toy parachutist which children could play with and enjoy watching it actually fly?

Within a week or two, the far-seeing entrepreneur had located a firm in Liverpool which was able to produce as many cardboard parachute-men as he required, following which he employed extra workers himself to make the parachutes and attach them to the little men. Once this novel product hit the shops, there was no stopping its success. Henry had to employ two hundred workers to cope with the orders that continued to roll in. He also had to ensure that his supplier of the cardboard parachutes kept the little men marching in.

"William, we're getting low on parachutists," exclaimed Henry as he strolled through the assembly-area of his factory during one of his regular tours of inspection. "Send a wire to Liverpool and tell them that I want 500,000 men at once."

William Sudbury was a conscientious and reliable Works Manager and always responded to his boss's requests without delay.

"It's as good as done Henry. I'll do it right away."

It wasn't until the next day that the Post Office contacted William to say that they had held up the telegram due to its unusual request for half a million men. The Boer War had just begun and the Post Master felt that such a request should have rightly come from the War Office. Needless to say, Henry was furious at the delay.

"I can't believe their stupidity, William. I expect they thought I was intending to have a private war on my own!"

Despite this hiccup, sales of this little man, who could float gracefully across any kitchen, dining room, bedroom or back-yard, continued for many years, with the millions of them that were made putting a welcome bob or two into Henry's already bulging coffers.

During the almost frantic first year of these sales, Elizabeth had given birth to their second son, Frank, which had put some pressure on the need for a bigger house. As a result, Henry decided to buy a beautiful cottage called Rose

Villa in Wood Lane, in the rural village of Stannington. When the family moved into this new home in the May of 1890, the fruit trees in full blossom looked a picture nestling at the bottom of the well-stocked garden. Henry Junior, Alice and baby Frank found the large green lawns an absolute delight to play on, and Elizabeth was over the moon with her country abode. In fact, within a couple of years, she had successfully evened-out the sex inequality in her family by having a second daughter Emily, who was born in these idyllic surroundings.

THE BIRTH OF THE SALVATION ARMY

The birth of Henry and Elizabeth's fourth child in 1892 also coincided with another birth in Sheffield; in Thomas Street to be exact.

A parade of kindly looking men and women in smart black suits and caps was just beginning its march down to South Street, where it would turn left and join the Moor as far as the Crimean war memorial at Moorhead. Between the regular thuds of a large drum supported by a surprisingly

Derelect Salvation Army Citadel, Cross Burgess Street, 2008

small gentle-man, concertinas and tambourines provided the melody for the enthusiastic singing of hymns which accompanied the whole ensemble. This was the birth of the Salvation Army in Sheffield, which was led by a very determined and dedicated man by the name of General Booth.

Unfortunately, a significant element of the population at that

General Booth

time didn't take kindly to a group of drum-banging strangers walking up their main streets preaching the gospel and asking for money to support the destitute and the poor. The General and his followers were pelted with stones and other objects by young tearaways, who shouted abuse and jibes at them. History, of course, shows that neither sticks and stones nor hurtful words could stop the determined march of this army which, over the last hundred years or more, has given help and hope to thousands of people who have fallen on hard times. Today, particularly at Christmas time, we can still look forward on a cold, dark evening to the trumpeted arrival and singing of this happy group of people, who continue to light up our lives with their joyous renditions of Silent Night, Away in a Manger and many other well-known Christmas carols. Long may they continue.

HENRY THE FAMILY MAN

However, let's get back to Henry Dixon and see what he's been getting up to. Five years had now passed since he had established his home in Stannington. His firm was continuing to do well and he wanted for nothing financially. However, success had brought with it extremely long working hours and little time to spend at home. As Henry himself put it when asked about his busy life: "Sometimes for weeks I never saw the children awake from Sunday night to Saturday noon."

This was no life for a family man or his wife and children, so he resolved to change it. In addition to this problem, his factory was by now far too small to cope with its expanding business.

Henry's first decision was, therefore, to buy a large building at the corner of Love Street and Spring Street which had been originally built for a firm of cutlers and silversmiths. This building, which he called 'Britannia Works', became the centre of his success for many years to come, and was the birth-place of the famous 'Dixons Mint

Rock' which is still enjoyed today. We will talk about this later in a little more detail.

The second and perhaps more important decision he made was to sell the family's beloved Rose Villa and move back to Sheffield where he bought a large house at 59 Wilkinson Street in Broomhall. Although it was a great wrench to move from their rural Stannington residence, the family benefited by Henry being able to pop home whenever it suited him, to see and spend more time with his wife and children.

The location of Rose Villa did have one other disadvantage while the family lived there. The two older children, Henry Junior and Alice, had spent a year or two at a boarding school in the country but, on returning home to Stannington, had found that travelling to a school in Sheffield was not all that easy. Henry Junior, for example, had started at Newell's school in Paradise Square (called Pot Square by the locals), which had involved a long walk down from Stannington Village to Malin Bridge. From there, the horse-tram took him to West Bar, leaving him to walk the remainder of the way up to his school.

"Did you know, Henry," his father said to him the day before they moved to Wilkinson Street, "in that row of cottages you pass each morning down at Malin Bridge, there's one in which a baby boy was born on the night of the Great Flood of 1864. The poor mother's bed was floating on the water at the time, and it was a miracle that both she and the baby weren't drowned."

"I didn't know that, dad. It must have been a terrible time."

"It certainly was son. Nearly 700 million gallons of water poured down Loxley Valley that night when the Dale Dyke Dam burst its banks. There were nearly three hundred people killed, you know, and thousands of houses damaged or destroyed."

"That's awful. What happened to the baby, do you know?"

"Well, from what I hear, he survived and his mother called him Noah. With a name like that and a 'miracle' birth, I think we can presume that he was intended to live, don't you?"

But, of course, that walk for Henry Junior would be no more, as Wilkinson Street was just a ten minute stroll away from his school in Paradise Square. This area, which was located more or less behind St. Peter's Church, was well known at the time for the large number of solicitors who worked there. On the western side of the square, a row of tall, posh houses had been converted into offices, nearly all of which were occupied by these learned men of law. These offices were referred to by all and sundry at the time as 'The Devil's Row in Paradise', a description which lasted for many years, and gives some indication of the reputation that these gentlemen had earned for themselves in those days.

WORK, RELAXATION AND RELIGION

Henry's large Britannia Works in Love Street was located in an area full of factories and workshops, and was only a stone's throw away from the Don Confectionery Works in Bridge Street, which was owned and run by the two sons of a fellow confectioner, George Bassett. It was also an area occupied by a large number of public houses, a fact of significance to Henry with him being a staunch believer and supporter of abstenance from the 'demon drink'. He was often heard to say: "Given eleven cricket balls, it was possible to hit eleven public houses from the roof of my works."

Many of the large number of manual workers who toiled away in the hot, dusty and cramped conditions in this area, which encompassed steelworks, rolling mills and grinding wheels, had only one thing on their minds in the evenings which followed their long hard days; a trip to their favourite pub or club. One such place was The Grand, a Music Hall at the end of Spring Street, opposite the Packhorse Inn.

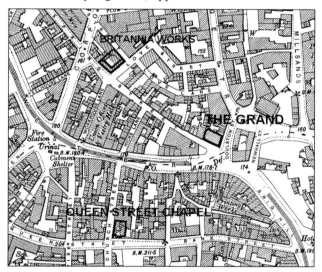

View looking down Snig Hill in 2008 showing the new buildings on the site of the old Grand Music Hall

The portly gentlemen standing outside this music hall, which was known locally as the flea pit, was doing his best to deafen anyone who chose to be passing by.

"Two's and four's this way; early doors a penny extra."

His barrel chest and ample stomach strained desperately against the posh, tight-fitting blue and gold uniform which he was wearing, and it would have been no surprise to anyone if one of his shiny gold buttons had popped off during one of his announcements.

"Seats in the boxes, madam? That entrance over there, and only a shilling each. It's better than being at 'ome madam."

Henry never frequented this building which was regularly filled with alcohol fuelled singing, laughter and boisterous shouting, all competing with a seven-piece orchestra. Most mornings, however, as he strolled past on his way to work, he watched the sawdust and debris being swept into the street, and wondered just what it was like inside this place which was so popular with so many people. Because he never went in to tell us all about it, we'll never know, will we?

What we do know is that he was still very active both in his business, which began to make filled Christmas Stockings and Christmas Novelties very successfully, and also at Queen Street Chapel, where he was elected a Deacon. Sadly, it was only a few months after being elected as one of the youngest ever to this position that his mother Sarah Ann died at the age of 68. Sarah had been a guiding-light and a source of great strength and comfort to her son who, still only 36 years old, was greatly affected by her passing. As is often the case at such difficult times, he chose to cope with his sorrow by putting even more effort into both his work and his church activities. In particular, he formed the Federation of Wholesale Confectioners, was elected as a delegate to the Yorkshire Union Church Aid and Home Missionary Society, and became Treasurer of the Sheffield and District Branch of the Colonial Missionary Society, a post he held for thirty four years.

Within a year or two, his eldest daughter Alice, now 15, joined her father's firm as a secretary in his office, and it was a comfort to him to have her there. Sadly, however, another tragedy was to hit Henry and his children only two years later. His youngest son Frank, who had been ill for some time, died at the age of 15. This was a crushing blow to the distraught father, and prompted the return home of his eldest son Henry Junior, who was just completing an apprenticeship in Scotland with a high class confectionery manufacturer. His son's return was not only a tremendous help to Henry as a grieving father, it also heralded in the beginning of a new era in the history of Dixons. It was also probably one of the most important periods for the business. Under the direct supervision of Henry Dixon Junior, the firm commenced, for the first time, the manufacture of sweets in 1905.

It's strange to think that we've actually covered twenty one years of Henry Dixon's involvement in the confectionery business, during which time he only factored (bought as a wholesaler) sweets which he obtained from manufacturers and sold to shops at a profit. As his name is synonymous with mint rock world wide, my expectation was that this confectioner made his own products throughout his sweet career. Well, now we know that Henry

Henry Dixon Junior

Junior was the first Dixon to hold that privilege, he being the only family member to have actually learnt the trade by apprenticeship. It is at this stage that the story fans out to cover two equally important Henrys, father and son.

Although only 19 years old, Henry Junior had the same drive, energy and abilities as his father who allowed him to use these, in combination with his sweet making training, to expand the business into a dual confectionery manufacturing and wholesale operation. As you would expect, Henry Senior was still at the helm, a position he never voluntarily relinquished, but, with his considerable external interests, he had no option but to give his son a bit of rope to make some key decisions in the business.

This is probably a good time to have a look at one particular activity in which the 'old man', now 45 years old, was involved. This was known as the Croft House Settlement.

THE CROFT HOUSE SETTLEMENT

Henry Senior, as we know, was an active member of the church and had been involved with the Queen Street Congregational Chapel, where he was a Deacon, for many years. William Blackshaw had been the Minister of this

Chapel for about six years, from 1899, and was a good friend of Henry's. Although deeply committed to the church, the Reverend's main aim was to help others, and community-service was his priority in life. He was particularly concerned about the appalling conditions which existed in a residential area known as The Crofts, acknowledged at the time as being the most deprived in the city.

This area, which included streets such as Hollis Croft, White Croft, Simms Croft, Hawley Croft and Lee Croft, was notorious not only because of its physical deprivation, but also because of the 'disposition' of some of the people who lived there. It was regularly said by many local Sheffield people at the time that 'from Saturday to the

1 White Croft 2 Hollis Croft
3 Simms Croft 4 School Croft
5 Hawley Croft 6 Lee Croft
7 Garden Street 8 Croft House
9 Queen Street Chapel

Monday, no respectable person dare pass through unprotected'. It was not likely, of course, that many would have wished to wander through its small courts and filthy yards where many died of hygiene-related diseases. There were, for example, at least seven two-roomed houses in one of the Crofts which actually accommodated sixty-two people at a rate of nine people per house, with only one privy (outside toilet) between them. With water only available for a few hours on three days a week, the whole combination was one of squalor, stench and disease.

It was against this backdrop that William Blackshaw, supported by Henry Dixon, decided to do something to help these unfortunate residents. His first task was to find a suitable building in which to base an organisation which could serve the various needs of the poor community. At that time, the Congregational Chapel in Garden Street, which formed the southern boundary to The Crofts, was being considered for sale. Following discussions between

this Chapel and that at Queen Street, the congregation of Garden Street agreed to move to its sister Chapel, leaving the building to be used by the community organisation known as the Croft House Settlement. After carrying out extensive repairs and alterations to the Garden Street Chapel, which then became known as Croft House, it was officially opened by the Lord Mayor of Sheffield, Alderman George Senior, on the 26th October, 1902.

With William Blackshaw's link as Minister of Queen Street Chapel and Founder of Croft House Settlement, Henry Dixon, together with his Deacon Colleagues from Queen Street, had considerable involvement in the Settlement's development, both in terms of financial need and hands-on activity. The Reverend's approach to his task

of community help can best be summed up by an article he wrote at the beginning of the new venture: "Our work is not a trick to fill any churches, but to help men and women living in hard circumstances to fulfil better, and with more hope, a normal human life."

The Settlement began its long journey, which to date has lasted over one hundred years, by teaching basic house-keeping skills to the women of the area, whilst the men were trained for jobs. The children of these families were all given schooling (a basic education), and the families themselves all given meals in order

The Revd William Blackshaw

that they could simply exist. Following the introduction of these basic needs, a Boys' Club was opened with two hundred boys signing up as members, and a gymnasium (complete with instructor) was created. The gift of a ping-pong table at that time was also gratefully received.

Another significant decision was made in that exciting and busy first year. The Settlement Committee agreed to the formation of a Musical and Dramatic Society, which would give concerts once every two weeks on a Saturday evening. This was the beginning of the well-known Croft House Operatic Society, which in due course was closely linked with Constance Grant as Choreographer, and later with her daughter Judith Silvester as both Choreographer and Producer.

By the end of the first year, the Settlement included further activities such as a Men's Club, a Discussion Class, a Library and a Choir. A Girls' Class was also introduced a little later. Both the Boys' Club and the Men's Club had their own football, cricket and fishing teams, which proved to be very popular with the residents and their respective supporters.

To complete the picture, Reverend Blackshaw led Sunday Worship, which included Sunday School, an adult Bible Class, a Christian Union, a Mothers' Meeting and the Band of Hope. With regard to the religious activities, the Reverend was acutely aware of the stigma attached to the wragged clothes worn by the Crofts' residents, who could not afford to buy any decent ones, let alone 'Sunday Bests' such as bonnets, silk top hats and smart suits. To get over their understandable reluctance to turn up at church in their torn trousers, dirty shirts and toe-less boots, he held well

attended services outside in summer in all the courts in turn, virtually preaching on the residents' own doorsteps.

Such was the consideration of this kindly 'man of the cloth', who remained as Warden of Croft House for eleven years, that for the first time in their lives, the hitherto 'untouchables' of the Crofts realised that someone really cared for them, and was actually concerned enough to do something meaningful to improve their devastatingly poor quality of life. Although his stay in Sheffield lasted only about fifteen years, his remarkable contribution to the city's poorest was a legacy which will last forever.

As for the Croft House Settlement today, it is still going strong as a Youth and Community Centre, providing Sheffield citizens with various facilities and services to carry out a wide range of sports, arts, music and educational activities. It is also interesting to note that the first Scout Troop ever formed in Sheffield began in Croft House, which now remains home to music groups, craft groups, sporting groups and faith groups. Long may it continue to do so. Perhaps I should just conclude on the subject of the Croft House Settlement, that the 'Henry Dixon' connection with it still continues today, but I shall tell you more about that later.

THE TWO HENRYS CONTINUED

In order that we don't lose the thread of the sweet-makers' story following the Croft House diversion, let's nip back to where we left off in 1905 with both Henry Senior and Junior working together. Over the next few years, sweet production continued to grow, with Dixon's Mint Rock capturing the local market closely followed by Aniseed Rock, Butter Mints, Cough Drops and Chocolate Flavoured Limes. The names make your mouth water, don't they?

During this time, Henry's daughter Alice married, and her place as his personal secretary was taken by his other daughter Emily, who by now was 17 years old. Henry Junior was also determined to be in on the marriage scene and he began courting a lovely girl called Gertrude Fox who

he married when he was 25. A short time afterwards, Grandpa Fanshaw Dixon died at the ripe old age of 84 just as rumblings of war were afoot between Great Britain and Germany.

THE IMPACT OF WORLD WAR ONE

In 1914, war broke out and Henry Junior, along with thousands of other eligible men, was sent overseas to fight for King and country. Despite the monumental losses suffered by the British forces, young Henry (though now 28) was one of the lucky ones who survived. He was able to return to both his anxious father and his desperately worried wife, not only with his life, but also with stories of the incredible experiences he had encountered.

His war travels had taken him to South Africa, Mesopotamia, Turkey, Palestine, Egypt, Italy and France, and, armed with the new 'must have' invention of recent years called a camera (as well as his rifle), he was able to bring back and send home hundreds of photographs to bring his stories alive. Indeed, having made two or three hundred of these into lantern slides, he gave many an illustrated talk to interested groups in Sheffield and others around the country. It was obviously with great foresight and optimism that the budding young sweet-maker had decided to take his camera to war with him.

Despite Henry Junior returning safely home in the May of 1919, his father was not to be spared the sadness of loss yet again. As the war came to an end, his oldest daughter Alice died at the age of 31. There is little worse than suffering the loss of one's children, and Henry had tragically lost two. The grieving father, now 58, always managed to find comfort in his unquestionably strong Christian faith, but still had to endure the pain like anyone else.

The war years, of course, not only took their toll on the young men of the country, they also had a devastating effect on most businesses, in particular those who were dependent on sugar and other scarce raw materials. Henry Dixon, Confectioner and Wholesaler, was no exception. However, although the sugar allocation was reduced to just 25% of its pre-war level, the business managed to survive and still produce sufficient confectionery to prevent thousands of shops from closing down. Thereafter, the Government established home-grown sugar beet factories to minimize the problems which had been caused by the fact that all sugar, up to this point, had come from abroad.

The years following the war were very difficult for everyone. Henry Senior was now in his early sixties and his son was, in effect, running the show at the Love Street factory. However, despite having many other outside interests, the workaholic boss had no thoughts of passing on the reins of his company to Henry Junior. His control over the business was still absolute, and although the younger Dixon was still only 36 at this time, he was beginning to feel a little frustrated that his father refused to give him the status befitting his responsibility. Perhaps the time wasn't just right for such a change as the two of them had a lot on their plate during the post war period and into the early 1930s.

The reaction to the war had now taken hold, unemployment was rising and strikes were the order of the day. The country was gripped by a major depression. Frustratingly, Germany and Japan were allowed to 'dump' goods into the country, whilst many home-grown small manufactures went out of business. This was compounded by the fact that our Government and her allies even allowed Germany to cut us out of their export markets. Henry summed up the situation rather well when he said: "We won the war and lost the peace."

But, of course, life goes on and, with hard work and dedication Dixons continued to supply what the public wanted; sweets and more sweets. In the midst of this rather depressing time, Henry Senior had several things to celebrate and cheer him up. It was 1928 and he was now 68 years old, and was planning to have a break.

"You deserve a good holiday, father," his son remarked a few days before the planned departure. "You never seem to stop working, and it will do you good. The business will be in good hands while you're away, and if I dare to suggest it, this seems to be a good time to retire and let me take over. What do you think?"

The few seconds which followed seemed an age to young Henry as he watched his father's face change from one of concerned shock to mild amusement.

"Did you say retire, son? Me retire and hand over to you? Why, you're only a lad, and I've got years left in me yet. Ask me again when I'm 80, and I'll think about it."

Although the answer was what Henry Junior had expected to hear, it was, nevertheless, disappointing and frustrating for him, particularly as his father had only been 24 years old when he started and ran the business on his own.

However, completely unphased by his son's suggestion, Henry and his wife Elizabeth embarked on a long holiday with friends, following in the footsteps of the Pilgrim Fathers and their historic trek to America. On their return, the Sheffield Congregational Association held its 50th Jubilee, during which Henry introduced and organized a 'Festival of Golden Years' in honour of members who were 70 years or older. With a turn-out of two hundred and fifty such 'oldies', the enthusiastic sweet-maker-cum-churchman declared the event to be "the most successful affair I have ever organized." Last but not least during these depression years, his daughter Emily, who he had always lovingly called Emmie, got married at the age of 37. Unfortunately for her father, she and her husband chose to live in Leeds, which resulted in her leaving her father's office where she had been his 'right hand' for twenty years. Despite her departure from the business, Henry was thrilled that she had found a good man to marry at last.

HENRY AND ELIZABETH'S GOLDEN WEDDING

As we know, time never stands still, and it seemed to move on at a remarkably fast pace for the present star of our story. The late 60's turned into the early 70's in age terms, and in 1935, at the age of 75, the Golden Wedding Anniversary of Henry and Elizabeth was the talk of the town.

As you might expect on an occasion such as this, the morning sun was shining through the east-facing window of Henry Dixon's rather grand dining room as the family sat down to breakfast. The silver service, which proudly adorned the table around which they were sitting, teased the

sparkling rays by reflecting them onto the surrounding walls which were adorned with some fine looking paintings more befitting an art gallery than a dining room. Everyone was relaxed and happy, and Henry Junior felt that the time was right to raise a sensitive issue once again.

"Happy Anniversary, father. I don't wish to upset your special day, but have you given any further thought to…"

"Don't mention it son. I'm staying on for as long as I can. I'll let you know when the time comes."

This short, sharp exchange was another blow to the ageing sweet-maker's son, who felt that his father, who spent more time outside the firm than in it, should step down and allow him to develop the business with his own ideas before reaching retirement age himself. It wasn't that he considered his father to be any less able due to his age; it was simply that the longer the wait, the less enthusiasm and energy he would have to pursue his own dreams.

TYPICAL LIFE IN THE 1930s
A Journey through Hillsborough

Nevertheless, worrying about it wouldn't solve anything, and Dixons carried on regardless. Life in the 1930s was still very difficult, however, and many people were on 'relief' (a bit like social security payments today). Take Eric Carey, for instance, a young Hillsborough lad whose mother used to collect her money on Thursdays. That day became the once-a-week treat for them both with a visit to the Hillsborough Kinema House to see the latest film. A tram ride started the exciting night out with fares each way costing 1½d.

Eric and his mother were sitting on the top deck of the swaying tram which clanked fairly smoothly along the steel tracks which nestled

within the surface of Middlewood Road.

"Aren't we there yet, mam? We'll miss the beginning if we don't look sharp," said Eric, his nose jammed against the nearside window as the

Hillsborough Library came into view within the green parkland which they had been passing by.

"Whose house is that, mam? It's a big 'un'," he continued after waiting in vain for a reply to his first question from his mother.

Mrs. Carey often let her son's chatter drift over her head as he always seemed to have something to say or ask. This time, however, his question about the house in the parkland had struck a chord.

"It's funny you should ask that, Eric," she responded with unusual enthusiasm. "Your grandad was only telling me the other day that it was built over one hundred and fifty years ago. It was called Hillsborough House then, and there was open countryside all round it."

"Yes, but mam, whose house is it now?"

"Well, it was owned by a man called Thomas Stead, but he sold it to a man called John Wilson who then sold it to someone called John Rodgers who for some reason changed its name to Hillsborough Hall."

"Yes, but mam…"

Hillsborough House-now Hillsborough Library (Photo 2007)

"Oh, but that wasn't the end of it, Eric," she continued with persistence. "Mester Rodgers sold it to a silver plater called John Dixon, and when he died his son then sold it to the Corporation."

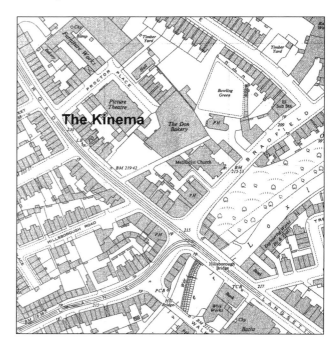

The look on her son's face should have told Mrs. Carey that she was boring the young lad to death.

"Mam, I didn't really want a history lesson tonight. It's bad enough having one at school. But I still don't know who lives there now."

"Don't be silly, Eric. Nobody lives there now because it's a lending library. Don't they teach you anything at school?"

Eric decided that it wasn't worth trying to say anymore in case his mother got cross with him. In any case, the tram was passing through the Hillsborough shopping centre, and their's was the next stop.

"Come on, mam, we're here."

The excited young lad almost fell down the metal stairs which spiralled down to the bottom floor of the tram which was grinding to its usual shuddering halt.

"Mam, look sharp or we'll be late," he shouted as he launched himself off the tram platform and scurried down the road before turning into a little side street known as Proctor Place where the cinema was located.

Although this picture-house, which was known locally as The Kinema, was a bit off the beaten track, it was enticingly attractive. Its brightly coloured main entrance had just been modernised, and you couldn't help but want to rush inside and enjoy a few hours viewing once you got there.

There was also one other attraction about Proctor Place. It was the main access to the huge Don Bakery which was situated just behind the cinema. Not only did this factory produce wonderful freshly baked breads, cakes, buns and pies, it created the most mouth-watering aromas imaginable which drifted tantalizingly over the whole of this area for most parts of the day.

However, Eric's mother had other things on her mind at this time.

"He'll be the death of me, our Eric will," she muttered to herself as she arrived breathlessly at the pay-box after trying to catch up with her son. "He's always in a rush, that lad."

As she gazed round the rather posh looking entrance area, a cheeky-looking face appeared at the side of the sweet counter a few yards away.

"Which seats are we going in, mam? Oh, and can I have some of these?"

"If you want some spice to eat while we're in there my lad, we'll have to go in the pit. I can't afford posh seats as well as sweets you know."

Admission to the pit, where numb-bums and neck strain were the order of the day, was 4d for mum and 3d for her son. As far as sweets were concerned, Eric made a bee-line for a quarter pound of Dixons Mint Rock at 2d a bag, whilst his mother went for the 2oz bar of Bourneville Chocolate at the same price. The whole evening for the two of them, including the tram fares, came to 1s 2d (one shilling and tuppence), which is 6 pence in today's money. Even allowing for raging inflation, that's as cheap a night out as you'd get anywhere these days.

It's strange, isn't it, how memories flash back into your mind when you're writing about someone else. The night out with Eric and his mother is a true account, of course, and it reminds me of my own experience in the early 1950s when, along with my brother John and my sister June, we were all running down to the Kinema past Hillsborough Park to catch the next episode of 'Flash Gordon'. The large cinema at the other end of Middlewood Road where it meets Catchbar Lane, which was called the Hillsborough Park Cinema, was showing the X-rated horror film 'King Kong',

Brothers and sister in the early 1950s

so we weren't allowed in. We couldn't afford the tram fare to the Kinema, hence the mad dash by the three of us. What really sticks out in my mind is my younger sister June shouting out: "Wait for me, wait for me," as we passed the Hillsborough library on our left.

"What's up June?" I shouted. "You're not tired are you? We'll miss the film if we don't hurry."

I stopped running and looked back at my dear little sister, who had tears welling up in her eyes.

June in the 1960s

"I can't run," she sobbed. "The elastic's gone in my knickers and they keep falling down."

I recall not knowing whether to laugh or cry at the time, before walking back to console her. All went well in the end, however, as my older brother John went on ahead to save us some seats whilst we strolled along together at a pace where good 'knicker control' was achievable. To make up for the traumatic start to our outing, we sat through the whole programme twice as film shows were screened on a continuous basis then. Those were the days, weren't they?

HENRY SENIOR: 80 YEARS OLD
WORLD WAR TWO ARRIVES

However, having inadvertently diverted from my Dixons story, let's catch up again with Henry Senior who,

80th BIRTHDAY CELEBRATION

HENRY DIXON
BORN JULY 27th, 1860.

QUEEN STREET CONGREGATIONAL CHURCH
SHEFFIELD
JULY 29th, 1940

you will recall, had just celebrated his Golden Wedding anniversary at the age of 75, and was still steaming ahead at full throttle. With such energy, time sped by and, in what seemed like no time at all, he was celebrating his 80th birthday. This milestone, which he described as 'one of the biggest events in my life', was celebrated by a large reception at the Queen Street Congregational Church where Mr. Henry Dixon was the guest of honour.

It is interesting, at this stage, to look at a facet of this man's character that was, perhaps, more understandable at that time than it might be today.

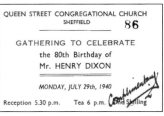

QUEEN STREET CONGREGATIONAL CHURCH
SHEFFIELD 86

GATHERING TO CELEBRATE
the 80th Birthday of
Mr. HENRY DIXON

MONDAY, JULY 29th, 1940

Reception 5.30 p.m.   Tea 6 p.m.   One Shilling

Such was the importance attached to Henry Dixon by the church, of which he was a very senior member and life-long Deacon, that the reception which was planned was not only by personal invitation, the guests invited had to pay one shilling each for the honour of attending. This was a most unusual arrangement which, it would appear, Henry was aware of and also supported. To some degree, he appears to have been caught up a little by his own importance. I wonder what his friends and colleagues really thought about the idea of having to pay to go to this wealthy man's birthday party hosted by his wealthy church?

The reception itself was very formal, and took the form of a 6.00pm tea, followed at 7.15pm by a meeting addressed by nine speakers, including Henry himself. A vocal and musical accompanist concluded the meeting. Strangely, despite his reputation as a major wholesale manufacturing confectioner, no mention was made of this aspect of his life in the biographical notes which were included in the printed

Order of Service which accompanied the event. Perhaps this reflected his priorities in life, although he still chose to rule the roost at his Britannia Works, much to his son's now resigned frustration.

In the midst of all these birthday celebrations on the 29th July 1940, one could be forgiven for forgetting that the country had been at war with Germany for about eleven months. The Sheffield Blitz, which began five months later, on the 13th December, brought the dreadful reality of the hostilities to everyone's attention with a vengeance. The devastating destruction that night, particularly in the city centre which was a raging sea of burning, twisted and crumbling buildings, left searing memories in most people's minds of the indiscriminate cruelty that war brought to everyone.

Elizabeth and Henry Dixon had been putting the finishing touches to their Christmas decorations at their home in Wilkinson Street that night, and were relaxing over a cup of tea when the bombings began. Being near to the city centre, the noise of the explosions appeared to come from only a few yards away, causing understandable terror and near panic in the household. Both Henry and his wife were 80 years old, and poor Elizabeth was already suffering from a mild heart condition.

Suddenly, an almighty blast ripped through their house, shattering some of the windows.

"Oh my God, Henry, we've been hit."

Elizabeth was in a bad way, gasping for breath as she struggled to hide under the large, oak table which stood defiantly in the centre of their dining room.

"It's not us, Elizabeth, it's next door. We've been spared. Thank God, we've been spared."

The house adjacent to their home at number 59 had received a direct hit. As Henry and Elizabeth gazed out of their broken windows at the smouldering pile of rubble, over which flickering orange and blue flames competed for space with snaking tongues of black smoke, they thanked God once again for their reprieve.

This, sadly, was the beginning of the end for Elizabeth, as she never really recovered from the effect that the blitz had caused to her heart. Over the next year and a half she deteriorated in health and, on the 21st of July 1942, at the age of 82, she passed away. Henry, distraught and saddened, was always good with words, and recalled fondly that "after 62 years courtship, 57½ years married, my dear and beloved wife was called to higher service. Though sad memories are often with me in my loneliness, yet the joy and sweet remembrance is my sustaining strength."

DIXONS DIAMOND JUBILEE

HENRY JUNIOR NOW MANAGING DIRECTOR

The loss of Elizabeth had, at last, made Henry think about his own mortality and the future of his business, which, due to the impact of the war, had suffered the enforced closure of its hitherto profitable Novelty Section. As a result, he decided to turn Dixons into a Private Limited Company with its shares being held by his family. Although he still chose to remain as Chairman of Henry Dixon Ltd, he promoted his son Henry to Managing Director, with his daughter Emily taking over as Company Secretary.

So, at last, at the age of 56, thirty-two years older than his father had been when he first ran his business, Henry Junior had some real clout in the company. The 'old man' still had overall control of course, and was still active enough to organise one more special event. This was the celebration of the diamond jubilee of the beginning of Dixons in 1884, which started off in a small rented shop before rapidly moving to 87-89 West Bar.

To celebrate the occasion, the company took all its employees by charabanc (an old-fashioned coach) on a special visit to the new Ladybower Dam which King George VI and Queen Elizabeth had officially opened only a few days earlier. Following this eventful and exciting tour of the area, Henry took everyone back to Sheffield for a

Ladybower Viaduct 2006

dinner at the rather posh Albany Hotel at the corner of Fargate and Leopold Street. Here, at a cost of 4s 6d (23 pence today) per head, the hungry employees enjoyed a well cooked three course meal, following which each of them was presented with a gift by the Chairman.

To finish the day off in style, a visit to the theatre was provided. Although the artist and venue for this finale are not known, perhaps it was Ted Ray they all went to see, as he was performing at Sheffield's famous Empire Theatre at the time. This extremely well-known and talented comedian would certainly have been on Henry's list of suitable

entertainers. It must be acknowledged, however, that as far as arranging events and celebrations is concerned, there was no-one who could do it better than Henry. This day was no exception, as the occasion was greatly enjoyed by all concerned. As the great man himself said at the time, "It was a great day in my history".

It's strange, isn't it, how some people manage to continue being very active in life right to the very end. Perhaps it is that very activity and determination to continue that prolongs their lives? This certainly appears to be the case with Henry Dixon. If we cast our minds back sixty years or so to the time just before he decided to start his own business, we will find that one of the main reasons for leaving his position at Wilsons' Toy Shop was that his health was suffering. Despite this, and the handicap of having only one good eye, he was still going strong at the age of 84 at a time when the life expectancy of most of Sheffield's workers was only 40 years.

HENRY DIXON SENIOR SAYS GOODBYE

However, even Henry Dixon, the 'Peter Pan' of Queen Street Chapel, and the 'everlasting' boss of Dixons sweet company, couldn't continue for ever. In 1949 at the incredible age of 89, he finally handed his company over to 'Junior' (now aged 63) as he said his last farewell to the world and went to meet his maker. A kind and sincere letter sent to him from an old business friend a year or two earlier is perhaps a fitting testimony to this remarkable man:

> "The occasions on which a man lives to see the sixtieth year of a business which he himself established must be rare indeed, and I feel sure that the congratulations of your friends and those connected with you must have been a source of great satisfaction to you, and also the fact of the great esteem in which you are held in the widest trade circles must cause you great happiness."

It was, of course, the 65th anniversary of his company when Henry Dixon died and, strangely enough, the only other businessman that springs to mind who could compare with this achievement is Samuel Johnson. This young man, who we have read about earlier, joined the then loss-making Bassetts sweet company in 1860. Firstly as a partner, than eventually as sole owner, he built up and developed the famous firm into what was recognised as the most successful company of its kind at the time. At his death in 1925, on the 65th anniversary of him joining and rescuing the company, 86 year old Samuel had himself set a longevity record very similar to that of Henry Dixon. The two men, both being confectioners, knew each other well as their business lives overlapped for forty years. Perhaps it's something in their mouth-watering, taste-bud tickling products which kept these 'giants' of confectionery going? Perhaps we'd better not let today's kids know this, however, or we might have Jamie Oliver on our backs.

PHASE TWO: DIXONS–PITCHFORK-MAXONS AND MERGES.

The second phase of our Dixons-Maxons-Pitchfork story introduces a family whose name is not as well known as the Dixons, but is just as important. This name is PITCHFORK.

Roger Pitchfork is the current Chairman and Managing Director of a local confectionery manufacturing company

which trades under the name of MAXONS on Bradbury Street in Heeley. The company makes old favourites such as Pear Drops, Rhubarb and Custard and Granny's Old Fashioned Herbals, as well as Dixons Mint Rock, Dixons Cherry Balsams and Jesmona Old Fashioned Black Bullets. There are, of course, many more such delicacies made in the modern Bradbury Street factory, but the selection identified above clearly shows a mix of differing famous manufacturing names now all grouped together. Let us have a look at how this has developed and who it really involved.

Perhaps we should start with Roger's grandfather, George, who was born in 1884, the very same year that Henry Dixon Senior first started his own confectionery business. George wasn't really into sweets, and for many years sweated it out in one of Sheffield's huge East-End Steelworks. However, at the age of 45, he was tiring of his rather unhealthy life amongst the noise, heat and dust, and, with a few savings he'd managed to build up, he bought a small newsagent shop on Chesterfield Road at Woodseats.

By this time, his wife Alice had given birth to three children, Edward (born in 1911), Ralph (born in 1913) and Edna (born in 1916). It was George's younger son Ralph who was destined to be the driving force in the Pitchfork family's venture into sweet-making, and when the time came for him to leave the Central School in the heart of the city centre in his early teens, it was through his father's connections in the newsagency business that he obtained employment, working for H. Turner & Sons Ltd., a wholesale newsagents company based on Bank Street.

Other than for a two year gap from the age of 18 when he was called up to do his National Service, Ralph spent the next ten years learning as much as he could about the wholesale business. This knowledge and experience would prove to be very valuable to him in future years. The Second World War took him away on active service with the Royal Air Force for about four years just after his 26th birthday, following which he returned to his employment at H. Turner & Son.

RALPH PITCHFORK: SWEET-MAKER

However, just like Henry Dixon Senior had felt nearly seventy years before, Ralph felt that he wanted to be his own man. So, in 1950 with the support of his wife Margaret he bought a small wholesale and manufacturing confectionery company by the name of Nadins, which operated at 62 Albert Road in Heeley, and became the proud owner of his very own sweet factory at the age of 37.

By a stroke of good fortune, a gentleman by the name of Gordon MacDonald was working for Leonard Nadin's company at that time. He had moved there after the war, following the collapse of his own sweet manufacturing

Ralph Pitchfork

company, Maxons, which had suffered dramatically from the loss of much of his labour force and the impact of sugar shortages and rationing during and after those terrible years of hostilities.

However, his experience as a sugar confectionery manufacturer was a 'godsend' to Ralph Pitchfork, who was more than happy to appoint him as a director in his new company. More importantly, even though Maxons no longer operated as a manufacturer, it still existed as a dormant company, which Ralph managed to purchase from Gordon MacDonald to complete his launch into the confectionery business. Thus, the wholesale side of Nadins changed to Ralph Pitchfork Ltd., whilst the manufacturing side changed to Maxons Ltd. A new era of Sheffield sweet-makers was born, and Ralph Pitchfork's career in the confectionery industry had begun in earnest.

Before its demise over the war years, Maxons itself had been in business for some time (although historical details of the company are a little sketchy) and, in the early 1930s, specialized in making toffee with a high butter content at its 'Garden Factory' at Bents Green. It also had an address on Eccelsall Road, which was presumably its retail outlet.

Following on from this specialization, it branched out into making rock and a variety of boiled sweets under the guidance of the MacDonald family of father and sons, from whence came the name 'Mac and sons', which finally emerged as Maxons.

It was about this time, the 1930s that the famous mint rock manufacturer, CHARLES BUTLER, who started his business in 1848 was up for sale. His mint rock, claimed on his advertising literature to be 'the most popular in the world' in the 1900s, was an obvious attraction. Dixons was the successful buyer at that time, probably because its own mint rock had acquired the same 'best in the world' acclaim, and the combining of the 'best' made good business sense.

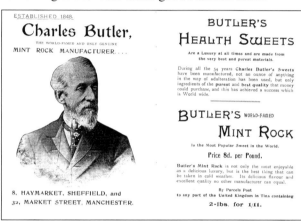

However, to return to Ralph Pitchfork's new career, he decided to expand his wholesale operations by taking over another wholesaler who operated under the name of Fred Robinson of Barnsley. Following this, in 1954 he opened a new showroom and warehouse on Lenton Street at the Junction of Shoreham Street and Duchess Road, which became the headquarters of the expanded Ralph Pitchfork Ltd. wholesale operation. Its promise of 'good service, the best products and speedy delivery' of mouth-watering sweets from manufactures such as Bassetts, Pascalls, Hollands, Fox's, T a v e r n e r s, Bellamys and Thornes, as well as its own Maxons products, made it a very successful enterprise.

The Maxons sweet-making factory was still located at number 62 Albert Road in Heeley, on the site of old stables which once housed horses which pulled trams from Sheffield town centre to its terminus at the Red Lion. The shell of the old tram shed itself is still visible at the bottom of Albert Road, where it displays the description 'Sheffield Tramway Company – 1878' in the old stone lintels set in the brick-arch facade leading to its cobbled courtyard. The Meersbrook Tannery, together with its

The Red Lion Public House, Heeley

supply reservoir, occupied the land between this tram shed and the adjacent Valley Road, and anyone travelling on the open-topped horse-buses which trotted out to the Big Tree at Woodseats at that time, knew well in advance when they were getting close to this foul-smelling factory.

The River Meer, which gave its name to Meersbrook and was formerly the old City and County boundary, ran behind Maxons' Albert Road factory, and it

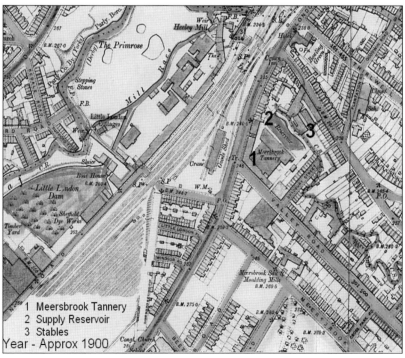

1 Meersbrook Tannery
2 Supply Reservoir
3 Stables
Year - Approx 1900

83

wasn't until the 1960s, by which time the river had been culverted (put in large pipes underground), that access was possible from Bradbury Street. The demolition of the old terraced housing in this street in the 1970s had enabled the company to expand its manufacturing site over a number of years until there was nothing left of the original Maxons (formerly Nadins) factory. The only evidence of the factory of the 1950s is a conspicuous gap between houses numbered 60 and 64 on Albert Road, although as you stand there, the sweet, strong smell of boiling sugars still stir the memory when the wind is in the right direction.

HENRY DIXON JUNIOR

But, what had Henry Dixon been doing during this time? Now, as both Chairman and Managing Director of his company at last, he felt free to manage without any interference, however well intentioned. His confectionery sales had, unfortunately, slowed down considerably due to rationing still being in place in those early years of the 1950s, although they did improve with a vengeance once it was lifted. Most importantly, however, his skilful and caring management of his workforce meant that very few people chose to leave his company, as loyalty was always uppermost in their minds.

An example of the loyalty of his workforce, and the esteem in which they in turn were held by their managing director, can be seen in one example from 1955 when, on Friday the 29th April, Mrs. Florrie Adsetts completed fifty years service with the company. Florrie had started working there as a young girl, and had worked her way up to the position of forewoman of the Wrapping and Bottling department. It wasn't just the job she loved; it was the companionship and friendship she had formed with hundreds of other women like her. To Florrie, Dixons was her second family with whom she spent the major part of her life, and she would be lost without it.

But of course, she was not retiring that day, only being honoured and thanked by Henry Dixon personally, who presented her with the latest new invention which she could

Florrie Adsetts receives her TV after 50 years service

never have afforded at that time - a black and white television. She was the envy of all her colleagues. Perhaps, with a gift such as this, retirement wouldn't have been such a bad idea after all?

DIXON PITCHFORK MERGER

Despite the rapid upturn in demand for sweets after rationing was abolished, Henry was feeling a little downhearted, and he decided to approach his good friend and colleague, Ralph Pitchfork, with a proposition. A business lunch at the Grand Hotel in Barker's Pool gave him the opportunity.

"You know Ralph, I waited so long to take over my company that I'm too tired to give it my best now. I'm 72, and Gertrude and I feel that we could do with some of the pressures of work taking off us. As you know, we've got a lovely daughter but, sweet though she is, she doesn't really want to run my factory, so I'm wondering whether you'd consider a merger between us?"

It was several seconds before Ralph lowered the half-full glass of red Merlot which he had been sipping as an accompaniment to his medium-rare fillet steak which graced the dining table at which he and Henry were sitting. A proposal of this sort obviously made good sense to the new Pitchfork/Maxons boss who, at still only 45 years old, was rightly ambitious to move on. Dixons' wholesale contacts would considerably broaden his own operation, and its well known manufacturing brands were an obvious asset.

"Henry, my friend," he replied with a tremor of excitement and emotion in his voice, "I'd be delighted."

Thus, in 1958, Dixon Pitchfork Ltd. was established, with Maxons Ltd. continuing as its manufacturing arm. Henry became Chairman of the new parent company in a basically non-executive capacity, and, with Ralph as Managing Director of both the wholesale and manufacturing operations, the future looked rosy.

The merger between these two confectioner friends was the catalyst which spurred on the joint company to buy a large new factory-cum-showroom at 290-300 Broadfield Road, with wholesale activities concentrated on the ground floor and manufacturing taking place upstairs. Production was moved there from the Britannia Works in Love Street, and the new showroom was acknowledged as one of the biggest and best in the country. It is interesting to have a look at the sweets and chocolate products that were being produced under both the Dixons and Maxons brand names at the time:

It is also interesting to remember that most of the sweets produced were actually contained in large, glass jars, which were a feature of the 1950s and '60s sweet shop shelves. Although similar plastic jars are still used today in some specialist shops, it was inevitable that the size and weight of such glass containers was going to be a major storage and handling problem as demand for sweets increased. It

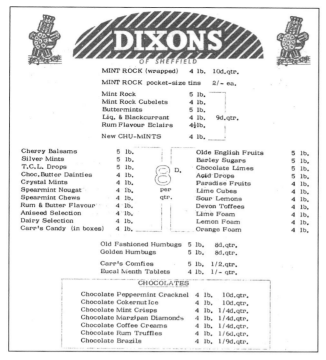

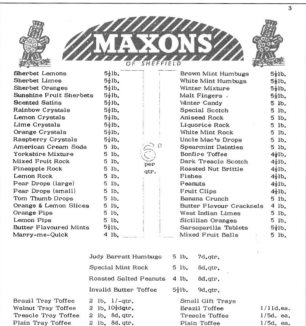

A background murmuring drifted around the puzzled faces of the board members who, unsuccessfully, tried to visualize if their MD's complex calculation was feasible.

"That really is a tall order, Ralph. But how many jars would you have in each 7ft stack then?"

"Well, I reckon that we'd have about 600 or so jars in each one, which would mean we'd have twenty piles of jars altogether."

There was no doubting Ralph's optimism and good intentions, but the weight of each 7 ft stack of sweet-filled jars, together with the space needed to store them, was mind-boggling. I wonder what health and safety inspectors would think about such a proposal these days? Nevertheless, what the boss wanted, the workers produced, and, with the whole of the loading bay at Broadfield Road occupied by these jars, and an equivalent area similarly occupied elsewhere in the factory, the predicted post-January sweet demand was met in full, with no disappointed customers. It just goes to show that the old saying 'If you don't try, you won't succeed' is really worth remembering. Ralph Pitchfork was obviously an advocate of this.

Before we roll the Ralph Pitchfork 'express' on further, let us just consider the wholesale aspect of confectionery in a little more detail. This is the business, you will recall, that

was, in fact, beginning to be a problem as early as December 1958, when Ralph Pitchfork was making decisions about the sweet stocks he needed to meet anticipated demand.

"Now then, gentle-men," he began, addressing his fellow directors at one of his monthly board meetings. "I would like to see about 25 tons of Maxons and Dixons sweets available in stock by the end of January."

"That's a tall order, Ralph. Are you sure it's necessary?" queried one of the directors.

"Absolutely Ken. I know it means that we'll need about 12,000 jars, but if we stack them on a 12 jar by 12 jar base, with two rows less in each successive layer, we should be able to stack up to 7ft high without much fear of them falling over."

Henry Dixon Senior set himself up in for the first twenty years or so. The wholesalers are the 'middle men', to whom most manufacturers sell their products in order that they can then be distributed far and wide to thousands of shops and other retailers, who then sell them on to the public. This system enables the manufacturers to concentrate on making sufficient sweet products (in the case of confectioners)

BARRATTS		
Count Lines—		
2d.	French Nougat	
1d.	Gob Stoppers	
1½d.	Everlasting Strips	
1½d.	Skipping Ropes	
2d.	Fountains	
2d.	Goldflake Cigs.	
2d.	Jolly Lolly	
2d.	Sherbert Suckers	
2d.	Choc Bananas	
1d.	Licorice Telephones	
2d.	Sweet Tobacco (Rolls)	
8 a 1d.	Aniseed Balls	
4Al	Aniseed Balls	
2Al	„ „	
2Al	Gob Stoppers	
2Al	Chinese Lanterns	
4Al	Shrimps or Clogs	
4Al	Ogo Pogo Eyes	
1d.	One Up Bar Asst. Flavours	
2d.	Sherbert Dab	
2d.	Disneyland Sweet Cigs	
2d.	Scout Pipes	
4d.	French Nougat	
2d.	Comforter	
Weigh-out—		
Qtr.		
6d.	Broadway Mixt.	
6d.	Liquorice Comfits	
6d.	Mixed Pastilles	
8d.	Theatre Mixture	
7d.	Chocolate Chewing Nuts	
8d.	Swiss Nougat	
6d.	Love Hearts	
6d.	Noah's Ark Cachous	
6d.	Nutty Bon Bons	
6d.	Crystallised Pears	5½ lbs.
6d.	Tom Thumb Mixture	5½ lbs.
7d.	Cough Candy Twists	4 lbs.
Pre-packed Lines—		
6½d.	Bags, Liquorice Comfits	2 doz.
6½d.	Bags, Pastilles	2 doz.
Jars.		
7d.	Nutty Nutty	4 lb.
6½d.	Bags, Licorice Allsorts	2 doz

	MISCELLANEOUS GROCERIES		Doz.	
1/11	Bovril (Bottles 2 oz.)		19/6½	Nil
3/6	Bovril (Bottles 4 oz.)		35/8½	,,
6/3	Bovril (Bottles 8 oz.)		63/9	,,
11/6	Bovril (Bottles 16 oz.)		120/3½	,,
4d.	2 oz. Bisto		3/2½	,,
7½d.	4 oz. Bisto		6/–	,,
1/2	8 oz. Bisto		11/2	,,
1/4½	Camp Coffee, Small		14/5	,,
2/6½	Camp Coffee, Large		26/7	,,
6/1	Camp Coffee, Cafe Size		66/3	,,
15/–	Horlicks Malted Milk	each	12/–	,,
			Doz.	,,
3/2	Horlicks Malted Milk Jars I		30/6	,,
5/6	Horlicks Malted Milk		53/–	,,
9d.	Horlicks Malted Milk Tin Tablets		7/2	,,
1/11	Horlicks		18/8	,,
1/–	Hax Real Lemon Juice		9/6	,,
1/3	Chappie Large	48/3 Case	12/0½	,,
8d.	Chappie Handy	38/8 ,,	6/5½	,,
1/7	Lassie Large	61/1 ,,	15/3½	,,
10½	Lassie Handy	50/9 ,,	8/5½	,,
9d.	Kit-E-Kat	43/2 ,,	7/2½	,,
1/11	Meat Large	74/6 ,,	18/7½	,,
1/1	Meat Handy	63/2 ,,	10/6½	,,
1/6	Ovaltine Tins		14/5	,,
2/9	Ovaltine Tins		26/5	Nil
5/–	Ovaltine Tins		48/–	,,
8d.	Ovaltine Tins Tablets		6/4	,,
2–2½d.	Oxo Cubes (Grossed Boxed)	Gross	12/6	,,
6½d.	Saccharine Tablets (Pkts.) Gross Lots			Nil
	58/– Gross	5/2	Doz.	,,
1/9	Vinegar 20 oz. Sarsons		16/6	,,
1/2	Vinegar 10 oz. Sarsons		11/–	,,
2/6	Bottles Lucozade		24/–	,,
	Bottles charged 3/– dozen Returnable			
8d.	Bottles Lucozade		5/8	,,
	Bottles charged 2/– dozen Returnable			

to meet demand across the whole country and, indeed, overseas, without the need to have to store vast amounts of products on their premises or employ huge fleets of vehicles to deliver to individual retailers direct. Many companies, including Ralph Pitchfork Ltd., had their own separate manufacturing and wholesale organisations. However, there was still the need to use other independent wholesalers who distributed goods in different regions of the country.

One such wholesaler of interest was Naylor Bros. of Aldershot, who stocked and distributed just about everything that the average family would need. Its mid-1950s brochure makes fascinating reading, as can be seen from the extracts from it printed on this and the previous page. In these lists, the initials R.P. means Retail Price, W/S P. Doz means Wholesale Price per dozen, and P.T. means Purchase Tax.

	CLEANSERS	Doz.	
1/–	Ajax	10/5	,,
7d.	Ajax	6/1	,,
1/2	Brobat Liquid Bleach	10/6	,,
	(Bottles Returnable at 2/– doz.)		
9d.	Brobat Liquid Bleach	7/6	,,
1/4½	Chemico Lavatory Cleanser	12/4½	,,
1/–	Chemico Hand Cleaner	9/–	,,
1/3	,, White ,,	11/3	,,
1/6	,, Household Cleaner	13/6	,,
2/9	,, ,,	24/9	,,
1/4	Dirty Paws	10/8	,,
10d.	Durazone Bleach	7/6	Nil
1/4	Durazone Bleach	12/–	,,
	(Bottles chargod 2/– doz. refundable)		
1 –	Gumption	9/–	,,
2/6	,,	22/6	,,
1/7	Harpic Size B	14/3	,,
2/8	,, ,, A	23/10	,,
1/2	Kleenoff	10/6	,,

Of interest in these product lists is the absence of any advertising of Dixons and Maxons products, despite many of their competitors advertising their ranges of confectionery. One reason for this decision not to advertise was that their own wholesale organisation, Dixon Pitchfork Ltd., was sufficiently widespread not to require the services of this independent wholesaler, Naylors.

R.P.	TOILET SOAPS	W/S P. Doz.	P.T.
7d.	Breeze Toilet Soap, 3 oz.	4/9½	30
1/–	Breeze Toilet Soap Bath Tablets, 6 oz.	8/2	,,
10d.	Bristows Lanolin Toilet Soap, 3 oz.	6/4	,,
1/8	Bristows Lanolin Toilet Soap Bath Tabs. 6 oz.	12/8	,,
10d.	Cussons Imp. Leather Toilet Soap, 3 oz.	6/3	,,
1/8	Cussons Imp. Leather Bath Tablets, 6 oz.	12/6	,,
10d.	Cussons Apple Bloss. Toilet Soap, 3 oz.	6/3	,,
1/–	Fields Buckingham Lav. Toilet Soap, 3 oz.	7/3	,,
1/3	Fields Buckingham Lav. Bath Tablets, 6 oz.	9/–	,,
1/3	Gerards Bath Tablets, 6 oz.	9/10	,,
3/–	Gerards (3 in box) Toilet Soap Asstd. Perfumes, Doz. Boxes	20/6	,,
11d.	Gibbs Vinolia Baby Soap, 3 oz.	7/4½	,,
9d.	Gibbs Astral Toilet Soap, 3 oz.	6/0½	,,
1/3	Gibbs Astral Bath Soap, 6 oz.	10/1	,,
11d.	Johnson & Johnson Baby Soap, 3 oz.	7/1	,,
7d.	Knights Castile Toilet Soap, 3 oz.	4/9½	,,
1/–	Knights Castile Bath Tablets, 6 oz.	8/2½	,,
7d.	Lifebuoy Toilet Soap, 3 oz.	4/9½	,,
1/–	Lifebuoy Bath Tablets, 6 oz.	8/2½	,,
7d.	Lux Toilet Soap, 3 oz.	4/9½	,,
1/–	Lux Toilet Soap Bath Tablets, 6 oz.	8/2½	,,
7d.	Palmolive Toilet Soap, 3 oz.	4/9½	,,
1/–	Palmolive Toilet Soap Bath Tabs., 6oz.	8/2½	,,
10½d.	Pears Transparent Toilet Soap, 3 oz.	7/2	,,
9d.	Pears Embassy Toilet Soap, 3 oz.	6/0½	,,
9d.	Vinolia Toilet Soap	6/1½	,,
9d.	Wrights Coal Tar Toilet Soap, 3 oz.	6/–	,,
1/5½	Wrights Coal Tar Bath Tablets, 6 oz.	11/8	,,

RALPH, ROGER AND ANOTHER MERGER

However, something else was afoot which probably influenced this decision. Ralph Pitchfork was considering a further merger, this time with a wholesale company called J.A.& P. Holland Ltd., based in Southport, Lancashire. Holland's were keen to establish a national chain of wholesalers to secure a good distribution of their own manufactured products and were keen to get Ralph Pitchfork on board to 'spearhead' this project under a subsidiary company called Holland Distributors Ltd. Before we see if he followed this course of action, let's pop back a few years to see what had been happening on the domestic front.

Ralph had married his sweetheart Margaret in his early twenties. They had met whilst they had both been working at H. Turner & Son Ltd. during the 1930s, and they had been subsequently gifted with the birth of three children, Graham, Eileen and Roger, during the early war years of 1939-41.

Roger, the youngest of these, had been in his last year of study at High Storrs Grammar School on Ringinglow Road at the western side of the city when his father had merged his company with that of Henry Dixon Junior. Although showing a keen interest in the confectionery business, before committing himself fully to his father's firm he wisely chose to go to the Borough Polytechnic in London to study food technology in detail, as well as availing himself of the depth and breadth of learning and independence which such establishments provide. However, whilst he was still studying there in 1961, the merger between Dixon Pitchfork and J.A.&.P Holland Ltd, which his father Ralph had been considering, actually took place.

HENRY DIXON JUNIOR RETIRES

But what of Henry Dixon, who was still Chairman of Dixon Pitchfork Ltd? He was now 75 years old, and the thought of being involved in another merger prompted his decision to call it a day and spend his retirement years with his dear wife Gertrude. Sadly, she was only able to enjoy four of these before her devoted husband died at the age of 79.

Whilst Henry Dixon Junior had lived to what was then a very good age, his life seemed to have been somewhat on hold for such a long time as he waited for his father to retire from the 'top spot' and pass over the running of the company to him. That is not to say, of course, that he did not enjoy his business life; it is only my presumption that it was probably tinged with frustration. What we do know, however, is that it was his knowledge, experience and enthusiasm in the field of confectionery manufacturing that caused Dixons to indulge in sweet-making instead of dealing only with the wholesale side of confectionery.

Henry Junior was, in fact, the 'unsung hero' in this tale of Dixons the sweet-makers.

It wasn't just confectionery that this gifted man was involved in, however. He was a great supporter of the Croft House Settlement and, indeed, ran its Swimming Club. His credentials in this sporting activity were second to none, and he had the honour of being appointed as a Swimming Judge at the Olympic Games held in London in 1948, Helsinki in 1952 and Melbourne in 1956. By the time the Rome Olympic Games arrived in 1960 he had been appointed to the position of President of the Amateur Swimming Association (ASA), a position which he held with pride.

To sum up what Henry Dixon Junior was really like, therefore, we can say with confidence that not only was he gifted in a business sense, but he was also a kind and caring person, a Sheffielder of whom we can be very proud.

J. M. GOLDSMITH TAKES OVER

However, the tale doesn't stop here, does it? Neither does it get less complicated. No sooner had Ralph brought about the Dixon-Pitchfork (including Maxons) merger with J.A.& P. Holland Ltd., then up popped a take-over bid for the Holland Group of companies by J.M. Goldsmith, the millionaire owner of Cavenham Foods Ltd.

Ralph was now Vice-Chairman and Managing Director of J.A.& P. Holland Ltd., and was well known and respected nationally for his knowledge and expertise in the manufacturing and wholesale confectionery business. This was the reason he was now being targeted by Cavenham Foods. But who, we can rightly ask, was this aggressor company of which James Goldsmith was Chairman and Managing Director?

Cavenham Foods Ltd. was formed as an alliance of a number of companies in the food industry. Most of these were old, established firms, some of which were encountering difficulties in adapting themselves to the highly competitive conditions being faced by this industry. In particular, the smaller companies, who had to fight it out alone against large groups, were finding life rather difficult. According to its Chairman, Cavenham Foods' aim was to combine 'What is best in the old, established traditional Companies with what is best in the modern efficient food group'.

RALPH PITCHFORK

M.D. OF CAVENHAM'S WHOLESALE DIVISION

At the time that James Goldsmith was propositioning Ralph Pitchfork, Cavenhams had an annual turnover of £27½ million, and employed 5,800 people in seven food factories, four paper and allied products factories, and 33 wholesaling companies. This company was, without a doubt, in the 'Premier League'. Holland Distributors Ltd. was one of the largest wholesale confectionery and tobacco groups in the United Kingdom, and was an obvious key target for the millionaire. But what was in it for Ralph? Well, he was offered a place on the Cavenham's Group Board of Directors, and the position of Managing Director of the Group's Wholesale Division. This indeed was a real promotion into a food and confectionery giant at a time (1965) when the British public ate £319 million worth, or 597 thousand tons, of sweets (including chocolate confectionery) each year, bought from 200,000 sales outlets and 1,500 wholesalers. In fact, this mammoth amount of sweets consumed by we Brits was more, per person, than any other country in the world. What a greedy lot we were.

Not surprisingly, Ralph took the job offered to him and became a big fish in a big sea, whilst both Dixon Pitchfork and Maxons were absorbed into Cavenhams' Wholesale and Manufacturing Divisions respectively. Ralph was now 52 years old, and his 23 year old son Roger had finished his study and was gaining practical experience with both Maxons and Hollands during this time of change. Life at the top was hectic to say the least, and demanded an enormous amount of Ralph's time, much of it away from home. He'd reached the pinnacle of his speciality, and all he could see ahead was work, more work and less time with his family. To cap it all, he'd now been asked by his Chairman to move to London. This wasn't really what his idea of life was all about.

After only two or three years with the company, therefore, Ralph Pitchfork decided to resign from Cavenhams and buy back, with James Goldsmith's blessing, his old firm name of Dixon Pitchfork Ltd., which he mothballed, and Maxons Ltd., which he continued as an independent manufacturer once more. Roger was equally happy to be moving back to being a family business, and the mothballing of the now dormant Dixon Pitchfork wholesale operation enabled the two of them to work together and concentrate on their preferred manufacturing operations.

MAXONS RE-EMMERGES
RALPH PITCHFORK - THE END OF AN ERA

Ralph was 56 when he bought back Maxons Ltd. and the dormant Dixons Pitchfork Ltd. from the Cavenham Group. Although he had many more goals in life, he had no wish to return to the day-to-day running of a business, so he took on the role of Executive Chairman, with Gordon MacDonald being Managing Director and his son Roger assisting them both. This decision enabled him to guide Maxons forward for the next eighteen years or so whilst also pursuing other outside activities. It also enabled him to take a well-deserved holiday or two with his wife Margaret, and just enjoy the simple pleasures of life without the constant pressure of time and targets to consider. Sadly, he passed away in 1988 at the relatively young age of 74, having reached the pinnacle of his profession as one of the most knowledgeable and respected wholesale confectioners in the business.

Despite his incredibly active life, Ralph Pitchfork had always found time to get involved in voluntary work. This included a spell as Chairman of the Community Health Council for the Northern General Hospital, Chairman of the League of Friends for two hospitals, and many voluntary activities related to his keen involvement with Rotary International. There is no doubt that his contribution to Sheffield in one way or another has been considerable, and it is with our great thanks that he had the foresight to retain the exciting sweet manufacturing business of Maxons as a still thriving Sheffield gem.

ROGER PITCHFORK IN CHARGE

At the relatively young age of 38, Roger Pitchfork took over as Managing Director of the company on Gordon MacDonald's retirement as a full-time director in 1979. He later became Chairman, in 1988, on the death of his father Ralph. On his appointment as Managing Director, he had been married seven years to his dear wife Tricia, and with five year old Christopher and two year old Stuart to look after, life was busy to say the least. Fierce competition in the confectionery industry also meant even greater pressure at work had to be accepted to be successful. Despite this, however, the factory at Bradbury Street was able to be expanded in 1979 in the February of Roger's first year in charge of Maxons. This set the scene for a successful future.

MAXONS MINT ROCK KING KIDNAPPED

However, there were times when things went wrong in a manner which could never have been anticipated. Such an event occurred one dark night, three years later, in 1982.

It was mild and muggy on that dark August night in Bradbury Street. Three hooded figures in black clothing were creeping nervously towards the gated wall which butted up to the gable of the nearest building which formed Maxons' sweet factory, pausing only to steady the long ladder which they carried between them.

"Come on Tom, let's put this up and get it over with before anyone sees us."

Within a few minutes, all three figures were busily helping to lean the ladder up against the main factory wall. There, just above the top rung, clinging happily to the brickwork where he had lived for many years, was 'The Mint Rock King', Maxons' mascot who was affectionately

referred to by the local Sheffield press as 'Mint Rock Man'. Unbelievably, the four foot tall, smiling figure was about to be kidnapped by a group calling themselves the Pyramid Gang.

When Roger arrived the next morning, humming cheerfully to himself as the early sunshine tantalizingly played on an extra clean patch of factory wall, his thoughts were anywhere but on 'The King'. It was only when the foreman burst into his office half an hour later that the news broke.

"I can't believe it, boss, he's not there. I just can't believe it. Come and look for yourself."

"Just a minute, Bert. Who's not there? What are you talking about?"

"It's 'The King', boss. He's disappeared into thin air."

Roger strolled out of his office calmly, wondering whether the pressure of work was getting to Bert. How could a four foot high wooden figure clamped to a brick wall twelve feet up just disappear? It was nonsense.

To say that Roger was gob-smacked when he viewed the bare patch of wall a minute or two later would be the understatement of the year.

"Bloody 'ell. I don't believe it!"

To be fair, Roger wasn't a man who swore very often, and he probably uttered his disbelief under his breath. He was obviously stunned.

Time passed on and no sign or word of the famous mascot was seen or heard of for the next two months or so. Then, on a cold, grey morning in October, a letter dropped through the office letter box to explain it all. Perhaps you'd better read it for yourself:

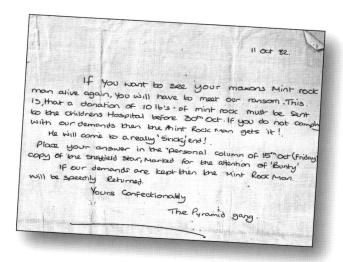

11 Oct 82.

If You want to see your maxons Mint rock man alive again, you will have to meet our ransom. This is, that a donation of 10 lb's of mint rock must be sent to the childrens Hospital before 30th Oct. If you do not comply with our demands then the Mint Rock Man gets it!. He will come to a really 'sticky' end!.

Place your answer in the 'personal' column of 15th Oct (Friday) copy of the Sheffield Star, Marked for the attention of 'Bunty'. If our demands are kept then the Mint Rock Man. will be speedily Returned.

Yours Confectionally

The Pyramid gang.

Roger wasn't sure whether to be relieved or annoyed with the note, although as the ransom was for a charitable gift to sick children, all earlier concerns were erased and the demands were happily met. The entry in the 'personal' column of the October 15th issue of The Star read: "BUNTY. Terms agreed – Dicky Mint", and the following final response from the Pyramid Gang concluded the kidnappers' negotiations.

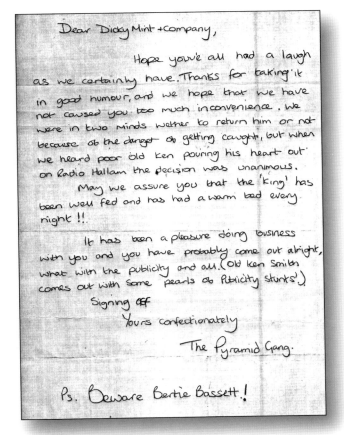

Dear Dicky Mint + company,

Hope you've all had a laugh as we certainly have. Thanks for taking it in good humour, and we hope that we have not caused you too much inconvenience. We were in two minds wether to return him or not because of the danger of getting caught, but when we heard poor old Ken pouring his heart out on Radio Hallam the decision was unanimous.

May we assure you that the 'king' has been well fed and has had a warm bed every night!!

It has been a pleasure doing business with you and you have probably come out alright, what with the publicity and all. (Old Ken Smith comes out with some pearls of publicity stunts')

Signing off

Yours confectionately

The Pyramid Gang.

Ps. Beware Bertie Bassett!

The delivery of the ransom to the Children's Hospital a few days later was a joyous affair for all concerned, as the sick children gratefully accepted 10lb of mint rock sweets plus a giant 3 ft stick of the popular seaside delicacy from Maxons. The return of 'The King' himself was reported in the press as also being delivered to the hospital where, under cover of darkness, he was handed to a night porter

for safe and anonymous delivery. Whether you know Maxons' mascot as Mint Rock Man, The Mint Rock King, The King of Mint or even The King of Rock (with Elvis's permission of course), you must admit that this daring and exciting kidnap probably did everyone a power of good, particularly Maxons who inadvertently gained valuable publicity for its wonderful products.

A TOUR ROUND MAXONS FACTORY

Well, I think we've come to a point in the Maxons story when a look round its sweet-making factory would be a good idea. Why don't you join me?

The wind was blowing around my ears on that late October morning as I stood at the door to Maxons' office block, waiting for someone to answer my ring for attention. I was several minutes early for my appointment, and this had given me time to take-in the cluster of buildings which nestled at the cul-de-sac end of Bradbury Street which formed the manufacturing confectionery business. The Mint Rock King mascot, which was perching on the factory wall again with his crown jauntily placed on his head, had welcomed me through the open gateway with a smile, and I was looking forward to an interesting tour of his works.

"Morning Bob. Nice to see you."

It was a cheerful Chris Pitchfork who had answered the door and ushered me into the office, where an equally friendly greeting from his father and Managing Director, Roger Pitchfork, was offered.

"It's good to see you Roger. It's a bit windy out there, although I don't suppose it's bad for this time of year, is it?"

I guess it wouldn't be normal if we Sheffield folk didn't spend the first few minutes talking about the weather, despite the fact that it's often boring to do so. Nevertheless, a nice cup o' tea and a bit more chit-chat later, during which time we put the world to rights, led us into the main purpose of my visit.

Chris, who'd popped out of the office for a few minutes, suddenly returned with an armful of protective clothing which he offered me with a smile on his face.

"Here, Bob, put these on. We all have to wear them when we walk round the factory."

A blue hair-net covered by a smart white cap, which seemed to perch on my slightly smaller than average head, was complemented by a thick, knee-length white coat to complete my 'health and safety pack' issue. I felt more like a hospital doctor than a sweet-factory visitor, particular with my camera slung around my neck like an oversize stethoscope.

The statutory hand-wash was completed before we left the office block to make our way across the yard to the 'operating theatre' on the ground floor of the nearest factory building. The opening of the door to this wonderland of sweet-making was a revelation, as a mixture of warm, sweet-smelling odours rushed over to meet us and settle mischievously in our noses and throats. Cheerful faces glanced up from several busy workers, whilst bright lights tantalizingly illuminated what at first appeared to be two red flying-saucers, huge sausage-making machines, steel operating tables, and a large pot of bubbling stew.

Cooling Carousels

"Wow! This is fantastic, Chris."

I couldn't really say much else at the time as I was busy clicking- away with my posh camera, trying not to miss any of the exciting events taking place. Perhaps we should calmly start at the beginning and digest each activity in turn.

On that particular morning Clove Rock was being made, a speciality that was enjoyed by many people in Ireland, where it was sent in large quantities. A large, over-size saucepan with its tall, domed lid was a key participant in this process. It was sitting proudly on a hot gas-cooker at one end of the room and had just been filled with a combination of sugar, glucose-syrup and water. Within minutes the powerful jets of flame beneath it had begun to warm up and combine its ingredients which, by now, had begun to merrily burble amongst themselves. Ten to fifteen minutes later, with steam belching out of the top of its lid, the whole mass was a sea of boiling bubbles which burst frantically on the surface as if trying to escape.

The temperature gauge on the wall adjacent to the boiler was already showing 148 degrees, and, with its lid now removed, the pan of porridge-looking lava, which would have done Mount Vesuvius great credit, was almost screaming to get out. It was not to be disappointed, as two white-coated 'sweet-doctors' wearing heat-proof gloves carefully grasped the four, long metal handles which were attached to the pan and carefully lifted the whole ensemble off its tormenting flames.

Whilst all this heated excitement had been developing, two sturdy, six foot long, steel operating-tables, which were situated adjacent to each other only a few feet away from the boiling mixture, had been prepared for the next stage. The nearest table, with a neat two inch upstand all around its edge, had been cooled to a pre-determined temperature by means of a water jacket built-in beneath it. The second table, however, had been warmed up with its built-in gas heating system, again to a pre-determined temperature.

"Are you ready, table?" hissed the unbelievably hot, sweet, sticky mass as it approached its foe and hovered menacingly above it."

"Never been more ready", whispered the thick, steel plate coldly. "I'll soon sort YOU out."

A carefully controlled tilt of the seething saucepan by its two handlers commenced the battle as millions of raging hot bubbles attacked the waiting table like an erupting volcano. With huge white clouds of steaming defiance, they charged everywhere and, within seconds, occupied the whole surface, doing their best to break down the surrounding steel barrier which contained them. Still frothing and bubbling, they sizzled their victory-song as their amazing heat was retained.

Suddenly, the frantic activity began to subside, and, within a few minutes, you could almost hear the patient, cool table saying "got you." The energetic fluid, although

still hot, was now turning into a thick, pliable, syrupy sheet, and the two sweet-doctors began treating its surface with liquid flavouring whilst at the same time adding red colouring fluid to about two thirds of it. Doctor One now decided that he had to operate quickly. He needed to separate the red-coloured part of the sheet from its untreated, creamy-brown coloured partner, otherwise all was lost. Still wearing his heat-resistant gloves, he cut

across the quivering mass using a huge pair of scissors, pausing only to mop his brow as the severed ends curled up in protest after the successful operation.

Now was the time that the sweet-doctors' years of experience, skill and judgement were needed. The two separate, pliable masses needed to be folded, turned and massaged until they took on the form of large bulbous pancakes. The larger of these was, by now, a streaky red

colour, whilst the smaller of the two was more creamy in appearance. Unfortunately, they were both beginning to cool down.

"You feeling a bit chilly, Creamy?"

"Not 'alf, Red," came the reply.

The doctors were, of course, aware that their patients were now beginning to feel the cold, so they carefully transferred them onto the adjacent warm table where they were able to sink down in comfort onto the heated steel plate. The red pancake was still a little streaky, so Doctor Two was required to carry out a little more surgery on it. Out came the large scissors once again, and before you could say Jack Robinson, it was in two pieces. This was only a temporary measure however, as following more folding, turning and massaging, the two were reunited into what was now a consistently red pancake.

By now the creamy pancake had been taken to the stretching and aeration chamber, which looked like a large

microwave oven, for the gold-star treatment. Here, it was stretched out like a piece of soft chewing gum and draped around several, discreetly placed metal rods which slowly began to move and rotate. This steady, repetitive action gently pulled and stretched every sinew and muscle that Creamy possessed, and culminated in quite an amazing transformation. Not only had he increased in size because

Stretching and aerating machine-Creamy brown mixture inserted

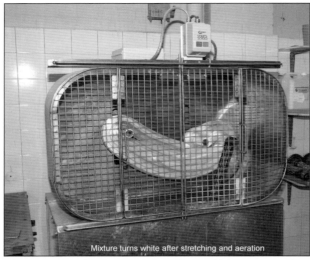

Mixture turns white after stretching and aeration

Extruded strips of rock awaiting chopping

of the aeration, his texture was softer, and his creamy colour had turned to white.

"Hey Red, just look at me now," he shouted as he was taken out of the wonder- machine and gently flattened out into a thick, two foot square of 'pastry' on yet another table. "Why don't you join me?"

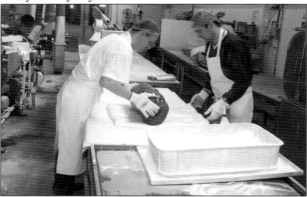

Red needed no further asking and, with the help of his white-coated friend, who had formed him into the shape of a short, thick sausage, he joined him on the table. The red and white soul-mates were reunited at last, and as Doctor Two rolled them together into a large, fat sausage-roll, their transformation was almost (but not quite) complete.

"You know, Red?"

"What, Whitey?"

"I think we need to slim down a bit, don't you?"

"I agree. Let's ask the docs. They'll know what to do."

The two, caring white-coated doctors who had created and transformed the sweet-tasting sausage-roll, now passed it over to the 'slimming and finishing' section. Here, with the help of a specially geared, cone-shaped extruding machine and the skilful hands of a lady physiotherapist who expertly massaged the extrusion, the fat, red and white sausage-roll was transformed into an attractive, long strip of delicious rock. Now cooling rapidly, this strip was cut into metre lengths and fed into a final machine which chopped it into small pieces. As they tumbled out into the round, mesh-bottomed collecting basket, laughing and riddling with delight, these little delicacies knew that they would now be packed into large plastic jars before being bought by delighted children and adults, to whom they would give extreme pleasure. That was their destiny in life, with success their only reward. Perhaps there's a message in their philosophy somewhere?

Well, I don't know about you, but I feel a bit exhausted after all that excitement in the Rock Shop. I think a more relaxing stroll around a few other areas is now in order, perhaps starting with the adjacent Packing Section.

As we passed the two, red flying-saucers on our way out, I was advised by Chris Pitchfork that these were, in fact, large Cooling Carousels, which use blown air to cool-off many of the boiled sweets which were also made in this room. Why didn't I think of that, I wonder? Perhaps it just wasn't as exciting as thinking that it was something from outer space.

We soon arrived at the entrance to the packing area where, after entering through its glossy green door, the first image that met us was a huge pile of multi-coloured Yorkshire Mixtures waiting to be weighed. Alison, who was

Sweet-wrapping machine

standing at the far end of this seemingly endless rainbow of sweets, was busily scooping up the delicacies and putting them carefully into a shiny gold dish which sat like royalty on its weighing-scale stand. She enjoyed her job, even though it was rather repetitive, and she always gave a satisfied smile when she poured the correct weight of sweets into double-layered polythene bags, which she subsequently sent on for packing.

At the other end of the shop, the bagged sweets were enjoying a pleasant ride on a conveyor belt which took them through a short tunnel within a metal-detector machine before arriving at the packing station. Marsha, another smiling lady, was in charge of this area, and she was able to fill a cardboard box with the continuous flow of little bags in no time at all.

After a pleasant, brief chat with both ladies, I was taken upstairs to another two work areas. The first of these contained complex-looking machines which, with their stubby white wings projecting each side of a cockpit of complicated controls, wouldn't have looked amiss in a Royal Air Force design centre. These, believe it or not, were the sweet wrapping machines. Although a significant proportion of Maxons sweets are of the traditional type and are dispatched in old fashioned plastic jars to the delight of thousands of children, some are wrapped and boxed to cater for different customer requirements. These clever machines are able to quickly cover each sweet with a clear, cellophane wrapper, and either bend or twist its ends to form a seal. It's amazing what they can do nowadays, isn't it?

Around the corner from these RAF look-alikes, was a second room in which stood two large machines, each of which incorporated two steam cookers containing ingredients similar to those in the clove-rock shop. These were linked by pipes to a large, central, covered bowl which, by the magic of vacuum suction, enabled the eventual boiling contents of the cookers to travel through

Steam cookers in the Black Bullets production area

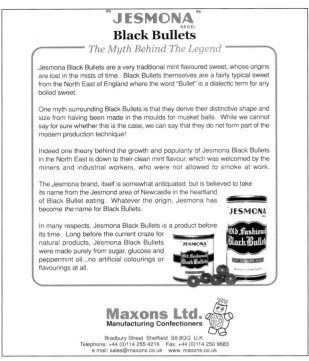

the pipes and fill it. Once there, protesting or otherwise, the bowl of sizzling sugars was able to gently glide down twin metal guides and tip its contents out onto steel tables similar to those described earlier. This more automated system, which doesn't require the same degree of complex processing necessitated by multi-coloured rocks and boiled sweets, is used for the manufacture of Maxons famous Jesmona Black Bullets which, when completed, are stored and stacked in their easily recognised black and white tins. It is interesting to just have a brief look at the history behind these famous sweets, which Maxons have kindly set out as shown above.

Last, but not least, we had a quick look at the Pear Drops, Chocolate Limes and Sherbet Lemons production area. All these boiled sweets are manufactured on the same principle as that used for rock production, with just two or three specific differences. The Pear Drops, for example, are produced in three blended colours, which necessitates the splitting of the boiled, then cooled, ingredients into three pancakes, each of which are coloured separately before being blended and then reunited. The sausage-machine

Special gears used for moulding and shaping sweets

process is then carried out as before, with the pear shapes being obtained by passing the extruded and pulled, long thin strips of candy through a specially geared machine capable of moulding and chopping any shape required.

The Chocolate Limes and Sherbet Lemons are similarly produced incorporating Lime or Lemon flavouring, whilst their chocolate or sherbet centres are simply added to the product at the time the fat sausages are rolled and formed.

We could, of course, go on for ever, but I think we've all now got a flavour of the methods used by Maxons to make its wonderful sweets. This whistle-stop tour of its factory has really brought to life the magic of sweet-making, and it's a pity we have to leave such pleasures to conclude our profile of the Pitchfork family. However, that is what we must do.

Two happy workers

LOOKING FORWARD

Roger has now reached pensionable age, and his son Chris, who is in his early thirties, is already Operations

Director with one eye on the Chairmanship. Maxons is not, of course, in the same league as their Sheffield neighbours Cadbury Trebor Bassett, but as a family run business, it is one of only a few these days who can claim to be still going strong with a bright future ahead. What they lack in size, they certainly make up for in quality, and their large range of very popular and mostly traditional sweets, many of them originating a century or more ago, still titillate the taste-buds of Sheffield folk, young and old, and will continue to do so into the foreseeable future.

The Pitchfork family, in their usual modesty of not seeking fame for themselves, continue to run their sweet-making business in the interests of their customers, both in the UK and in countries across the world. Indeed, internet sales have opened doors which were locked before, and this combination of tradition and modernity plays a large part in Maxons' continuing success.

Roger, like his father before him, has also kept up the Dixon tradition of serving the community, having served as Chairman of Croft House Settlement for seventeen years from 1984 to 2001. This position was held by Henry Dixon Junior in the 1950s, whilst Henry Dixon Senior, you will recall, was a founder of this organization with the Rev. William Blackshaw in 1902. Putting people first has been a long-held belief and tradition of Sheffield's sweet-makers, and the Sheffield family of Pitchforks is certainly no exception.

But, what about the future? Chris Pitchfork came into the company in 2003 with a degree in economics, two years experience with a stockbroker and four years experience with a merchant bank. His knowledge and understanding of finance is essential in this hi-tech business world, and, together with his five years of experience to date in the hands-on operations of sweet making, gives him an excellent base from which to run Maxons in the future. In addition, to guarantee a continuation of the family name in the confectionery manufacturing industry, he has obligingly become the father of a baby son, William Ralph, who, no doubt, will follow in his father's footsteps. In fact, I wouldn't be surprised if the first words he spoke were "Mint Rock" or "Pear Drops"!

However, it is an unfortunate fact that whilst the names of such confectioners as George Bassett and Henry Dixon are well known to the buying public, most will confess to never having heard of the name Pitchfork when it comes to sweet-making. Nevertheless, this family of 'dark-horses' has won every prize possible in their continuing race for satisfaction and success, and if there was ever to be a Grand National for sweet scrumptiousness, I know who I'd put my money on. Long may such Sheffield folk continue, as there's really nowt like 'em, is there?

Old Sheffield Characters

In this Section, we look at the life and times of some old Sheffield characters who have wandered about our streets over the last 150 years or so.

Many of these characters led different lives to the average Sheffielder and, in some instances, were a little different by virtue of their appearance or because they had a disability.

They were, nevertheless, the 'salt of the earth', and represent a life that many people today are probably unaware of.

Some of the characters have only a brief story to tell, while others share much of their lives with us. I hope you will find them all interesting.

Fagey Joe

Let us begin by going back about 150 years to the 1850s when a well-known character by the name of Fagey Joe was running a butcher's business in the centre of Sheffield.

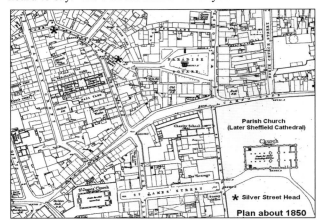

Joe was a stocky, powerfully built man with a face which resembled chiselled granite. Standing behind the counter of his shop located in Silver Street Head, just below Campo Lane, he made an imposing and somewhat intimidating figure, particularly when wearing his blood-stained apron and holding a chopping cleaver in his hand.

In a way, being a butcher was a somewhat strange choice of trade for Joe, as he was well known as a great animal lover. His interest in animals stemmed from his younger days as a small boy when, following the early death of his father, he left his birth place of Leicester and came to Sheffield with his mother and two sisters. Here, he devoted much of his younger life to the keeping and care of small animals and birds with whom he was easily able to relate.

"He's a kind soul is my little Joe," his mother was often heard to say. "He's a real animal lover you know."

Parish Church
(Later Sheffield Cathedral)

★ Silver Street Head

Plan about 1850

However, times were hard for Joe and his fatherless family, and the young man felt that he should try to earn a few coppers to help his family out. Now a young teenager, he decided to use his exceptional talents for this purpose and chose to breed champion birds. These were no ordinary birds, however, as with their vivid red combs dancing proudly on their heads above wild, darting eyes, they fought to the death using their powerful, curved beaks and razor sharp talons. This was the age of cock-fighting, and money could be made and lost from the betting which accompanied it.

"You ought to be ashamed of yourself, Joseph Taylor," his mother would retort upon Joe's successful return from an evening match. "How on earth can someone who's supposed to love animals be so cruel?"

"But mam, mine usually win. I look after the cocks when they're injured, and we do need the money."

Needless to say, whether it was a touch of conscience on Joe's behalf, or a few clips round the ear from his mother, Joe eventually gave up his fairly lucrative hobby and chose a different, albeit related, career instead.

Now aged 25, he was a successful butcher, and the cattle, sheep, pigs and poultry which he handled had been slaughtered for him by someone else. Competition was, nevertheless, quite keen as the Fitzalan Market, which was known as the Shambles and extended between Market Place and Haymarket, provided excellent covered accommodation for butchers' stalls which were very popular with the public.

The Rules and Regulations relating to the Shambles did, in fact, give an interesting insight into the hygiene standards

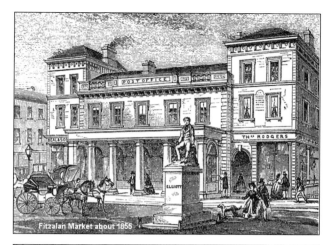
Fitzalan Market about 1855

SLAUGHTER HOUSES

Plan About 1850

in place in these days, as they forbade butchers from 'whetting and sharpening their knives upon the stone Pillars' upon the penalty of one shilling for each time of offending. The seventh regulation was particularly interesting and stated that 'for Decency sake and cleanliness of the said Market, no person having any Holding in the said Market shall at any time piss against the walls of the said Market'. That just about says it all, doesn't it?

But, of course, standards of hygiene in general were very different in those difficult days of the mid-1850s when Joe ran his own butcher's shop. Although a new livestock market had been built at Smithfields adjacent to the River Don, together with the construction of Blonk Street Bridge to give easy access to and from the Wicker, the nearby slaughter-houses were a disgrace. The Killing Shambles, as

Slaughter Houses

they were called, had been built several years previously and were now dilapidated and insanitary. No butcher could guarantee his customers that their meat would be fresh and disease free, and this was of great concern to Joe.

It was this concern which prompted him to confide in his close friend, Bill, who had popped into the shop during a quiet lunchtime period.

"You know Bill, I'm not happy with the way these animals are killed and cut up at the slaughter-house. There's no proper control down there you know, and it's dead filthy."

Joe had known Bill for many years, and he was one of only a few people whose views he respected.

"I don't know about you Joe," Bill responded, "but I'd get out of this business and move into something more suitable. I tell you what. Yon pub just down the road's just come up for sale. It'd suit you down to the ground."

Joe couldn't believe his ears. He'd often thought that running a pub would be a good business venture, particularly in these times when drinking was about the only entertainment or relaxation that the average person could afford and have time to pursue after a long day's work. This, he thought, could be the opportunity of a lifetime.

Once the reluctant butcher had made up his mind to do something, there was no stopping him and, within a month or so, the Blue Bell in Silver Street had acquired a new landlord. In addition, with Bill helping him out behind the bar, he had time to spend on his real hobby, looking after animals. He had bought himself two young, pedigree dogs by this time which, like himself, had short stubby legs and powerful shoulders. They were his pride and joy.

Not only did Joe care for his own dogs, but he was often called upon to give advice on those owned by other people. Indeed, such was his interest in animals, that by the age of 26, he had earned himself the reputation of being one of the best judges of dog, horse and bird in Yorkshire.

This reputation had not missed the ears of a local minister of the church, Canon Sale, who, wanting a dog for himself, had gone to Joe as the expert.

"Perhaps you could get one for me, my son. I will leave the choice to you."

Now although Fagey Joe was the acknowledged expert in his field, he was not in the same field as the eminent Canon when it came to honesty and integrity. This was evidenced by his whispered response to Canon Sale's enquiry.

"Just tell me whose dog it is you want, father, and I'll personally see to it that you get it."

Although quite taken aback by Joe's whispered response, the understanding minister retained a quiet dignity.

"I think we're talking at cross-purposes, my son. I do not wish you to steal one. I just want you to find a good, healthy, even-tempered dog that I can buy."

"It's as good as done father," Joe replied with some degree of embarrassment. "I was just trying to save you the money, you being a kind man of the cloth and all."

It wasn't that Joe was a dishonest man by nature. He was helpful to the extreme when it came to animals, and his respect for men of the church knew no bounds. However, upon reflection he did accept that his offer to steal a dog for the minister was rather over the top in this instance.

Although the Blue Bell was Fagey Joe's first venture in life as a publican, he was very successful and ran a very orderly house. He liked a drink, but never allowed himself to get drunk whilst on duty. In particular, he disliked any fighting or violence in his pub, and strictly banned such activities, which was a brave thing to do in those days.

"If there's any fighting to be done in my pub," he would regularly say, "then it'll 'ave to be with me."

There was no exception to this rule, and in general Joe's tough, uncompromising reputation was enough to prevent any such trouble. A glance at Joe's lived-in face, which displayed several scars and the hint of a once broken nose which sat defiantly over thick leathery lips did, nevertheless, suggest that he'd had to do more than just intervene on one or two occasions.

There was one evening, however, when this no-nonsense landlord's house-rule was really put to the test. It was the year 1854, and England's most successful bare-knuckle fighter, Tom Sayers, was in Sheffield to box a benefit match. This famous Light Middleweight Champion, who weighed-in at just under 11 stone (150lbs) and measured 5ft-8½" in height, was recognised as the toughest fighter in the country. He had only lost one fight in his career, a 61 round thriller with the then English Middleweight champion, Nat Langham, this fight only being stopped because Tom Sayers had both eyes swollen shut and was unable to see. Such  was the state of boxing in those days that this tough little fighter regularly fought others much heavier than himself and, during a dynamic, though sadly short life, he also became the country's Heavyweight Champion by beating 14 stone Bill Perry. To cap it all, at the age of 34 he even took part in the first ever World Heavyweight Championship match against the American Heavyweight, John C. Heenan. This brutal fight, which lasted 42 rounds and ended in a draw, resulted in both contestants being badly beaten and suffering broken limbs.

However, to get back to our story, this particular evening in 1854 saw Tom Sayers enter Fagey Joe's pub. The boxer was extremely well known and the Blue Bell was full to bursting with people hoping to get a glimpse of him. Because of his relatively modest stature for a champion fighter, would-be bullies, always the worse for drink, were often ready to take him on. That night was no exception as a burly labourer issued an abusive challenge. Tom Sayers

had not earned his reputation by being diplomatic, and was ready in an instant to 'beat the living daylights' out of the foolish challenger until the landlord stepped in.

"Not in my pub, you don't."

Joe's words cut through the smoky, noisy gathering with chilling effect, and you could almost hear a pin drop.

"And just who are you?" growled the irritated pugilist as Joe placed himself between the foolish, drunken hulk and the little, honed man of steel.

"I'm the landlord, and I don't allow fighting in my pub, OK?"

The two men were very similar in build, with Joe being just that bit taller. Both had faces that had seen life, although Tom's was that bit more battered. Perhaps most importantly, neither man had ever been known to stand-down.

Seconds ticked away in the now deathly silence as 'granite' and 'steel' stared into each others eyes. A minute passed by, and now all but these two men were sweating with apprehension and anticipation.

Suddenly, as if a light had been switched on, a smile appeared over Tom Sayer's face and a gnarled, muscular hand snaked forward in offer of friendship.

"You're the first man who's ever had the nerve to stand up to me outside the boxing ring," he roared. "Put it there."

Two strong hands gripped in mutual respect, and a new friendship was made. Cheers rang out around the pub, and everyone relaxed. As for the burley labourer, he was nowhere to be seen. I don't blame him, do you?

Fagey Joe's brief brush with fame and new-found friendship was a rare bit of excitement at the Blue Bell, and eventually faded into the past as the publican directed his interest towards a venture involving his dogs. He had heard over the grapevine of an activity involving his four-legged friends which was rapidly gaining popularity, whilst at the same time creating money and excitement for those involved. The only fly in the ointment was that he would need more space to develop the idea. Luck was on Joe's side, however, as the Jolly Bacchus public house in Holly Lane, just off Barker's Pool, was put up for sale a few months later.

"I reckon the Jolly Bacchus will just do me fine Bill, what do you think?"

"Well, if it's more room you need, inside and out, then it's just what you're looking for Joe. But are you sure it's what you want to do?"

"Too right I do, Bill. I've got it all worked out in my mind. It'll go down a bomb, you'll see."

So, what was Fagey Joe's idea that was so important to make him need to change pubs? The answer was RATS. For the past few years, Joe had been catching and handling rats as a hobby, and also developing his skills as a professional rat-catcher. His uncanny relationship with all animals had enabled him to breed and tame some rats which he allowed to crawl about him, inside his shirt on his bare skin. There

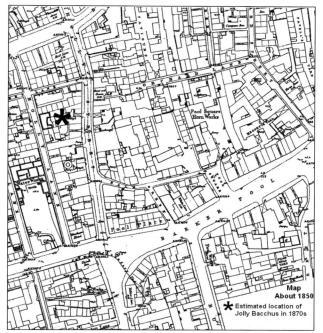

Map
About 1850
★ Estimated location of
Jolly Bacchus in 1870s

was many a time, whilst taking a stroll in the street, that he would, upon meeting a friend, respond to a greeting by offering a hand-shake. Unfortunately for the friend, Joe's hand would contain a rat which he had casually pulled out from under his shirt, causing, as you might expect, great laughter for Joe and fear for the recipient of his prank.

Well, we've established that Joe's latest idea involves rats, but what part do they play in his master-plan? Within a couple of months of successfully selling the Blue Bell and subsequently buying the Jolly Bacchus, everything was clear. He had built a large rat-pit in the rear courtyard in order that competitors from near and far could bring their dogs to take part in rat-killing competitions. This was the new craze spreading round the area which involved excitement, betting and personal wagers, and Joe was to be in the thick of it.

You could reasonably ask, at this stage, why the tough, yet kind, animal-lover wanted to promote such an activity, which involved encouraging one type of animal (dogs) to kill another kind (rats). In answer to this, I suppose we should look at how people actually lived in the 1850s and 60s. Average wages for the thousands of people working in the cutlery and silver works or the heavy-steel works were about £2 a week, working-class houses consisted mostly of back-to-back terraces with primitive outside toilet facilities, water was available only by pump in back yards for two or three hours a day, and poverty was rife. As for entertainment, football for the masses did not take off until 1867 for Sheffield Wednesday and 1889 for Sheffield United. In addition, with appalling working conditions, poor sanitation and a high rate of infant mortality during the first half this century, the average age at which people died in Sheffield was 24 years old.

It is hardly surprisingly, therefore, that people living under these conditions grasped hold of life, excitement and opportunities as they arose. Today's society would, quite

rightly, condemn Fagey Joe's decision to carry out these blood sports at the back of his pub, but, with rat infestation being a major problem everywhere, killing them as part of an exciting sporting contest presented no moral dilemma to most people at the time.

Within a few weeks, rat-killing competitions at the pub were well known and attended, and money exchanged hands very rapidly, often in Joe's direction.

Take the time, for example, when the owner of Jet, the Attercliffe rat-killing champion, challenged Fagey Joe's dog one evening at the Jolly Bacchus.

"Come on Joe. I bet you 2 guineas that my dog can kill more rats than yours in three minutes."

"Not a chance," grinned the confident landlord. "You do know that you are challenging my dog, Bullet, don't you? He's the Sheffield champion now."

"I'll let Jet do the talking if you don't mind," growled the burly steelworker trying to control the gasping bundle of black muscle straining at the chain-link collar attached to his worn leather leash.

Brown Rat

The challenge had not gone unnoticed in the packed pub, and its eager customers quickly made their way to the edge of the circular pit where the 'contest of the year' was to take place.

"Watch your backs. Here they come."

Joe appeared dragging his large cage of rats and casually dropped a hundred or more of them into the pit to the tumultuous cheering of the watching crowd and the deep throated baying of both dogs. A coin was tossed, and Jet was placed in the arena and let loose as the stop watch was started. The pit floor immediately became a cauldron of boiling, black energy flavoured with darting, razor-toothed brown bodies, all stirred together with a crescendo of blood-curdling growls and constant high-pitched squeaks.

As Joe watched the seconds and minutes tick by, he couldn't help but recall his mother's words of many years gone by.

"You ought to be ashamed of yourself Joseph Taylor. How on earth can someone who loves animals be so cruel?"

"TIME," roared the rather portly, bearded man holding the stop-watch. "Retrieve your dog."

Jet's handler jumped into the pit and bellowed at his dog to stop before managing to slip a chain over his bulging neck. A quick count showed fifty-one furry bodies with broken necks, which met with a roar of approval from the viewing crowd.

Joe quickly put his mother's words out of his mind and concentrated on removing the dead rats from the pit and replacing them with live ones. He whispered in Bullit's ear and calmly lowered him into destiny as the stop watch was started.

The minutes seemed to pass more quickly this time as the host chewed a little anxiously on an old cigar butt as he watched his dog perform.

"Fifty-five," roared the crowd as time was called, and the man who always liked to be a winner hugged Bullit as though he were his son.

Fagey Joe's fame now spread far and wide. Bullit went on from strength to strength and set a new rat-killing record of 200 rats in 13 minutes. Being an expert breeder of dogs, Joe continued his success with further champions and also expanded his interest into dog-fighting as well as rat killing. His success in this field was equal to that of his first venture, and his favourite dog, Cribb, stood as Sheffield's Champion Fighter for 12 years.

However, not satisfied with handling and breeding dogs, the ever-searching landlord also decided to breed badgers in captivity and, according to news items at the time, was the only man to do so in Sheffield, and probably in the country. He also converted a large beer barrel into a kennel for his largest badger, and encouraged men to bring their fighting dogs to his pub to try and draw the badger out of the barrel. The dogs were goaded to try and attack the animal and entice him out, success in this venture supposedly being a test of the dog's courage and fighting qualities. Needless to say, the dogs always failed, and Joe,

once again, came out the financial winner of the wagers that were made on each occasion.

You'll notice from what you've read so far about Fagey Joe, that he liked to be a winner. He promoted his rat-killing venture with dogs that nearly always won, his fighting dogs likewise were always champions, and his badger never actually fought or was seriously injured. His animals were always well treated, well trained and professionally cared for if they did receive modest injury. And, to cap it all, his little muscular friends made him a lot of money. If there's one thing we can say about this man, he certainly was no fool.

Now for a man like Joe, you might think that there was little else for him to expand into. But you would be wrong. Take that day in February 1866, for example.

It was a cold, wintry afternoon when the city centre street scene was dramatically interrupted by the arrival on High Street of a lumbering, brown bear which was on tow at the end of a long pole and rope. Its owner, who looked remarkably like his charge, shuffled along in heavy, well-worn boots over which a long, rather tattered, hairy coat was draped. The hunched shoulders of this unusual figure supported a large, furry hat, under which a pale, bearded face could just be made out. A slightly nervous crowd began to gather around the unusual pair.

"Wot's that bear doin' 'ere, mister?"

"Is it fierce?"

"Where're you both from?"

"Somebody fetch Fagey Joe. He'll know what to do."

More people were joining the enquiring crowd, and the barrage of questions continued, interspersed by the yapping and growling of two or three mongrel dogs which had been roaming the streets as usual.

"Stand back you lot. You're frightening the poor bloke."

The stocky figure of Fagey Joe pushed through the mingling throng and confronted the bemused, hunched figure.

"Now then mate. It's not often we see a bear walking down our streets. What are you doing with it?"

A pair of dark, piercing eyes confronted Joe's enquiring stare whilst a few mumbled words forced their way out of cold, cracked lips.

"What was that?" exclaimed Joe. "Did you say you were trying to sell him?"

After several minutes of difficult discussion, Joe established that the hairy man was a Russian, although how and why he had arrived here in Sheffield remained a mystery. More importantly, the discussion had culminated in the animal-loving publican buying the bear, in the middle of High Street of all places, and at a price he refused to disclose. The bemused crowd which had gathered looked on in amazement as Joe took his new friend back to his pub, whilst the solitary, hunched figure ambled back into the unknown from where he had come.

The Jolly Bacchus now resembled something of a zoo as dogs, badgers, rats and now a bear adorned its premises. Joe obviously liked animals, but his financially alert mind never missed a trick. The bear was quite a crowd-puller at opening times, and the extra pints he sold probably more than compensated for the amount he paid for his new furry friend.

How long the bear lived at the pub is uncertain, but rumour had it that it was only a year or so before it died. Whilst Joe was genuinely sad at his loss, he was aware that bear-grease was the new, wonder cure-all for most ills and ailments at that time. With his butcher's skills, he went into the bear-grease-making business, and was able to produce and sell vast amounts of the 'genuine' product for many months to come.

It is interesting to note that Joe was able to produce far more of this wonder product than the total weight of the bear itself. This, of course, leads us to conclude that he was obviously making not-quite-so-pure bear-grease whilst at the same time making a lot of money. Although he was being less than honest with his customers, the extra large number of people who benefited from using it probably balanced the 'honesty versus quality' equation at that time. I only say this because from what we know about bear grease, it probably provided little medical benefit for any of the ailments it was meant to cure, although its perceived benefit probably did a lot of good to a lot of people. That, after all, is life, isn't it? If you think something is doing you good, you actually feel better in yourself, don't you?

After the excitement of the Russian bear, life steadied up a bit for Joe, although he still continued breeding dogs and badgers at the Jolly Bacchus for many years, as well as running his rat-pit. He even had time to get married and have a son, although there is little recorded information about such events in his almost totally male-dominated life at that time. As he grew older, however, he gave more time and attention to treating and curing illnesses in animals, particularly dogs, and was reputed to be 'the best in town' in this activity. Had there been such a profession in those days, he would undoubtedly have made a wonderful vet.

By the time Fagey Joe reached his early 50's, he was hankering for a slightly more steady life, and decided to grasp a further opportunity and

move from the Jolly Bacchus to the Social Tavern public house in Bailey Street. Although he continued to breed dogs, and for a while his badgers, his life-style changed, and he could often be seen strolling around town looking every inch a gentleman in his smart, velveteen suit, bowler hat and riding crop. Whether or not the riding crop was just for show is uncertain, but on a gentle Sunday morning stroll along Fargate and down High Street, he was certain to 'tip' his bowler with it many times when he encountered many of the hundreds of friends he had made over the years.

But, of course, as life goes on and we get older, our bodies begin to weaken a little. Not that Fagey Joe subscribed to this notion, as he continued to manhandle the heavy barrels at his pub as though he was still in his twenties and thirties. One day, however, at the age of 58, he injured his knee whilst doing just this task.

"I'll be reight enough, lass," he exclaimed in exasperation when his concerned wife suggested he should let up a little and seek some medical advice several weeks later.

Unfortunately, he wasn't 'reight enough', and the injury developed into a diseased bone and poor old Joe had to be admitted to number 2 ward at the Sheffield Public Hospital (later the Royal Hospital) on West Street. Hospital hygiene and medical knowledge was sadly lacking in those days (1880s) however, and Joe had to have his leg amputated just above the knee to save his life. To a rough, tough, yet kindly war-horse like him, you would have thought that the loss of a limb would have been a terrible blow. However, our ever-grateful hero shrugged it off and even presented the two surgeons involved in the operation with a little Airedale puppy each, which they aptly named Fagey and Joe.

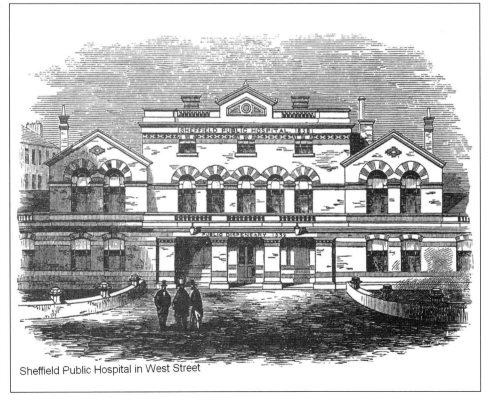

Sheffield Public Hospital in West Street

Despite the apparent success of the operation, this larger than life man never really fully recovered, and on 2nd October, 1886, Fagey Joe died at the age of 60.

Joseph Taylor, as he had been christened six decades earlier, had most certainly been quite a character and, as Fagey Joe, had become Sheffield's favourite, Victorian-age publican. Despite his involvement in what are now considered to be cruel blood sports, he was truly an animal lover who gave his healing services to animals freely. Many an elderly person was grateful for his success in curing their four-legged companions of various ailments, injures and even distemper when no known cures for most of these were available at the time.

Fagey Joe was, in fact, a rough diamond, and was sadly missed. He was different, of course, but, aren't we all? That's what makes us so special, isn't it?

THE CROSSING SWEEPERS

The next two characters we have a brief look at couldn't be more different to the rough, tough, action-man image portrayed by Fagey Joe.

The work they did was not only very different, it was also very necessary during the time in which they lived.

I'm sure that most, but possibly not all, of you will find their claim to fame rather interesting.

During the mid to late Victorian times, it was very difficult to find work and many unskilled men had to accept the most demeaning jobs you could imagine. One such job was that of a Crossing Sweeper. If you consider that the main modes of transport in those days were horse-pulled buggies, horse taxis, horse trams and horse omnibuses, it doesn't need much imagination to realise that the thousands of horses clip-clopping up and down the cobbled streets of the town will leave tens of thousands of 'trade-marks' on the road surfaces as they pass by.

Crossing to the other side of the road in these days was, therefore, a perilous affair as pedestrians tried with difficulty to pick their way through obstacle-courses of horse droppings as they went about their every-day business. Wet weather was particularly challenging in this respect.

However, in an attempt to make life easier for

Horse drawn taxi-cabs at Sheffield Midland Station about 1900

Sheffield's pedestrians, crossing-places were identified at strategic locations along the many routes into and within the town centre. These crossing-places were manned by Crossing Sweepers who shovelled up the forever-occurring heaps of manure and then swept the road surfaces to keep them relatively clean.

Take the routes from Walkley and Crookes to town, for example. Those who travelled from Walkley walked down Crookes Valley Road and Winter Street, crossed over Brook Hill and continued along Leavy Greave until they met Glossop Road. There, they were joined by the residents walking to town from Crookes.

For the Walkley walkers, a wonderful character by the name of PUNCH was the Crossing Sweeper at Brook Hill. This dedicated man, who worked from eight o'clock in the morning to six o'clock in the evening, was only four feet six inches tall. Although he was poor and only earned a few coppers a day, he always kept himself as smart as he possibly could. A well-worn, knee length coat over-laid an equally well-worn, almost shiny, waist coat which he always buttoned up carefully each morning. A dark cap, which sat proudly on his broad head, peeked mischievously over his rather bushy eyebrows, beneath which two deep-set eyes seemed to constantly twinkle. He was a happy man, but never more so than when thanked by the people who passed by him everyday.

Punch

"Thank you, ma'm, thank you, sir," he always responded whilst standing stiffly to attention and saluting each and every one of them.

Although Punch was given a modest wage by the Town Council to keep its streets clean, he depended on the generosity of the people who benefited from his work to enable him to earn enough to live on. Whilst most of the people who used his crossing point were pleased to be able to do so without messing up their shoes, it was the ladies in their long dresses, skirts and coats who were most grateful. These 'customers' were happy to give the cheerful sweeper an odd copper or two to keep their trailing hems free from the smelly mess which unavoidably built up.

Punch carried out his job at Brook Hill for many years and continued sweeping there until the late 1890s. By that time, the writing was on the wall regarding the use of horses to power public transport, as electric trams were taking to the streets, motor cars had made their first appearance, and

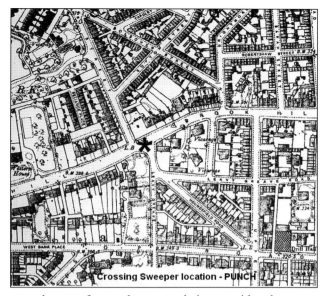

Crossing Sweeper location - PUNCH

even the use of motor buses was being considered.

At the same time that Punch was sweeping his crossing at Brook Hill, another character by the name of SNOWBALL was sweeping the crossing at the junction of Glossop Road and Convent Walk, just beyond Glossop Road Baths.

Snowball was totally opposite to Punch in most respects. He was a very tall, thin man with long, jet-black hair and a black moustache which drooped despondently down either side of a remarkably thick, upper lip. He was always shivering with cold, which was not helped by the thin, threadbare coat and trousers he always wore. His pale face looked almost white beneath his black locks and somewhat resembled a ball of snow which had been placed on his shoulders and carelessly adorned with black cokes and twigs to form his features.

Despite his generally miserable look, Snowball was a conscientious worker, being rather quiet but polite. Like Punch, he kept his crossing remarkably clean, and the people who used it were always grateful. With his crossing point being located on Glossop Road, which covered both the Walkley and Crookes routes to town, he was known to practically all the inhabitants on the west side of town. Indeed, he took pride in the fact that he held the record for the longest length of service in the crossing-sweeper

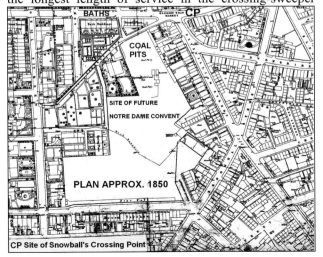

PLAN APPROX. 1850

CP Site of Snowball's Crossing Point

business, having taken up this job after bronchitis had compelled him to leave his first job as a forgeman in Sheffield's East-end steel-works after only working there for a few years.

Snowball

Although Snowball had been sweeping at this location for many years, he did on occasions move to the crossing site at the top of Northumberland Road in Crookes Moor. Whilst there, a kind-hearted lady noticed his constant shivering and gave him a good, warm set of clothes to wear to keep out the cold. When passing a few days later, she noticed he was still shivering and wearing his thin, old clothes.

"Why are you wearing those thin clothes, Snowball? Where are the warm ones I gave you?"

"Well ma'm, I hope you don't mind, but I'm keeping them for when I go to church on Sundays."

Such is the way of the world, but it was characters such as these two gentlemen who made it go round.

It's worth mentioning here, that although Punch and Snowball's jobs of constantly shovelling up horse droppings was not the most ideal type of work to be carrying out, they had a friend whose job was far worse. He was a dung collector (known for some reason in those days as a pure collector) who, not surprisingly, was self-employed. His job was closely connected to the Tanning business which, in essence, is the conversion of cattle hides into leather. During this process, the freshly stripped hides were placed in pools of urine known as tanning sumps, into which dog, cat and chicken droppings were added in order that the hides could be de-limed in the bacteria infused concoction.

Fred Dung's job (we don't know his real name, probably because he wanted to keep the nature of his work to himself) was to walk and often crawl around the town's streets picking up the more solid pieces of cat and dog droppings which he put into his large coat pockets or the knapsack which he carried over his shoulder. A few pocketfuls of these not-so-delicate packets of poo paid very well, as the Tanning bosses were always in need of this key ingredient for their processing plants.

Fred didn't, understandably, have many close friends as, in the absence of modern devices such as pooper-scoopers or even polythene bags, his job was literally a hands-on affair. Few people, if any, were prepared to offer him a friendly handshake, and even being near him was a rather unpleasant experience.

The dung collector did, nevertheless, make a reasonably good living and, despite the unpleasantness of his job, he usually felt better when he reflected on the obnoxious activity which the Tanner's assistant had to put up with. This involved the poor lad climbing into the pool of foul smelling mixture in his bare feet and treading the hides in order to allow the bacteria to do their work more effectively and thus convert the raw product into usable leather.

I suppose the moral of this part of the story is that there is usually someone worse off than yourself and, perhaps, that we should be grateful to have a job at all. As far as Fred Dung was concerned, he was happy with his lot and, being a Sheffielder, knew the importance of every person in the chain playing his or her part in achieving success. Good luck to him, I say.

UPSY DAISY

It was during this late Victorian period of the 1870s to 1890s, when Punch and Snowball were sweeping their crossings to make things easier for the walking public, that various well known street-sellers were carrying out their trade. Leather laces were popular items to sell at that time as the poor could rarely afford new shoes, and the laces in their old ones always needed replacing. Walking was still the main mode of transport for most people, even though horse-drawn buses and horse drawn trams were in use on main routes.

So, at a time when extreme poverty was still rife in Sheffield, street trading had long been the only alternative to the workhouse. One such trader walking the streets of Sheffield in the 1870s was a gentlemen by the name of Herbert Moss or, as he was known to most Sheffielders, Upsy Daisy.

This kind and honest man sold garters, brushes and Old Moore's Almanacs as well as the long laces which always hung around his neck. At five feet tall he was rather small for a man so he wore a black, silk top-hat to make himself look taller. Upsy Daisy bought his hats from Mr. George Hewitt, a hatter with shops at both 31 High Street and 33 Snig Hill, where he could always guarantee finding the largest size available.

For such a small man, Upsy Daisy had an rather broad, flat forehead overseeing two, rather narrow-set eyes. His thick, pointed beard grew roughly round his wide set jaw and gave him the rather odd appearance of having no neck. He presented an unusual figure as he shuffled around the town centre, particularly when he chose Pinstone Street as his pitch in front of St. Paul's Church where he tried hard to attract the attention of the mainly posh Sunday morning congregation hurrying home after prayers:

"Long leather laces, a penny a pair,

The more you grease 'em, the better they'll wear,

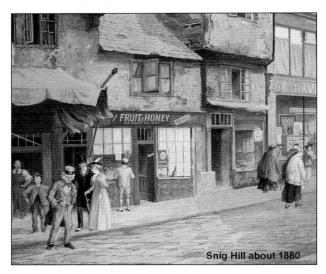

Snig Hill about 1880

Long leather laces, a penny a pair."

As his sharp, clear voice penetrated the crisp, morning air, one or two worshipers were always willing to part with penny or two at a time when kindness to others, as well as worn-out shoe laces, was on their minds.

"Here you are, Upsy. Can I have a pair of garters as well please?"

The rather frail, little old lady holding out her bronze penny seemed an unlikely customer amongst some of the more affluent townsfolk who chose to worship at St. Paul's. Her tightly fitting head-scarf which draped onto an old, tweedy-looking over-coat two sizes too big for her, contrasted sharply with the wide brimmed hats and the colourful, long-flowing dresses and coats worn by most of the ladies leaving the church.

"Thank you dearie, and God Bless you," Upsy whispered in gratitude, knowing that he was still a long way short of the nine pence target he set himself to earn each day. He really struggled to make a living, but managed to survive by never smoking or drinking.

Being a non-smoking teetotaller was, of course, something of a barrier to making meaningful friends in those days as most, if not all, of his acquaintances spent much of their time in the pub. Take, for example, his friend Joe who he often bumped into whilst on his travels.

"Just pop in for a quick one, Upsy," he would say. "It'll do yer no 'arm. In fact yer can sell some of yer laces in there. They'll buy 'owt once they've 'ad a pint or two."

Upsy's less than refined friend was well meaning, of course, but his insistence was lost on our kind, yet determined street-vendor.

St. Paul's Church about 1900

"I'll roll yer a cig if yer want an' all," Joe continued. "Yer not telling me that yer've never smoked a cig."

"Listen 'ere Joseph," Upsy replied, a little indignantly. "If God had meant thee to smoke, he'd a' put a chimney on top'n thee 'ead, wu'nt he?"

Upsy Daisy was often heard making this response to those who tried to persuade him to take up smoking, and it always did the trick.

Although he was rather slow at walking, he covered a lot of ground in his quest to make his nine pence or more a day. Not only did he trudge up and down the main town centre streets, he ventured out into the townships such as Crookes on the western side of Sheffield.

One afternoon, whilst strolling past Crookes Endowed School situated on the main Crookes road, several pupils emerged from the school after lessons were over and began to taunt him because of his unusual appearance. In particular, they condescendingly ran up to him and patted the top of his silk hat whilst mimicking his song "long leather laces, a penny a pair…". To their astonishment, however, this small, but proud, man was able to turn on a

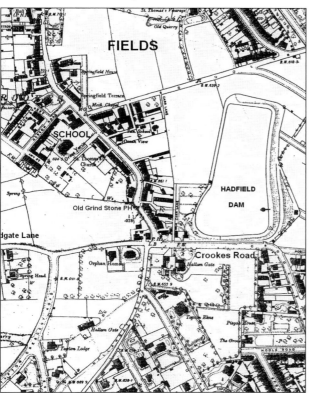

fair burst of speed and chase the unkind schoolchildren through the village until they took off over the fields to Walkley.

This type of experience was not, unfortunately, unusual, particularly the hat-hitting whilst being greeted in the street by those he met. It wasn't that he minded the greetings; it was the fact that all his hats (of which he had several) ended up, in Upsy's words, "looking like concertinas". Eventually, he decided that a visit to Mr. Hewett's hat shop was required.

"I'm fed up wi' folk 'itting me 'at, Mr. Hewett. Can yer do owt about it?"

After much discussion, Mr. Hewett agreed to provide a new hat for his unusual, but valued, customer. The sizes he provided ranged from 6 5/8inches to 7 5/8inches, with the broad-headed street-seller always needing the largest size. However, in this instance, Mr. Hewett decided to introduce his secret weapon to alleviate the problem that Upsy was experiencing. He sowed dozens of black pins into the crown of the silk hat so that only their points protruded.

Upsy Daisy was delighted with his new hat and, after paying for his latest acquisition, ventured out with confidence. He didn't have long to wait to see if the hatter's solution would work. It was just after lunchtime and customers were turning out of the Old Blue Bell public house just behind Mr. Hewett's shop in High Street, and they were all in good spirits.

"Na' then, Upsy me ow'd mate. 'Ow's tha goin'?"

The friendly greeting from the burly grinder who lurched past the smiling little man was, as usual, accompanied by a pat on the top of his black-hatted head. The roar of pain which resulted from this action proved to all and sundry that Upsy's new 'pointed' hat was a success, and life thereafter was more bearable for him as everyone became aware of his novel defence-system.

Although Upsy was well known for his top hat, his selling jingle and the long laces hung around his neck and shoulders, his kindness was probably his most well-known asset, particularly towards children. If ever a child was wishing to cross the road whenever he was anywhere nearby, he would rush over and always see them across. If very young children were there he would carry them across to ensure their safety.

It was from such acts of kindness that Upsy Daisy got his name which, strangely enough, is still used today. In those Victorian times, many people used to call their children Daisy, meaning delicate or small and precious, and many a proud parent would refer to their small child as being 'Such a Daisy' when talking about them to their friends. When such children fell down, their mother or father would gently help them up saying "Up, my Daisy".

Now, when Herbert Moss lifted up the small children to carry them safely over the road, he always did so whilst saying "Upsy Daisy", a derivation of "Up my Daisy". Apart from this expression being used as Herbert Moss' nick name, it gradually caught on and began to be used regularly when parents picked up fallen children. Nowdays, we say Upsy (or Upsa) Daisy when we see a small child fall down, and then console them whilst picking them up. It's amazing how names and habits stick over the centuries, isn't it?

So, our special, small gentlemen left not only a legacy of kindness in those difficult Victorian times, he was the inspiration for one of the most common Yorkshire sayings used today. Life in those days was rarely long-lived, however, and no-one really knows what age Upsy was when he departed this world. What is known is that as a non-smoking teetotaller with no known vices, he also left £300 upon his death.

Bearing in mind that he only earned nine old pence a day, which relates to about £13 a year, assuming that he actually spent half of such income to live off, he must have been saving for about 40 years to build up his nest-egg. That would have taken some doing for a poor street vendor in those late Victorian times. Perhaps it's that Sheffield grit and determination that spurred him on. Whatever it was, Upsy Daisy proved to be a real character with qualities that would be envied by many today. Perhaps we could all learn a lesson from him?

LONG SAMMY

Affectionly known by the name of Long Sammy, Samuel Cattell was born in the mid 1880s and lived for many years in the West Bar area of Sheffield with his mother. At 6'- 7" tall, Sammy certainly lived up to his name. Although he was, unfortunately, deformed in both legs, he did not let his affliction affect him and was a cheerful man, always ready with a smile and a kind word.

He rose to fame as a Sheffield character by virtue of the job he did; a walking advertisement for Suggs of Angel Street, a prominent firm of sports outfitters in town. As a sandwich-board man, he paraded the town centre streets for many years.

Although Sammy was a very respectable character, he did fall foul of the law on one occasion, as the following incident illustrates.

"'Ello 'ello! Wot 'ave we 'ere, then?"

The local bobby had stopped him one fine afternoon, just outside Cole Brother's store at the bottom end of Fargate. Sammy's tall figure was fully decked out with his large advertising boards which sandwiched a very smartly dressed man wearing a soldier's uniform.

"You do know it's an offence to wear an armed-forces uniform for advertising purposes, don't you m'lad?" boomed the rather intimidating looking policeman who had quietly strolled up while on his town centre beat.

Policemen in those days, more commonly known as 'bobbies', were nearly always big and burly as this was, in part, a requirement of their job. Their very presence commanded respect, and their undoubted authority to uphold the law was never questioned. They were also given the power to use their initiative and discretion as they thought appropriate, which meant that many an offence or disturbance could be successfully nipped in the bud. Wouldn't it be wonderful if such common sense could prevail today instead of the poor coppers having to concentrate on achieving targets and writing reports?

However, let's get back to Sammy's dilemma.

"Well, no. I'm afraid I didn't know that, officer. I'm very sorry, really I am."

"No 'arm done this time m'lad," the policeman replied kindly. "Just take this as a warning and get back to yon shop on Angel Street and change that uniform of yours."

Poor Sammy, although relieved at only being given a mild telling off, was in a bit of a tizz as he ambled back to Suggs to tell the gaffer all about it.

"I didn't know I was breaking the law, Mr. Sugg. Nobody told me anything about such a thing."

"Now, now, Samuel, don't fret. We both made a mistake on this occasion," his employer replied whilst trying to console him. "Just go home and rest and you can start your rounds again tomorrow wearing your normal clothes."

Sammy was eventually reassured and, in accordance with Mr. Sugg's wishes, went home and returned to his store the next morning wearing more normal clothes. The tall man's idea of normal was, however, a little different to that of Mr. Sugg, for he turned up dressed as a Boy Scout, complete with trumpet. Whether it was by design or accident no one really knows, but Sammy always managed to wear outlandish outfits which attracted attention which, after all, was what his job was all about.

Being a provider of sports outfits, Mr. Sugg was anxious for Sammy to advertise his products in areas where sporting enthusiasts were in abundance. The obvious choice was at Bramall Lane or Hillsborough where Sheffield United and Sheffield Wednesday were keeping the city's football fans entertained. Sammy was always happy to oblige as he usually managed to sneak into the grounds just before the matches started thanks to the generosity of the officials of both clubs.

Take Christmas 1918, for example. The First World War was in its final throes and many men were still away from home. Wednesday and United were keen to keep the spirits of the sporting population high, and a double-bill of Local Derbies was arranged for Christmas Day and Boxing Day. Mr. Sugg was obviously keen to take advantage of the opportunity to advertise his sporting gear.

"I know it's Christmas, Sammy, but I'll pay you double if you do a stint at Hillsborough on Christmas Day and at Bramall Lane on Boxing Day. How about it?"

After a little thought, the sandwich-board man responded.

"Well Mr. Sugg, as it's you I'll do it."

Despite Sammy's seemingly half-hearted agreement, he was actually delighted inside. Although he loved spending Christmas at home with his mother, he could rarely afford to buy her a decent present. Two afternoons at Christmas-time on double pay would make all the difference, not to mention two free, exciting matches between both of his favourite football teams.

The game at Hillsborough started early so that spectators could get home in good time for their Christmas dinner. Sammy strode purposefully amongst the thousands of people who thronged the streets around the stadium. At 6'-7" tall, he stood head and shoulders above most of them, and, with his advertising boards extending another two feet above his head, just about everyone knew the name of Suggs that day.

Sheffield Wednesday - English Cup Winners 1907

Sammy, apart from being a kind person, was also fair. When he was at Hillsborough, he always supported the Owls and when he was at Bramall Lane, he always supported the Blades. Today, December 25th 1918, Sammy's luck was in and Sheffield Wednesday thrashed their neighbours by four goals to nil. Our long friend was

Sheffield United - English Cup Winners 1899

delighted and he went home with a song (and double pay) in his heart.

Boxing Day at Bramall Lane was equally busy, with excitable Wednesday fans wanting more of the same, and desperate United fans wanting revenge. By some miracle of coincidence or intervention, the hand of fate dealt a fair pack of cards that day and the Blades duly thrashed the Owls by three goals to nil.

So, a happy Christmas was had by all, especially Sammy. Both of his teams had won, he had enjoyed both games to the full, his boss was delighted and he had extra money for his mum. He couldn't ask for more, could he?

Although being badly crippled, Long Sammy had tried, with success, to live a meaningful and happy life. Sadly, his legs gradually let him down and he was seen less and less on the streets. He had made lots of friends and had walked the length and breadth of many of the town's streets over the years. Following the death of his mother, who he had cared for and shared his 'ups and downs' with for most of his life, he slowly deteriorated, and his charismatic life came to an end two years later at the age of fifty.

Sheffield had lost a great character, but the town was the richer for the life and times of Long Sammy who, despite his problems, had become everyone's friend. His contribution to Sheffield's history will not be forgotten.

WILLIAM WARD

The next four characters who bring old Sheffield back to life for us were, to varying degrees, all blind. This affliction befell many people in Victorian times when medical knowledge and treatment of this condition was limited. Let us start by meeting William Ward.

It was Saturday evening in Sheffield town centre and the light was gently fading as William Ward and his pretty little wife Mary slowly made their way along Fargate. It was 1893, and rumour had it that the City Council was thinking about demolishing New Church Street, which ran adjacent to St Paul's Church, to make way for a new Town Hall. William was not happy about the idea.

"I don't know what they want a new Town Hall for, Mary. It's a waste of good money if you ask me."

"Well Billy, now that the Queen says we can call ourselves a city, it's supposed to be a great honour. They've even made the Duke of Norfolk our Lord Mayor and I suppose he wants a posh new building to sit in."

"A posh new building? What's up the one we've got in Waingate? Any road up, where am I going to go if they

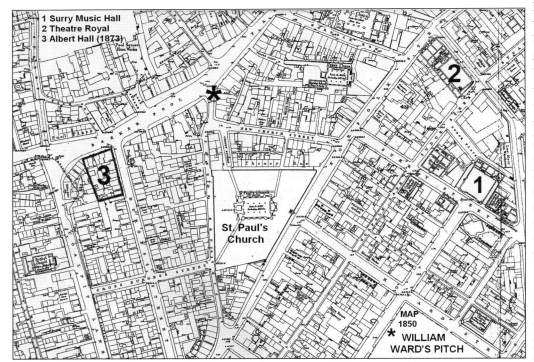

knock down the Old Green Man and the Cutlers Arms in New Church Street? It's disgraceful."

"If you don't mind me saying so, Billy my love, that's the least of your worries. Your pitch at the corner of Pinstone Street and Fargate will go as well, you know."

Without any forewarning, Billy suddenly stopped walking, and the weird, old fashioned instrument perched perilously on a makeshift shelf on wheels which he and Mary had been pushing clanked its annoyance at the sudden stop which had almost made it topple over.

"Now then Billy, don't have one of your turns. There's nothing we can do about it."

Waving his arms in frustration, William Ward, or Blind Billy as he was known to everyone, cursed the fact that he had lost his sight and was subsequently less able than most to influence what was happening in his home-town.

He hadn't always been blind. In his younger days he'd been a bit of a tearaway with a strong 'attachment' to handcarts and wheelbarrows. Unfortunately, this attachment had not been appreciated by their owners from whom he had stolen them. As his eye-sight had gradually deteriorated, however, his wildness had subsided and he had even started to attend St. Matthew's Church where the vicar had befriended him.

"Listen here, Billy," the vicar had said one day. "You'll have to earn a living to help support both yourself and that good lady of yours. I'm prepared to lend you ten shillings (now 50p) to buy yourself an organ so that you can entertain the public in an evening and earn a few coppers."

With his ten shillings, which he managed to repay at six pence a week, Billy had bought the barrel organ which he and Mary were now pushing and, in order to personalise it, he had christened it his Tingleary. He had also managed to secure a good spot at the end of Surrey Street from which he could play his music every day and try and persuade passing pedestrians to give him money in return.

Billy's new-found career was, in fact, rather like that of the street musicians you see nowdays in Fargate with their

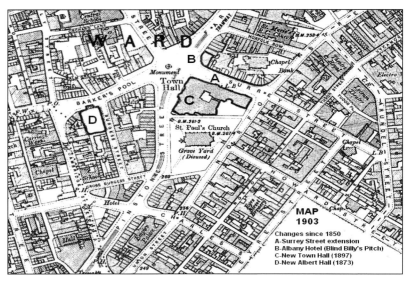

guitars, violins and other more sophisticated musical instruments. Fortunately, very few of them today are blind.

However, William Ward was very concerned about the City Council's proposals and he made sure that his wife knew about it.

"I can't afford to lose my pitch, Mary. Everybody knows which corner I stand on most nights. I'll lose all my regular customers if I have to move. I'm just not 'aving it."

Billy had a point, of course. It wasn't just that his pitch was slap bang in the middle of town, it was actually situated at the junction of several important pedestrian routes.

Take the route to the hugely successful Surrey Music Hall, for example. Most people going to the Surrey, which

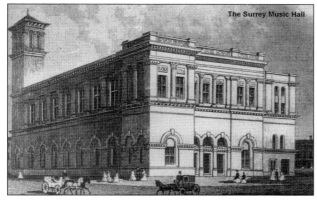

The Surrey Music Hall

was situated in Surrey Street on the site now occupied by the Central Library, had to pass Billy and his Tingleary in order to get there. And it wasn't just the numbers of people that mattered. This rather high-brow theatre produced concerts of classical music and poetry readings which attracted the well-to-do's and professional people of the day. In fact even forty years earlier it had been charging the extremely high prices of seven shillings and six pence (now 37p) and ten shillings and six pence (now 52p) (equivalent to more than a week's wages in those days) to see Charles Dickens performing in a play co-written by himself and the then Editor of Punch. With a capacity of up to 1,000 people, the amount of wealth which chinked past Billy's battered old money tin was very considerable. Even if only a very small percentage of it managed to find its way into the tin, our blind friend would have done very well.

Billy wouldn't have known, of course, that within ten years this music hall, which had been in Surrey Street for 70 years, would have closed down and been converted into a carpet warehouse for Messrs J.G. Graves and an Army Recruiting Office in the war years of 1914-1918 before becoming the Central Library.

However, it wasn't just the Surrey Music Hall which brought him customers. The Theatre Royal in Tudor Street was only a stone's-throw away, having been built there over 100 years earlier, and this wonderful theatre was equally as successful as its neighbour. Nightly performances of operas, plays and pantomimes attracted Sheffield folk by the hundred, and the huge variety of acts presented, which even included performing animals and birds, ensured a large cross section of visitors. Once again, many of these would

stroll past Billy's barrel organ to and from their evening's entertainment, usually in a happy frame of mind. This happiness more often than not created a generosity in the theatre-goers which William Ward welcomed with open arms. After all, having paid between two shilling and six pence and three shillings for their seats, a few coppers in Billy's tin was not a lot to pay for a contented mind and a better future for a blind man, was it?

When Billy and Mary had originally chosen the location for their barrel organ pitch, they had obviously done so very carefully. Not only was it en-route to the Theatre Royal and the Surrey, it was also perfectly positioned to catch theatre-goers visiting the Albert Hall, which had been built only twenty years earlier in Barker's Pool.

This music hall, which was previously the site of the home of Ebenezer Elliott, the Sheffield poet known as the Corn Law Rhymer, was acknowledged by many as probably the most prestigious place of entertainment in the city. Boasting a huge 125 feet long by 60 feet wide main hall and a 2,000 seating capacity, musical concerts and operas attracted the better-off residents of the city who were only too willing to part with a few coppers after a good evening out. Strangely enough, thousands of Sheffield folk have been prepared to part with some of their hard-earned cash when visiting the building which later succeeded the Albert Hall on this site, as in 1963 Cole Brothers built its very popular new store there. Now, instead of Blind Billy asking for alms, Big-Issue vendors sell their interesting magazines in order to keep them out of the poverty trap.

However, to get back to Billy's reaction to the thought of losing his pitch, his caring and patient wife Mary understood her husband's tendency to flare-up occasionally when he felt threatened. With her help, he usually calmed down quickly, and tonight was no exception as within ten minutes or so the couple had reached the corner of Surrey Street and set up Billy's Tingleary with which he could entertain passers-by for the next few hours.

"I'm off now love," called out Mary as she set off home to their little terraced house in Carver Lane. "I'll be back about 10 o'clock to pick you up. Best of luck."

Billy raised a hand and waved in the direction of the disappearing voice, then turned to his old fashioned barrel organ. A small rod had been attached to its handle so that he was more easily able to reach it and turn the barrel to produce its music.

To most people, however, describing the noise which came out of the open lid as music was, to say the least, a rather generous description. The weird looking, old fashioned instrument emitted equally weird, old fashioned tunes and, as Billy usually accompanied the music with a doleful ditty and an equally doleful expression, the whole experience was destined to either make you laugh or cry. Most people passing by were, in fact, amused by what they saw and heard and gladly dropped a copper or two in Billy's tin as he plaintively sang out: "Kind friends, please to remember the blind."

To many people, particularly children accompanying their parents, it was the barrel organ itself which was the main attraction. Looking rather like an old fashioned shop till when its lid was open, its partly glazed front was covered by an interesting painting which included a man doing conjuring tricks with cups on a table, another figure beating a bell to music, whilst another was doing a step dance. This fairly colourful scene, albeit a little faded and chipped, always caused interest amongst the children which, to Billy's advantage, usually caused their parents to stop and donate something whilst they were waiting.

The pinnacle of Billy's entertainment programme was, however, at coming-out time at the nearby theatres. As the happy theatre-goers meandered their way home, our blind hero gave the handle of his barrel organ an extra strong turn to ensure that its main tune, That Old Arm Chair, together with a gutsy rendition of the words by himself, could be heard by everyone passing by.

No-one quite knows how much money William Ward was able to make with his Tingleleary but, with the modest income his wife Mary was able to earn from doing domestic work, they managed to live a relatively simple, but comfortable life which, hopefully, was able to compensate to some degree for his blindness.

As history shows, Billy's pitch at the corner of Pinstone Street and Fargate was lost within a year or two as work associated with the new Town Hall commenced. Whether or not Billy chose to move elsewhere or simply call it a day, we don't know. What we do know is that for many years Blind Billy was one of Sheffield's best known characters, whose plaintive cry of alms and his occasional vocal accompaniment combined magically with his weird looking and weird sounding Tingleary to give pleasure to thousands of Sheffield's people.

William Ward might have been blind, but he rarely let his disability get the better of him. He was determined to succeed and do his best, a quality which personified most Sheffield folk at that time.

New Town Hall - 1897

CHARLIE HYDE

Charlie Hyde, known locally as Blind Charlie, was a jolly, round-faced newsvendor who lived in St. Philips' Road, near to Fawcett Street, on the north-west side of town. His long curly hair, which always tumbled down casually over his ears, blended well with his equally curly beard and gave him the appearance of a brown-haired Father Christmas.

Charlie Hyde

His dress was equally distinctive. Regardless of the weather, his thick long jacket was nearly always left open to reveal a brown waistcoat of imitation sealskin. It was, however, his heavy corduroy trousers which created his rather comical appearance. They were obviously several sizes too long and resembled the bellows of a large concertina whose folds became thicker and heavier as they settled down over his rather large feet.

Charlie was, however, proud of his clothes, as, indeed, he was of his shiny black shoes. Unfortunately, the shoes were also shiny underneath, being somewhat the worse for wear, and he had to wrap them in flannel cloths in winter to stop himself slipping down. At this time, as you can imagine, his feet looked twice as big and did nothing to help his appearance. As he shuffled along the town centre streets with his cane, kicking his feet out with each step he took, he looked every inch like the sad little tramp known to the world today as Charlie Chaplin.

Strangely enough it was during this period, when Charlie Hyde was walking the streets in this fashion, that Charlie Chaplin appeared at the Empire Theatre in Charles Street with Stan Jefferson (who later became the thin half of Laurel and Hardy). As part of the Fred Karno's Company which had come to

Sheffield, he was playing a red-nosed drunk in the play called Mumming Birds in the July of 1899. He would probably have taken a stroll around town during the day whilst he wasn't working, at which time he could have spotted our Charlie doing his comical shuffling walk. I wonder if that gave him the original idea for creating his famous little tramp? You never know, do you?

The public loved Charlie Hyde, and whenever his infectious grin broke through his bewhiskered face, those who met him were always pleased to pass the time of day with him.

"You're looking very smart today, Charlie."

"Thank you sir," he responded proudly as he padded on up the street with his walking stick.

Although Charlie was classed as blind, he did have some small degree of sight and held down a good job with the Sheffield Evening Telegraph and Star as a travelling newspaper vendor. His paper-round extended right out to Barber Road at Crooksmoor, which necessitated him carrying not one, but two waterproof bags full of papers across his broad shoulders.

"Evenin' Paper," he would bellow in his loud, bass voice as he trundled along, collecting a penny for each one he sold.

The walk to Barber Road was, however, by no means easy, especially when carrying the heavy bags. Although Charlie was able to catch a horse-tram back to town, the need to sell his papers en-route prevented him doing the same on his outward journey. The walk was, nevertheless, quite an interesting one which he enjoyed, especially when accompanied by his friend Joe who often kindly volunteered to became his 'eyes'.

The pair of them set off one fine summer's afternoon from no.17 High Street, the home of the Telegraph and Star in those days.

High Street about 1900

"Now then Charlie," warned Joe, "just watch out for them there horses pulling them great contraptions on steel rails in the middle of the street. It's just like a race track on 'ere."

"Oh, you mean the horse-trams," his friend replied. "They're all right. They make such a racket that I can always hear them coming."

"I'll tell you what," Joe added as they continued along Church Street. "That there church could do with a bit of a clean if you ask me. They reckon it's been there for hundreds of years and I bet it's never been washed."

Joe was, of course, referring to the building which we now know as the Sheffield Cathedral, although it didn't acquire this status until the year 1913.

Parish Church in mid to late 1800s

"Well, being a newspaper person," responded Charlie, puffing out with pride, "I happen to know that it's been there seven hundred years or more, and was built in 1280. The previous one was burnt down, you know, about a hundred years earlier as far as I remember."

"There's not much you don't know Charlie, is there?" commented Joe as he nodded to an elderly beggar sitting patiently on an upturned box which leaned conveniently against the church's boundary railing.

Progress along this part of their walk was always very slow as Charlie had to pause on a regular basis to sell his papers to the many shoppers who wanted to buy one. However, it wasn't just the sales that pleased him; the gradual reduction in weight of the bags slung over his shoulders was particularly welcome. Although Joe had offered to carry one

Today's beggar?..., ...or is it Father Christmas on his day off?

of the bags himself, Charlie had firmly but kindly refused his friend's thoughtful gesture as he always insisted on being as independent as possible.

It wasn't long before the chums found themselves walking along West Street, once again having to step aside to allow a clip-clopping-clanking horse-tram to sway by. A few passengers on the open top deck recognised the newspaper-man.

"We'll see you at Barber Road, Charlie, if you manage to get there under that weight," one of them shouted as they passed by.

Joe and Charlie both smiled and gave a quick wave whilst enjoying the friendly banter which tumbled down onto them.

Suddenly, a clatter of hooves took them both by surprise as a horse and a rather dilapidated open trap rushed past in obvious haste. Joe managed to glimpse a white faced figure draped carelessly behind the anxious driver who was making excessive use of a twitch of birch on the rump of the sweating old nag which was pulling the trap. The poor animal was well past its sell-by date, but was obviously doing as good a job as it could.

"What's all the commotion about, Joe? Sounds like the Crookesmoor Derby to me."

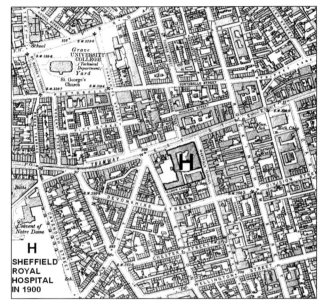
H SHEFFIELD ROYAL HOSPITAL IN 1900

"Looks like an emergency, Charlie," came the worried response as the make-shift ambulance came to a shuddering halt a few yards up the road outside the imposing, but daunting, structure of the Royal Hospital.

This hospital, which started its life as a small dispensary for the sick-poor on the site of the present Central Library in 1832 before moving to West Street a year later, was known as the General Hospital in 1860 and the Sheffield

The Royal Hospital in West Street about 1900

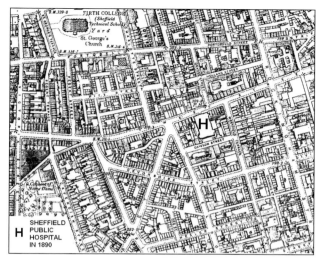

Public Hospital in 1875. It was ultimately rebuilt as the Royal Hospital in 1895. However, like most hospitals of the day, it was both welcomed and feared by the public, as healthcare, medical treatment and surgery were still very primitive in those days.

"Somebody's being taken into the 'ospital, Charlie. He looks a bit rough to me."

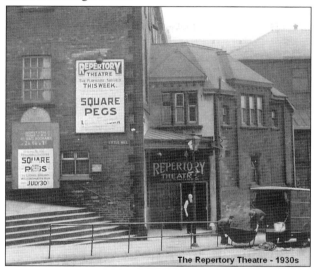

The Repertory Theatre - 1930s

Joe's blind companion stood still and couldn't help but reflect on the time when he'd been forced to visit the old Public Hospital on this site. It was in the 1880s, and Charlie was well known at that time for his magnificent bass voice and often sang at the Saturday night concerts held in the Victorian Comrades Temperance Hall in Townhead Street (later to become the Repertory Theatre and, in 1938, the Playhouse Theatre).

Just imagine the scene in this large, packed hall which had been built in 1855. Its rather posh balcony had seats for 222 slightly better-off customers, whilst the large saloon was able to seat 319 noisy, yet contented punters whose priority was cheapness rather than comfort. At the opposite end of the hall, which had also been the British Legion Headquarters at one time, a small orchestra was tuning-up in the pit directly in front of the brightly lit stage upon which the Master of Ceremonies was pacing up and down impatiently.

"And tonight, ladies and gentlemen," boomed the authoritive figure of Alderman Clegg, the chairman of the evening meeting, "we have your friend and mine, Charles Hyde, the best bass singer in town."

Charlie rose from his seat at the front of the large hall and made his way to the stage where the equally well known figure of Mr. Holroyd, the hall's permanent accompanist, awaited him. To rousing cheers, Charles Hyde's rich, deep tones drifted majestically and penetratingly to all corners of the concert hall, although as he gazed out over the admiring audience to whom he was singing, he was concerned to note that the smiling faces in front of him were rather blurred.

That evening was the beginning of a progressively difficult time for the singer, and a visit to the Sheffield Public Hospital a few weeks later to investigate his declining vision was to be of no real comfort. As he sat there on that dull Monday morning in the large, overcrowded

waiting room amongst dozens of sick and injured patients, he shuddered at he thought of having to come into such a place for anything really serious. "After all," he thought to himself, "It's only a bit of blurred vision I've got. I'm sure a few of them new fancy eye-drops that you can get nowdays will do the trick."

"Charles Hyde," shrilled a startlingly officious voice which jolted the unhappy singer back to reality.

Charlie glanced over to his left in the direction that the call had come from and slowly rose to follow the blurred image of a little white hat perched perilously on a small, bobbing head which was rapidly approaching him. He could just make out a dark blue dress and a shiny white collar supporting the bobbing head, which led him to correctly presume that it was the doctor's nurse who wanted him to follow her.

"We haven't got all day, Mr Hyde!"

A pale, stern-looking face directly in front of him had now replaced the previous image and confirmed his view that he was expected to move rather more quickly than he was doing, despite his affliction.

"I'm coming lass," mumbled poor Charlie as he stumbled over the outstretched feet of a waiting patient sitting next to him.

It was with some trepidation that he entered the rather cold-looking consulting room a few minutes later. The eye specialist, who looked a bit lost sitting behind his large desk, was about as welcoming as Miss 'bobbing-head', his impatient nurse. The subsequent examination with some new-fangled gadgets and lights did temporarily give Charlie some encouragement, but that exploded when the doctor presented the poor man with his diagnosis. Charles Hyde, bass singer and exceptionally cheerful chap, had an incurable eye disease and was slowly going blind.

"Are you all right, Charlie?"

Joe's anxious question suddenly brought his friend back from his thoughtful reminiscing and urged him to move on, past the hospital entrance through which the horse and trap passenger had just been carried by the driver.

"Let's make haste, Joe. I've got papers to sell."

A little more thoughtful than usual, the chums moved on, along Glossop Road. As they approached Convent Walk, the tall, gangling figure of Snowball appeared with his broom.

"Evenin' gents. If yer just 'ang on a minute, I'll make sure yer can cross wivout gettin' muck on yer shoes."

"Hi Snowball, it's always good to see you," came the cheerful response from Charlie, who wished like mad that he really could see his friend.

The two characters had been friends for some time as they usually met each other on a daily basis at Snowball's crossing point. Instead of giving the crossing-sweeper the odd copper to supplement his very poor daily wage, Charlie gave him one of his newspapers, for which he was always very grateful.

"If yer see Punch up at Brook Hill, give 'im my regards," piped the tall man as Charlie and Joe continued on their journey.

As expected, little Punch was there at his crossing, making sure that everyone could safely cross the Brook Hill Junction.

"Hi Punch. Me and Charlie are doing his Barber Road round today," called out Joe. "Do you fancy a paper?"

"Yesss Sir!" responded Punch, clicking his heels to attention whilst saluting Joe and his blind companion as they made their way over the clean road en route to Winter Street.

Charlie never minded this paper round, despite its length, as he always managed to bump into friends.

Unfortunately, one of them had been admitted into the Borough Hospital for Infectious Diseases on Winter Street (later to be called City Hospital), situated directly opposite the rear entrance to Weston Park.

"Let's pop in and see him, Joe. He doesn't get many visitors these days."

"Well, we're a bit short of time this afternoon, Charlie. I tell you what. We'll pop over in the morning when you're not so busy."

Nodding his head, Charlie walked slowly onwards, hoping that tomorrow wouldn't be too late.

This hospital, later renamed Winter Street Hospital, also specialised in chest and lung problems and to some degree was feared by many who went in there. Although the treatment and care was as good as was available in the late 1800s, the severity of the illnesses which necessitated admittance there often ended tragically. Nevertheless, the medical profession did its very best with the knowledge and resources available, and many a grateful patient did make a good recovery. Nowadays, the hospital is used for medical teaching purposes and is a key part of the Sheffield Teaching Hospitals facilities.

The last stretch of the paper round, which culminated in the busy Crookesmoor housing area around Barber Road, took Charlie and Joe onto Crookes Valley Road. This road was a natural vantage point which stood high above the large Crookesmoor recreation ground to the right and the Old Great Dam to the left. The late afternoon sun was still quite high in the sky, and the summer heat was beginning to take its toll on the newsvendor and his mate. As Joe glanced down towards the glistening, blue water of the dam which magically mimicked the blue of the sky above, the sun's reflection appeared as a ball of fire in the water.

"Looks like the dam's on fire from up 'ere, Charlie. I've never really noticed before what a fantastic view it is. Mind you, I'm not sure what that building is just beyond it. Do you know?"

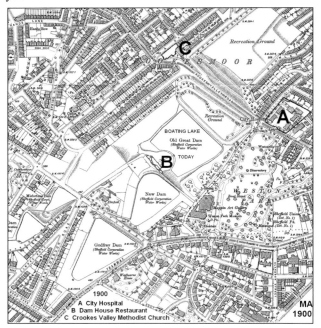

Sheffield Teaching Hospital - Winter Street

Despite his blindness, Charlie knew what building his friend Joe was referring to. The heat to the side and back of his head told him that the sun was in the south east and that the building beyond the dam must be the Dam House Restaurant. This rather posh establishment, which was destined to be gutted by fire many years later, was a favourite eating place for many of the better-off residents of the town in those days, and has now been restored to its former glory for those wanting a slightly up-market breakfast, lunch or evening meal with a beautiful view.

"Come on, Joe," his friend chided. "Let's sell some papers 'els gaffer'll shoot me when I get back."

A few yards further on, the two tired men arrived at a huge stone church which stood at the junction of Crookes Valley Road and Crookesmoor Road. This impressive

Crookes Valley Methodist Church today

building proudly formed the gateway to Crookesmoor and Walkley beyond, and with Barber Road rising steeply from this point, was a natural location from which Blind Charlie could rest and set up his pitch to serve the hundreds of locals in the area.

After an hour or so, with the sun gently sinking in the evening sky, Charlie had nearly sold all his papers.

"I think we'll call it a day and catch a tram back if you don't mind, Joe. My papers have nearly all gone and I'm feelin' tired now."

As the Walkley tram slowly lurched down Barber Road towards them, restrained by the driver's brakes to allow its team of horses to move freely, Charlie gave a contented sigh as another working day came to an end. Selling papers might not be the most sophisticated of jobs, but meeting people and 'borrowing' eyes from good friends from time to time made life go round as well as it could for a sightless person.

As we've seen, Charlie Hyde lost his sight later on in life than many. Making the adjustment to blindness must have been despairingly difficult, but he always managed to remain cheerful and optimistic. He hadn't got much money, but he had a wealth of friends, most of whom he had made as a consequence of him losing his sight. For that richness, he was eternally grateful, and it is to him that we are also grateful for allowing us to join him on his interesting walk through the past. Perhaps we'll join him again one day. Who knows?

OWEN WING

It was the mid 1880s, and Owen Wing, a man of modest height and slight build, was sitting on his three-legged stool in Market Place at the bottom of High Street, adjacent to the thriving Fitzalan Market Hall.

The Market Hall was a huge building commonly known as The Shambles, and extended three hundred feet or more

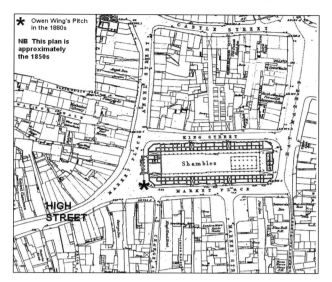

along the full length of King Street on one side and along the bottom section of High Street (then known as Fruit Market) on the other.

Markets in Sheffield at this time were held every Tuesday and Saturday, with live markets for calves and sheep held every Friday and for fat cattle every Monday. They generated large crowds of eager shoppers, and for someone like Owen, who was totally blind, they presented an opportunity for him to earn a few pence with which to eke out a modest living with a small degree of independence.

Unlike many similarly unfortunate people, Owen was not a street vendor as he had nothing to sell but his voice. Whilst his talents were both vocal and instrumental, he considered himself to be a very religious person and, as he sat there on his stool, he often read aloud from a large, Braille bible perched on his rather bony knees protruding in front of him, pausing only to ask for alms.

"Spare a penny or two for a poor, blind gentleman."

Owen's plaintive cry punctuated his biblical readings on a regular basis, but often fell on deaf or

Owen Wing

uncaring ears. However, there were some people who were listening.

"'Ere you are, Owen. 'Ave some of this instead."

A group of several, mischievous boys had gathered around the blind beggar intent on teasing him. A handful of grit was suddenly thrown onto the page of his bible which resulted in a torrent of language from him which was anything but biblical.

"And God said to Moses, *** those ****** lads, they're at it again!"

Roaring with laughter, the boys ran off, having achieved what they had set out to do. Sadly, there were few places of entertainment for the town's youth in those days, and playing practical jokes on people like Owen was a common pastime for the bored, younger population.

A kindly old lady, having witnessed the frustration and anger created in the rather despairing little figure trying to retrieve his bible which had fallen to the ground, walked up to him and tapped him on the shoulder.

"You must learn to ignore those children my dear. They don't really know any better. Why don't you sing for us? You've got a lovely voice you know."

Owen slowly glanced up into the gentle darkness that had replaced his despair. The noisy hustle and bustle of hundreds of busy shoppers intermingling with the shouts of street trades and the clip-clop of horse drawn carts faded slowly into the background as the kind words tumbled over him.

"Thank you ma'm. God bless you ma'm. What would you like me to sing?"

"You choose, my dear, you choose. Any of your lovely hymns will do very nicely."

The chink of metal hitting the bottom of the rather battered tin cup perched on the ground between Owen's feet was a welcome sound, as the grateful street entertainer had not only received kindness, which was good for his soul, but also money, which was good for his stomach, each contribution being as important as the other.

The scene in Market Place on that late Saturday morning was in fact something to behold. Owen, in response to the kind lady's request, now sat with pride on his three legged stool, pulling and punching a rather battered concertina in time with a powerful rendition of All Things Bright and Beautiful which competed quite

Market Place about 1880's

successfully with "Fresh oranges, three a penny" and "Best 'taters, tuppence a bag" which drifted like a noisy cloud over the whole area.

Complementing Owen's entertainment, gentlemen on horseback, ladies in a variety of horse-pulled carriages and dozens of passengers on horse-pulled tramcars all battled for road space along with excited shoppers scurrying along like ants, criss-crossing the area to get to their favourite shops. There was, of course, no 'Hole in The Road' (which appeared about 80 years later) or any posh supertrams (which frequent the site of the old Market Place now), but even in those days traffic jams were common place and occasionally reached the status of 'gridlock'.

It was, nevertheless, a magical scene which poor old Owen could only imagine in his mind. Behind him, as he sat with his back to the magnificent stone-built Market Hall with its huge pillars supporting the roof to its grand entrance, rich, well-dressed ladies and their men folk mixed with poor, working class women and their spouses with the same intent in their minds: to fill their bags and baskets with fresh meat, fish, fruit and vegetables.

In front of him, 'J. Jones and Son, Carpeting and Furnishing Warehouse' was emblazoned on the two multi-storey buildings which faced each other across the bottom of High Street at nos. 63 and 72. A little further up High Street, John Walsh was developing his business and he too occupied even larger buildings opposite each other at nos.

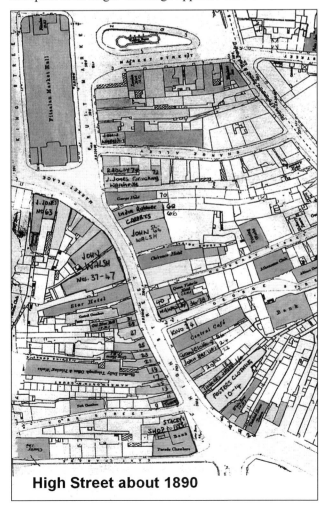
High Street about 1890

54 to 64 and 37 to 47. His rise to success was quite remarkable for, having worked as a buyer at T. B. and W. Cockayne from 1866 to 1875, he left to sell baby linen and outfitting in a small shop at no. 39 High Street, (opposite his later, huge department store now occupied by T.J. Hughes). Within 15 years he had acquired and amalgamated the six shop units on each side of High Street and was possibly the largest retailer in the city at that time.

It wasn't just on Market days that Owen chose to beg on the City streets. During the 1890s, most shops were open from 8 o'clock in the morning to 9 o'clock at night every weekday, whilst on Saturdays they stayed open until 10 or even 11 o'clock. Half-day closing on Thursday afternoons after 2 o'clock had, however, been introduced by John Walsh who had successfully persuaded other shops to do the same. Friday night was a good time for a bit of special Blind Owen singing or preaching, particularly as working men and their wives, having been paid that day, used the evening for their main late-night shopping spree. Many also poured into the shops after a few hours in the pubs and, with extra money in their pockets and a bit of beer in their bellies, their generosity to Owen's pleas for financial help increased significantly.

Another favourite spot used by Owen was in Fargate at its junction with Norfolk Row. With John Rennie's hosier shop at no. 47 on one corner and William Taylor, carver and gilder at no. 51 on the other corner, Owen was well placed

Fargate in the 1880s

to attract the attention of the hundreds of passing shoppers and businessmen with his vocal talents.

Fargate itself was a hive of activity in those days, as indeed, it is now. It boasted many a good shopping facility, including the now famous Cole Brothers (Drapers) at nos.

Fargate in 1907

Coles Corner in the 1880s

2 to 8 at its junction with Church Street. Diagonally opposite Owen's pitch, Arthur Davey (Provision Merchants) was a particularly attractive shop from which emanated an aroma of baking bread, buns and cakes which drifted tantalizingly across the road to seduce the blind man's extra sensitive nostrils. The largest retailer on the street was Robert Ramsdon who occupied two shops at nos. 7 and 42 as a hat maker, a shop at no. 44 as a victualler, and a shop at no. 46 as a boot and shoe dealer. Other shops in Fargate included confectioners, ironmongers, butchers, photographers, joiners, and many more.

The variety and extent of the shopping facilities on Fargate attracted shoppers and business people from all walks of life, and Owen usually enjoyed a modestly successful day singing, preaching and begging when he chose this street as his pitch.

Variety of location was also essential for his success, and he rarely occupied the same pitch two days running. Apart from working in Market Place and Fargate, he also worked in New Pinstone Street and Barkers Pool. In fact, if we move on about one hundred years or so for a moment,

G4　　City Hall steps

we find that other singers still use this area as a platform for future success. The well known group G4 of X-Factor fame were a good example of this.

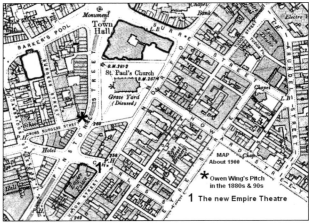

MAP About 1900

★ Owen Wing's Pitch in the 1880s & 90s

1 The new Empire Theatre

One of his favourite locations, however, was in Cross Burgess Street at its Junction with Pinstone Street. From there he had 'sight' of the new theatre being built at the junction of Charles Street and Union Street. The old Alhambra theatre, which had stood there for many years, had been demolished and was being replaced by Sheffield's new 'Jewel in the Crown', the Empire Theatre.

As the huge 3,000-seat building slowly rose out of the ground in magnificent splendour, Owen would ask the passers-by, who kindly stopped to talk to him, to describe the progress by 'painting' a picture on his permanently dark canvas. Opening night, on November 4th 1895, was a special night for him. Cora Stuart was appearing in The Fair Equestrienne, and a full-house was expected to occupy seats varying from sixpence to two shillings (2½ p to 10p), with private boxes going at one and a half guineas (£1.57½p). There was also an additional standing area in the gallery where 1,000 people could squeeze in for 4d (1½ p) each.

With up to 4,000 people making their way to The Empire that night, Owen made sure that not only was he at his pitch in good time, but that he also brought with him a

friend who could tell him what was happening and who was passing by.

It was cold, but dry on that exciting November night, and the local constabulary was out in force. 4,000 people converging on the new theatre on foot, in buggies, horse taxis, and horse-drawn trams demanded careful and sympathetic control, particularly as many dignitaries and people of considerable wealth and position were attending.

Ladies in fine, long dresses and coats accompanied by gentlemen in evening dress and top hats glided by in their posh, horse-drawn carriages as hundreds of ordinary folk dressed 'up to the nines' proudly made their way to the

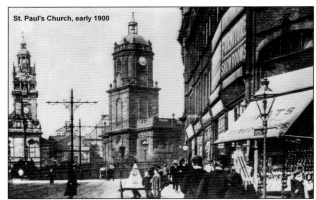

St. Paul's Church, early 1900

grand opening along the thronged Pinstone Street past the magnificently domed St. Paul's Church. Everyone was feeling happy, particularly Owen as coins were continually tossed into his tin in response to his dramatic pleas.

"If the-er-blind man hadn't ast for-er-er-sight," Owen regularly explained to those who walked by, "he wouldn't 'av got it; therefore if i-er-didn't never ask-er-for your money, I-er-should never-er get any, should I?"

His nervously put biblical argument for alms was always followed by a powerful rendition of an appropriate hymn which, with hands held high and sightless eyes turned upwards, usually proved too much to resist for many of the passing theatre goers who almost felt obliged to make a contribution.

"Tha's dun well tonight, Owen lad. Keep it up and tha'll be better off than them lot goin' to' theatre."

Owen's friend, Joe, who had accompanied him that night, was a kindly soul often to be seen by his side giving him encouragement and support. He had little or no money himself, but his gift of friendship meant more to his best mate than any amount of coppers which rattled into his tin. They both lived in Duke Street in the Park District and had known each other for many years, struggling to survive, like many others, in the tiny back-to-back terraced houses which lined many of Sheffield's streets at that time. A night like tonight was not just an opportunity for someone like Owen and Joe to make extra money, it was also an exciting and pleasurable night out which brightened up the tedium of everyday living and gave them memories to cherish in years to come.

Following this special and memorable evening, the two friends were able to visit the blind man's pitch on many more occasions, and Owen was able to enjoy the magic of 'seeing' (with Joe's help) celebrities such as Marie Lloyd (of 'Oh Mr. Porter' fame), Harry Houdini (the amazing escapologist), Fred Karno's Company (which included two relatively unknown artists by the name of Charles Chaplin and Stan Laurel) and the cheeky chap with a banjo, George Formby. Joe developed into quite an artist painting pictures of these and other celebrities in his friend's mind which, undeniably, helped our well-meaning blind beggar to have a more colourful life than might otherwise have been the case.

Marie Lloyd

George Formby

Laurel and Hardy

However, despite his relatively young age, Owen was not a person who enjoyed good health. His lifestyle of poverty combined with hours of sitting and begging in cold, wet and miserable conditions eventually took its toll and he died before he reached his 50th birthday.

Although Owen Wing was blind and poor, he was by no means a loser. His enthusiasm for life, his determination to help himself and his genuine (albeit sometimes a little misplaced) belief in the scriptures were qualities that many a more fortunate person would have been proud of. He was, if course, a Sheffielder, and that explains a lot, doesn't it?

THOMAS ANDERSON

Thomas Anderson was a typical young lad living in late Victorian Sheffield and, like many others at that time, started work at the age of 12 or 13. His father worked in the local silver trade and Thomas, who showed a natural aptitude for this type of work, happily followed in his footsteps.

Sadly, at the age of 15, this capable apprentice silversmith became blind. The cause of his misfortune is unknown, but the effect was drastic. He was unable to follow the trade he loved and had no option but to attend a blind school in York in order that he could learn an alternative trade such as brush-making.

Following a short spell at this school, Thomas was grateful that he was able to transfer back to his home town and attend the Sheffield School for the Blind which had just been built on Manchester Road.

Tapton Mount 1996

Before we follow him into this innovative new school to see how he went on, let us have a quick look at how and when such an establishment came to be built in Sheffield in the late 1870s.

Although the building itself was to be funded by the public of Sheffield, its upkeep and maintenance was to be funded privately. This arrangement dated back to 1869 when the late Daniel Holy of Newbold in Derbyshire left property worth £25,000 (which equates to about £1million today) to the Sheffield Town Trustees. The income derived from this very large sum of money by way of interest and profits from investments was, at Daniel's request, to be paid to the Sheffield Blind Institution upon condition that a suitable building for the blind, including furnishings etc, must be provided within five years of the marriage or death of his sister Caroline.

Six years later, in 1875, Caroline Holy died and a public appeal to Sheffield's residents and businesses for the funding of the proposed new Blind School raised £12,564. Of this total sum, £8,864 was spent on building the new Tudor-style stone structure, which still exists today, £2,100 was required to buy the land upon which the School was built, and £1,600 was thus available for equipment and furnishings. With the funding of annual maintenance and running costs now guaranteed by the Blind Institution out of Daniel Holy's original bequest, the future of the new school was assured.

The location of this prestigious building obviously needed a prestigious site. Sheffield's public was not to be disappointed as two acres of prime building land within the rural west end of the town had been made available for the project and, on the 24th September, 1879, the Sheffield School for the Blind opened in all its glory. It had been designed to accommodate fifty boys and fifty girls who would, it was claimed, receive an equivalent education to that given in the best national schools. This education would also be supplemented by moral and industrial training.

It was against this background that Thomas Anderson arrived at the school the day after its official opening with both excitement and trepidation. Despite it being a bright and sunny morning, he shivered a little as, arm-in-arm with his mother, he walked up the driveway which led him to the large oak doors of the school's main entrance at the front

of the building. Although he was now 16 years old, he had only been blind for just over a year and he understandably felt nervous and rather vulnerable in this new environment.

As the couple entered the impressive entrance hall, two signs invited them to make their first decision; Boys' Department to the right or Girls' Department to the left. Mrs. Anderson guided her son to the right where they were soon greeted by a kindly looking, middle-aged lady of modest stature.

"Good morning Mrs. Anderson. Good morning Thomas. I'm Mrs. Carter, the school secretary, and I've been expecting you."

This rather quiet but positive greeting washed gently over Thomas' ears and filled him with confidence and relief at his first encounter with the school staff.

"If you'll come this way to my office," she continued, "we can sort out your paperwork before I introduce you to the Matron."

Thomas' confidence suddenly disappeared as quickly as it had arrived at the mention of the word Matron, as it conjured up a picture of stern intolerance in his mind. He was not to be disappointed. The office door suddenly burst open with a flurry of navy blue cloth which bedecked an ample frame of agitated authority. Despite his blindness, Thomas could almost feel the penetrating glare which darted towards him.

"Well, Mrs. Carter," she trumpeted. "Who have we got here?"

Matron's abrupt manner, even towards her colleague Mrs. Carter, was an indication of what was to come, and Thomas' heart sank as the conversation continued.

"This is Mrs. Anderson and her son Thomas, Matron. I was just going to…."

"Yes, yes, yes. I'm pleased to meet you both. Now, come along Thomas, I haven't got all day."

As you might expect, the blind teenager's head was swimming as he tried to adjust to the sudden confrontational attitude of the most important and influential member of his new home, who now turned her attention to his equally concerned mother.

"You can go now, Mrs. Anderson. Thomas will be fine here," she rasped while trying to force a reassuring smile which failed miserably to light up her stern looking face. "We'll let you know when you can visit him."

It's difficult to know exactly how long it would be before Mrs. Anderson was allowed to see her son again. This was the year 1879, and even seven decades later the parents of blind inmates were only allowed to visit their children on a Saturday, once a month. We can only assume that, in Thomas Anderson's case, visiting rights would be at least, if not more, restrictive.

It is with no surprise, therefore, that we find both mother and son very upset. A gentle, tear-stained kiss on Thomas' cheek and a long, desperate, clinging hug heralded the last contact between them for many weeks. As the retreating tap-tap of his mother's worn shoes on the uncarpeted corridor faded into the distance, the new resident of the Sheffield School for the Blind took a deep breath and prepared himself for an uncertain future.

Thomas, you will appreciate, was one of many blind children at this school. It is possible that he was the oldest there, as the school took in children from the age of four. You will recall that he had actually started work by the age of 13 and had probably only received a rather limited education before going blind. His admission to Sheffield's new school for the blind at the age of 16 to enable him to gain a good education was, you might say, a small piece of silver lining in his otherwise dark cloud. Let's see what he thought about it.

Thomas' mother had now left the building and Matron turned her attention back to her latest resident (more often than not simply called inmates in those days).

"Follow me to the assembly hall, young man, and you can meet Mr. Wood there with the rest of today's new arrivals."

With an about–turn befitting a sergeant major in Her Majesty's Army, Matron Gover (as Thomas later found out she was called), swished out of the secretary's office and, for a few precious moments, peace and quiet reigned supreme. It didn't last for long, however, as an angry retort in the distance demanded to know why Thomas Anderson wasn't following directly behind her.

At this stage, the calm voice of the secretary, Mrs. Carter, took over and reassured both Matron and Thomas that she would see to it that he would be escorted safely to the assembly hall. There, along with many other nervous and frightened children of all ages, he learned from Mr. William Wood, the School Superintendent, that the offices, the dining room, the kitchen, the classrooms and the

Washroom in 1996

committee rooms were on the ground floor of the school, whilst the dormitories, washrooms, lavatories and sick rooms were located upstairs on the two floors above. To his horror, he also learnt that the school's large communal baths were located in the basement of the building, which he later found out was like climbing down into the bowels of the earth.

Armed with this knowledge, Thomas and his fellow inmates were given a conducted tour of the building and reminded that from that time on, they had to find their own way around the school, as well as doing just about everything else that previously they had been helped with. This induction into a regime of total self-help and self-preservation was a huge shock to all the inmates there, particularly those of much younger years who found the whole experience almost impossible to bear.

To bear witness to the conditions that prevailed there all those years ago, let's just leap forward to the middle of the next century when an even better known Sheffield character was experiencing exactly the same dreadful treatment as he entered the same school at the tender age of four. The name of this young child was David Blunkett and the year was 1951.

It would be in-appropriate for me to write about David Blunkett's life in this book about Sheffield folk, although he would have been a perfect candidate in my opinion. His life story as written in his autobiography 'On A Clear Day' typifies the determination, courage and understanding that most Sheffield folk embrace, and his sincerity of wishing to help others is unquestionable.

However, I would like to borrow a quote from his autobiography which directly relates to the rigid Victorian attitudes and discipline which would have been experienced by Thomas Anderson more than 70 years earlier. I'm sure he won't mind.

Dining Room in 1996

Music room in 1996

Lounge

Playroom in 1996

Bedroom in 1996

Bedroom in 1996

David had this to say about the school's policy of parents being told to bring their children in to the school's assembly hall on their first day, bid them a quick farewell and then leave them to it:

"Obviously this has a profound effect on an infant, who feels totally abandoned and terrified, and particularly when he cannot see who or what is around him. It was one of the worst experiences of my life, as it was for my parents."

There were several special schools for the blind around the country during the time that David attended the Sheffield School for the blind, later renamed Tapton Mount School. Many, it would appear, applied similar strict controls to those applied in Sheffield. My research has identified feelings of despair and lasting psychological effects such as continuing insecurities and anxieties caused by the austere and sometimes cruel regimes in many of these old-fashioned, blind boarding schools. However, David Blunkett managed to climb this thorny tree of adversity and reach the top. Perhaps he was stronger than most and was able and determined to get the best out of the system and not let it beat him. Unfortunately, I suspect that some weaker mortals succumbed and are still suffering.

However, times have changed, and throughout the 1960s to the 1990s things improved dramatically at Tapton

Mount. Testament to this was the huge turnout which occurred when the school held a Reunion Day on the 29th June, 1996. On that occasion, at which I was privileged to be present, hundreds of ex-pupils attended to express their gratitude for the kindness and help shown to them during their stay there. The resident blind children, who were still attending classes that day, also joined in the activities and were clearly happy and content, and the caring headmistress and her large staff were an absolute pleasure to meet.

In my capacity as a photographer on that occasion, I was also allowed to do a tour around the whole building which, with the exception of the disused but interesting communal bathing area in the basement, was more akin to viewing a 4-Star hotel than a school. Outside, within the school's spacious grounds, excellent recreational play facilities were available for use by the schoolchildren, and an environment of genuine care and kindness seemed to permeate the whole school.

Sadly, but for very good reasons no doubt, this Reunion Day was a precursor to the closure of the school which took place a short time afterwards. Educationalists had obviously come to the conclusion that integrating disadvantaged children, such as those at this school, into mainstream schools was now in their best interests, and Tapton Mount School for the Visually Impaired has now been converted into a block of luxury residential flats. Whilst I'm not criticizing this decision, it just seems to be the way of the world these days, doesn't it, that just as something is working really well, then someone has to find a reason to change it. Perhaps it's my age, but I think there's a lot of common sense in the saying: 'If it's not broken, why try and mend it?'

However, let's get back to our friend Thomas Anderson who we left some time ago starting this newly built school in 1879. Whether it was due to his age or his dislike of the rigid regime at the school I'm not really sure, but he chose not to stay there for long. Instead, he decided to try and make a career out of singing. He had a very good baritone voice and, with the help of his family, managed to secure regular singing engagements in Morecambe.

During this stage of his life he met and married a local Sheffield lass, following which the happy couple were able to set up home in a small but respectable house in Oxford Road, just off Ecclesall Road in the rapidly growing town. Life, however, was never going to be easy for a blind man in those days, and following the birth of the couple's baby a year or so later, Thomas had to take to the streets in order to earn enough money to live on. This was obviously quite a blow for the independent-minded man who had always wanted to make his own way in life. However, with his singing engagements being mainly in the summer months in Morecambe and his family commitments requiring that he be in Sheffield as much as possible, he really had no other option.

Thomas Anderson

Being the kind of man he was, Thomas put his heart and soul into his new venture, and his golden voice together with his accomplished accordion playing was able to earn him enough money to live a very modest but comfortable life with his wife and child. As life moved on, unfortunately, street singing became his only source of income, but with his wife earning what she could, the couple managed to struggle into old age without complaint.

Although I've not been able to cover Thomas Anderson's life story in much detail, I thought it was worth including for two reasons.

Firstly, he was a Sheffield character who overcame, with great determination and a smile, the adversities of sudden blindness, the consequential inability to pursue his chosen career in the silver trade and his eventual decline into relative poverty. He was an inspiration to all Sheffield folk during his life-time.

Secondly, Thomas' brief stay in the Sheffield School for the Blind enabled me to give you an insight into this prestigious building and its history of Victorian and modern teaching attitudes which have spanned 117 years. It is unlikely that we shall see its like again.

POND STREET NORA

To many people in Sheffield, particularly in the 1950s, 60s and 70s, the tall, determined lady who propelled herself with huge strides through the city centre streets during the day and around the central bus station by night was quite a sight to behold. Her long, mousy coloured hair was usually tied back to expose a strong, lived-in face with high cheek bones and a larger than usual nose. Sadly, she appeared to be homeless as she was often found to be sleeping on benches or in doorways in and around Pond Street.

As a result of this, our lovely lady became known to all and sundry as Pond Street Nora and, because she was different, became the butt of ridicule and taunting remarks, particularly from children who, sadly, should have known better. To compound the public perception of her, Nora usually responded to any such taunting by letting rip a string of swear words at her aggressors, often chasing them away. Her long, powerful legs were often a match for the agile youngsters and, as her large feet clad in white plimsolls smashed down onto the footway closely behind their heels, jeering faces sometimes turned into frantic concern as a swishing carrier bag zipped close to their ears.

But, how realistic was this perception of Nora? Let us look back and see what she was really like.

It was 1942, and 19 year old Dolly Wattan was sitting in the driving seat of the overhead crane in the girder shop of Tommy Ward's Albion Works in Savile Street. Two sets of riveting hammers were banging away in constant torture, doing their best to deafen all those within ear-shot. In many cases they succeeded.

Amidst this deafening mayhem, Dolly did her best to accurately control her machine which was cutting up six inch steel plates, pausing only to scan the sea of activity below her. It was war time, and everything was wanted yesterday.

From her elevated position, Dolly was able to see a door open at the far end of the shop through which a tall, willowy figure in a dark boiler suit appeared. A fairly deep voice rose purposefully above the girder-room dim.

"Giz a fag then, love."

Nora had nipped out of the adjacent shell-turning shop for a few welcome minutes to beg a cigarette off one of the men sweating away in the girder shop.

At 21 years old, Nora Melbourne had managed to get a job at the local steelworks across the road from where she lived at 12 o'clock Street with her brother Charlie. Jobs weren't easy to find at that time, but Nora could hold her own with any bloke and was easily able to operate the capstan lathe which produced shells for the 25- pounders used on the front line.

Working in this environment amongst the steelworkers meant that she had to be able to cope with their rough ways, and she learnt a whole new vocabulary of straight-talking during the three or four years she worked there. The whole experience at Tommy Wards taught her never to give in to

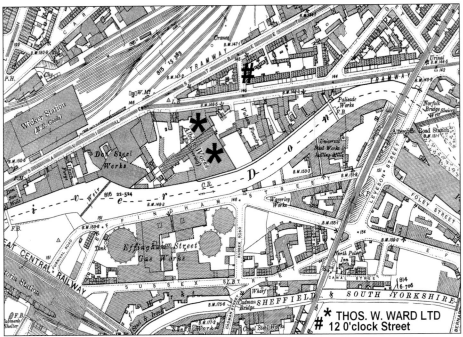

* THOS. W. WARD LTD
\# 12 0'clock Street

"Oh, that's my little 'un," said Nora casually. "She sometimes helps me on my rounds."

No more was said, and Dolly never did find out what Nora's daughter was called as her good friend refused the offer of a cuppa' and left a few minutes later to get on with her window cleaning round. In fact, she never saw the little girl again as it was only at holiday times that she helped her mother with the windows.

Strangely enough, Dolly did see Nora again not long afterwards whilst she was taking a stroll in her local recreation area just off Abbeyfield Road, not far from Burngreave. The locals knew this area as Abbeyfield Park in those days and it was amply provided with seats and a wooden shelter for its visitors to use. It was in this shelter that Dolly saw her friend sleeping rough on several occasions, and she wondered then if that was Nora's permanent residence for the time being. Her daughter, thankfully, was never with her, and was probably being cared for by friends and supported by the small amount of window cleaning money her mother earned.

It was not long after this time that Nora moved her 'residence' to the city centre, and in particular to Pond Street. It was during this period, in the late 1950s to early 1960s, that the local postman, David Mowatt, met her.

David was about 30 years old at the time and was one of three brothers who had shot to fame in the 1930s as being the first triplet boys to be born and survive in Sheffield. All three, David, Alister and Ian, are, in fact, now in their mid 70's and are living proof of the excellent and dedicated care

those who felt that they were better than she was (usually men) and never to be bullied. With this training, she became the person we know, and for those of us with this knowledge, we learnt to respect her.

After the war, Nora had to find another job but, with little employment available, she eventually set herself up as a window cleaner working in the Burngreave area of the city.

It was during that time that Dolly Wattan met her again. It was a pleasant, sunny morning in the mid 1950s and Dolly, who happened to live in Burngreave, was making herself a cup of tea having just finished her washing.

Suddenly, a friendly smiling face appeared at the kitchen window of her terraced house and was then immediately lost amidst an explosion of frothy white bubbles which slithered laughingly down the glass pane. Then, as if by magic, a long rubber blade sped horizontally across the streaky, white window leaving behind it a crystal clear view of that same smiling face again.

"My goodness," gasped Dolly. "It's Nora!"

Dolly ran outside and hugged her friend who she hadn't seen since those war years.

"How are you? It's lovely to see you again."

Before Nora could reply, a small cheerful face peered round the corner of the outside kitchen wall.

"Come on mam. I've finished my window."

The little face broke into a cheeky grin, than disappeared again as quickly as it had appeared.

Dolly looked at Nora questioningly, and whilst not wanting to pry into her friend's life, she was obviously interested in the auburn-haired little girl who momentarily had appeared from nowhere.

Pond Street in 1967

they were given in their birth-place, Nether Edge Hospital (now closed), all those years ago.

Postman David used to deliver letters in the Pond Street area and worked both day and night shifts. When working on nights, he did part of his shift at the Midland Station where the Newcastle-Sheffield-Bristol mail train arrived late at night and in the early hours of the morning.

The postmen called it the TPO (Travelling Post Office), and David and his colleagues spent an hour or more each night unloading and sorting bags of mail from the train, as well as sorting, bagging and tagging new post before loading it onto the train. It was a demanding job which required good organisation, efficient marking and acquired experience to ensure that the right post went into the right bags in the right carriage to arrive at the right destination at all times.

It was during these night shifts that David often encountered Nora, either sleeping on the forms in the bus station, or in the doorway of the Murco petrol station in Pond Street. She was hardened to this rough living which force of circumstance had imposed on her, but she never complained.

During the day when David was delivering post in the area, he often stopped and had a brief chat with her, and she rarely failed to come out with her favourite request:

"Giz a fag then, love."

Cigarettes were probably one of Nora's rare comforts and, despite their long term dangers (unknown in those days), they kept her going. What she did during the day in and around Pond Street is a little uncertain, but she always started off the day with a wash-and-brush-up in the ladies' toilets located down the long concrete stairway under the Pond Street Bus-Station platform.

Pond Street wasn't, however, the only city centre location she frequented. She was often seen striding past the Town Hall, along Fargate and down to the Hole in The Road where she was sometimes given a mug of tea by a kindly vendor or was given a cigarette by, of all people, Dolly Wattan who, with incredible coincidence, she met up with again.

The Duke of Darnall

Dolly actually worked at Leeson's Newsagents kiosk

in the 'Hole in the Road' for about fourteen years from 1969 to 1983 and, due to Nora's frequent visits there, was able to continue her on/off acquaintance with her friend.

It's worth mentioning at this stage that during her many jaunts around the city centre, Nora must have encountered another Sheffield character who was rather conspicuous by the way he looked and the way he acted. This person was a rather eccentric, smartly dressed, elderly gentleman who was known locally as the Duke of Darnall. He would often be seen strolling around wearing a bowler hat on his head, white gloves on his rather large hands, and white spats over his highly polished shoes. To complement this attire, this rather solemn looking man usually wore a white carnation in his lapel and always carried a stout walking stick which he used to great effect.

The primary example of this was his regular habit of trying to control traffic in the Waingate and Haymarket area of the busy city centre, despite no-one asking or wanting him to do so. Drivers and pedestrians alike were rather amused by his well-meaning antics which were dominated by confusing gestures made by waving his walking stick about. As far as I can recall, however, I don't think the local police were very impressed with this unofficial traffic cop on point duty.

Although I have no way of knowing whether or not Nora passed the time of day with the Duke when they met in the street, I like to think that they became friends.

However, let's get back to our story. Despite all her wanderings, Nora was still keen to get a job and pay her own way in life. She had been in her late forties when she encountered Dolly working at the newsagents, but a year or two later saw her working in the kitchens at the Claremont Nursing Home on Sandygate Road in a fairly posh area of town. To get there she caught the Lodge Moor bus from Pond Street which passed Claremont en-route. By another amazing coincidence, postman David Mowatt had been transferred to the Lodge Moor area to deliver his post, and he caught the same early bus as Nora.

125

Middlewood Hospital in the 1950s

It was a fine, but chilly, start to the day in Pond Street when David humped his bulky bag of letters and small parcels onto the bus that morning and manoeuvred his way to a convenient seat (the entrance/exit was at the back of the bus in those days). Suddenly, a familiar a voice rang out.

"I remember thee. Tha gave me fags in Pond Street, didn't tha?"

Startled, David looked up and there, sitting directly opposite, was none other than Nora.

"What are you doing on this bus, Nora?"

"I'm goin' to work of course. I've got a job at the Claremont Nursing Home in the kitchens."

"Good for you lass. I'm right pleased for you," beamed David.

Nora was never inclined to say too much, being a very private person, but both she and our friendly postman were pleased to have each other's company that morning and pass the time of day with a bit of friendly chit-chat and a quick fag during their journey.

Its uncertain how long Nora worked at Claremont as the hospital was taken over by another medical organisation some years ago, at which time all the hospital records relating to those who worked there were lost. She must have liked it there, however, as in her early fifties she managed to find similar work at the Middlewood Hospital for some time. She had always been an understanding person, and enjoyed helping others more than anything else. To work in a hospital amongst people less fortunate than herself seemed to appeal to her, probably because she was able to empathise with them.

Sadly, details of Nora's life beyond this point appear to have been lost in the fog of time and change and, being such a private person, she probably wouldn't have wanted us to search much deeper in any case. It's uncertain as to whether or not she's still alive, although opinion is that she is not. If she is, however, she would be in her late eighties now. The whereabouts of her daughter is also unknown. We can only presume she is still alive and would now be in her early sixties. I can only hope she approves of my decision to write about her mam.

It's clear to see, however, that Nora Melbourne, alias Pond Street Nora, had a difficult and challenging life which she coped with remarkably well. She was not gifted with beautiful looks by today's demanding standards, but she had an underlying beauty of character. Unfortunately, simply having a child out of wedlock in those days was considered to be a sinful act for which she was probably treated as a bit of an outcast. Today it is a common-place occurrence for which good financial and social support is always available for both the mother and child. How times have changed.

Nora was, nevertheless, a kind person, albeit very tough and single minded with a vocabulary which was imprinted on her mind during the war years at Tommy Wards Steelworks. This toughness probably helped her to cope with the unfair treatment she often received from society in the 1950s, 60s and 70s.

If I were to describe Nora in a brief sentence, I would say she was a rough diamond whose sparkling character was a delight to behold, but whose strength of mind was one to be wary of and respect. That was Nora Melbourne. God Bless her.

4

Well Known Sheffield Characters

This Section of the book follows the lives of three characters who will be well known to most readers.

They have all managed to climb the ladder of success from the bottom rung to the top by hard work and determination, and their stories make interesting reading.

Tommy Ward

Queen Victoria was in the sixteenth year of her 64 year reign when Tommy Ward was born in 1853. Bulk steel production in Sheffield was rapidly developing and companies such as Charles Cammel's Cyclops works, Thomas Firth and Sons' Norfolk works and John Brown's Atlas works were at the fore-front. Self employed craftsman with specialist skills, known as Little Mesters, were busily producing cutlery in their small workshops, whilst water-powered works in mills along Sheffield's rivers were producing quality cutting edge tools. Forgers and Smiths were able to earn between £1 and £2 a week if they were lucky, grinders were paid up to £2.50 and the hardworking burnishers and finishers (usually women) only managed to take home about 10 shillings (50d). On top of this, housing conditions for the working class were generally appalling, and poverty and sickness was at its peak.

It is within this backcloth of life that young Tommy experienced his childhood. He was fascinated with the huge, noisy steelworks that were dominating Sheffield's east-end, but he yearned to work in a more pleasant environment. It was with great pleasure and anticipation, therefore, that at the age of 13, he was able to begin his working life at a mill called the Walkley Bank Tilt in the beautiful Rivelin Valley on the western side of town.

Life for the young lad was, however, much harder than he had expected and he had to put in 12 hour shifts from 4-o'clock in the morning to 4-o'clock in the early evening. Let's join him and see how he went on.

When he first walked into the dimly lit stone buildings which formed the Walkley Bank Tilt, Tommy was somewhat taken aback by the dust, noise, and vibrations which seemed to enfold his whole body. He was barely a teenager, and the excitement of getting a 'real' job had led him to create an image of what to expect. After all, he was going to make farm tools out of steel, and that shouldn't be too difficult, should it?

The coke-fired forge in the corner of the first room he entered was burning fiercely, and the strong-armed workman bent over it was carefully withdrawing a glowing, red-hot steel bar with long handled tongues held firmly in his gloved hands. A few feet away, a huge wooden hammer with a wrought iron head was pounding a similar bar, held by a second workman, into a flat, slightly curved shape, thus creating deafening thuds each time it did so.

Disused water wheel-2004

127

It was, however, the constant repetition of the noise which Tommy found so mind blowing. As he looked more carefully, he could see that a huge wooden shaft, the diameter and length of a small oak tree, was part of the offending noise-producing machinery. Along with an assortment of iron tyres and gears attached to it, it rotated quickly and steadily to keep two hammers incessantly banging away. As if to say "hey, it's not all my fault," the shaft seemed to point to a hole in the stone wall through which an adjacent shaft passed. This shaft, to which was connected an enormous geared wheel, gleefully turned in unison with an equally large water wheel on the outside of the building. To the delight of this whole contraption of shafts, wheels and gears, water from an adjacent dam slopped and slurped into the ever thirsty 'pockets' of the outer wheel, keeping it rotating with a slow, but constant groaning of content.

"Clever stuff, this is," the young apprentice thought to himself. "All this power, banging and shaping caused by a drop of water. I think I might enjoy it here after all."

"Come on lad, stop thi gawpin'. I'll show thi rest of place and then get thi started."

Slightly flushed and taken aback by the blunt approach of the gaffer who suddenly appeared at his side, Tommy was shown to an adjacent room. There, a row of three

rotating grindstones screeched their annoyance in harmony as shaped and welded wrought iron and steel strips were cruelly pressed against their very hard surfaces by three determined looking grinders. The round stones threw up clouds of dust in protest, but their attackers carried on regardless.

"This is the grinding hull, lad, where me sickle and scythe blades are made. That first stone over there is used for rough grinding, then the blade's passed onto the second fella who does smooth grinding and then passed onto the third 'un who polishes it and gives it a reight sharp edge. I'll let thi try one o' stones out later on. In the mean time, tha can mash us all a mug o' hot tea to keep us goin'."

The poor boy heaved a sigh of relief at the last request. Looking at the hunched up figure of the first grinder, whose body was shaking with a racking cough whilst his tired,

bloodshot eyes tried to peer out through fine, grey dust which settled on his face, it was very obvious that this job was seriously unhealthy. Little did he realize that many a grinder failed to make it to the age of 40 in those days.

For twelve, long hard years Tommy worked in the forges in Rivelin Valley gaining a variety of skills and experience in tool making. During this extended apprenticeship, he had managed to put aside a small amount of his wages each week in order to try and achieve his dream of working for himself one day. Despite the long hours, poor conditions and hard work, the experience had beneficially hardened him to the long, tough working culture which existed in the mid to late1800's. This experience, combined with a natural enthusiasm and ambition to succeed and a fortunate small loan from a caring Aunt, enabled him, at the age of 25, to set up his own business as a coal and coke merchant with his 15 year old brother, Joseph, as his assistant.

It was with great pride, therefore, that on a beautiful spring day in 1875, Tommy and Joseph were able to stand outside number 39 Norfolk Street in the town centre and look proudly up at a sign which was attached to the building's second floor window.

"Well. What do you think, Joseph? That's us, T.W. Ward - Coal and Coke Merchants. I can hardly believe it."

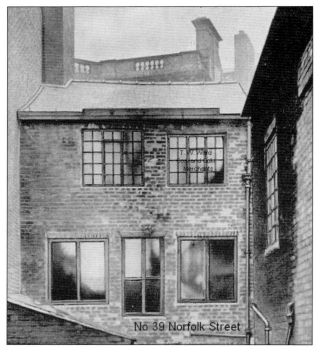

No 39 Norfolk Street

It was only a small room at number 39 that Tommy had rented as his office, but it was a start, and we all know the saying 'large oak trees from little acorns grow', don't we?"

As part of his business activities, Tommy regularly visited many of the cutlers' small forges which existed in the town in order to get orders for his coal and coke supplies. It was during these visits that he noticed the scrap steel plates that cluttered up their yards, these being the remnants of the plates from which knife blades had been punched.

To the cutlers, these scrap steel plates were simply a valueless nuisance, but to the quick minded Tommy Ward they were the beginning of his future huge empire. He knew that if the plates could be handled easily, he could buy them very cheaply and sell them for a good profit to the foundries at the city's steelworks.

Showing great initiative, he invented and patented a hydraulic press which crushed the plates into manageable bundles which were easily able to be transported to the foundries. Thus, as far as we are aware, he became the first Scrap Merchant in Sheffield, and, possibly, in the country.

Working sixteen hours a day, six days a week and now also employing his youngest brother Arthur, Tommy steadily increased his business. Within four years he moved to larger premises in the Corn Exchange and then, in 1888, to Fitzalan Square. By 1902, at the age of 49, he had built the huge Albion Works in Savile Street, the headquarters of Thos. W. Ward Ltd which still exists today. The Ward Group, which developed from these very humble beginnings into a multi-million pound industry, had offices throughout the country and was responsible for more then sixty subsidiary companies. Many of these were located in other countries around the world and resulted in the Group employing a staff of about 11,000 by 1971.

Albion Works

A STROLL ALONG RIVELIN VALLEY IN 1903

Whilst Tommy Ward worked almost non-stop on those six days a week building up his business, he sensibly enjoyed some recreation time on his day off.

Typical of this was probably a stroll along the Rivelin Valley, taking in the tranquillity and beauty of the area he loved, whilst at the same time re-kindling memories of his early working life in the area. Let's join him, shall we?

Such a stroll would likely start at the Corn Mill located adjacent to the meandering River Rivelin just beyond Rails Road. This imposing building, nestling amongst an old-world hamlet of houses and surrounded by mature trees, had two large water wheels, each of which drove three pairs of grindstones.

WATER-MILLS ON THE RIVELIN.

Rivelin P.O.
RIVELIN MILL.
UPPER COPPICE WHEEL.
SECOND COPPICE WHEEL.
THIRD COPPICE WHEEL.
PAPER MILL.
FRANK WHEEL.
WOLF WHEEL.
SWALLOW WHEEL.
PLONK WHEEL.
HIND WHEELS.
UPPER CUT WHEEL.
Glen Bridge.
NETHER CUT WHEEL.
HOLMEHEAD WHEEL.
LITTLE LONDON WHEEL.
ROSCOE WHEEL.
THE NEW DAM.
SPOONER WHEELS.
RIVELIN BRIDGE WHEEL.
WALKLEY BANK TILT.
MOUSEHOLE FORGE.
GROGRAM WHEELS.
Malin Bridge.
River Loxley.

The Corn Mill

Existing small dam on the original Corn Mill site

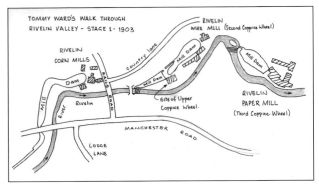

TOMMY WARD'S WALK THROUGH RIVELIN VALLEY - STAGE 1 - 1903

On a bright summer's day, the cheerful sun would send teasing streaks of light through the swaying branches of the towering trees so that they playfully made ever changing patterns on the dusty pathway on which Tommy was now walking. Although it was now the early 1900's, the more mature Thomas W. Ward would still have been enjoying these delights of nature, whilst also listening to the gentle

The Upper Coppice Dam and the old Packhorse Bridge

rumbling of the grind stones which softly and respectfully sent out their greetings as he strolled by.

About two hundreds yards down the valley, after crossing Rails Road and the quaint, stone-arch Packhorse Bridge which heralded in the next dam, the buildings of the Upper Coppice Wheel and the Second Coppice Wheel came into view. Upper Coppice was a wire mill at this time, whilst the adjacent buildings of the Second Coppice Wheel were busy making scythes and saws to the pounding 'music' of what would resemble a heavy-rock band these days. Tommy would have thus quickened up his pace as he strolled past the sparkling dam which kindly gave up its

Walk to the Second Coppice Wheel

water to the thirsty water-wheels driving the hammers and grindstones.

Around the next bend in the river, about another hundred yards downstream, the buildings of the Third Coppice Wheel appeared from behind the leafy trees which

The Wier approaching the Third Coppice Dam

The Third Coppice Dam in 2008

stood proudly to attention on the bank-side. Flag irises rose majestically through the surface of the water of the adjacent dam which, combined with the sparkling reflection of the blue and white summer sky above, looked more like a magical painting than the working-water of the people who laboured there. Although starting out life as a cutler's wheel with four troughs, this wheel was now a paper mill incorporating other buildings such as drying houses, a rolling store, stables and a cow shed. As with other wheels in this valley, it is obvious that this one was used as a home as well as a work place, with horses being the main mode of transport and locally produced milk ensuring the working family was fairly self-sufficient. Perhaps the young apprentice who worked here learning his trade became a travelling milk-boy along the valley first thing each morning, making a few extra bob for his gaffer?

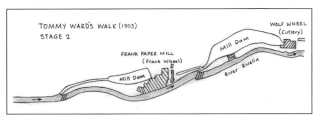

TOMMY WARD'S WALK (1903) STAGE 2

The dam of Frank Wheel was the next vision which shimmered enticingly to the wanderer beyond a further bend of the playful, meandering river. Around it, a coppice of tall, slender trees linked arms and shook their bushy, green heads as they discussed the weather and the day-to-day happenings which took place beneath them. The

Head goit entering the Frank Wheel Dam

The Frank Wheel Dam in 2008

assembly of stone buildings which emerged through this magical forest was also a paper mill, although in its hey-day, in 1815, its two owners paid £5-0-0 each in rent to the Lord of the Manor for the thirteen cutler's troughs which employed 14 or more men there. Sadly, the waterwheel was to stop turning within the next two years or so following the famous man's nostalgic stroll, as by 1905, the mill was only a silent, empty reminder of those magical days of yesteryear.

But, of course, Tommy wouldn't have known that as he soldiered on for another quarter of a mile to the Wolf Wheel

Approach to Wolf Wheel Dam

Wolf Wheel Dam in 2008

with one of the largest dams in the valley. The building itself housed nineteen troughs (with three grindstones in each), seventeen of which were devoted to the manufacturer of knives and two to the manufacturer of razors. It was common knowledge that Wolf Wheel had the largest single grinding room on the Rivelin which, with its huge iron water-wheel, was a feast of vision which Thomas W. Ward would particularly appreciate. He had just built his huge Albian Works housing the latest in technology, so this comparison between the 'biggest and best' of the old with the 'biggest and best' of the new, would have been a delight to this man who had experienced both. He would have realised, of course, that with the way technology was improving he was strolling along a valley of innovative water-powered engineering and manual skills that would probably be a valley of history within 25 years.

Nevertheless, this delightful summer's day was still his to enjoy, with many more wheels spread over the second half of his walk. As it was some distance to his next port of call, I think we can presume that he chose to rest a while at the next bend in the intoxicating water-way and have a welcome bit of snap. Of course, as Chairman and Managing Director of the Ward Group, we might presume that his snap would consist of a hip flask of mature port to wash down delicate strips of pheasant or wild boar. In practice, I suspect he actually had cold tea in the hip flask and tasty cheese sarnies to eat, more in keeping with the environment which he loved and the background from which he came.

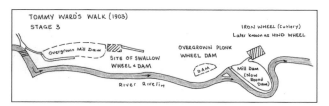

Approach to Swallow Wheel Dam

The Swallow Wheel Dam in 2008

The next two wheels, covering half a mile of sun-drenched waterway, were the Swallow Wheel and the Plonk Wheel, both originally accommodating cutler's troughs. Unusually at this time (it was 1903), they now existed only as silted-up dams overgrown with lush green grasses and weeds with no sign of the once busy grinding hulls.

The Round Dam in 2008 (Previously the Hind Wheel Dam)

The old Hind Wheel

In contrast, Hind Wheel (also known as Iron Wheel and now known as the Round Dam) was still turning away about 200 yards or so further down the valley. The huge, iron water-wheel (hence its name) serviced 8 cutler's troughs where grinding, smoothing and polishing of forged steel plates provided knives for the public of Sheffield. Its large Mill Dam, which stored the water for the wheel, was overlooked up the valley's northern embankment by the Rivelin Hotel and the adjacent cottages known as Albion Row which sat proudly high above the valley bottom. On the opposite (southern) side of the valley, a steep rise behind the Dam levelled out to where the three Hagg Lane Cottages stood in splendid isolation. Maybe some of the cutlers lived there? They certainly would have had a short but very tiring walk home at the end of a hard working day if they did.

It was another quarter of a mile to the Upper Cut Wheel, where a rough country lane (now Rivelin Valley Road) petered out just above its narrow, pear-shaped dam. The

The wier-head and approach to Upper Cut Dam

Ruins of old Upper Cut Wheel adjacent to Dam

well-trodden footpath linking the Iron Wheel with the Upper Cut Wheel nestled tightly between the burbling river and the happily swishing stream of supply water (which is

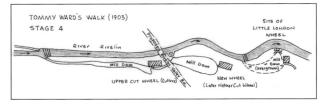
TOMMY WARD'S WALK (1903) STAGE 4

called a head goit) which kept the Dam's lazy waters topped-up as it released its contents onto the relentlessly turning water-wheel. Approaching the dam, whisps of white smoke curled out of the dark chimney projecting proudly above the stone roof which covered the extensive yet quaint buildings of the forge with its 8 cutler's troughs. Tommy would have recognised all too well the mixture of rasping and high pitched screeches which escaped from the open windows as the cutlers produced their fine Sheffield Steel wares.

Nether Cut Wheel

At the other end of the dam, not more than a hundred yards away, the grinders of Nether Cut Wheel (also called New Wheel by this time), were doing their best to out-do their neighbours in volume and quantity of noise. This, they managed to do, as it was scythes which were being ground here at this time, not cutlery.

The Nether Cut Dam in 2008

Along this section of the valley, the river meandered around three s-bends which originally had a mill hugging the bottom of each. During Tommy's summer walk however, the middle wheel of these three, Little London

Footbridge over the old sluice to Little London Wheel Dam

Wheel, was in ruins. Despite the beauty of the area, with dragonflies displaying their shimmering blue, green and gold wings with graceful sweeps over the still dam waters, the successful businessman must have felt pangs of regret at the gradual yet relentless decline of these wonderful local industries run by highly skilled, dedicated craftsmen. Not only was it these very people who gave him his early training and inspired him to create his global company, it was also they that gave the city its reputation as the world's finest producer of quality steel goods which were recognized internationally by the wording 'Made in Sheffield' stamped with pride on each item.

The raucous overhead call of an agitated rook, followed

quickly by the excited chattering of a pair of happy blackbirds playing follow-my-leader amongst a nearby cluster of bushes, broke the pensive silence around the tumbled ruins. Tommy was not a man to dwell on the past, and he would probably have quickened his pace a little, turning round the next bend in the meandering river to face the long tail of Holme Head Wheel dam. This dam, again

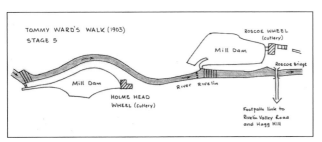

TOMMY WARD'S WALK (1903)
STAGE 5

ROSCOE WHEEL (cutlery)
Mill Dam
Roscoe Bridge
Mill Dam
HOLME HEAD WHEEL (cutlery)
River Rivelin
Footpath link to Rivelin Valley Road and Hagg Hill

Wier at the head of Holme Head Wheel Dam

Holme Head Wheel Dam in 2008

The site of Holme Head Wheel

The old Holme Head Wheel

in excess of 100 yards in length and shaped like a shrew's head, glistened in the blistering sun like a giant blue sapphire. Swallows were chasing the myriad of multi-coloured flying insects which hovered about just above the surface of the dam, whilst on a mischievous branch reaching out over the water, a startlingly blue kingfisher sat in its full majesty, patiently waiting to dive for an unsuspecting fish. This was the breathtaking beauty of the valley that Tommy so much enjoyed, and which gave him the peace of mind and relaxation that he needed away from the hectic and highly responsible working life he led.

133

Roscoe Wheel, with its huge dam about 150 yards in length and 50 yards across at its widest point, would have presented Tommy with his next environmental delight. Nestling amongst the hundreds of trees forming the Roscoe Plantation on the sloping hillside of Roscoe Bank, the dam and wheel seemed to be in a wonderland of their own.

The existing ruins of Roscoe Wheel

The old Roscoe Wheel

Amidst a chorus of birds singing and a playground of squirrels chasing each other up and down sturdy trunks and wildly swaying branches, the whole scene was reminiscent of Disney Land, with the reflections of the swathe of green-topped trees reflecting in the mirrored surface of the water to complete the magical tapestry.

"Where on earth could I go to get more wonderful views than these?", Tommy would probably have muttered to himself. "It really makes me appreciate life."

Such was the attractiveness of this area, that it was becoming a favourite place for weekend visitors to have their picnics, these being supplemented by the sale of 'hot water for teas' by the business minded tenants of the three Mill cottages standing adjacent to the wheel.

Even the quaint, stone-arched Roscoe Cart Bridge, which linked the wheel to a small hamlet at Clough Fields a short distance up the very steeply sloping valley side, was

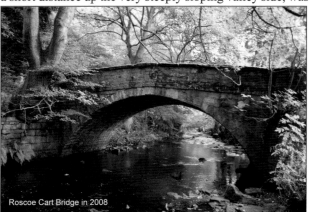
Roscoe Cart Bridge in 2008

a delight to behold. Its sturdy stone shoulders reached protectively over the sun-drenched river which resembled sparkling diamonds tumbling over each other as they raced to be the first to pass under the welcoming arch.

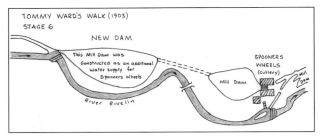
TOMMY WARD'S WALK (1903) STAGE 6
NEW DAM
This Mill Dam was Constructed as an additional water supply for Spooners Wheels
SPOONERS WHEELS (cutlery)
Mill Dam
Mill Dam
River Rivelin

Our good friend Thomas Ward would, by now, have completed three quarters of his journey and, no doubt, would have been feeling relaxed and stimulated by his nostalgic adventure. A quick swig of cold tea and a couple of sweet-cakes would have refreshed him for the final stage which would take him past the large New Dam adjacent to

Footbridge adjacent to the overgrown New Dam

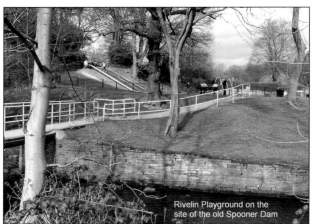
Rivelin Playground on the site of the old Spooner Dam

Rivelin Valley's Old Quarry. This dam was simply a feeder, via an underground stream, to the Spooner Dam 200 yards or so downstream which fed two imposing water wheels. Tommy would have been fascinated to watch their huge paddles gratefully gulping in the crystal-clear water from above before plunging down in a great arc to empty their contents into the dancing stream waiting patiently below.

Accompanying this spectacle, the great wheels slowly turned the shafts and gears of two grinding hulls to the music of powerful timbers flexing their muscles and a chorus of saws, files and knives trying to blend their different pitches in some form of harmony.

It would, indeed, have been music to an ex- Rivelin Valley apprentice, once again opening up many little

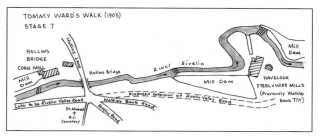

memory-doors of yesteryear. As he stood there, taking in the magic of the moment, his eyes would have rested on the

Rivelin Paddling Pool adjacent to the the site of the old Hollins Bridge Dam

Rivelin Bridge Corn Mill (later renamed Hollins Bridge) in the distance, behind which proudly stood the old stone arch from which the mill took its name.

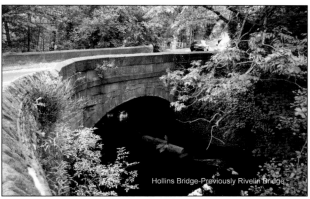

Hollins Bridge-Previously Rivelin Bridge

As he slowly walked past the busy mill, recollecting that in many years past it had been used for grinding fenders, cutlery and even optical glass, Tommy's heart must have skipped a beat as he realized that a few hundred yards further on, the winding river would make a dramatic s-bend turn around the very forge at which he first started his working life.

Havelock Dam in 2008
Previously Walkley Bank Tilt Dam

The Walkley Bank Tilt had, however, now become the Havelock Steel and Wire Mills, with wire drawing being its main function. The dam was a little over-grown in parts, but the good old water-wheel was still turning. Little did the nostalgic gentlemen realize that this dam would be one of only four dams along the Rivelin Valley which would still be preserved a century or so later. Fishermen sit on its bankside now, and the mill buildings themselves have disappeared to make way for a car park. Indeed, Tommy wouldn't at that time have known what impact the motor car would really have in the future, as they had only made their appearance on the streets three years previously.

The penultimate dam on this, by now, quite tiring walk, was about 200 yards long and provided water for the huge

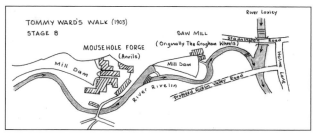

The grand entrance to the Mousehole Forge complex

The Mousehole Forge buildings in 2007

The old Mousehole Forge and Dam

135

Mousehole Forge complex which utilized four large waterwheels. These wheels provided the energy for driving two forge hammers, the furnace bellows and a heavy grindstone, all of which were required to produce the iron anvils for which it became famous. Although called a forge, it was more akin to the industrial works with which Tommy was now familiar, and the heavy pounding of the hammers was as imposing as that heard in his metal-breaking yards in Savile Street. Nevertheless, he marvelled at the size, complexity and efficiency of the working hamlet, and probably wondered to himself whether this too would suffer the fate of some of the smaller forges which had already become only a memory.

As he stood with his back to the huge cast-iron gates of this complex, a relatively small Saw Mill only a stone's throw away beckoned him over to complete his wonderful day out. This mill, originally known as the Grogram Wheels (the Groggy to those who worked there), had the benefit of

The old Grogram Wheels

two water wheels, one of which had the honour of being the largest wheel on the River Rivelin. This was now 'loaned' to the Mousehole Forge to drive its furnace bellows when one of its wheels was required to be closed down to conserve water for its remaining forge wheels. Tommy would have noticed the massive iron pipe skirting the Grogram dam which linked the two works for his purpose, probably acknowledging that progress inevitably means more intrusion into the landscape as demand for steel products continued to rise.

So, as the 50 year old industrialist rested by the last forge, the River Rivelin gushed gleeful by into the equally excited river which had been rushing down Loxley Valley eager to meet its sister. This reminded him how close he was to his siblings and how much they depended on each other in his early days. His brother Joseph had joined him at the beginning of his business career whilst his youngest

The converging of the rivers Rivelin and Loxley

brother, Arthur, had joined him four years later in 1882. Families are important, he thought, as he let the tranquil sound of the rippling waters take him back in time for a few moments.

As he pondered over his life so far, he felt fairly pleased with what he'd achieved, although he always wanted to do more. Little did he know that within the next fifty years his company's value would increase one-hundred fold, with a turnover of £330,000 in 1903 increasing to £33,000,000 in 1953. Employee numbers were also destined to rise tenfold during that period from 1100 to 11,000, and two world wars would utilize his company's resources and skills to the utmost.

I think it would be interesting at this stage to take a look at the Tommy Ward operations which developed and assisted the war effort over this period. His scrap steel recovery and supply activities, for example, provided 1000 tons of much needed steel a day to the country's hungry steelworks during the first world war. Other significant activities which were vital to the efficient operation of the country during this period and which promoted Tommy Wards to a major player on the domestic scene in general included such activities as Ship salvage, breaking and dismantling; Works dismantling; Railway line purchase and redistribution; Iron and steel production; Quarrying and road material supplies; Portland cement supplies; Construction and maintenance of roads, runways and railway sidings; and Reconditioning and maintenance of machine tools.

A particularly important achievement was that relating to the company's huge war-time task of moving and reinstalling the hundreds of machine tools and ancillary equipment used at the many plants of the nation's aircraft factories. In order to make such vital plants less vulnerable to enemy bombing, the government had decided to move them all en-bloc to secret sites, a task which was given to Tommy Ward's company. Lord Beaverbrook, Minister for Aircraft Production in 1940-41, described the successful venture at that time as "the most gigantic of its kind in history".

We could go on, as the company's achievements under Thomas Ward's leadership and guidance were seemingly endless. However, let us conclude our story by mentioning just two more achievements for which the great man was well known.

Firstly, and most gratifyingly for him, was his election to the office of Master Cutler in 1913, Sheffield's premier accolade for its industrialists. This recognition by his peers was probably the highlight of his working life.

Secondly, on a more humorous note, when horses were requisitioned nationally by the government during the First World War for use by the armed forces, Tommy needed to quickly find an alternative to pull the company's heavy wagons and castings which, up to that time, had been the duty of several dray horses. So, what did he do? He found an elephant. Lizzie the elephant became a well known Ward

employee in 1914, much to Tommy's delight and to that of those who lived and worked around Savile Street at that time.

Thomas W. Ward didn't, unfortunately, live to see the Second World War, as he passed away in 1926 at the age of 73. He had requested that he be buried in Crookes Cemetery under a tree overlooking the Rivelin Valley when his time came. It is only befitting, therefore, that we have told his story around this beautiful location which encompassed the exciting memories of his earlier years and his subsequent recreational visits there as he grew older.

He was a remarkable Sheffield man who started life at the bottom of the heap, who always looked forward, and who, with sheer grit and determination, made his way to the top. His contribution to Sheffield and the country as a whole was enormous, and he is remembered with great pride. After all, he was a Sheffielder, wasn't he?

J. G. Graves

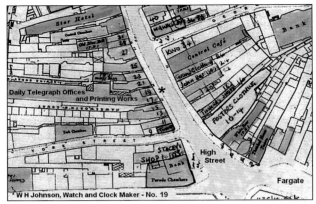

W H Johnson, Watch and Clock Maker - No. 19

Most people in Sheffield will be familiar with the name Graves. Some will associate it with the city's largest park in the Meadowhead and Norton area, while others will immediately think of the Graves Art Gallery which is housed in the Central Library in the middle of town. The Graves Trust Houses will also spring to mind for many people, particularly those who have enjoyed the benefits of living in them. We will have a more detailed look at all these associated links to John George Graves shortly.

However, before we do so, let's go back in time and see just who this man is and what influences in his life resulted in him being acknowledged as probably the most generous benefactor that Sheffield has ever known.

It was 1866 when baby John popped his head out into the world with a gusty cry. Although the rolling landscape of rural Lincolnshire where he was born was a pleasant place in which to spend his infancy, his parents eventually moved to Batley (which lies between Leeds and Huddersfield) where the youngster went to school. During these formative years, he developed a fascination with clocks and watches. In particular, taking them to pieces to see how they worked was always a challenge and a delight

to him, particularly if they still worked after he had put them back together again.

Being an adventurous sort of chap, however, once he had finished school he decided he would like to move to an exciting industrial town where everything was happening. His parents probably also had a say in the matter, but regardless of whose decision it was, the young teenager, now 14 years old, arrived in Sheffield looking for work. By a stroke of good fortune, which everybody deserves once in their life, a vacancy for an apprentice was being advertised at a well-known watchmaker's shop in town. John decided to apply for the post, and it was with great delight that he received a request to pop in for an interview.

It had been raining that morning when a rather nervous John Graves made his way across the slippery, cobblestoned road surface towards the rather imposing shop front of William Henry Johnson, Watch and Clock Maker at number 19 High Street. With its well stocked window display, the shop was sandwiched between the front entrance to the Sheffield Daily and Weekly Telegraph's Offices and Printing works at number 17, and John Thompson's neat little tailor's shop at number 21. The sudden ding of the bell over the doorway which rang out as the young job-seeker tentatively entered the premises didn't help to calm his nerves at all, and was in sharp contrast to the rather soothing and intriguing mixture of ticking noises which engulfed the shop interior.

"Can I help you, young man?"

The elderly gentlemen who was sitting behind the highly polished counter at the far end of the shop had a magnifying glass cupped to his right eye, and was obviously the owner of the shop. However, his apparent reluctance to move, other than raise his head and speak, was a little disconcerting to the anxious teenager.

"Excuse me, sir," John blurted out. "I'm here for an interview with Mr Johnson."

It was at this stage that the shop owner seemed to spring into life.

"Ah. You must be master Graves. You look a bit younger than I expected. I hope you're not one of those layabouts that are here today and gone tomorrow, because it takes seven years to learn the trade properly as an apprentice, you know."

"Of course not, Mr Johnson, sir. I love working with clocks and watches. I'd stay as long as you needed me."

The watchmaker's sharp blue eyes seemed to twinkle as they peered penetratingly into John's honest face whilst the young man spoke eagerly at length of his experience and interest in clocks and watches. A short period of silence then followed, during which time John's heart seemed to beat louder than anything that the mischievous clocks around him could muster. Eventually, after what seemed to be an age, Mr Johnson slowly stood up, extended his hand and spoke the words which the 14year-old was so desperate to hear.

"The job's yours, John Graves, if you want it. I don't pay much while you're learning, you understand, but I can guarantee you the best experience in the business. You can start today if you wish."

Shocked, but overjoyed by the instant decision, the excited youngster wasn't really sure whether to laugh or cry. Regardless of which he did, this was the beginning of a long apprenticeship which he was looking forward to with great enthusiasm and anticipation.

Although seven years training was a very long time, even for someone who loved his job as John did, he stuck at his task on a very modest wage with great determination and acquired considerable knowledge and skills in the process. By the time he reached 21 years old, however, the young man felt that it was time to move on in the world and possibly develop a business of his own so that he could try and make a contribution to society. Mr Johnson, recognising the ability that his ambitious employee had developed, did not want to stand in the way of his future progress. It was with sadness and pride, therefore, that the two watch and clock makers bade each other farewell in the spring of 1887.

Success for John in his endeavour to go-it alone was, however, easier said than done. For the next two or three years he worked long hours from home, both selling and repairing clocks and watches for customers he'd canvassed by knocking on doors while walking round the growing town for hours on end. Showing great determination and patience, his hard work was eventually rewarded and his reputation as an honest and knowledgeable trader brought him more and more custom.

By the age of 24, he had developed such a good and reliable customer base that he was able to open a small shop on the corner of Furnival Street and Porter Street, opposite the Crimean War Memorial at Moorhead. It was a good location for this new, young entrepreneur as Moorhead was a centre of transport activities. It was not only the terminus for the horse-tram services to Nether Edge and Heeley, it was also awash with horse-drawn taxicabs. John used to love to watch people of all shapes and sizes, both rich and poor, bustling around like ants on their respective journeys or simply resting a while in the adjacent tramway waiting rooms.

Moorhead about 1900

Across the main road, where Pinstone Street began, the huge furnishing and drapery store of T. & J. Roberts, which opened in 1862, stood proudly between Carver Lane and Cambridge Street. Boasting 200 employees and 3 acres of floorspace, Roberts Brothers, as it was known, attracted

Roberts Brothers Store

customers from all walks of life due to the availability of its huge range of products. One particularly interesting claim which the store made was that it was able to completely furnish a house at a cost that would suit all sections of the population. Its four all-in price levels of £75, £125, £175 and £235 for this complete furnishing service proved to be very attractive to customers.

It was, however, the lonely figure of an old woman who sat at the bottom of the war memorial from dusk to late evening that intrigued John the most. History tells us that the memorial was erected in 1863 to commemorate the memory of sailors and soldiers from Sheffield who died in the war with Russia, and rumour has it that this lonely woman started sitting there as a much younger lady about that time, possibly having lost a loved one in the fighting on the front line.

But, you might ask, why did she still sit there? She was, in fact, a very well known character of the time known as Hot Taties, a seller of hot roasted potatoes. These delicacies were very popular with Sheffield folk any evening of the week, particularly in cold weather, and were often the only hot daily

Hot Taties

meal that some of the poorest members of society were able to afford at that time.

On a winter's evening, Hot Taties would usually be seen sitting close to the rails of the monument on a hard wooden seat under which a bucket of fresh potatoes would be kept. On the coldest and wettest of nights, a small portable lath and canvas shelter provided her with some protection from the elements, whilst a small, glowing brazier, on which sat a battered, open oven, gave her some warmth as her potatoes were roasting.

It was, however, her appearance which also interested John. Her stern, almost tragic looking face usually peered out from under a hat that looked more like a woollen bag pulled well down over her ears, whilst her hunched up body was draped in green gingham shawls and wraps which almost engulfed the tattered old coat she was wearing.

The little lady's most famous and recognizable feature, however, was her shrill, piping voice which called out with regular monotony, advertising her wares.

"Hot Taties. Hot Taties."

This cry, which cut through the cold air with ease, enticed scores of hungry customers to give up their odd coppers for a hot roasted potato or two each evening. A small salt box at the side of the oven was available for them to dip their potatoes in, whilst her tatie-can on the footpath beside her always welcomed in the falling coppers with a ding of delight. There was many an evening, in fact, when young John Graves was such a customer, although I suspect that on many occasions it was his desire to help the lady rather than to sample her hot potatoes that influenced his purchase.

During the early years that John was at his shop at Moorhead, he gradually developed the idea of not only repairing and selling clocks and watches there but also of giving his customers the opportunity of buying other household goods as well. He expanded on this by handing out leaflets listing his products which customers could read in the comfort of their own homes before buying or ordering items of their choice. Furthermore, he encouraged customers to choose to pay for their goods over an agreed time period if they so desired, thereby allowing less well-off Sheffield folk to buy things they would otherwise be unable to afford. This idea gained momentum like wildfire, and in 1897 J.G.Graves moved his innovative business into

a large, stone building at the corner of Division Street and Holly Street which had been built thirty years earlier as the offices of the Sheffield Water Company.

This move heralded the official beginning of what is reputed to be the country's first mail-order company, pioneered by this enthusiastic and gifted Watchmaker and Jeweller, who by now was 31 years old. Division Street was now the headquarters of an organization which employed 2000 people, many of whom being agents who ran catalogues from which goods were selected and paid for in monthly instalments. This mail-order system totally revolutionised shopping for hundreds of thousands of Sheffield people, and was as significant then as on-line internet shopping is now.

It is interesting to have a brief look, at this point in our story, at how successful John Graves' business really was. A newspaper advertisement in the local press at that time showed that he was receiving a massive ten to fifteen thousand orders every single week at his Division Street headquarters. A key selling point in his business which

related to these orders was that every item ordered was delivered with a guaranteed promise that if the customer was not fully satisfied with any product received, it could be returned at the expense of the company. This unique promise, which in later years also became the corner-stone of every other mail-order company which was formed nation-wide, was a brilliant piece of marketing initiative introduced by John Graves and was some indication of the sharpness and agility of his mind.

A few examples of the types and cost of products included in the J.G. Graves mail-order catalogue are shown below and make very interesting reading.

Despite the enormous size of the company's headquarters on Division Street, demand for John Graves's sale-or-return products grew so rapidly that additional storage space was soon necessary. He decided, therefore, to have new, larger accommodation built on Western Bank opposite the large University of Sheffield complex which was being slowly built at the time. By 1903, two years before the University was completed, he opened his grand

University of Sheffield

new headquarters, which he named 'Westville', and within a year he had moved his whole business there, vacating the Division Street block in 1904.

During this period of building and change, the Surrey Music Hall had closed down in Surrey Street and, by 1903, J. G. Graves had also established a drapery, tailoring and carpet warehouse there to ease the burden caused by a shortage of space.

The country's first mail-order company was now doing a roaring trade at its posh Westville headquarters, which is occupied today by Sheffield University's Octagon Centre, and life for John G. Graves was most certainly rosy. Apart from his undoubted business success, he had also been successful in love as he had met and married his wife during those hectic years at Division Street. Shortly after settling into his new building, by which time he was able to relax a little and delegate much of the running of his empire to his highly competent managers, the happy couple were gifted with their one and only child, a beautiful baby daughter who they named Ruth.

John was 39 years old at this stage, the year was 1905, and King Edward VII had succeeded his mother Queen Victoria on the throne of England. He was now a rich man, but had always held the view that if you made money, then it was best to use it where it could do most good. To date, he had ploughed most of his earnings back into the business in order for it to succeed. This had resulted in him being able to employ 3000 Sheffield people at its peak, at a time when life was hard and jobs were scarce to come by. With some of his wealth he had also gradually fed his hobby of collecting paintings, mostly 19th century English landscapes. He went on to amass about three thousand of these over his lifetime.

However, he was now wanting to do something more positive to help others, and with this in mind he successfully became a city councillor, with the welfare of all Sheffielders being uppermost in his mind. He was genuinely a caring man and this quality was evidenced in his early years when, shortly after arriving in the city, he witnessed mob attacks on Salvation Army members who had no other thoughts but to help people less fortunate than themselves. John George Graves decided to join this Army himself, and he adopted its principles of selflessness, generosity and fair play for the rest of his life.

Life hadn't all been a bowl of roses for the mail-order boss, however, and a particular incident, which you may find of interest, occurred shortly after his company had moved to Western Bank. This proved to be a good test of his patience, determination and sense of fair play.

It was 1904, and JG (as he was commonly known) was spending about £1000 every month on postage, with the post office collecting hundreds of parcels and letters from his warehouse daily in order that they could be delivered. This very satisfactory and efficient arrangement with the post office had worked well for many years until a new Post-Master had been appointed at the Head Post Office at the Junction of Commercial Street and Haymarket. Despite much resistance and argument from John Graves, the officious Post-Master demanded that all the mail had to be brought to him in future rather than it be collected.

"That is totally unreasonable," retorted the rather irate businessman when this demand was imposed on him. "I'm

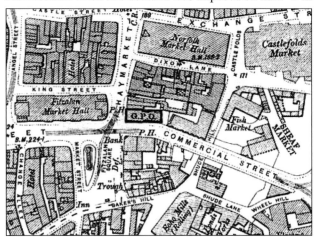

not in the transport business. That's why I use the post office service. In fact, I'm their best customer."

Suitably aggrieved, and thinking that this was officialdom gone mad, he gathered together two hundred of his employees and explained the situation to them.

"Listen here, folks. I'm a fair man, but I don't like this new, unreasonable attitude taken by the Post-Master. To make a point, we'll all take a parcel or two each down to the post office and queue up like everyone else. This should make him see the error of his ways."

At 5-o'clock the next evening, the two hundred employees, complete with their parcels, boarded a fleet of horse-drawn cabs, buggies and buses which proceeded down West Street, Church Street and High Street before turning into the rather narrow Haymarket where they all parked to allow their passengers to alight. After alighting, the Graves employees formed an orderly, but extremely lengthy queue within and outside the post office in order that their parcels could be paid for and posted in accordance with post office rules.

Needless to say, due to the narrowness of the streets in the city centre and the large number of horse-drawn vehicles standing in such streets, total traffic grid-lock occurred, with most of the new electric trams which were now running on Sheffielders streets being caught up in the chaos. The massive and unmanageable congestion within the post office and the long queues outside were also an embarrassment to the Post-Master, and the whole situation caused much concern and annoyance to the travelling public.

Shoppers were beginning to pour out of the adjacent Fitzalan and Norfolk Market Halls to see what the commotion was all about, and others walking in the thronged streets stopped in their tracks to question the situation.

"What are all these horses, cabs and buses doing here mam? Are they having a race or something?"

"Has somebody important arrived? Is it the King, or what?"

"They say someone's been murdered. I hope its no-one we know."

And so the rumours and questions spread as the biggest event in town for some years engaged the public's minds. But did it do the trick? Did the Post-Master take notice? I don't think he really had any choice, do you?

To the relief of all concerned, normal-service was resumed thereafter, and JG's mail was once again collected as before. Needless to say, this was not just one-upmanship being practised by the mail-order boss. He just wanted fairness and common sense to prevail.

To get back to our interesting story of this good man, we now have to follow his career in local politics, in an area where his knowledge, experience, wealth and opportunity enabled him to pursue his dreams of helping the citizens of Sheffield in a positive and everlasting way.

Following many years as a city councillor, John G. Graves was made an Alderman of the city in 1925 (an honorary position bestowed on him in recognition of his dedicated services), and the following year, at the age of 60, he was appointed as Sheffield's Lord Mayor. He had already reached the pinnacle of his profession as a business man, and now he had been honoured as the city's top public servant. He was now able to do something positive, and began using his accrued wealth in many wonderful ways.

With his knowledge of the city and its workings, he was acutely aware that opportunities for the average Sheffielder to access and enjoy recreational and leisure facilities were very limited. With this in mind, he firstly bought and

presented to the city the beautiful Graves Park, the former gardens and estate of Norton Hall. In subsequent years, he bought and gave other areas of beauty for the use and benefit of Sheffield's citizens including Concord Park, Blackamoor, Ecclesall Woods, Forge Dam and Tinsley

Entrance to Graves Park

View over Blackamoor

Forge Dam

Playing Fields. Even a small parcel of land at the corner of Manchester Road and Lygate Lane in Crosspool, formerly part of Lydgate Hall grounds, was bought by him and presented to the city in order that the trees there could be preserved.

Education and learning were also high on JG's list of access needs which he felt should be more freely available to the public. With this in mind, he proposed the building of the Central Library and Graves Art Gallery in Surrey Street in the centre of town, and provided one third of the cost of such a venture (£90,000) from his own money. Such was the importance and esteem in which this venture was held, that the Duchess of York (later to become Queen Elizabeth, the Queen Mother) honoured the city by personally opening the building following its completion in 1934. A brief tour round the well-stocked Art Gallery by her Highness would have revealed that hundreds of the paintings on display had in fact been donated by John Graves from his own collection.

Its strange, isn't it, when you look back and realize that this magnificent public building, which is now used daily by thousands of Sheffield folk, is located on the site of the very popular Surrey Music Hall which, before its demolition in 1930, also hosted J. G. Graves' large carpet warehouse. I suppose it's fitting in a way that a site which once was visited by thousands of Sheffield folk for the purpose of entertainment and, later, carpet sales, should now be used again for entertainment and learning, with books on shelves and pictures on walls to look at instead of people on stages and carpets on floors. Such is the wonder of change!

Our John, as you have probably gathered by now, was quite unique as a Sheffielder. His concern for his fellow citizens knew no bounds, and the more money he earned, the more he gave away.

In all, it has been estimated that he gave away over £1 million to Sheffield causes (which is about £40 million at today's prices), included in which was the funding to establish Sheffield University's Student Union. Part of the Union building is still known as the Graves Building.

Of particular concern to this generous benefactor, however, was the plight of the poor and the elderly at this time. Unemployment was still high in the 1930's, and many Sheffield folk were struggling to keep a roof over their heads. With this problem in mind, he founded the Graves Trust, into which he poured much of his wealth. This trust has provided, and continues to provide today, small communities of houses which have benefited thousands of poor people all over the city. Known by everyone as Graves Trust Houses, their highly subsided rents have meant that those people who are most vulnerable have been able to enjoy the privilege of calling somewhere their home, a privilege which most of us take for granted. This legacy is, perhaps, the one which truly demonstrates John George Graves' deep understanding of people's needs.

Although we have only skimmed the surface of this great man's life, we can see that his contribution to the life and welfare of our city is immense. As we have already acknowledged, he wasn't born in Sheffield, but as an adopted son he probably did as much if not more than any other person has for its citizens. To quote the Star newspaper in 1997 on the occasion of the death of his daughter, Ruth, at the age of 92, "His catalogue of gifts to the city of Sheffield reads like a shopping list for the ideal town."

But what became of the huge, innovative mail-order company that he built up? Well, after John Graves' death in 1945 at the age of 79, it was transferred to another well-known mail-order company known as Great Universal Stores. Even this event was strangely linked to the first large store in Division Street that young John Graves occupied in 1897, as he had aptly called it The Universal Supply Warehouse. Perhaps there was some link. Who knows? What we do know, however, is that John George Graves will never be forgotten, and as far as Sheffield folk are concerned, he was undoubtedly a good 'un, wasn't he?

Graves Park entrance

Constance Grant
QUEEN OF DANCE

The year was 1905 in the small, front bedroom of a modest sized terraced house in Khartoum Road which nestled comfortably just below the bottom entrance to the Botanical Gardens in the district of Ecclesall. A French dressmaker and her husband, a Scottish carpenter by the name of Grant, were anxiously awaiting the arrival of the local midwife. Mrs Grant was expecting her seventh child, nearly a quarter of a century after her first had been born. During that intervening period, Queen Victoria had ended her sixty four year reign, her son Edward had taken over as King and her Grandson George (later to become King George V) had married Princess Mary.

But of course, the anxious couple were not thinking

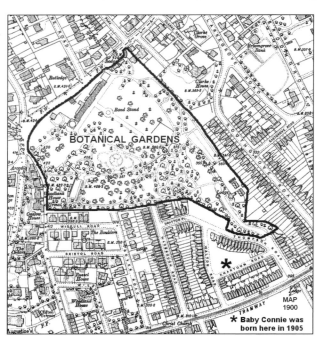

about the past, only the present.

"I think we'll make this the last one, lass," her husband said kindly as he saw how tired his wife had become on this occasion.

"We've already got six beautiful children, and this one'll make seven, so I think we've done our bit now, don't you?"

The experienced mother managed a wry grin and a nod of her head amidst a longer than usual contraction which caused her to cry out slightly, sending her husband into a fit of anxiety and concern.

"I wish that woman would make haste and get here. She must know that you've not got long to go, mustn't she?"

There was, of course, no need to worry. The kind, experienced midwife had timed things to perfection for the first six children, and this latest one would be no exception. This baby was, however, determined to have its full allotted time in comfort, and it extended its warm stay inside its mother for several more long, tedious hours.

Knowing what we know now of course, the new parents wouldn't have expected any different, as the tiny bundle of energy which finally arrived, a strikingly pretty, dark-haired baby girl, started life as she meant to carry on: determined, self-willed, strong and self-assured.

"By-gum lass!" exclaimed the overjoyed carpenter. "She might be little, but she's got a pair of lungs on her that would deafen an army."

And so began the life of Constance Grant, known as Connie to her family and as the Mighty Atom to her friends and peers later on in life.

Constance had a happy childhood and, being the youngest of seven children, had older brothers and sisters who were always on hand to help and care for her when the need arose. Her hardworking parents had to struggle to make ends meet, however, with her mother taking in as much sewing and dressmaking as possible whilst her father

Botanical Gardens in mid to late 1800s

earned what he could as a carpenter. The young girl rarely went without, mind you, and was fortunate enough to live close to the beautiful and intriguing Botanical Gardens. She spent many an hour with her family there, chasing squirrels across the well kept lawns, talking to the colourful parrots in the large aviary, and even throwing pretend buns to the two pretend brown bears which had lived in the deep bear-pit at the top end of the gardens forty years earlier.

It is interesting to note that these wonderful gardens, which have recently been restored to their former glory, formed Sheffield's first public park when it was opened in

The Botanical Gardens in 2007

1836, although it was not until the gardens were transferred to the Sheffield Town Trust in 1898 that the public could enter without payment. Even then, uniformed commissionaires guarded the garden's two entrances to ensure that no 'undesirable' people could slip in unnoticed. Although the Grant family were certainly not undesirables, it was always left to mum to make sure that everything was in order before they set off for their excursion into the park.

"Now then children," she would say. "I want you all to be spanking clean and tidy before we go. Remember, there'll be no shouting or bad language allowed and Connie, please try and walk like a young lady occasionally instead of skipping and dancing around everywhere."

It wasn't just that Mrs Grant liked her children to be polite and well behaved when they were out and about, the rules of entry to the gardens were designed to discourage certain sections of the public. I've reproduced one such rule below to give you some idea of what I mean:

'No person of notoriously bad character shall enter… nor any person in a state of intoxication, or suffering from any contagious infection or loathsome disease, or so dirty in clothes or person as to be an annoyance to the public.'

I don't think they'd get away with such rules nowadays, do you?

With regard to young Connie's fantasy game at the bear pit, this was based on local knowledge handed down over the years which identified that bears had lived there from the day the pit was built in 1836. It was about thirty four years later in 1870, however, when a tragic incident took

Modern-day bear in the Botanical Gardens bear pit

place. It would appear that a large pole with branches and platforms rose up the centre of the pit, and that children threw bread and buns onto these platforms to encourage the bears to climb up. Sadly, according to a letter sent to a newspaper at that time, a nurse had held a child over the railings to get a better view of the bears which, either deliberately or accidentally, had clawed the poor infant to death. That incident had, understandably, heralded the removal of the animals from their place of public entertainment.

It is unlikely that little Connie knew about this tragic incident as her excursions into the gardens were always ones of happiness and delight. In particular, she loved to skip down the wide, five hundred foot long promenade path from the glass domed conservatories to the magnificent circular fountain which was always an attraction to both adults and children alike. The glistening waters which tumbled into the crystal clear pool below were always a temptation for tiny little fingers to play in, and this little bundle of energy was certainly no exception. Strangely enough, this fountain was replaced by the Crimean War Memorial in 1961 which itself had been removed from its original position at Moorhead, although as part of the recent restoration works during the period 2001 to 2006, a fountain has once again been established there.

However, let's continue with Constance Grant's early life. The young child's favourite activity, as we have gathered, was dancing. She never seemed to stand still, and any opportunity to exercise her twinkling feet was always grasped with enthusiasm, whether inside her home, out in the street or anywhere else for that matter.

At the important age of five, however, her happiness was suddenly shattered by the unthinkable; she had to go to school.

Constance hated school. You had to sit at a small, wooden desk and try and learn things. You couldn't talk, sing or even laugh in class, or the stern-looking teaching lady would send you to the headmistress for punishment. And worst of all, you had to walk quietly everywhere, and never run, skip or dance about. 'It must be worse than being in prison in here', the unhappy little girl thought to herself at the end of her first day. 'I'm going to leave school as soon as I can.'

It was, of course, to be another nine years before the determined young girl got her wish. During that time, however, she decided not to let the grass grow under her twinkling feet and began to pursue her interest in dancing more rigorously. With her older brother Ernest, to whom she was very close, she spent many evenings and weekends dancing at the Greystones Ballroom on Ecclesall Road, this inspiring her to follow her love for dancing more seriously.

By the age of 14, and still only four feet and a bit in height, the little bundle of energy and ability had made a decision. It was time to leave school and, without a qualification to her name, she had to find employment. As a natural and enthusiastic worker in the areas she enjoyed, being unemployed was not really an option for her. The only opportunities available at that time, however, were a job as a buffer-girl in the silver and cutlery trade, or as a tea-girl in a solicitor's office. It was no surprise when she chose the latter.

For someone who never liked school, Constance had a very sharp mind. She realised that if she could progress in the solicitor's office and thereby earn and save money for a year or two, she could couple this with early, before-work dancing lessons. This she did under the excellent tuition of a local, well-known dancing teacher called Madame Enderby.

By the end of the first year at work, she had shown such enterprise that she had become an articled clerk, with a little more money going into her wage packet. More importantly to her, however, was the fact that she had made such rapid progress learning dancing with Madame Enderby that she began teaching dancing herself, giving lessons at home in her mother's front parlour. These lessons, which were mainly given to neighbours' and friends' children, took place after work and were often based on the dancing tuition and techniques she had learnt that same morning. So, our determined and enterprising Mighty Atom established her regular routine of 'learn in the morning at 8 and teach in the evening at 6' until she had earned enough money through her dual jobs to realise her dream of having her own dance studio.

Amazingly, within two years of leaving school and still only 16 years old, Constance Grant's dream came true. Gone was the front parlour for teaching dancing as the enterprising young lady set up her own studio above Madame Waldon's dress shop in Division Street. Although it was only a large, plain rather scruffy room, she was fully aware of its potential. With her dad's help as a carpenter, and with mum, brothers and sisters helping with cleaning, decoration and creative decor, the whole family converted the drab room into a vibrant dance studio which was to inspire many students for years to come.

The final transformation, however, was with the young lady herself. Gone was Connie or Constance to her pupils. In their place arose Miss Grant, by which name all her pupils referred to her for the rest of her life. The dancing fraternity and eventually most of the population of Sheffield grew to acknowledge Constance Grant's School of Dancing as the best in the city, with its Principal now emerging as a teacher of exceptional knowledge and skill. These qualities, as you might expect, had to be earned and were the result of many years of further study with experts in London on all aspects of dance until she had attained the highest level of qualification.

This then, was the real beginning of a most remarkable career and life for this dedicated lady. Not content with simply teaching dancing, she was keen to produce dancing shows. Within a relatively short time she had hired the Roxy Ballroom at Firth Park where she presented a show she was producing. Her father was, as you might expect, roped-in

to make all the scenery and props, while mum, inevitably, made all the costumes for the dancers.

But, of course, if you have a show you need a dance band, which Constance duly advertised for in the local press. Significantly, the pianist in the band which was subsequently hired was a gentleman by the name of Harry Silvester, a colliery store-manager from Barnsley by day, and a musician by night.

Constance had a shine for Harry who, likewise, had fallen for the dynamic dancing teacher and, within a year or two, they were married. So, we now have a dynamic duo, with Harry not only being her husband, but also being the business manager of the partnership as well as playing piano for all their classes and shows. Together, their reputation and their business grew, and their married home which they had bought at 182 Psalter Lane was partly converted into a dance studio, with the large downstairs room being used for this purpose.

Psalter Lane, however, was not just a house-cum-studio. More importantly, it was the birthplace of Constance's only child, Judith, who was born in 1937 when her mum was 32. Caring for a child was, of course, certainly a challenge for our Mighty Atom who was still ambitious to take her dancing school and career to even greater heights. Fortuitously, although under sad circumstances,

Constance Grant Dance Centre, Psalter Lane - 2008

Constance's sister Ethel, older than herself by 20 years, was able to come and help to look after the baby at Psalter lane, having lost her husband due to illness a little time earlier. Judith was thus brought up by both her mother and her Aunt Cis (as Ethel came to be known), to the benefit of all concerned.

As the years slowly passed by, demand for both theatre dancing and ballroom dancing expanded rapidly, putting a strain on the limited accommodation at the Dance Centre in Psalter Lane. Not to be beaten by the problem, Constance popped out one fine morning, unbeknown to her husband and business manager, and secured a lease on premises over Kenning's Garage in West Street. This was an extremely ambitious and expensive move, which Constance probably made in the knowledge that her husband Harry would have disapproved of it had he been consulted. We don't really know what his reaction was at the time, but as the top floor room was duly transformed by the Grant family into the highly successful Cavendish Ballroom, I don't suppose he was at all surprised that his wife's judgement had been a stroke of genius once again.

All ballroom dancing was now concentrated at the Cavendish, whilst theatre dancing remained at Psalter lane. Many thousands of Sheffield folk will fondly remember the time spent learning the basics of ballroom dancing with Constance Grant, which opened the door to a vast new social life for them which, in many cases, will have impacted on their lives forever. I wonder how many romances, marriages and subsequent families this remarkable lady was responsible for?

However, it wasn't simply the ability to dance that Miss grant taught her pupils, many of whom were only young children ranging from three or four years old upwards. She taught them Life-Skills, and was proud to do so. In particular she treated her pupils like a large family and encouraged them to be friendly, to work as a team, to do their best and respect others. This stood them in good stead

Constance Grant's School of Dancing

Teamwork at Showtime

in their lives thereafter, and many a pupil went back to the great lady twenty years or so later and thanked her for her guidance, despite having complained about the discipline and effort demanded of them by their teacher in their younger years.

It is very encouraging to see that the Constance Grant Life-Skills approach to learning was continued by her daughter Miss Judy and has now been taken into the 21st Century by her grand-daughters Karen and Tracey.

But let's pause for a moment. We seemed to have raced up to the present time whilst Constance's husband Harry had been working hard in pursuit of the couple's plans to expand their dance business. Following the establishment of the dance studios in Psalter Lane and West Street, the partnership bought the Empress Ballroom in Mexbrough, leased the Carlton Ballroom in Rotherham and bought the Roxy Ballroom at Page Hall as a Bingo and Gaming venue. The latter acquisition was intended solely as a business venture, as was the later purchase of a cafe in Mexbrough, both of which Harry felt would give additional financial security to their dance interests.

However, whilst the development of Constance Grant's business portfolio was essential at that time in order to secure longevity of the dance schools and meet the ever growing demands from all age groups of Sheffield folk, we are really focusing here on the dancing dynamo herself.

Let's have a look, therefore, at what else she got up to apart from running her dance classes and producing her shows. In particular, let's look at what influenced the rapidly growing interest in dancing, not just in this country, but over much of the developed world also.

The key influence, which emerged in 1941 during the Second World War, was the broadcasting media. At this time, the BBC started broadcasting dance music and dancing lessons on the wireless (we call them radios now) as part of a show called the BBC Dancing Club. This decision by the British Broadcasting Corporation was taken in an attempt to brighten up the lives of not only thousands of service-men and women who were away from home, but also of those waiting patiently at home for their loved one's return. Victor Silvester (no connection to Constance's husband), who was World Ballroom Dancing Champion in 1922, presented the broadcast whilst his dance orchestra provided the music.

The big breakthrough, however, came in 1948 when the programme was transferred to television and viewed by a rapidly growing audience. The result was a huge increase in dancing schools across the country. Just about every town and village had a dance hall, these varying from simple church halls to posh ballrooms with sprung floors and rotating coloured lights high up in creatively painted ceilings. It seemed like the whole country wanted to be like the professional dancing couples who floated gracefully across their small black and while television screens bringing sparkling glamour into their living rooms.

The success of Victor Silvestor's BBC Dancing Club prompted the television company to introduce its equally successful televised ballroom-dancing show which it called Come Dancing. This show, which ran on and off from 1949 to 1995, became one of television's longest running shows, and was helped enormously by the introduction of colour. The full benefit of cascading rainbows of delicate silks, chiffons and sequins which now filled the screens was there for all to see and marvel at, and thousands of dreams were made for young women and men across the country who aspired to belong to this exhilarating dream-world. Now, the extremely glamorous Strictly Come Dancing TV show, which is a dancing competition featuring well known celebrities and sports personalities, has taken the country by storm and is watched by millions of viewers every Saturday. The photographs displayed give you some idea why it is so popular.

It was a gentleman by the name of Eric Morley, of Miss World fame, who created Come Dancing, and it was presenters such as McDonald Hobley, Peter Dimmock, Sylvia Peters, Terry Wogan, Angela Rippon, Michael Aspel and Rosemary Ford who brought the whole show alive for our enjoyment. In amongst all these household names arose that of Constance Grant who was one of the first adjudicators on this programme, a position which now brought her to the attention of the British public.

It was during those early war and post-war years that she had, with great vision, established her dance studios, and it was during those later successful television broadcasts of Come Dancing in colour in the 1950s when she began to pursue her next aims. The highly popular television show not only attracted huge audiences in this country, it appeared in both Australia and America under the name Dancing With the Stars, where millions of viewers absorbed its delights like a global sponge.

This interest on an international scale was the catalyst which Constance sought, and with determination and sheer talent, she studied and worked hard to get to the top of her field. She obtained Fellowships in Ballroom, Latin American, Sequence, Ballet, Stage, Tap, Musical Theatre and Classical Greek Dancing before moving on to become

The Constance Grant Formation Team - Cavendish Ballroom, 1949

an external examiner for the Imperial Society of Teachers and Dancing (ISTD). Her contribution to dancing was now recognised internationally, and to cap it all she pioneered the hugely popular Formation Dancing which has given so much pleasure to so many world-wide. It was, in fact, with great pride that she was able to present her own dancers as the first formation team to appear on television.

The busy lady's workload was now spread between coaching dancers for local, national and international competitions (including many British champions), exhibition dancing, and the judging of many top dance competitions. She was also in demand for her excellent choreography skills, which included a post she held for many years as choreographer for the well-known Croft house Operatic Society. This society, which is a spin-off from the large Croft House Settlement charitable organisation, presented its shows at the Lyceum Theatre and the old Empire Theatre until 1960, and at the Montgomery theatre, the City Hall and the Lyceum Theatre thereafter.

This special, proud lady was also a three times winner of a Carl Alan Award, the dancing fraternity's equivalent of an Oscar, and whilst abroad on her many travels she became

Connie and Harry's Golden Wedding Anniversary, 1982

the first woman to judge dancing in Japan, where she also produced exhibition-dancing shows. You'd never believe it, but she was even asked to judge a Zulu dance competition (probably in Africa), although I believe she drew the line when asked to participate in the dance herself!

Having only one pair of feet, one pair of hands and only having 24 hours in a day like the rest of us, you'd think there was very little else this Mighty Atom could squeeze into life, wouldn't you. But, of course, I'd forgotten about her amazingly analytical mind which led her to put on paper the dancing techniques which she had either learnt, devised or developed over the years. She was no stranger, therefore, to many would-be dance experts, particularly abroad, to whom she often gave fascinating, technical lectures on the Technique of Dance.

Constance Grant had now reached the pinnacle of her chosen career. She was renowned, respected and loved world-wide, and had reached her goal in life. But she still loved the involvement, excitement and challenge of giving to others what she enjoyed herself. It was not until the age of 74, therefore, that she finally handed over the running of her dance studios to her daughter Judith, and even then she couldn't help popping in to help out for another two years or so. But, even the Queen of Dance had her limits, and for the last eight years of her eventful life she actually relaxed a little and enjoyed the pleasure of having more time to spend with her husband and her two grandchildren.

Sadly, at the age of 83, three years after her dear husband had passed away, Constance Grant, probably the greatest ambassador of dancing that this country has ever seen, peacefully died. The world of dancing had lost its Mighty Atom.

Fortunately, our story doesn't stop there. The great lady had created a dance-scene of almost unparalleled success, and ensured its continuation into the foreseeable future through her one and only daughter, Judith Silvester. Miss Judy, as she is known to most people, was 52 years old when Constance died, by which time she had acquired all the skills, qualities, qualifications and enthusiasm of her mum. Her appetite for work and her determination to achieve success mirrors that of her mother, and although outside the dancing fraternity she is perhaps less well-known than Constance Grant, inside it she is respected as her equal, both nationally and internationally.

By 1989, when Constance finally 'left the stage', the dance scene had been changing dramatically, and only the Psalter Lane and Cavendish Studios remained. Although public interest in dancing was still high, society itself was changing rapidly. Cinema houses, which had often doubled up as dance halls, were disappearing in droves as colour television, videos and other in-home entertainment was made possible by rapidly improving technology. A night out now became a visit to one or more of the new modern pubs or restaurants which were sprouting like mushrooms, and a visit to the local hop became old-hat.

Recognising these rapidly changing consequences of a high-tech promoted society, Miss Judy decided, in 1992, to close the Cavendish on West Street and consolidate her dance studios at Psalter Lane, both floors of which are now used for that purpose. Fortunately, television still creates considerable interest in dancing through programmes such as Strictly Come Dancing, which enjoys huge audiences. These subsequently continue to create demand for lessons, and the Constance Grant Dance Centre in Psalter Lane is always a busy, thriving place with pupils of all ages dancing their hearts out.

Now, of course, Miss Judy has crept past her official retirement age, and has handed the studio to her daughters,

Miss Judy with her daughters Tracy and Karen - Early 1980s

Karen and Tracey. However, like her mum before her, she still carries on doing many of the things she loves best such as adjudicating, lecturing and coaching.

Perhaps to conclude this story, I hope you will indulge me giving my view of what dancing is all about. To me, dancing appears to be something that is inherent in all of us, although it often needs teasing out. When we go to a wedding reception, an anniversary celebration, or just a pub or club playing music, most of us want to get up and 'jig around' a bit. It is a habit which is centuries old, and is probably enjoyed in one way or another in every country in the world. You might say that music and dance are as closely linked as Roast Beef and Yorkshire Pudding. They just need a good chef to blend them together with all the right ingredients. Constance Grant was such a Master-Chef, as is her daughter Judith now. Let us carry on enjoying their wonderful, varied menus forever.

5

Everyday Sheffield Folk

In contrast to the previous Section, we now follow the lives of three Sheffield folk who, in their own particular ways, have made an impact on many lives without knowing it.

They are ordinary people, known only to their families and friends. Their stories are, however, typical of thousands of others who have just done their best in life without getting or seeking recognition.

Each story is quite different and takes us on a journey through time and places which I hope you will find interesting.

Can I go home, please?
EDNA'S STORY
A VISIT TO THE NURSING HOME

It was a typical cold, November evening and Jon had decided to visit an elderly friend who lived at the nearby Rivelin View Nursing Home.

A tormenting breeze was doing its best to make him stumble and slip on the carpet of rusty, damp leaves which carelessly covered the winding drive down to its main entrance.

"I must be mad coming out in this weather," Jon chuntered to himself. "She'll not remember that I've been, so I don't really know why I bother."

He did know, of course, for he was very much aware of how lonely all the residents felt in the home, and how much they valued a visit, even if they didn't often show it.

As he stood there in the semi-darkness of the almost empty car park which surrounded the large and imposing building, he shuddered a little before entering through the front door which was usually unlocked at this time. A small table on the left-hand side of the bright hallway in which he was now standing contained an open signing-in book alongside a type-written notice which asked all visitors to enter their name, the time of day and the person they were visiting. There was a conspicuous absence of names on the almost empty sheet on this occasion, and Jon wondered whether it was the cold, raw weather which was the cause of this or the usual lack of a pen or pencil with which to write. It was probably a combination of both, he thought, as he struggled to try and find his small trusty biro which had slipped down into the torn lining of his inside coat pocket.

His next task was to gain entry to the main reception area which was visible through the half –panelled glass door to which Jon had now turned. A quick press on the well-thumbed button in front of him soon brought a kindly member of staff to let him in.

However, although being let into the care home was rarely a problem, experience told him that coping with the invisible reception he sometimes received when he entered could be rather daunting. That evening was such an occasion.

"Good grief, not again," he muttered as he stepped inside and was nearly knocked out by the competing aromas of disinfectant and stewed minced beef, carefully blended together by a stifling hot atmosphere more befitting a sub-tropical aviary than a residential home.

"Are you all right love?" purred the very pleasant lady who'd let him in. "You seem to have gone a bit flushed."

"Yes, yes thank you," Jon managed to choke. "I must have got a tickle in my throat."

It was, unfortunately, meal preparation time when Jon arrived, and as the home had to be kept warm and scrupulously clean, this was not really the ideal time to visit. However, taking two or three deep breaths, Jon bravely strode forward to begin his early evening adventure. He tried to forget the invisible battle going on around him as the pungent disinfectant droplets screamed CLEANLINESS in one ear whilst the highly flavoured stew juices sent clouds of soft, mouth watering droplets to whisper enticingly in the other ear. Both aromas fought for Jon's approval and battled it out under his sensitive nose. Neither, of course, could win, and Jon just wished that they would call it a draw and stop bothering him. He did, nevertheless, manage to reach his next hurdle.

"It's just like Fort Knox in here," he muttered to himself, as he now had to contend with the first of two combination-lock inner doors which protected each end of the staircase which gave access to the upper floor where his elderly friend was located. Despite being unable to find anyone for several minutes who knew the combination of the security locks, he eventually emerged from the upper door with a triumphant smile on his face, now ready to face anything.

Suddenly, a shrill scream sounding like the death cry of a werewolf pierced the silence of the corridor leading from the door to the home's large, brightly-lit lounge, and Jon was jolted back to reality.

"That'll be Agnes having one of her do's," he thought to himself as he sought out Edna, the purpose of his visit at this time.

Edna was a very good friend of Jon's, and he had known her for many years. Due to a combination of circumstances, this kindly, elderly lady in her mid-eighties now found herself being cared for in a nursing home, and Jon was her regular visitor.

He glanced over to the corner of the room where she usually sat, and the forlorn, pale-faced figure hunched to one side in the pale pink leatherette chair looked rather sad.

"Hello Edna," beamed Jon as he approached, wondering why she looked so different. She was, unfortunately, gradually deteriorating, but today she looked older.

"She's just had a shower," explained a helpful nurse who suddenly appeared on the scene having noticed Jon's obvious concern. "She's misplaced her glasses, and her teeth are still in her bedroom."

Of course, that was it. Edna's eyes were heavy, rather pink and a little watery, aspects of her appearance which were usually fairly well hidden by her thick lensed

Edna and her friend Joan at Rivelin View a few years earlier

spectacles. Her mouth also drooped without her teeth and, combined with her damp, flat hair, conspired to make her look older and less well than she really was.

Despite the extreme warmth of the room, Jon shivered a little as he watched his dear friend sitting there, gazing into space, only managing on this occasion to respond with a weak smile to her friend's greeting. At nearly 86 years old, she wasn't the oldest by a long way amongst the seventy or so residents cared for at Riveln View, but she was feeling sad and vulnerable and appeared to be losing interest in herself.

A sudden gust of wind outside rattled a slightly-open top window a few feet away from Edna's chair, and clammy fingers of cold, damp mist desperately tried to claw their way into the welcoming warmth of the lounge.

"There's a gale blowing down my neck," bellowed Thelma, a straight-backed, grey haired old lady with an uncharacteristically deep voice who always sat in a window seat.

"And another thing," she continued, "I'm thirsty and I want a cup of tea…NOW!"

Jon had to smile to himself as Thelma's forthrightness dispersed his temporary feeling of sadness. This was, after all, a home for the care of frail, confused, elderly people where few, if any, could be said to be actually happy. None were able to properly care for themselves and, therefore, all had lost much of their independence. Most had developed varying degrees of dementia which manifested itself as forgetfulness, the inability to understand, fear of the unknown, anxiousness, stubbornness and varying degrees of aggression. Combined with this, most experienced some difficulty in walking, and many were incontinent. This, then, was old age, a stage in life which most, if not all, people aspire to reach. Do they really know what it might hold for them?

Suddenly, Jean, a kindly care-worker who had been looking after elderly people for over thirty years, appeared in the lounge doorway with the first of several wheelchairs. It was 'first-sitting' time, when the less able of the residents were given tea with more personal attention from the staff on duty.

TIME FOR TEA

Slowly but surely, in response to much prompting by care workers and nursing staff, a straggly, struggling line of residents began the exodus from the lounge and embarked on their daunting journey to the dinning room.

As Jon slowly helped Edna to her feet, he glanced up at the shuffling, muttering group which was led by Nora who sounded like a giant grasshopper as she hobbled and swayed to the tempo of the rapid drill-like noise she created by the constant grinding of her teeth.

Little Clara on her Zimmer-frame wasn't far behind, but she wondered why she was going there at all as she followed in sheep-like fashion muttering constantly to herself on her tedious journey.

Elsie and Emma, struggling in the middle of the pack, were supported on the helping arms of two carers. Both residents looked as though they had been in a boxing match with bruises and cuts showing prominently from behind plasters and bandages which adorned their wrinkled, kindly old faces. Unfortunately, it wasn't unusual for elderly residents to fall and damage themselves, particularly in their bedrooms, as they were encouraged to have as much independence as possible in order that they could keep some dignity and self respect.

Jon, meantime, had Edna on one arm and her friend Ruby on the other, and was bravely trying to make progress up the corridor as several members of the leading pack decided to change their minds and return to the lounge against the flow, causing grid-lock in the process.

This, however, was a typical day, and in due course about fifteen first-sitters had made the twenty yards or so hazardous journey to the dinning room in just under 10 minutes and were more or less settled in their seats.

Eating, however, had yet to begin.

Nora, who was sitting at a table in the corner of the dining room, was still grinding away, punctuating her highly irritating habit with an occasional, equally irritating, high pitched screech which would do justice to the mating call of an anxious tawny owl.

"Silly sod," muttered Ruby as she glanced towards Nora whilst balancing precariously on the edge of the dining-chair arm which Edna was already sitting in.

Jeannie, a quiet, plump, unassuming lady, had been brought to her seat in a wheelchair and, unluckily for her, was Nora's table-mate. Having been presented with a plateful of minced beef, mashed potatoes and liquidized carrots, she gratefully plunged her spoon into her food with excited enthusiasm.

It was, however, to be short-lived as Nora, who had ordered sandwiches, suddenly snatched the plate away and began devouring Jeannie's soft meal using her fingers.

"Oi," shouted Clive, the burly male-nurse in charge. "Stop it."

He had spotted the misdemeanour just as a very impatient Madge, who was sitting at the other end of the room, flicked, with great skill and accuracy, half a spoonful of tasty gravy into his left ear from a distance of at least twelve feet.

Cursing quietly to himself, Clive was in two minds as to who to deal with first.

He didn't have to think long however, thanks to big Ted, a second-sitter who had drifted in almost unnoticed to join his friends at the table nearest the door.

"Bloody-'ell," Ted roared, suddenly standing up and taking the whole table cloth and contents with him.

Crashing crockery and flying sandwiches soon concentrated the minds of Clive and two young lady carers as they lurched forward to try and prevent total chaos.

"What's up?" boomed Ted yet again as his 6'-3" frame towered intimidatingly over the keen but rather diminutive figures below him who were trying to salvage the mugs and plates whilst Clive attempted to calm the big man down.

"You're not supposed to be in here Ted," retorted Clive. "Go back to the lounge and wait your turn."

After a few more bellows and rantings, Ted departed the battle-scene and left the staff to clean up the mess and re-assure the other residents.

The excitement, however, had been a little bit too much for Madge who had slammed down her half-finished mug of tea into a bowl of soft blancmange sending messages of fresh cream to all and sundry.

Jon, meantime, was trying to relax on the chair next to Edna, who had spent the duration of the mealtime mini-war steadily eating her sandwiches, whilst trying in vain to dislodge Ruby from her chair arm with the aid of the sharp end of a well aimed, silver fork. Ruby, however, was well padded, and only gave up her perching-place when she was firmly but tenderly escorted to an empty seat at the other side of the table.

But what of little Clara who had earlier Zimmer-framed her way to the chair at the other side of Jon, thus denying poor Ruby her original choice of seat? She hadn't even started her meal, despite not having eaten much for the last two or three days.

"Clara, you must eat something or you'll be poorly," advised the very pleasant nurse who had calmly strolled over to help her.

"I can't eat. I've not got any teeth in," she responded quietly, her almost angelic face turning appealingly towards the nurse.

"Now, now, Clara, you've not had any teeth in for over a year. Your gums are as hard as nails. Let's see if you can have a bite of one of these egg sandwiches."

The angelic face turned once again and a soft, pleading response followed.

"I just can't. I don't know how to."

Jon by this time was feeling very sorry for the sweet old lady.

"Clara, can I help you?" he offered politely.

Clara slowly turned her head, and her wide, almost tearful eyes gazed into Jon's for a few seconds before she spoke in a quiet, though surprisingly firm, voice.

"Sod off and mind your own business. I'm just not 'ungry."

The sweet old lady was not so sweet after all, and poor Jon never failed to be surprised by the sudden mood changes of those around him. He decided, therefore, to escort Edna back to the lounge and leave them all to it.

Their relatively short walk back to the lounge was not, however, destined to be easy as the couple soon encountered dear little Alice on one of her many strolls up and down the corridors.

"I want to go to bed," came the plaintive, high pitched cry which echoed round the walls for at least the three hundredth time that day.

"Will you take me to bed?" she continued, her lovely but amusing face contorted into impossibly rubbery shapes whilst her tongue casually wrapped itself around the end of her nose.

Now Alice was a real character. To look at her she resembled on elderly, grey- haired, female version of Charlie Chaplin with her feet turned outwards and her big toes pointing skyward through the end of her sandals.

"'Av you brought me a can o' beer?" she suddenly asked when she realized it was Jon who was approaching her.

Jon had seen Alice every week for the past four years or so and, in casual conversation with her, had discovered her liking for a drop of the hard stuff. What had turned out to be a one-off treat had developed into a weekly event, as after gratefully accepting the first can, the elderly lady had remembered with remarkable regularity to ask for one on every subsequent occasion.

Alice

"Is it a can o' Stones," she shrilled as Jon carefully took the drink from his overcoat pocket.

Now whilst Alice liked a drink of beer, she was quite discerning and always asked for her favourite brew.

"Of course it is Alice. What else would I bring?"

"Can I go to bed now?"

"Not just yet Alice. How about having your tea first and then you can go to bed afterwards. Ok?"

"Yes," came the response after a short pause.

Alice stood for a minute thinking, swaying back and forth as she always did when standing up.

"Can I go to bed now?"

Jon smiled to himself as he looked into the heavy lidded eyes of that incredibly character-filled face in which every line seemed to tell a story, and thought what a fascinating life she must have lived.

A sudden tugging on Jon's sleeve brought him back to the present and he realized that Edna was weary of standing and urgently needed to sit down.

"Come on Alice. Come with me and Edna to the lounge until your tea's ready."

So, arm in arm, the three of them made their way along the corridor, Jon trying to balance the upright, rapid shuffling gait of Alice with the more stooped, lurching movement of Edna. Needless to say, the return journey was equally as daunting as that they had encountered making their way to the dinning room, as by the time the threesome had nearly reached the lounge door, the second-sitting invasion had begun. However, with deft footwork, much patience and the help of one or two care-workers, the safety of the lounge was eventually reached, their entry there being heralded by a shrill greeting from Florence who was bringing up the rear of the departing second-sitters.

"I'm just going to the shops. Do you want anything?"

"Just got me a packet of polo's if you don't mind, Florence. I'll play you later."

Jon's parting comment to the sweet old lady was about as much as he could manage at the time, and with a supreme effort he finally guided a grateful Edna and Alice to their respective seats.

RELAXING IN THE LOUNGE

With so many of the lounge chairs having been vacated by the second-sitting residents, it enabled Edna's very tired visitor to flop down in comfort for a well earned rest…well, for two or three minutes at least.

Little Nellie (most of the residents appeared to be rather small) had yet to be taken for her tea, and was still sitting in her usual chair banging its wooden arm with a spoon. As if this wasn't annoying enough, she always accompanied this habit by counting every blow that the spoon made in a rather monotonous, irritating voice:

"973, 974, 975, 976…Hey, don't knock me, I've lost my place now. 1, 2, 3, 4…"

Clive had come into the room with a wheelchair in order that he could take the budding mathematician for her tea, and had tapped her on the shoulder to gain her attention.

"Come on Bingo," (Nellie's nick-name apparently). "Don't start counting again, for heaven's sake."

"Where are we going?" she enquired quietly. "Is it somewhere nice?"

"It's tea-time Nellie, so you can put that spoon to some good use."

Jon gave Nellie a wave and a smile as they passed and noticed that kindly Ernest and a lady companion were lagging behind the rest. Now Ernest, better known as Ern', was always helping the ladies and had waited patiently for shaky Emily to find and put on one of her slippers which had accidentally found its way into her hand bag. Eventually wearing both slippers, she hung gratefully onto Ern's strong arm as they 'chased' after the fast-disappearing pack ahead of them.

Ernest was one of only four men amongst thirty women in this wing of the nursing home, a clear indication of how much longer women live than men do. In his early days he had been a red-hot football star playing for Sheffield Club. As Tiger Smith, he had been a much feared and respected centre-forward, and had played when the game was simply a sport rather than a business. I wonder what he would have thought of players of his ability earning in the region £40,000 a week or more about fifty years later? Like most people nowadays, he would probably have considered such a wage to be outrageously undeserving.

Looking at Ernest, Jon thought how proud he must have felt to have played for the oldest football club in the world. Established in 1857, Sheffield Club first played their football when four goal posts and a crossbar formed the shooting area at each end of the pitch. If a shot on goal went between the outer two posts, a near-miss, called a rouge, was recorded, whilst any ball passing between the inner two posts was recorded as a goal as it is now.

By the time Ernest played for the club, of course, the conventional two-post goals were used, and his right footed pile-drivers often tested the quality of the netting hung behind them. But, of course, Tiger Smith was only a memory, and good old Ern' had to follow the pack nowadays like everyone else.

Another tug on Jon's sleeve brought him out of his day-dreaming as he realized that Edna wanted his attention.

"Have you dropped off or what," she complained. "I thought it was me who was supposed to be old and tired."

Suitably rebuked, and a little more refreshed, Edna's good friend leaned forward to speak just as the lady in the next chair (whose name he could not quite catch) let rip with an accusation which she hurled straight at poor old Edna.

"Is that my handbag you've got? I bet it is, and it's got all my jewellery in it."

Edna shrank back into her seat and clutched her tattered old bag tightly to her chest. The most valuable things in her bag were, in fact, a couple of stale biscuits, one of yesterday's egg sandwiches and about six packets of polo mints.

"Don't be such a fool. This is my bag."

It was most unusual for this sweet, grey-haired lady, who was noted for her quiet, polite demeanour, to respond in this way. But, of course, there is nothing more precious to an elderly, lonely person than her memories and her handbag, and no-one was too surprised when she continued.

"She's stupid she is. This is my bag."

Altercations of this type weren't, of course, unusual in these surroundings, and as Jon glanced round the warm, well-lit lounge and watched the elderly residents chatting to each other, he realized that it was the choice of each and every visitor as to whether or not to laugh or cry at the behaviour which inevitably unfolded.

Freda, for example, a roughly spoken, rather brusque elderly lady sitting a few feet away from Edna and Jon, had just turned to the demure, bespectacled lady sitting next to her.

"Where's George?" she asked.

"I don't think so," came the reply.

"Have you seen him?"

"I think its Tuesday, isn't it?"

Hardly able to contain his urge to laugh, Jon turned his face towards Ethel and Nellie who had returned from the dinning room and were sitting comfortably near the back wall of the lounge. Inevitably, a relaxing conversation began between these two friends also.

"It's cold today, isn't it?"

"Bingo."

"Is that window open?"

"Bingo."

"I'll ask mother to close it."

"Bingo."

At least, Jon now knew why Clive called Nellie 'Bingo' when he had taken her to the dining room for her evening meal!

By this time, Edna was nodding off and Jon thought that it was about the right time to say au revoir to his dear friend. He'd enjoyed her company as usual, and the entertainment provided by the remaining residents was always a wonderful mixture of pathos and humour which genuinely brought tears of laughter and sadness to his eyes. He bent over and gently kissed her on the cheek before whispering a quiet goodbye in her ear. Edna opened her eyes and, with an imploring look at Jon, said what she usually said at such a time as this.

"Can I go home, please?"

"Of course you can Edna. I'll try and sort it out for you."

As Jon slowly left the warm lounge and made his way down the stairs to the entrance hall, he did so with mixed feelings of relief, sadness and despair. He was of course, happy that so many elderly people were so capably cared for at a time when neither they nor their families could reasonably be expected to cope.

He was, nevertheless, sad that their mental and physical condition left only a few of them able to achieve any reasonable degree of independence which could give them a meaningful quality of life. Despite this, however, many residents were, for much of the time, oblivious to the problems and anxieties which existed all around them, and this, strangely enough, enabled them to be content in their own, private way.

The most important, natural gift given to the elderly, however, is their unique ability to delve back into the depths of their past lives, an occasion which usually brightened up many a quiet, lonely day. These memories of nearly a century past can suddenly become real again and can stimulate even the saddest of people if the catalyst of a genuinely kind and enquiring friend or relative is introduced.

As these thoughts filtered through Jon's mind, he recalled fondly the wonderful stories that Edna had told him over the several years that he had been visiting her. These stories not only related to her life, but also to those of her

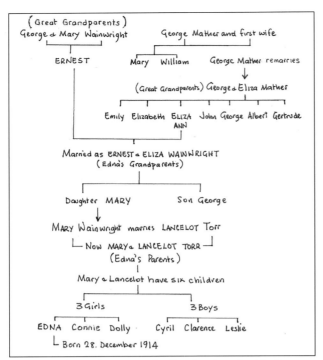

(Great Grandparents)
George & Mary Wainwright
George Mather and first wife

ERNEST
Mary   William   George Mather remarries
↓
(Great Grandparents) George & Eliza Mather

Emily Elizabeth ELIZA John George Albert Gertrude
ANN

Married as ERNEST & ELIZA WAINWRIGHT
(Edna's Grandparents)

Daughter MARY   Son George
↓
MARY Wainwright marries LANCELOT Torr
— Now MARY & LANCELOT TORR —
(Edna's Parents)

Mary & Lancelot have six children

3 Girls   3 Boys
EDNA Connie Dolly   Cyril Clarence Leslie
└ Born 28. December 1914

parents and grand parents who lived and worked in the once rural village of Norton many years ago. Before Jon forgets, let's just ask him to share with us those long-gone memories of yesteryear as they were told to him. It should make fascinating reading.

Before we begin, I think it would be helpful to briefly look at Edna's family tree to see how everyone fits into the picture Jon is about to paint.

Jon didn't mind recounting Edna's memories that evening as it gave him the chance to sit down and relax for a few quiet minutes on a chair just inside the nursing home's front entrance. It was chilly and very dark outside by this time, so as he sat back and closed his eyes in the warmth of the home, he was able to let his own recollections of their talks together come flooding back.

EDNA'S GREAT GRANDPARENTS ELIZA AND GEORGE MATHER IN NORTON

It was a cold November morning in 1869 when Edna's 50 year old great grandfather, George Mather, a dedicated farmer and carter, was busily feeding the dairy cows on a small farmstead in the leafy suburb of Norton in the County of Derby. The huge, rolling green landscape which formed the grounds of Norton Hall (later to be called Graves Park) formed a magnificent backcloth to the farm's stone out-buildings and those of other farms which clustered around the sharp bend in the rough track which bordered the estate. This cluster of farm buildings, together with a row of seven quaint little cottages a hundred yards or so

further along the track where George lived, was known locally as Little Norton, and was the only sign of life in this area within a radius of half a mile or so.

George had left his young wife, Eliza, tucked-up in bed in their little cottage an hour or two earlier under the watchful eyes of his daughter Mary and his son William. Mary and William were children from his first marriage, and it would appear that his first wife had died within a few years of the birth of their son. George had moved to Little Norton with his two young children while still in his mid-thirties, and it had been there that he had met and married the 20 year old Eliza. A year after their marriage, Eliza had a daughter, Emily, and four years later another daughter, Elizabeth. She was now pregnant with her third child, which meant that the small two-bedroomed cottage at Little Norton would be home to mum and dad Mather, 16 year old Mary, 13 year old William, 5 year old Emily, one year old Elizabeth and a new baby whose birth was expected any time now.

It was no surprise, therefore, that George was feeling a little anxious as he broke open a bale of tightly packed hay which he had harvested a few months earlier during the gloriously hot August of that year. The heat hadn't really been suiting Eliza, but George was thankful that the present year's summer weather had not reached the unbearable levels of the previous year, 1868, when shade temperatures of 91 degrees F and temperatures in the open of 125 degrees F had been recorded. This intense heat was reported to have set fire to the wheat fields and local woods in this and other areas of the city following the long drought which accompanied the heatwave. I wonder how many people in those days thought that such temperatures were the result of a condition that politicians nowadays call Global Warming, a phenomenon which today's governments of the world blame on man-made carbon dioxide emissions being released into the atmosphere.

It's strange, isn't it, that similar or less severe weather conditions which occur today, one hundred and forty years

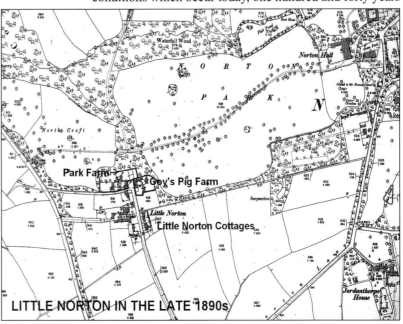

LITTLE NORTON IN THE LATE 1890s

on, are considered to be an indication of a disaster which is about to destroy our planet and our very existence in the not too distant future unless we take significant steps to change the way we all carry on living. Perhaps if Edna's great grandparents, George and Eliza Mather, had enjoyed the benefits of sophisticated technology and the opinions of thousands of highly paid climate-change experts that we have today, they too may have been persuaded into thinking that the end of the world was nigh. Thankfully, no such benefits were available to them, and they continued to enjoy long hot summers, droughts and even exceptionally long periods of rain and flooding without being frightened and bullied into changing their way of life as happens in today's society. Perhaps they just accepted, like many eminent experts do today, that climate change has always taken place and will always continue to do so.

You will have gathered that I am a little sceptical about the cause, timescale and magnitude of the global warming disaster which is predicted to engulf us all, and I trust that you will forgive me for incorporating my opinions in Edna's story. We'd better get back to Little Norton, however, because George's private thoughts had been dramatically interrupted as Joe, one of the farmhands, had suddenly appeared, shouting loudly and waving his hands.

An unknown farmer/farmhand

"What the heck's the matter, Joe?" asked George with a concerned look on his face. "What's all this shouting about?"

"It's your missus, Mester Mather. I think the baby's coming."

George, of course, was no stranger to births, but his wife Eliza was not all that strong having only just recovered from the difficult birth of their daughter Elizabeth the previous year.

"Joe, fetch Mrs Bradbury," he gasped as he slithered across the muddy yard towards the farmhouse gate. "She'll know what to do."

Mrs Bradbury lived in one of the old cottages in Greenhill Village about a five minute buggy-ride away. She was a lady of considerable experience, and apart from having had children of her own, she had delivered many babies when called upon to do so by friends and neighbours in the area. Getting a doctor out to this rural setting, particularly in bad weather, was never achieved quickly, but, thankfully, Mrs Bradbury was always willing to step in and help.

It was only a short distance to George and Eliza's cottage along the stone track, later to be known as Little Norton Lane, but to the anxious farmer it seemed to take an

age to get there in his heavy, muddy boots. Eliza was equally anxious, and it was with great relief that she greeted her husband when he eventually arrived.

"Oh, George. Thank heaven you're here. I thought you might be out in the fields."

"You've nothing to worry about m'dear. I'm here now. Everything's under control, and I've sent Joe to fetch Mrs. Bradbury to give us a hand."

Eliza had been sleeping in the small, back room of the cottage for the past week or so where the benefit of a log fire in the old cast iron fireplace in the outer stone wall had been a comfort during a particularly cold November spell. Normally, this room would be rather cold as most activity would be in the larger, stone-floored kitchen at the front of the house. With its large, black range fired up twenty four hours a day and a constant supply of hot water from the black kettle which sat almost permanently on the hob, this was the hub of the household.

It was Mrs Biggin, Eliza's helpful neighbour, who had popped in as usual that morning to look in on their four children whilst George was at work. Finding Eliza in labour, she had sent their 13 year old son William scurrying to the farm to alert George, and kindly old Joe had done the rest. Once George had arrived, Mrs Jones had taken the children back to her place until the baby arrived.

A sudden cry from Eliza coincided with the welcome arrival of Mrs Bradbury, a kindly-faced lady of ample proportions. Her very presence created reassurance and confidence, and both mother and father-to-be knew that they were in good hands.

It was about two hours later that George, having provided the kindly mid-wife with some sheets, towels and hot water as and when requested, found himself pacing up and down the kitchen in a somewhat dazed condition. The mug of strong tea clenched in his fist had gone cold and just slip-slopped all over the stone flooring in time with the anxious farmer's sudden turns and other movements. Bruce, the usually docile Border Collie who normally claimed the warm spot in front of the fire, was skulking around wondering what catastrophe had occurred which had caused his master to be so agitated. The orchestra of moans, shouts and the occasional high pitched screams which had played to both man and dog from within the back room over the last few hours had descended into silence at last. Whilst being relieved at the welcome peace which had arrived, both of the prowling males stopped in their tracks and stared at each other with air of expectant anxiety.

Suddenly, another cry cut through the air like a freshly sharpened arrow causing George to release his automatic hold on his battered tea mug and make a lurch towards the back-room door. It was touch-and-go who would reach the already opening door first; a frantic new father or a tea-drenched, scared out of his wits Collie dog.

Bruce won the race by a whisker, diving straight between the sturdy, widely placed legs of Mrs Bradbury who, with a grin from ear to ear, was now standing in the open doorway. Looking more like the laundry lady than a mid-wife, she was tightly holding several layers of white towelling in her arms, in the midst of which peered out a tiny, deep pink, puzzled little face.

"She's arrived, Mr Mather. She's arrived!"

Hardly daring to breath, George gingerly took hold of the delicate bundle and gazed adoringly into the beautiful little face.

"By gum, lass. Yer just like yer mother."

As the unofficial, albeit highly skilled midwife stood to one side to allow the new dad to see his brave little wife, the grandfather clock in the corner of the kitchen began to chime 12 o'clock. George bent over to kiss her.

"She's beautiful me darlin', just like her mum."

A solitary tear rolled down a weather-beaten cheek and landed lovingly on the delicate, pale face lying on the pillow beneath him. Tired eyes gazed adoringly upwards and, for those first few magical moments, all thoughts of the hours of hard work, effort and pain that Eliza had endured were banished.

The last chime of noon was sounding and, in this peaceful far-flung region of what then was the County of Derby, another life had begun.

Eliza Ann Mather, Edna's grandmother, had made her way into the world at approximately 12 Noon on November 15th, 1869. For the next 86 years she would, like hundreds of thousands of other Sheffield folk, make her particular contribution to life. So, what was so special about her, or about Edna for that matter (who had not yet arrived on the scene)? Did they have exceptional abilities? Were they extraordinary in any way? Were they gifted with many talents?

The answer to all these questions is no. But it is this answer itself which makes them so special. They were typically caring, loving, hard-working people from whom kindness and unselfishness flowed as a matter of course. Their names would never be up in lights, but their everyday contribution to life was a typical example of ordinary folk who deserve to be remembered as much as those who achieve fame and fortune.

Let's take a brief look, therefore, at how Eliza Ann became part of Edna's special memories.

EDNA'S GRANDMOTHER, ELIZA ANN, IN NORTON

Nearly two years after Eliza Ann's birth, a baby boy was born on June 16th in the middle of the hot summer of 1871 in a small cottage in nearby Dronfield Woodhouse. Mary and George Wainwright had become the proud parents of a son, Ernest. In common with Eliza Ann's father George, Ernest's father (also called George) worked on a local farm as an agriculture labourer. In those days, with agriculture and farming in general being the main activities in these rural areas (although a few of the menfolk took up file-cutting), most farmers and farm workers got to know each other well. It was no surprise, therefore, that young Eliza Ann met Ernest during their childhood.

However, during those early years, Eliza Ann's mother was very keen that her daughter should receive as good an education as possible, which meant that going to school

Norton Free School

every day left little time for new friendships outside the area in which she lived. However, Eliza Ann always enjoyed the ten to fifteen minute stroll to the little school just beyond Norton Grange on what later became known as Matthews Lane. This walk, which she did with her friend Emmie in each direction every week day, began at the cinderpath which ran up the side of the end cottage, four doors away from where she lived. To the left, tall, leafy trees formed a proud protective boundary to the huge Norton Park beyond, whilst open fields to the right were decorated with clusters of brown and white cows and fluffy white sheep.

Beyond this path, which ended at its junction with Norton Lane, a stroll up this road took the two chums past the very posh Norton House on the right and Norton Parish Church on the left.

Norton House

It was on one such fine and sunny morning when the two girls had reached this point that Eliza Ann made a suggestion to her friend.

"If we nip through the church yard and round the side of Norton Hall, Emmie, we might be able to see the deer roaming in the top field. What do you think?"

"Ooh, I'm not sure about that Eliza. I don't think we're supposed to go round there. Anyway, we might be late for school."

Norton Hall

"Don't be such a scaredy-bum, Emmie. We've got plenty of time, and I've done it loads of times before."

Emmie didn't really have much choice in the matter, as her brave friend had already opened the church gates and was skipping down the pathway.

"Wait for me Eliza, wait for me."

It only took two or three minutes to arrive at a gap in the trees through which two pairs of twinkling eyes could gaze in anticipation of seeing a deer or two frolicking about. They were not to be disappointed.

"Look, there they are Emmie! Aren't they beautiful?"

The delicate pale-brown figures which appeared before them as if by magic were indeed a wonderful sight. Their slender legs carried gracefully formed bodies on which their whitish fluffy tails looked almost comical. Large, soulful eyes stared out from gently pointed faces, and they all seemed to be looking at the two girls in disbelief.

"I think they've seen us Eliza. What shall we do?"

"I think we'd better make a run for it, Emmie, or else we'll be late for school."

The two seven year old girls scampered back through the churchyard and dashed along the country lanes to their school where, no doubt, a rather stern-looking headmistress would have been waiting for them.

But, of course, time passes on and by the end of 1882 Eliza Ann was of working age, having now reached her 13th birthday. She, like most other youngsters, had to help her parents at home and, when necessary, on the farm. In addition, and importantly for her, she could see a bit more of her friend Ernest, although with him being two years younger than she was, it was some time before romance blossomed between the two of them.

During those years when the couple were growing up from childhood to adulthood, a few changes took place in the Norton area. Most prominent of these was the building of the large Stone and Brick Works in the old quarry halfway up the steep section of Chesterfield Road, which was later to be renamed Meadowhead. These works were very welcome in the area as they offered employment to those who might otherwise be struggling to find a job.

As far as work was concerned, both Ernest and Eliza were keen to find employment once they were seeing each other on a romantic basis, as any thought of marriage needed the security of an income. Steelmaking was big business across the border in the thriving town of Sheffield, and a steady walk down to the Big Tree public house in Woodseats enabled them to catch a horse-bus ride into town to search for suitable jobs. It was, in fact, to be a longer treck than the couple thought as it was to be in the Attercliffe Township on the eastern side of the town where jobs were on offer at the huge, noisy, air-polluting steelworks. Ernest did, nevertheless, manage to get himself a job as a steelworker and annealer at one such works, whilst Eliza was able to secure a job as a steelworker's labourer at the same place. Although the days were long and

hard, with a lot of time spent travelling, they at least spent time together and were able to save for that magical day when they could be married.

It wasn't, of course, all work and no play for the courting couple, as the nearby, thriving village of Greenhill had two very attractive public houses, the White Swan and the Old White Hart, which provided a very nice pint to

relieve their parched throats on many an evening as well as providing friendly social gatherings every day of the week. It is interesting to note that both of these pubs are still in existence and are still doing well.

ELIZA ANN MARRIES GEORGE WAINWRIGHT

By this time, Eliza and Ernest were in their mid twenties and, on the 21st November 1895, they decided to tie the knot and get married. The wonderful, although rather cold, wedding at St. James Church in Norton was a sight to behold. The trees which surrounded the beautiful stone church were in their multi-coloured autumn clothes which contrasted magically with Eliza's white, flowing wedding

St. James Church, Norton

dress which shimmered in the strong sun casting playful shadows over the loving couple as they left the church hand in hand. Even Ernest's more sombre charcoal-coloured suit seemed to glow in recognition of this happy occasion, which was witnessed by a host of shivering yet happy family members and friends.

Now proudly called Mrs Eliza Ann Wainwright, the new bride needed somewhere to live with her husband Ernest. She had also been concerned for some time about her father's fragile health which had deteriorated over the last ten years or so since his retirement from farming and his move into a less demanding job as an egg and butter dealer. With both these considerations in mind, she had kept her eye on the rented cottage next door to where she and her

parents presently lived in the run-up to her wedding, as she knew it was likely to become vacant in the not too distant future.

Eliza Ann had spent the first twenty six years of her life with her parents and siblings in their modest size cottage, during which time her mother had been gifted with four more children, John, George, Albert (who sadly died at the age of one), and Gertrude. That made seven children in total which her mother Eliza Mather had given birth to by the age of 43. This had ensured that life within the Mather household had been a little bit like living inside a tin of sardines, with little or no privacy for anyone. Getting a home of her own, but also near to her tired parents, had for a long time been a very high priority for this 26 year old.

Strangely enough, by the time that her marriage to Ernest took place, all the children except herself and her 10 year old little sister Gertrude had fled the nest, and it was only with moderate difficulty that the newly-weds spent the first few months of their married life in the greatly reduced Mather household.

However, within six months of their marriage the adjoining cottage became vacant and the newly-weds were fortunately offered the opportunity of renting it. It was with great delight that they accepted the offer and at last began their independent married life together.

Little Norton Lane Cottages

EDNA'S MOTHER, MARY WAINWRIGHT, IS BORN

Number 51 Little Norton Lane, as their cottage later became known, was a cosy little home with a dining room and a small slop kitchen downstairs and one bedroom upstairs. Eliza Ann felt secure and settled there and within a year gave birth to a baby daughter, Mary, to the delight of her parents Eliza and George. Sadly her father died about a year and a half later just before her second child, a baby son who she named George after him, was born in 1899. Although George Mather's passing was not unexpected, it

Stone cottage, Little Norton Lane

was a desperate blow to Eliza Ann to whom her family meant everything. She was so thankful that she had been able to move into the cottage next to her parents as her mum would need her help and comfort more than ever now.

Baby George's birth did, as you might imagine, create the same type of problem with cramped accommodation that Eliza Ann had been forced to put up with nearly all her life, and it occasionally got the better of her:

"It's all right for you, Ernest," she would say in frustration when one or both children regularly woke her up during the night for a feed or just to be comforted. "It's always me that has to look after them because you have to get up very early so that you can go to work in those awful steelworks in that smoky old Sheffield every day."

She knew, of course, that her husband had no choice in the matter as jobs were hard to come by in those days. It was simply the lack of space in their cosy but tiny cottage which was the problem. They had tried to improve the situation by hanging a large curtain across the centre of their bedroom in an effort to try and minimize any disturbances and create some semblance of privacy. Whilst this helped to some degree, it only served to shut out prying eyes whilst leaving keen enquiring ears to create their own picture of what was going on in their parents' area. You can imagine what problems this caused as they grew older, can't you?

Despite these nightly accommodation problems, life ran pretty smoothly in the Wainwright household. Young Mary and George were happy children and, like their mother before them, attended Norton School with the other youngsters in the area. They did, however, begin to feel rather claustrophobic as they grew older in their small home with their parents.

Not surprisingly, as they moved into their teenage years they were desperate to have their own space and identity. Mary was the first to move out. She had just reached the tender age of 17 as the rumblings of war were in the air, and she was going steady with a local lad by the name of Lance Torr. She also had something important to tell her mum and dad. The opportunity came one evening as all the family sat down together for a late tea-

Mary in her early 20s

cum-supper. The meal was lamb hot-pot, and Mary knew that her dad was usually in a good mood when a plate of this, his favourite food, was placed before him.

"I don't want either of you to get upset," she started as her parents tucked into their welcome meal, "but me and Lance have decided to get married."

It was as if time had stood still for a few moments in this delightful, rural family setting. You could have heard a pin drop, even on the multicoloured peg rug which draped itself carelessly over the stone-flagged floor of this cosy room. Mary's dad, Ernest, simply sat there as though paralysed with a look of shock on his face, whilst her mum tried unsuccessfully not to choke on a forkful of lamb she had just put into her mouth.

It was her 15 year old brother George who was the first to break the silence.

"You? Getting married? Does that mean you're going to move out and give me more room? Great!"

"Be quiet," thundered Ernest as the reality of the situation hit him. "Don't tell me that young Lance has got you into trouble already, my girl. I'll —"

"Now now, Ernest, calm down," interrupted Eliza Ann. "Let's just listen to what she has to say. After all, she is 17."

Mary's mum was always the calmer, more understanding member of the Wainwright family, and the job of keeping peace nearly always fell on her. To be fair, it wasn't unusual for girls to marry at 17 or 18 years old in those days, and Eliza Ann had been the exception to the rule when she married Ernest at the age of 26. In addition, large families were also the order of the day, with many wives having five, six or even seven babies within a relatively short time-scale, probably whilst they were young enough and strong enough to look after them.

However, on this occasion Ernest's suspicions were well founded as a tearful Mary eventually admitted that she was about two months pregnant.

"I do love him, you know, mum," she suddenly blurted out to a rather shocked, but not totally surprised, Eliza Ann. "Lance will take good care of me and we can live at his house in Harboard Road in Woodseats. It's only small but it will be alright for the two of us and the baby when it arrives."

Mary turned to look at her father and, as the two of them gazed into each other's tearful eyes, Ernest knew that there was no point in him objecting to this marriage. His daughter obviously needed the security of both a caring husband and a home for her and her baby to live in. Most importantly, however, they appeared to be in love. As far as security was concerned, Lance already had a job at one of Sheffield's large East-end Works as a steelworker's labourer and was bringing home a modest but regular wage. It was with great relief, therefore, that mum, dad and daughter decided to rejoice at the prospect of a new baby in the family, and they now turned their attention to planning the forthcoming wedding.

However, on August 4th of this eventful year, Britain declared war on Germany, a war which was to take hundreds of thousands of young men from the comfort of their homes and plunge them into the horrors of carnage and loneliness as they bravely fought for their country. Naively, many, if not most, of these young men were only

expecting glory and success, and their departure to the battlefields took place amidst feelings of excitement and optimism of a quick and easy victory. History tells a different story, as we all know, and it is to all these brave soldiers, sailors and airmen that we owe an everlasting debt of gratitude for their eventual success.

MARY WAINWRIGHT MARRIES LANCELOT TORR
EDNA IS BORN

Despite the arrival of what was to become World War One, Mary and Lance were married on September 5th at St. Peter's Church in Fitzroy Road in Heeley. The happy couple were grateful that Lance's employment in the steelworks meant that he wasn't drafted into the forces to fight, as jobs such as his played a vital role in providing steel plate and shells for use in the devastating war.

Our story now, however, concentrates on another important event, the arrival of Mary and Lance's baby daughter on December 28, 1914.

Edna, the main character of our eventful tale, had arrived at last.

The next stage of the story now briefly follows Edna's life up to the age of 40.

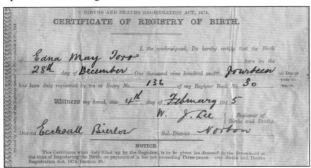

Unfortunately, its beginning did not start too well as her mother, Mary, was ill for some time following a difficult birth. To compound her problem, she went on to have a second child eleven months later and a third child ten months after that, resulting in her being too tired and ill to look after her three children properly. Fortunately, her parents Eliza Ann and Ernest kindly offered to care for baby Edna, who was still only 21 months old, at their cottage in Little Norton until their daughter improved. This decision was also influenced by the fact that Mary's husband, Lance, had now received his call-up papers for service in the Army. On the 19th May, 1917, Private 73867 Eugene Lancelot Torr joined the West Riding Regiment and for the next two years only saw his wife and children when he could get away on leave.

However, Mary and Lance's fondness for children was to influence Edna's destiny, as over the next few years they had three more children which not only put great demands on the very limited amount of space they had in their rented accommodation, it also put greater demands on Mary's rather frail health. An important decision was made, therefore, which enabled the family connection with Little Norton to continue unbroken. It was decided that Edna should continue to live with and be brought up by her grandparents on a permanent basis.

Edna at 51 Little Norton Lane

Before we wander through Edna's early life, let's have a quick look at what Mary's brother, George, was doing at this time. Surely he wouldn't have welcomed the arrival of a young baby in his parents' house after his sister's marriage and departure had given him a degree of freedom at last. Well, the answer lies in his schoolboy dreams. He had always dreamt about the glamorous life he could lead as a soldier in the British Army, and World War One gave him the opportunity he sought. As two year old Edna moved into No. 51, her Uncle George moved out and signed up for King and country, and the little one-up, two-down at Little Norton was now home to a cute baby girl and her doting grandparents.

It's strange, isn't it, how Eliza Ann seems to have been destined to share her home, and in particular her bedroom, with other family members nearly all her life. Before getting married she had shared a room with her brothers and sisters for twenty six years. Following her marriage, she and her husband had enjoyed about six months to themselves in their new home before Mary and then George arrived. After Mary left about seventeen years later to get married, George stayed with his parents for another two years before leaving to join the army, only to be followed a few weeks later by the arrival of Edna.

It's obvious, therefore, that the dividing curtain in the little cottage's only bedroom barely had time to be taken down and washed before it was put back up again, allowing the shared sleeping area once again to be alive with the sounds of cries, gurgles and laughter at all hours of the night. This curtain was in fact destined to form the flimsy boundary between Edna's and her grandma's sleeping areas for the next thirty eight years. Such was life in those days when the shared needs of families usually came first.

Coinciding with Edna's move to Little Norton during this time of the war, an enormous army camp of prefabricated offices, workshops and living quarters had been built for the Women's Auxiliary Army Corps just beyond the little row of cottages in which she lived. This not only brought the reality of the war to this otherwise quiet rural area, it also brought some excitement for Edna and her young friends as they grew up amidst the activity generated by this mini-village. A few years after the end of the hostilities, the Army Corps left the camp and the women's living quarters provided homes and gardens for severely wounded ex-servicemen. These men, despite having suffered terrible injuries, were able to work producing fabric and clothing incorporating different designs in existing buildings within the camp that had been converted for this purpose. The whole complex became well known in the city as Painted Fabrics, this name being displayed in large letters on the workshop roof for all to see.

Edna was about 9 years old by this time and was fascinated by this massive enterprise on her doorstep. She would often wave and chat to the servicemen and their families working and living there as she strolled along Little Norton Lane (although not yet named) on each side of which the complex had been built.

It was now 1923 and other changes had taken place in the area. The steep section of Chesterfield Road from Abbey Lane upwards had changed its name to Meadowhead and a block of dwellings incorporating one detached, three pairs of semi-detached and eleven terraced houses had been built

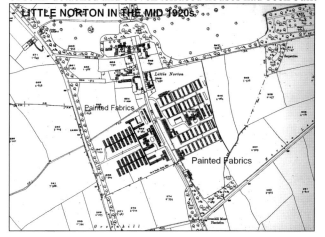

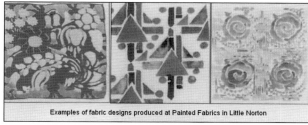

Examples of fabric designs produced at Painted Fabrics in Little Norton

on this road just above the Brick Works. Below the brickworks, particularly around the junction with Abbey Lane, the last twenty five years had seen a huge increase in housing with row upon row of terraced streets edging their way along Norton Woodseats, creeping along Abbey Lane and moving part-way up Meadowhead. Churches were still being built in those days instead of being knocked down as they are nowadays, and the Roman Catholic Church of our Lady and St. Thomas took its place adjacent to the densely packed terraced housing of Harboard Road and Green Hill Road above Abbey Lane.

However, let's get back to Edna. During the day, of course, she was at school, but work was hard to come-by for her granddad which meant that very little money came into the household. Second or third-hand dresses, together with worn-out, ill fitting shoes and no socks, made the little girl's schooldays somewhat difficult, although she was one of many in this situation.

Conditions generally were very primitive, with fresh water only being available from a pump a hundred yards or so up the road. Neither gas nor electricity supplies had reached this remote area, and the local residents had to make do with candles, paraffin lamps and log fires for their daily heating and lighting requirements.

In the absence of running water, toilet facilities were only offered by outside middins which were swilled down with buckets of water and collected and emptied by the local authority once weekly.

Despite these conditions, which were obviously the norm in those days, Edna enjoyed life, and meeting up with her friends for her daily walk to school was quite a treat. You will recall that her Grandma Eliza's walk to school with her friend Emmie about forty five years earlier had been a real delight and adventure. Now, young Edna and her friends were making the same journey along the same route where time seemed to have stood still. The cinderpath (later to be known as Serpentine Walk) was still there, and the open views over the parkland were as beautiful as ever. There was one other special thing that had not changed.

"Look Edna," shouted one of her little friends as they gazed across the rolling parkland bordered by the narrow lane known as Bunting Nook which meandered upwards from the side of Norton Grange. "There are some baby deer over there. Aren't they cute?"

The beautiful, speckled brown youngsters, which have been immortalised by Walt Disney's Bambi for every child these days, were frolicking around in the morning sunshine and causing as much delight to their audience now as their forefathers had caused Edna's grandparents nearly half a

Deer Park in the grounds of Norton Hall

century earlier. Such is the pleasure of living in the countryside where nature is oblivious to most change and life carries on as it has done for decades. Edna and her pals even had to make a mad dash for school just as Eliza and Emmie had. It just goes to show that people don't change much either, do they?

It's interesting to note that Norton Park, which was bought by J G Graves and presented to the City in the late 1920's, has lost little of its beauty. In fact, five generations later, Eliza Ann's great-great-great grandson, Thomas, is now enjoying its delights along with thousands of other Sheffield folk.

Graves Park Lake in 2006

The end of Edna's school years at the age of 14 coincided with an exciting event in her life. It was a pretty normal start to the day with grandad going off to work after

gobbling down his bowl of porridge and drinking a mug of sooty tea which usually formed his breakfast. Grandma had also been trying in vain to pour some water into her own mug from the heavy, black kettle which had been hissing angrily on the hob. Edna had noticed her predicament.

"I'll fetch the water today, grandma. The kettle seems to have run out."

"Thank you, dearie. My legs are a bit wobbly these days, so I could do with some help."

Grabbing hold of the sturdy handle of the well-used wooden water-bucket in the corner of the room, the helpful teenager waltzed out of the front door into the welcome sunshine of a beautiful summer's morning. A couple of geese strutting in front of a small-holding across the road gave her a noisy greeting as she passed by, whilst some inquisitive cows temporarily stopped their incessant grinding of freshly chewed grass in the paddock area adjacent to the cottages.

Little Norton Lane

The old well and its tiresome pump, which had provided water in this area for as long as people could remember, had just been replaced by a new modern tap which Edna was looking forward to using. She noticed, as she approached, that someone was already there filling a bucket, and as she got nearer she was delighted to see that it was her friend.

"Hi, Dorothy. Looks like you got here first. It's great isn't it, not having to push that big old pump handle any more."

"Hi, Edna. Just look at this. It's dead easy now, although if you're not careful you'll put more water in your bucket than you can carry."

Thanking her friend for her advice, Edna half filled her bucket in no time at all and proudly staggered down the road with her wet load.

Within a few minutes she arrived back at the old wooden gates to her home where she put the bucket down and rested for a while. As she stood there with her back to the little row of quaint, stone cottages and looked around her, she couldn't help but feel how lucky she was to live in such beautiful and exciting surroundings where happy memories were made. She loved to watch events such as the hay-making in the fields and Mr Hunstone taking his cows from Park Farm just up the lane to and from the fields

Park Farm

at milking time. Mr Goy's pigs were also a delight to watch as they could always be guaranteed to squeal with delight every time she approached them at his farm which was only a stone's throw away. What Edna particularly liked, however, was chatting to the hissing geese, the squawking hens, the quacking ducks and any other small, lost animals which had been placed in the small enclosure (called a Pinfold) opposite her front door while awaiting collection by their owners.

I think we can confidently say, therefore, that despite her primitive standard of living and being rather isolated from her parents and her brothers and sisters, she was happy and contented. She was also a bit of a day-dreamer.

"Edna, what are you doing standing there? Are you all right?"

Her grandmother's call from the doorway behind the young teenager quickly snapped her out of her dreams, and she hurriedly scooped up her bucket and staggered into the cottage with it.

"Here we are grandma. I've not been long, have I?" she chirped. "I'll make you a pot of tea if you like."

"I don't know what I'd do without you, dear," came the response. "No one could ask for a more helpful grand-daughter."

Helping her grandmother in the home was something that Edna had got used to doing from a very early age. The experience gained from this would prove to be very useful now that she was beginning her working life, as employment for most young ladies in the early 1900's usually meant working as a domestic servant, doing cleaning, sewing, shopping, cooking and anything else that men didn't like doing. Edna, of course, was no exception, and the only employment available to her was that of a house-helper in the Little Norton area doing such jobs.

She was a very good worker and managed to earn about five shillings a week (25p in today's money) which she gave to her grandmother to supplement the money she herself tried to earn taking in sewing, knitting, washing and ironing. Grandad Ernest, now 58 years old, had been made redundant from his job at the steelworks several years earlier and was not in good health. Although he managed to get the odd job or two labouring, he was mostly on the dole and provided very little money for the up-keep of his family. Unfortunately, by the time he reached his 66th birthday he was suffering badly from the long term effects of the appalling conditions which he had endured in the steel industry over many years. Sadly, on the 17th March 1938, three months before his 67th birthday, he died of his ailments, leaving his widow Eliza Ann and his now 24 year old grand-daughter, Edna, to cope on their own.

By this time, Eliza Ann was 69 years old and had been drawing her ten shillings (50 pence) a week pension for four years. When added to Edna's five shillings a week and another few shillings she was able to earn taking in domestic chores, this amounted to about £1 a week total income, which equates to about £30 a week today. It's not a lot for two people to live on, is it?

There was one other interesting job that Edna really enjoyed but rarely publicised. She did a bit of baby-sitting for Derek and Sylvia Dooley. Derek was the best and most popular footballer that Sheffield has ever known, and Edna was quietly proud of the fact that she had been entrusted to work for them in this capacity.

It was another eighteen years later in 1956, when Edna was forty, that her grandmother died at the ripe old age of 86. During that time, her health had deteriorated and she had become rather frail which had necessitated Edna fitting in the tasks of full-time carer with any domestic employment she was able to find.

Edna, aged about 40

However, as we look back over Grandma Eliza's somewhat ordinary life, when simply managing to exist presented quite a challenge, we suddenly find that this ordinary lady had in fact been touched with fame in the latter years of her life. Let's see how this came about, shall we?

The year was 1947 and the country had recently emerged successfully from the dreadful traumas of the Second World War. In addition, the winter of that year had produced the country's worst snowfall on record leaving the population of our small but proud island shell-shocked in more ways than one. On November 20th, Princess Elizabeth decided to brighten up the country by marrying Philip, the

Newly married Prince Philip and Princess Elizabeth

Duke of Edinburgh. This colourful and exciting occasion raised the spirits of the British population and resulted in many friends of the royal couple sending them gifts of food parcels to celebrate their wedding.

You might ask at this stage what Elizabeth's wedding has got to do with Eliza Ann Wainwright. Let's go back to the beginning of the war to find out. During those traumatic times, Eliza had spent many long hours knitting and making clothes for the British soldiers fighting on the front lines. Her efforts had unexpectedly been rewarded by the delivery to her modest home in 1947 of a food parcel sent to her by Princess Elizabeth (later to become Queen Elizabeth II). Accompanying this parcel was a letter written and signed personally by Elizabeth. This has been treasured and saved

over the last sixty years, firstly by Edna and latterly by her niece. It is a bit of history to be cherished. I wonder if the Queen, as she is now in her 83rd year, remembers sending both the parcel and letter to Eliza, who was probably one of several kindly Sheffield folk who quietly did their bit for the war?

BUCKINGHAM PALACE

Many kind friends overseas sent me gifts of food at the time of my wedding. I want to distribute it as best I can, and to share my good fortune with others I therefore ask you to accept this parcel with my very best wishes.
Elizabeth

EDNA ALONE

But, of course, time moves on and so must we. The 40 year old subject of our story now found herself alone and totally independent. Caring for others had been the only way of life she had known so, predictably, she successfully applied to work at an elderly person's care home in the nearby Low Edges area.

Edna was a hard-working and dedicated employee at this home where she spent nearly twenty years carrying out both domestic and caring duties. She was extremely well thought of by both the management staff and the residents. Her understanding of elderly people and her ability to empathize with them was second to none, and she often recalled the many happy times they spent together and the almost daily supply of sweets they gave her in appreciation of her kindness. It's unfortunate that the home no longer exists as I would have liked to have gathered a few interesting stories about her stay there.

However, we'll have to be content with the knowledge that Edna, who never sought thanks or special recognition, simply did her very best to help others and ensure that she "was never a nuisance to anyone", as she put it.

It is interesting to note that her rent at 51 Little Norton Lane was 11 shillings and six pence a week (57p in today's money) when she started work at the care home in the mid 1950s, and the following costs of a few household goods available in the shops at that time should also make interesting reading:

1/2lb Cheese: 1s/3d   1lb Sugar: 4d   1/4lb Tea: 1s/6d
1/2lb Margarine: 5d   Loaf of bread: 1s/9d   1lb Potatoes: 3d
Jar of Camp Coffee: 1s/4d   Tin of Ovaltine: 1s/6d
3oz Pears transparent Soap: 10d
3oz Wright's Coal Tar Soap: 9d
Omo, Rinso, Oxydol and Persil Washing Powders: 11d
Tin of Vaseline: 6d   Small Jar of Brylcreem: 1s/10d
Tin of Mansion Floor Polish: 1s-0d   Tin of Vim Cleaner: 7d

During Edna's first few years at the care-home, she walked to work from the quaint old cottages on Little Norton Lane where she had lived almost all her life. The mid 1960s, however, brought a shock to this caring lady as the Council decided to demolish the whole row of seven historic buildings and redevelop the area. By this time Edna was in her early fifties, and the wrench of moving, even to more modern accommodation, was a very stressful ordeal for her. The move took her to the top floor of a 4 storey block of maisonettes on the Lowedges housing estate. This accommodation, pleasant though it was, necessitated climbing 39 steps every time she returned to her new home from work, shopping trips or any other occasion. I wonder if Alfred Hitchcock got his idea for his well known thriller after hearing about these maisonettes which had no modern conveniences such as lifts?

By the time Edna reached the retirement age of 60, she had climbed about 140,000 steps just getting to her home. If you combine this with the 140,000 steps she first had to climb down each time she went out, I think that the flat she was given was designed for the ultra-fit, don't you. It was, in fact, a kill or cure situation which gradually ensured that going out at all was a momentous task for her to undertake.

Fifteen years and a further 420,000 steps later, (totalling almost three quarters of a million steps negotiated in the twenty five years she lived there), 75 year old Edna could no longer cope and she went to live for a time in Crookes with her younger sister, Connie. Ill health soon overtook her, however, and after several months in hospital she found herself in Riveln View Nursing Home, now being cared for by others. Life had gone a complete circle, and she didn't really like it.

Edna

Edna's sister Connie in her mid to late 70s

BACK AT THE NURSING HOME

Jon suddenly looked up and realised that he'd been sitting in the hallway of the home for nearly an hour, allowing his mind to drift round Edna's reminiscences which had gathered there over the years. It was time to get up and move on.

Trudging up the winding driveway which was now covered with a layer of early snow, he turned up the warm collar of his coat to keep out the oppressive dampness which was trying to wrap itself around his exposed neck.

"Chuffin' weather," he gasped as he reached desperately for the nearby handrail as his feet slipped and slithered to the shrieking delight of the gusting wind.

"It's got worse. No wonder there's no-one else visiting. There's no-one daft enough to be out in this lot."

Suddenly, he felt guilty. At least he had the choice. He could still hear Edna's despairing plea to him which she always made when it was time for him to leave her: "Can I go home please?"

Even though Jon always left promising to sort things out, he knew that the answer to her question was always going to be no; or was it?

Thoughts, questions and doubts tumbled around in his mind as he slowly trudged on homeward.

"She's lucky really," he muttered to the thickening snowflakes which were now swirling in front of his face. "After all, she was only given three days to live five years ago when she was taken into hospital suffering from depression, self imposed malnutrition and a very nasty ulcer."

Jon was right in a way, of course. Edna was indeed lucky to be alive. The quality of hospital treatment she had received at the Northern General was second to none. Special diets, constant care, the use of an expensive air bed and the application of the latest surgical techniques had literally brought her back from the brink of death. After months of such treatment she had been found a place in the nursing home.

"But was she really lucky to be in there? Was she really pleased to be alive?" he shouted at the ever teasing wind which moaned through the trees lining the street before once again shrieking with laughter as he almost fell to the ground after slipping off the edge of the kerbstone camouflaged by the thick, yet very soft snow.

As jumbled thoughts continued to confuse Jon's mind, misty-white shapes danced before his eyes and tormented his pounding head, making him gasp a little. He paused and peered into the dank, eerie darkness through which the tall, sombre street lamps shed their mysterious orange light on the whiteness below, offering the hint of a little warmth.

"The home she wants to return to doesn't exist any more," Jon explained carefully to the white-capped post box which suddenly appeared in front of him smiling broadly through its rosy red cheeks, "and she wouldn't be happy living with me."

He knew, of course, that it wasn't true. Edna would have loved to live with her kind friend and his family, but Jon also knew that they couldn't give her the specialist, twenty four hour care she actually needed. Such was the extent of his dilemma.

With head bowed to shield his face from the still driving snow, he made his way slowly along the white, unspoilt carpet which extended as far as he could see in front of him. His eyes suddenly rested on a crumpled, white paper bag which had somehow sunk into the soft sparkling crystals forming an irregular shaped crater around it. It was of little significance really, but that evening the sight of carelessly discarded litter (which proved to be a partially eaten meal from the local fish and chip shop) irritated Jon more than usual. How dare anyone spoil the magic white carpet that Nature's hand had so carefully painted?

But the young man's thoughts were fluttering between reality and pretence. The cold, swirling darkness had made him feel miserable and rather sad, whilst the pure-white vision of the snow also made him appreciate the wonder of life. The 'message' left by the discarded litter had simply said 'value and enjoy what you experience in life, but don't expect perfection.'

Edna certainly hadn't got perfection, he thought to himself, even though she is well cared for. She simply wants to go home.

Jon paused to avoid treading on a discarded, empty coke can which protruded defiantly from the snow in the centre of the footpath. This time, he accepted its presence with less concern, and by simply enjoying the magic of the evening he felt better.

"So, what's the answer?" he shouted suddenly as if to blame the still argumentative and irritating gusts of wind that continued to do their best to confuse him.

He stood there, his arms wide apart and head flung back in defiance of the tormenting yet beautiful weather. Glancing back, he noticed that Mother Nature had carefully painted over the blemishes he had encountered, and everything looked beautiful again. He knew that by tomorrow heavy black tyres and rubber soled boots would destroy this pure, delicate picture and turn it into a sea of grey mud. But, that was tomorrow. Today, nature had done its best, and no-one could expect any more.

"Of course," Jon shouted almost excitedly. "That's got to be the answer. We can only do our best. Today I've tried to give Edna a bit of happiness and some hope. I think I've done my best and I will deal with tomorrow when it arrives. Yes, that's got to be the answer."

Jon knew that his small efforts could only influence Edna's quality of life to a small degree. But he also knew that no-one can do better than their best, and in this complicated, high speed world of the 21st century, just to achieve your best is almost a miracle.

Sadly, although upon reflection, possibly wisely, Edna decided to remove any conflict of views which Jon might still be harbouring. On the second morning after his visit she chose to stay peacefully asleep in her bed, comforted by the knowledge that Jon would arrange for her to lie with her loving grandmother Eliza who had reared and cared for her from being a small baby.

A SPECIAL MEMORY

Amy Johnson

We will all remember this kindly lady as an ordinary person who was a little old fashioned, rarely went anywhere, rarely did anything too adventurous and, as far as we know, never set foot out of Sheffield. She simply lived to help and care for others.

However, there was one event in Edna's life which I haven't touched upon which appeared to be totally out of character. I think that it's worth mention at this stage.

Let's just nip back to the 1930s for a few minutes, to October 1931 to be precise. Edna was only 17 years old at the time and she somehow had made friends with a young lady by the name of Amy Johnson who had recently completed her famous solo flight in an aeroplane to Australia. The two young ladies struck up a conversation during which Edna made a casual remark.

"You know, Amy. I wouldn't mind trying a flight in a plane one day."

Amy looked at her friend in amazement.

"Are you sure Edna? Wouldn't you be rather nervous right up there in the clouds with the birds?"

"Not really," came the rather casual reply. "You're not nervous, so why should I be?"

Edna, as we know, was a lovely, gentle, caring but somewhat naive lady. But today, she wanted to do something different, and flying was her choice.

"Ok. Come on then. Let's go over to the aerodrome, and me and Johnnie will take you for a spin over Sheffield." (Edna learnt half an hour or so later that Johnnie was the name of Amy's plane).

Amy Johnson

That day was one which would have been envied by probably only the most daring of men and women at the time but, as the small aircraft lifted off from Norton on a clear, sunny afternoon, it was our demure little Edna who waved to the world on her first and only adventure into the sky.

Strangely enough, she rarely spoke of the event to anyone, and I wouldn't be surprised if she didn't even tell her grandmother who would most certainly have been shocked at the idea. But, that was Edna all over. She took life in her stride. She did whatever wanted doing and enjoyed whatever presented itself to her. Calmness came naturally to her, and her only regret in life appeared to be that her grandmother couldn't afford for her to train to be a nurse, a job at which she would have excelled.

EDNA GOES HOME

The day of the funeral, the 28th December 2000 (her birthday), was one which no-one present could possibly forget. More snow had fallen as if to order, and a soft, silent blanket of white crystals covered everything in sight. In total contrast, two large, gleaming black limousines stood proudly in the street outside Jon's house, one of which carried a simple, light oak coffin bedecked in a glorious display of multi-coloured flowers which shimmered in the reflected light from the snow.

Although the journey to the cemetery was slow, the entry through its large stone- pillared entrance was breathtakingly beautiful. As the two cars glided silently along the snow-covered driveway towards the small, stone chapel in the distance, tall, elegant trees stood proudly to attention on each side and bowed their snow-capped heads to form a magical archway over the small cortege

After a simple but sincere service to celebrate Edna's 86 years on this earth (exactly the same length of time as her grandma Eliza), Jon, his wife and their children were joined by two kindly carers from the nursing home as they followed Edna to her final resting place alongside her grandmother. Not a sound was to be heard as the small group paid their last respects, alone in a huge, white wonderland. Edna had gone home at last and she would once again be able to swap memories with her grandparents with whom she could now stroll along the country lanes of their past.

God bless you Edna.

IN LOVING
MEMORY
OF A
KIND LADY

EDNA MAY
TORR
BORN 28·DEC.1914
PEACEFULLY
LAID TO REST
28·DEC. 2000.

Dancing Don

This story is about a man who, on the surface, appeared to be simply a typical, down to earth Sheffielder. However, Don Brookes was much more than that. His working life lasted 75 years, he was married for 61 years, and was still Rock-and-Rolling to Chuck Berry and other 1960s favourites at the age of 91. To cap it all, he was never known to say a bad thing about anyone, EVER, and as a friend he was more dependable than your right arm. Let's look back over those 91 years and get a flavour of his life.

Our Don, as he was affectionately known, was born on 24th May 1913, three years after George V ascended the throne of England. The last horse-omnibus had just vacated the city's streets to make way for the posh, new motor buses which could roar past the clanking electric trams with obvious delight. Motor cars had been making their presence felt for a dozen years or more, and were scaring everyone to death as they topped 15 miles an hour down High Street and Fargate. This, it seemed was the modern age, when new technology was really taking hold.

Alas, the pride (and sometimes concern) shown by Sheffielders in this new age was quickly overtaken by the outbreak of war with Germany in 1914, when our Don was only one year old.

Fortunately, at this tender age, Don was neither aware of nor interested in the impact that these hostilities had on the city or his family, and when his brother Geoffrey was born a year later, looking after him made the now 2 year old feel happy and (we presume) rather proud.

As children, the two brothers lived a life of poverty in common with most others at that time. Their caring parents struggled to make ends meet but, during the depression years of the 1920s, unemployment lay like a huge dark shadow over the city with more than half the adult men and women in the iron and steel trades being out of work at its peak.

However, Don considered himself lucky to have a younger brother with whom he was able to share his life during these difficult times. Wandering cheerfully down to school together barefooted even at the age of 8 and 10 was quite a normal experience for them both, although going without breakfast, and often lunch, did sometimes take the edge off their naturally happy dispositions.

"Save me the core, will yer?" was a regular request from Don as some of his more affluent mates actually brought an apple into school for break time.

The teachers at Abbeydale School, which sat a little uncomfortabley at the side of the Broadfield Pub on Abbeydale Road, were, nevertheless, very understanding

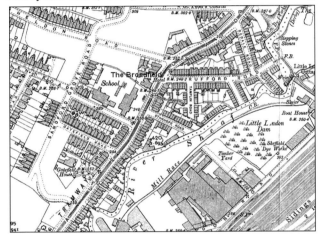

and often managed to provide a slice of bread or two for the desperate-duo to help them through the day.

Despite the difficulties, children in those days managed to find much pleasure in entertaining themselves. Hide and seek, cops and robbers, and cowboys and indians occupied many enthusiastic and energetic youngsters for hours on end, and Don and Geoff were no exceptions. They, like thousands of others, also enjoyed competing in games of

Abbeydale Primary School

skill. Don was a wiz at manipulating a yo-yo up and down its string, whilst both brothers were experts at whipping a top, playing marbles and throwing five stones (called snobs locally).

It was now 1924, however, and 11 year old Don had done well at Abbeydale School and had subsequently moved on to King Edwards. It was hard work there, and everyone had homework to do each night. Fortunately, Don enjoyed a challenge, and hard work was something he thrived on. In fact, it was his positive attitude to work and life as a whole that was to be the making of him as one of the most liked and respected people you could ever hope to meet.

However, life's challenges were still in their infancy, and his conversion from young lad to teenager in 1926 was a significant point in his life. To the city itself and, indeed,

King Edward VII School

to the rest of the country, this particular date was remembered as the year of the general strike during which unemployment was rife, people were starving and personal suffering was everywhere.

To 13 year old Don, however, this year represented the time that he very nearly lost his life. It was the morning of Good Friday when the problems started. Let's see what happened.

It was a fine April morning during which the rising sun was doing its best to brighten up the small, but neat little terraced house in Ashland Road where Don and his family lived. He had woken up to the dawn chorus of bird calls

with a twinging pain in his stomach. As daylight had silently crept into his bedroom through the half-open curtains, the pain had increased considerably and his moans of despair had awakened his brother also.

"What's the matter, Don? Are you alright?"

"Geoff. Go and fetch mam, quickly. I've got belly-ache and it's really bad."

Don's halting, tearful plea to his brother had taken the young lad by surprise and he almost fell through the bedroom door in his anxiousness to fetch help as quickly as he could.

Within a minute or two, the kindly, concerned face of his mother appeared at the bedside and a cool, gentle hand rested on his hot, sweating forehead. The sight of her son writhing on his bed, his pale face contorted with pain, told her in no uncertain terms that she had to act decisively.

"Geoffrey, nip down to the surgery straight away and ask the doctor to come as soon as possible. Don't worry, it's not far."

The half an hour or so which passed by before the doctor arrived seemed never ending to Don and his anxious mother, and it was with great relief when the smartly dressed, bespectacled figure appeared in the bedroom doorway.

"Can I come in?"

It only took a few minutes for the kindly physician to gently examine his young patient, and it was without hesitation that he made his diagnosis.

"Its appendicitis, I'm afraid, Mrs. Brookes. I think it may have burst, so we'll have to get him to hospital quickly."

"I'll be alright, mam, won't I?" sobbed the now rather fearful young teenager who, like most people, dreaded the mention of the word hospital.

Trying hard to hold back her own tears, the distraught mother managed to control her inner feelings and, despite her aching heart beating wildly in rhythm to a pounding headache, she reassured her son quietly and gently.

"Of course you will be, Don. A day or so in the hospital with those wonderful doctors and nurses will see you as right as rain."

A gentle sobbing behind her reminded the caring mum that young Geoff was also caught up in the trauma. Putting a comforting arm around his shoulders, she looked kindly into his big soulful eyes as tear drops welled up and rolled down his rounded cheeks.

"Now then, Geoffrey. Don't you worry. Everything will be fine. Just you nip along and tell your dad to come home as soon as he can while I stay with your brother. Off you go now."

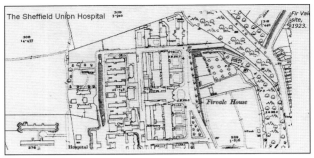

The Sheffield Union Hospital

It wasn't long before the heart-stopping tone of the ambulance's siren cut through the fresh morning air like an

Hospital main entrance

executioner's sword. Within ten minutes, patient and mum had arrived at the huge stone walls surrounding the Sheffield Union Hospital (later to become the City General Hospital and then the Northern General Hospital). Behind these walls, the Firvale Institution, part of the Firvale workhouse, still provided poor-relief and care of the aged and infirm, whilst the hospital itself provided treatment and care of the sick.

Unfortunately, mam's prediction of 'a day or so in hospital' was a slight underestimation. Poor Don contracted peritonitis (a serious inflammatory disease of the lining of the abdominal cavity), which kept him there from Good Friday to Christmas Eve of that despairing year. During those 8½ months, he had to endure five operations, including the removal of part of his bowel.

But, was our Don down hearted? Not on your life. He was given good food (albeit only liquids for the first month), and was cared for by one or two very 'dishy' nurses. He also befriended a deaf 70 year old coal miner by the name of Old Handley who had arrived in the ward with a bump on his head. This friendly old character stayed about two months and helped on the wards by doing polishing and cleaning. He should have been discharged after a couple of

weeks or so but, with the kind help of the ward Sister who very much valued his domestic activities, managed to overstay his entitlement by six weeks or so.

Christmas Eve, 1926, was, as you might expect, a joyous time for Don as he arrived home into the arms of his family. That night, two woolly stockings hanging up at the bottom of his and Geoff's beds were secretly filled by 'Father Christmas' with an apple, an orange and a new penny in each foot, and several small games bulging enticingly up each leg. As the fingers of the battered old clock in their bedroom noisily ticked their way round to 4.30 in the morning, Don, as if by sixth sense, suddenly sat bolt upright in bed and shouted "mam, he's been".

Like thousands of other children, Don's mind must have been programmed to wake up on Christmas morning at this unearthly hour just to ensure that his parents didn't manage to have a good night's sleep prior to the hectic activities of Christmas Day itself. However, Don's outburst in the blackness of the early morning was now predictable, and mam and dad Brookes had given him strict instructions several years earlier to help himself to just one of his presents when he woke, and to play with it quietly in order that they could grab a few more hours valuable sleep. This arrangement did, by and large, work quite well, although in earlier years the sheer excitement of the occasion had sometimes caused one or other of the two brothers to decide to be sick on the bedclothes much to the frustration of their tired mother.

Nevertheless, this Christmas worked out for all concerned. Don's shout had, not surprisingly, woken up his younger brother following which the two delighted youngsters grabbed hold of and examined their mis-shapen Christmas Stockings.

"Shh. Don't make a noise Geoff. We might wake up mam and dad. It's still dark outside, you know.

"Let's open one present then, Don. I'll go first."

"Alright then, Geoff. I hope my apple's better than last year 'cos it looked as though it had been in a fight with Joe Louis, Didn't it?"

Trying hard to stifle their giggles, the two excited brothers quickly tore the plain wrapping paper off one present each.

"Cor, look at this Don. I've got a new Snakes and Ladders game. It's great."

"Mine's even better Geoff. I've got one of those Ludo games. I can't believe it,"

This, then, was the beginning of Christmas. However, Don was still very weak, so after a few wonderful days with his family, he was sent to a convalescent home on the outskirts of town for two months or so to get his strength back. At the end of this recovery period, it was approaching Easter again, nearly one year on from that dreadful Good Friday of 1926. The Easter holidays were nearly upon them, and it was only a few weeks before Don would then be 14 years old. Education, therefore, has been non-existent during Don's thirteenth year, and as children left school in those days at 14, he was now of working age and raring to go out and earn his own money.

"I tell you what dad. You're into music aren't you? How about putting in a good word for me somewhere and getting me a job in the business. You know what a good singer I am, don't you?"

Now liking music was one thing, but claiming to be a good singer was another. You could understand the lad's

interest in music, mind you, as his father had built up a very successful dance orchestra which played both locally and abroad. Morecambe was one of its most popular local venues, whilst playing on the Union Castle passenger ship on its summer tours from London to Africa via Suez was as exciting as it was lucrative.

However, there was to be no such glamour for Don's first job.

"You can forget singing for the time being my lad. I've managed to get you a job helping out at the Glyco Petrol Company at the top of Woodbourn Road. The money's not bad, and it'll be good experience for you."

"But dad…"

"No buts, lad. Your mother needs the money while I'm away working and there's nowt else going as far as I can see."

Despite his young years, the would-be musician knew that he was lucky to have a job at all in these times of high unemployment. After all, he thought to himself when his father had explained to him what the company did, its offices were located near to the Sheffield canal, and it would be great fun watching the large fuel-barges bringing National Benzole petrol up the waterway. He would be able to watch the long fuel pipes snake over the side of the boats and make their way to large storage tanks on the bank-side where careful mixing and blending produced the then very well known National Benzole Mixture.

Canal Basin/Victoria Quays

It was one of Don's jobs, as office-boy cum tea-masher cum general helper, to take small samples from those 400 gallon tanks of fuel (which the company bought at 5d (two pence) a gallon) so that they could be tested for quality before the fuel was collected by special wagons for delivery and sale to garages where it was sold at the pumps for one shilling (five pence) a gallon.

His first day at work, however, was not quite as exciting as he anticipated. A cold winter had plunged into an exceptionally cold Spring, and Don found himself helping to light fires under the wagons to warm them up before their engines could start. But such was life. The warm Spring of 1926 had started with the chilling challenge of peritonitis, whilst the spring of 1927 had started with a chilling challenge of a different sort. However, if there was one thing that Don enjoyed, it was a challenge. That's what life was all about for this young man.

Life at home, meantime, continued to be a challenge for all the family also. In common with most households in those days, the coal and wood-fuelled kitchen range provided the downstairs heating and main cooking facilities. Luckily, mains water had been piped to this urbanized area of Abbeydale along with gas which fed a small ring in the kitchen. Electricity was not yet on hand, but candle-light was available to show the way to the two small upstairs bedrooms in which fire places waited in vain to burst forth with heat.

Now our Don was an enterprising young fellow who realized that in these hard times it would be of great benefit to all the family if he could earn a few extra bob (shillings). So, what did he decide to do? What else, but breed chickens! The little terraced home at Ashland Road probably wasn't ideal for keeping hens and chickens, but if money could be made from them, then the old adage 'where there's a will there's a way' applied.

In Don's case, he decided to keep a few hens simply laying eggs for morning breakfast and for sale to whoever wanted them, and two broody hens who, with the help of a neighbour's cockerel, laid fertile eggs from which chickens would hatch. Each hen laid twelve to fourteen eggs and, following twenty one days sitting, hopefully produced two dozen chicks between them, for which Don had established a good customer base.

However, contrary to the well-known saying 'never count your chickens 'til they're hatched', our young chicken breeder had to do the opposite and guarantee the number of young birds being supplied to his customers at least a couple of days before delivery. To do this, on the 19th day of sitting on the eggs by the mother hen, he had to entice her away from her clutch of eggs, usually by feeding her remote from her nest. During such time, he carefully removed all the warm eggs and placed them one by one in a bucket of warm water. Those eggs which bounced around in the water contained chickens, alive and kicking. Those which stayed perfectly still were, sadly, addled and contained dead chicks or no chick at all. The exact number of chickens which would hatch on the 21st day was thus established at this stage, and the still warm eggs were replaced in their nest without the mother hen knowing that they had ever been removed.

Not only did this enterprising young teenager earn himself the reputation of a skilled and reliable chicken breeder, he was also a dab-hand at building and repairing bikes. Cycling was a major form of transport in those days, but his parents were unable to afford to buy their two sons one to ride on. Unperturbed by this, Don taught himself how to repair old bikes he acquired for next to nothing, and then also proceeded to build bikes from spare parts he acquired from scrap yards and the like. 'Don'll mend it for yer' was a common comment from his friends when someone had damaged their bike or it had broken down due to a fault or wear and tear. The odd few coppers or more that he made from offering his repair service in this activity once again helped to keep the wheels of life turning more freely.

But of course, work didn't occupy all Don's time at this age. He enjoyed playing football in his back yard and his traffic-free street, or pretending to be a Len Hutton or Dennis Compton swinging an old wooden bat around in front of three chalked stumps on the house or boundary wall. At weekends in the summer months he particularly enjoyed doing a bit of camping with his mates, all of them arriving at their destination on their old but reliable (thanks to Don) bicycles.

As the teenage years rolled on, Don's interests centred more on music, dancing and films, and by the time he was 17, he was going out five or six nights a week. The Abbeydale Cinema was one of his favourite haunts, with 4d (4 old pence)

paying for a front row seat in front of a large, flickering screen or, better still, 6d giving entry to the local hop in the dance-hall on the floor below. Often, when Reginald Dixon was playing on the organ on a raised platform in the cinema, Don would stay and listen, enthralled by his music, and then nip downstairs for an evening of Jitterbugging with the other lads and lasses. Brincliffe Oaks, Nether Edge Hall, Greystones and the Star Cinema dance halls were also regular venues, and there were very few, if any, dances that Don and his mates were unable to perform.

But what of his vices? Surely this hard working, hard playing young man did things that were frowned upon? What about smoking and drinking for example? Well, he'd had what he called a sensible grounding in these activities. From the age of 13 or 14, his parents had allowed him to have an occasional drink or cigarette at home in the hope that by so doing it would dampen his urge to drink or smoke excessively elsewhere later. This rather forward-looking attitude worked for their son, and although he still enjoyed a pint or a cig or two in the company of others, it was in moderation that he enjoyed them most. Indeed, moderation in all things became a habit with our Don (except of course, with dancing which he enjoyed at all times), and a couple of pints of Gilmore's Dark Mild at 5d a throw in the tap-room (6d in the best room) plus a tuppenny packet of 5 woodbines (including 2 or 3 matches) was about his limit. A few of his better-off mates smoked Players or Gold Flake at 11½d for 20, but Don's money never really stretched to those dizzy heights.

The highlight of any year was, however, the annual visit to Blackpool or Bridlington which, by the age of 18, he was able to go on with his friends rather than with his parents. With Bed and Breakfast being £6 a week, there was always a bit left in the kitty to dance the night away every evening.

By the age of 19, however, Don was keen to progress in life and had joined Cravens, a delivery company in Darnall, where he took and passed his HGV (Heavy Goods Vehicle) Driving Test on a Leyland-Bull wagon. About this time, he also managed to get hold of a Ford 8 car which, in those days, you could have in any colour you like as long as it was black. As there were no car driving tests in those days, his HGV licence, which cost one shilling for three years, sufficed for any vehicle and continued to do so for the rest of his life. Whether or not Don would have passed a modern-day test to drive a car is difficult to say, but even at the age of 90 he could manoeuvre his faithful old red

Vauxhall into and out of seemingly impossible parking spaces without any problem at all.

With vehicles and driving becoming something of a passion, and now wishing to move on and better himself, this ambitious young man went to work for a local man by the name of Henry Speight who ran a combined coal and removal business. Mixing transport-related operations wasn't unusual in those days, and the use of a flat wagon for coal deliveries and an old 1920's Leyland van with hard tyres for his removals gave Mr. Speight some reasonable degree of flexibility.

Don enjoyed his work at Speight's, particularly as it involved meeting people as well as driving. After a few years, however, he become a little frustrated at the lack of ambition of his boss who had run his business without change for many years. With the confidence of a wealthy executive, instead of that of a 27 year old ambitious young man, he bought out Henry Speight in 1940 with a view to expanding the business. Although Don had managed to save up a modest amount of cash over the 13 years he had been working, it was certainly not enough for him to be able to buy any new vehicles. He decided, therefore, to go into partnership with Shirley's Haulage Company which also operated with one van and one flat wagon. An expanding company was now emerging with combined assets of two vans and two wagons which encompassed removals, haulage and coal deliveries.

Despite the success of this venture, Don realised that with fierce competition from the ever growing army of coal merchants and the increasing number of haulage contractors, it would probably make commercial sense to specialise in furniture removals. Demand for this type of service was steadily improving with the growth of housing in the new urban areas springing up and around the city, and Don's people-skills and honest approach to life would stand him in good stead in this area. Mr Shirley. However, wasn't too keen on change so there was only one thing for it. Don decided to buy him out also.

So, at last, our budding entrepreneur had done it. He now owned his own removals business. Within a short time he had sold the two flat wagons and used the money to buy an extra van. His three vans in their well recognised two-tone blue livery now buzzed around the growing city moving furniture and household effects seven days a week,

and the sincere thanks which Don received from hundreds of grateful householders made his dedicated efforts to give a good service much more worthwhile.

However, isn't there something amiss with this popular Sheffield removal business run by Don Brookes? On the

A later photograph of one of Don's vans on a windy day!

1962 severe gale in Sheffield

sides of his posh vans the words 'Henry Speight' jumped out for all to see, and indeed still do so today nearly seventy years after he took over the company from Henry Speight. Why didn't he change the name to 'Brookes Removals' all those years ago? I decided to ask him.

"Well, yer see, Bob, people had got used to seeing Henry's name on the van by 1940, and to be fair to the bloke, it was him who started the firm, wasn't it."

These few words spoken in his 89th year reflected Don's attitude to life. Fairness and honesty were his trademarks, and he didn't feel that it was right to get rid of his old boss' name, despite having dramatically improved and expanded the business. Don never did anything for personal glory; he simply wanted to do his best in a way that would help others.

But, let's not rush things. Despite his ambition to get on in life, our very special Sheffield character still retained his insatiable need to dance, which peaked when he met and subsequently married a lovely lass called Dora. It was at one of the local hops at Nether Edge Hall that they both met, and this vision of loveliness was sitting at the girls' side of the dance floor with her friends while Don, his brother and their friends were sitting at the other side eyeing them all up. That was the way things happened in those days, and it was usually both the attractiveness of the girl who had been spotted and the courage of the boy to get up and go over and ask her for a dance which determined progress from there on. With Don, however, the question of courage didn't come into it as he rarely stood on ceremony. If he liked a girl, he would simply go and tell her so, albeit in the politest possible way. However, as he strolled casually across the shiny dance floor which reflected a maize of coloured lights from the ballroom ceiling, he noticed that Dora looked a little apprehensive.

LAND'S END TO JOHN O'GROAT'S

SKILLED WORKMEN.
PERSONAL SUPERVISION.

HENRY SPEIGHT,
216 CROOKESMOOR RD.
SHEFFIELD.

Telephone—Central 1804.

BY ROAD, RAIL OR SEA.

"May I have this dance, please, Dora?"

A pair of sparkling eyes which were wanting to say 'yes' looked up at him for a moment or two before somewhat reluctantly glancing away.

"I'd love to, Don, but that nice chap over there has already asked me, so I've promised the next one."

Don could hardly believe his eyes when he realised that Dora was pointing directly at Geoff.

"You've promised the next dance to HIM! That's my young brother. I'm not having this."

But of course, true love rarely follows a nice, tidy line,

Don and brother Geoff in later years

and Dora was such a pretty little thing that it was no real surprise that both brothers fell for her. Fortunately for Don, she did in due course choose him and, following several years courtship, they married on May 25th, 1943, the day after Don's 30th birthday. It's strange, isn't it, how Don chose rather fraught times to make very important decisions. He arrived in this world just before the First World War began, and then got married just as the Second World War was at its peak. He didn't do things by half, did he?

However, we've only reached the time when Don and Dora got hitched. Over the next 50 years they were inseparable, spending as much of their spare time as possible dancing anywhere and everywhere that hosted a dance-floor or a ballroom.

During his working hours, which usually encompassed Monday to Saturday, Don continued to build up his removal business by concentrating on reliability, customer satisfaction and value for money.

The busy man had also developed a very keen interest in motor sports, and would travel miles around the country

with Dora, usually on Sundays, to watch motor-bike, stock-car, saloon car and formula-3 races. He even managed to get himself the job as a track Marshall which not only created more involvement and excitement, but also enabled him to influence the level of safety for both participants and spectators alike.

Surprisingly enough, in amongst their very hectic but enjoyable life, the happy couple did manage to find time to have a son, Michael, early in their marriage. Mick, as he is known to his friends, always enjoyed joining his parents on their adventures and became as enthusiastic as they were in due course.

But, as we know, life moves on and we all get a little older. As the loving couple reached the age of 80, Dora became less able to 'trip the light fantastic' than she used to be, and decided to call it a day as far as dancing was concerned. She did, nevertheless, encourage and indeed insist that her dear husband Don should continue being active for as long as he could.

"It will do you good, Donald," she always said. "You need to keep fit, even at your age. In any case I don't really

Later photo of Don and his son mick

want you under my feet all the time, do I?"

"Well, if that's what you want dear, that's what I'll do," was Don's usual reply.

And so, this remarkable man, at 80 years young, continued running his removals company six days a week, now of course ably assisted by his son Michael. At the end of each day he would relax by going out 'gigging' which always included meeting a host of friends, half of whom were lovely ladies (who he referred to as his daughters) with whom he would dance the night away.

"I'll tell you what, lad," he would say to me when I asked him how he kept so fit, "hard work, two pints of John

Don and his daughters

Smith's of an evening, and dancing eight nights a week is just the ticket. And what's more, lad," he added with a twinkle in his eye, "I've got at least twenty daughters that'll dance with me when I go out, so it's not a bad life, is it?"

Don's daughters, of course, were the wives and partners of his many friends and they felt it was a privilege to dance with such a caring, elderly (but not old) man. The problem was, however, that the lovable jitterbug-king nearly always insisted on doing the rock-and-roll, which more often than not tired his young partners out whilst he stayed fresh and lively.

Nemesis

Don with the Cadillacs

Red Rock

It was, in fact, the rock and pop groups and bands who Don insisted on following as they played in pubs and clubs across Sheffield, Chesterfield and many regions of Derbyshire. He'd been following The Cadillacs group, for example, for about 35 years and, indeed this group is still going strong 50 years after it was formed, now as a duo with Barry on vocals and lead guitar and Malcolm on vocals and rhythm.

Over the last ten to fifteen years or so, other bands and groups such as

Malcolm

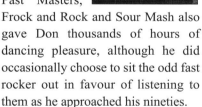
Barrie

Tequila Sunset, Nemesis, Red Rock, Twice Around, Look Twice, Jewel, Past Masters, Frock and Rock and Sour Mash also gave Don thousands of hours of dancing pleasure, although he did occasionally choose to sit the odd fast rocker out in favour of listening to them as he approached his nineties.

The 24th May was always a key day to look forward to for his legion of friends as they anticipated his annual birthday bash at a pub of his choice. From his 80th birthday onwards, he booked the Cadillacs to play for him and he always provided a tasty buffet for everyone in the pub. Dougie and Pat's at Holmesfield (also known as the Traveller's Rest) was his favourite venue. The caring

TEQUILA SUNSET

Pat, Dougie and Don

landlord and landlady there were 'one in a million', and nothing was too much trouble for them. Apart from providing a truly genuine, warm welcome to everyone who entered their 'home from home' pub, Dougie provided good beer and spirits at prices he considered to be fair (lower than

any other pub in the area), whilst Pat provided the best-you've-ever-tasted buffets as well as Saturday lunchtime home-made specials to die for.

Sadly for the customers, but deserving for the hardworking landlord and landlady, Dougie and Pat retired several years ago and the pub was converted to a restaurant. Don was thus obliged to move his birthday bash to another popular venue, the Sir William Hotel at Grindleford in Derbyshire where for fifteen years or so he had danced the night away every Sunday to many

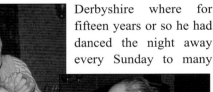

different rock and pop groups. The dance-floor there was bigger and better than most other places he went to, and he was always first up when the

music began. It was always with great affection that the musicians and the punters who sat at posh little tables all around the dance floor watched the slightly stooped, partly bald, grey haired man in his mid 80's choose a partner from those present. You couldn't help but feel proud to be a friend of this remarkable man who never seemed to look any different in this grey flannel trousers, striped shirt, posh tie and a beige (sometimes grey) cardigan. In fact, during the winter months he usually wore two or three cardigans which he peeled off one by one as he warmed up to the dancing.

"Come-on, lass," he would always say as he led his chosen 'daughter' onto the floor to dance. This was then followed by "thank you lass," as he escorted her back again when the dance had finished.

You might think that by the time he was approaching 89, that travelling to venues such as Grindleford or other locations in Derbyshire such as Bradwell, Tideswell and Chesterfield, might have presented him with a problem. Not on your life. He'd been driving since he was a teenager, and he wasn't going to give up now, 70 years or more later. He did, however, take the precaution of cutting his drinking down to 1½ pints on such occasions in order to make sure that he kept within the 2 pint limit imposed by the drink-driving laws.

It was not long after this time that Don had to reluctantly consider retiring from his full time job. He'd just turned 89 and, whilst checking oil levels in an overhead tank in his yard where his removal vans were kept, he fell off the ladder and broke his thigh bone adjacent to his hip joint. It was a bad break and required major surgery incorporating metal plates and bolts to repair the damage and necessitated a stay in hospital of six weeks. The prognosis offered by the hospital was not good.

"I'm afraid you'll not be able to walk properly again, Mr Brookes," he was told, "and you'll certainly never dance again."

Those chilling words from the staff-nurse at the Northern General Hospital, 76 years after his previous brush with death there, were probably the inspiration for another miraculous recovery. Determination had always played a major part in this long and eventful life, and this setback was to benefit by it also. Within two months of his accident he was walking well with the aid of crutches, and after three months he strolled into his local pub, the White Swan in Greenhill Village, with just one walking stick.

"Come-on lass," he said, grabbing hold of Elsa, one of his 'daughters', "let's show 'em."

Jewel, an upbeat rock duo, had just stuck up with their punchy version of Chuck Berry's 'Johnny B Good,' one of Don's favourites. Unable to resist the temptation, this amazing man discarded his stick and, although a little slower and stiffer than usual, went through his rock-and-roll routine with his apprehensive but very proud partner to the rapturous applause of the pub's customers. This was our Don, back in business as he had said he would be.

However, the enforced three months away from work had given the 89 year old rocker the taste for a little lie-in every morning and a more leisurely time in which to prepare the daily meals for his family which he had been doing for several years. His dear wife Dora, now 91 years old, spent most of her time in their bedroom as she found the stairs difficult to negotiate. Because of this, Don had been preparing breakfast and lunch for her before going off to work, although their son Michael had taken on the mantle of 'head cook and bottle washer' as well as trying to manage the removals business over the last three months. Don had also come to the remarkable conclusion that perhaps Michael, now in his early sixties, was old enough and capable enough to run the business on his own and thus allow him to retire. You can imagine the thoughts running though his head, can't you:

"I suppose after working all these years I could let Michael take over, although I don't know how well he'll manage without me. Still, it will give me more time and energy for my nights out dancing so it won't be all that bad, will it?"

So, after 75 years of constant full-time working, Don made his momentous decision to retire, although he did pop in to work from time to time to advise everyone how to do everything. However, with his eyes now set firmly on the future, this new man of leisure concentrated during the day on caring for Dora and doing chores such as cleaning, shopping, cooking and preparing meals. During the evenings, of course, he continued to do what he always did best, going out dancing 'eight nights a week' as he always put it.

He'd already booked the large Hill-Top Club in Dronfield, with a sumptuous buffet thrown in, for his 90th birthday bash, and as the day after would also be his Diamond Wedding Anniversary, he was expecting a good turnout for the dual event.

As always, The Cadillacs had been booked to play their inimitable rock and pop music, and on what was an

incredibly moving and exciting evening, Don danced the night away with just about every one of his twenty or thirty 'daughters'. It was a party to remember and this Peter Pan of Rock-and-Roll was in full flow with no indication of the trauma he'd gone through only a few months earlier.

He did, however, confide in me (when asked) that his hip still gave him 'a bit of jip' if he was on his feet too long!

As the tiring but memorable evening drew to a close, Don drew me to one side with a question only he would have asked:

"Where are we going tomorrow night, Bob? I hear they've got a good group on at the Miner's Club over yonder. How about it?"

Going dancing the following evening was just about the furthest thought from my mind that you could imagine. It was a few minutes before midnight, and after four hours of trying to keep up with Super-Don, I was feeling shattered.

"I'm not too sure Don," I recall replying. "I'll have to let you know if you don't mind."

"Never mind lad. It doesn't matter. I'll probably see you the following night if I don't see you tomorrow."

I think that said it all, don't you? Nine decades of work, excitement pleasure, struggle, trauma and success behind him, and he was still looking forward.

The White Swan in Greenhill Village and the Coach and Horses next to the Sheffield Football Club (the oldest in the world) in Dronfield bottom were his regular locals now, although he did still travel around many working men's clubs in the city of which he was an affiliated member. The 'Swan' was within walking distance, but was a bit on an uphill struggle, so he usually popped up in his old faithful Vauxhall Cavalier which had seen better days. The same car also took him to the 'Coach' a couple of times a week, where the 'home-from-home' landlord and landlady, Neil and Vicky, always gave him a good welcome. These two wonderful characters had, in fact, more or less taken over the mantle of Dougie and Pat as his, and most other people's, favourite publicans since the closure of the Travellers Rest.

It was during Don's 91st year that he caught the odd cold or two and seemed to slow down a little. His standard

Vicky and Neil

medication of half a glass of black beer topped up with hot water, a good measure of best rum and a spoonful of honey had always got him back on his feet quickly in the past, but it was taking a little longer this time. This slowing-down had also shown itself a few months earlier during his 91st birthday celebration at the Sir William in Grindleford at which time he had felt tired and actually sat a few dances out.

It was, however, in late October in the Coach and Horses one evening when, after dancing to a much slower Chuck Berry rock number with one of his special 'daughters', that Don actually complained for the first time of feeling a 'bit off-colour'.

The following week witnessed the rare event of him staying at home and, several days later, he was admitted to hospital with breathing difficulties.

November 12, 2004 was the day his family and friends will never forget. A hesitant, tearful voice on the telephone broke the news. Dancing Don had passed away peacefully in his sleep, and the world had lost a character who would never be able to be replaced. His legacy of honesty, kindness, laughter and sincerity lives forever in the minds of all those who knew him, and the memory of this man who had more dancing 'daughters' than you or I have had hot dinners will always stop us in our tracks whenever the strains of a Chuck Berry song hits the air-waves.

It is with both sadness and pride that I write this brief story of such a remarkable man who I had the privilege to call my friend. Don was a real Sheffield character who everyone loved, but none more so than his dear wife Dora and loving son Michael, to whom this chapter of Sheffield Folk is dedicated.

Au revoir Don.

Young Ron

This story, which is the last in our interesting look into the lives and times of a number of individual Sheffield folk, is different in so much that this 'young' man is still living. He is now 93 years old, and whilst he is not particularly ambitious to reach his century, I've got a feeling that he will manage it.

I'm telling you the story of young Ron because his life is not one of rags to riches like some of our characters, or spectacular self-made success like others. It is one of honest, hard work and an unselfish belief in pursuing those old-fashioned values of respect and discipline which used to make the world go round. He could in fact be your father or grandfather, as his story is simply that of a down-to-earth Sheffielder who always tried to give of his best.

Jessop Hospital

EARLY DAYS AND SCHOOL DAYS

Ron Cowen's life began on a cold winter's day at no. 26 Brightmore Street (now part of Netherthorpe Road dual carriageway), just a stone's - throw away from Sheffield's Jessop Hospital. It was the 7th January, 1916, slap bang in the middle of the First World War. Whilst his mum was panting, pushing and heaving to get the little pink bundle of joy into the world, brave British soldiers were sadly dying abroad on the front lines as they fought to retain the security and freedom of their country for the generations to come.

Following this dramatic start to life, you shouldn't get the idea that our Ron grew up into an innocent, sweet little child who did everything that was good and right. He was as mischievous and adventurous as the next kid, and even at the age of three, he created a major police alert and search by wandering off from home. He had just popped out to have a look at some horses which were kept in stables a few hundred yards away in Regent Court behind St. George's Church, a lengthy journey for a toddler which had

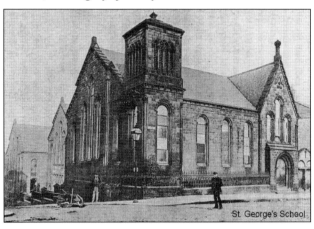
St. George's School

necessitated him having to cross two major roads en-route. As you can imagine, his parents were worried sick, but his mum still gave him a quick slap on the legs when the police eventually found him, just to make sure that her young son wasn't tempted to wander off again.

It was at St. George's Church of England School in Beet Street that, as a five year old, he later began his education. He actually stayed at that school for nine years or so (although not by choice), during which time he joined the Church as a choir boy, probably because there were a few lasses who he fancied doing likewise.

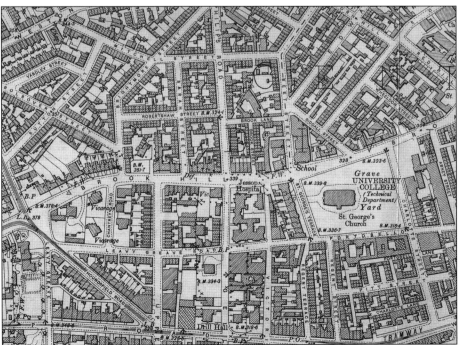

Beet Street
Site of St. George's School

Ron was genuinely keen on education, however, and had been looking forward to taking the Common Entrance Exam (later called the Scholarship or the 11-plus) at the age of ten or eleven which would have enabled him to progress to a Grammar School. King Edward VII School would have been his first choice. Unfortunately, when exam time came around he was not too well,

Girls
Choir   Boy

although in Ron's own opinion he was still well enough to take this important step in his life. However, despite pressure from his current teacher at St. George's, who had great confidence in young Ron's ability and drive, his mother flatly refused her son's desperate pleas to allow him to travel to the centre where the exam took place. So keen was the young boy's teacher for him to pursue this educational opportunity that he personally took over a pen, pencil and ruler to Ron's house and gave them to his mother to ensure that at least he would be properly equipped for the occasion. His mum, however, was not the type to be easily influenced.

"Ronald, you're just not well enough to travel and take these exams at present," she told her tearful son gently but firmly. "I know it's hard on you, but you'll just have to accept it."

To a lad in his eleventh year, desperate to give himself a better opportunity in life, it was a severe blow.

His mum's attitude was, to some degree, understandable. She was obviously concerned about his health (although Ron was adamant then and now that he wasn't as poorly as she made out) and life in 1926, the year of the National Strike, was very difficult. Her husband, a coalman, was struggling to make a living, and everyone else seemed to be on the dole. Many tried to drown their sorrows

in beer down at the pub with what small amount of money they could muster, and home-life was strained with everyone living on a knife edge. It was probably a natural first reaction of Ron's parents to want their son to stay at the school where he was so that he could not only leave when he reached the age of fourteen and earn some money, but could also continue to help his dad with his coal business as he had been doing for the last year or two. To some, this would appear to be a selfish decision taken by his parents, but both Ron and his younger brother Lewis, at ten and six years old respectively at this time, had obviously been unfortunate enough to be caught up in this web of poverty and decline which was slowly being weaved over society during those grim, dark days.

The stress of living in those difficult times combined with the loss of his only opportunity to pursue a significantly better educational route resulted in Ron having a prolonged nervous breakdown, which was identified as St. Vitas Dance in those days. As a result, he unfortunately lost about one and a half years of his education between the ages of ten and fourteen, this being another significant blow to the young schoolboy who was so desperate to get on in life and do well.

When Ron was at school, however, he really enjoyed it, particularly the English lessons in which he delighted at writing stories. This interest also led to him reading a lot of books which he regularly borrowed from the public library. His English teacher, Mr Paxton, was however a very strict man who expected nothing but the best from his pupils. He regularly gave the young scholars books and poetry to read and would either test them on the book's contents or insist that they recite the poems exactly during the last lesson on Friday afternoons. This was one lesson where all the pupils in the class did as they were asked, as Mr Paxton wouldn't let them go home from school until they were word perfect. I bet there were a few worried parents around as a result of this teacher's ruling in those days, although being home late was not really classed as such a danger as it might be nowadays.

"I can't stand that Paxton bloke," Ron would grumble to his mate Alf Marriot after they had both been kept back following an unsuccessful poetry test. "He's a right so and so, he is. How would he like it if we stopped him going home?"

If the two lads had thought about it, that's exactly what they were doing as their punishment for not knowing their poetry meant that their teacher had to stay at the end of school also, to supervise and re-test them.

Strangely enough, Ron now looks back at Mr. Paxton's classes in a different light, as he is now very grateful for the fact that this teacher persisted in making his pupils read and learn so much. That view sounds a bit familiar, doesn't it?

It's just worth mentioning before we leave Ron's schooldays that he chose to go to night-school to study Maths and English to make up for the education he had missed through his lengthy period of nervous depression, highlighting once again the young man's determination to succeed. It is also interesting to note that it was during this period than Ron saw a lot of the School Bobby, as he was known as then, who regularly called on him at home to check on his progress. Perhaps this lengthy association with him influenced his own career in the future? We will see later.

OUT OF SCHOOL ACTIVITIES

Before we move on to look at Ron's post-school days, let's have a look at what he got up to out of school during his childhood.

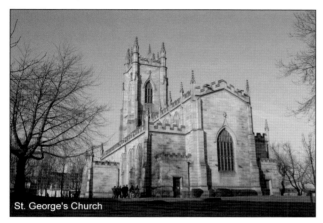
St. George's Church

During the years of 1924 to 1929, between the ages of eight and thirteen, Ron was a very active young lad. He had already joined the 101st scout group based at St. George's Church, first as a cub-scout, and then as a scout. Within this organisation he found that adventure, coupled with learning the art of living and independence, was available in abundance. However, he did have to fit in his scouting activities and other pleasures with helping his father to eke out a living as a coalman.

One of Ron's jobs at weekends, for example, was to walk around the streets visiting his dad's customers and collect half-a-crown a week from them (12½ p) which represented their weekly instalments for coal provided to them throughout the year. Whilst the young lad quite enjoyed the copper or two he was occasionally given by his dad for doing this job, he was always a bit nervous when he knocked on the customers' front doors.

Mrs Jones who lived just down the road in the house with the bright green door was one of his dad's more pleasant customers and usually opened her door in response to Ron's timid knock promptly.

"Excuse me, Mrs Jones," Ron said nervously on one such occasion, "I've come to collect the coal money and me dad says I've got to put a tick in this book against your name when you've given it me. He says I've got to put my name on your coal-card as well. He's even got me a posh new pen to use you know. It's nice isn't it?"

"All right, all right, Ron, don't go on love. I know what you've come for. You don't have to explain everything again every time you call, you know."

"Oh, all right then, Mrs Jones. I'm sorry. But what do you think of me new pen?"

What young Ron, the budding debt collector, didn't tell his customers like Mrs Jones, was that although his dad had bought his son the pen, he'd deducted the cost of it from the money he was supposed to pay the lad for his troubles. It doesn't seem fair, does it?

However, his father had another little venture which he put to his son which would help them both financially.

"Listen 'ere, son," he began as he sat down to his meal of bread and gravy one evening after a long day at work. "I want you to be especially well behaved at school and ask as many of your teachers as you can if they'd like to order their coal from me. You can tell 'em it's the best coal in Sheffield, and I'll give you sixpence (2½ p) for every permanent order that you manage to get. Don't forget now."

Although Ron was probably being used somewhat by his father, it did in fact benefit them both, with the young lad learning at an unusually early age what earning money and running a business was really all about.

It was during this period that the adventurous lad was hankering after owning a Haenel Air Rifle he had seen in the local gunsmiths. When he asked his father if he could have one, as many an optimistic eleven year old would do, he had been delighted with the reply.

"Dad. Can I have an air rifle like the one I've seen in the gunsmiths down the road? I'll be real careful with it, honest. It only costs five shillings (25p)."

"Five Shillings lad. There's no chance I can afford that, but if you can earn it, I'll go and buy it for you."

Glowing with enthusiasm, young Ron embarked on the difficult task of earning such a large some of money. He was, as previously mentioned, already getting the odd copper or two occasionally for collecting coal-money for his dad at weekends, and his mum kindly agreed to give him a penny a week to clean the cutlery for her at home. The big money-spinner for Ron, however, was from local coal deliveries to customers in the streets around where he lived. This entailed the small, but tough young lad delivering the coal in a wheelbarrow which held half a hundredweight (56 lbs) at a time.

"Chuffin' heavy, this is," he muttered to his mate Frank Capel who had popped over to keep him company. "You do realise, don't you Frank, that I've got to take a barrow-load to each house twice if they've ordered a full bag."

Frank was, understandably, very sympathetic towards his friend, and even offered to help him.

"You've got to be jokin' Frank. If me dad sees you helpin' me, he'll dock half me wages!"

The cost of a full, one hundredweight bag of coal at that time was one shilling and four pence (7p today) with tuppence (1p) extra for delivery. It was this tuppence that Ron was allowed to keep.

Things didn't always go well for the young lad however. Take the time that he staggered all the way round to Yardley Street with his load of coal and tipped it as usual (or so he thought) down the cellar grate of the house occupied by one of his dad's customers. Ron hadn't noticed the red-faced resident striding purposefully towards him.

"Oi! Wot the 'ell are you doin' shuvvin' coal down me grate? I 'avn't ordered any, so you can just take it out again!"

The irate and rather angry householder who had suddenly appeared at Ron's side had put the fear of death into him.

"He's only delivering coal, mester. He didn't mean no 'arm, really."

Frank was quite defensive of his friend Ron, who at first was lost for words. He did eventually, however, manage to speak.

"I'm afraid I've got the wrong grate by mistake, mester. Shall I come in and get it out again?"

"Come in?" the angry man retorted. "Come in to my house covered in black coal dust? I don't think so. Yer'll 'afto climb down the cellar grate and get it back the way it went in."

Ron almost swallowed his tongue as he drew in his breath at the thought of squeezing down the small square hole which, through a short, sloping chute, spewed the coal out onto the cellar floor below. But, he had no choice. If he left the coal there, the householder would give him a clip round the ear 'ole (whilst also being pleased to keep the coal at no cost), and his dad would likewise and give him a clip round the other ear 'ole and make him pay the one and fourpence income he had lost.

It only took a few minutes for the unhappy delivery boy to scurry back home and collect an empty coal sack from his dad's wagon parked outside. His plan was simple. He would throw the sack down into the cellar, slide down himself and partly fill the sack by hand before pushing it back up the hole onto the pavement above. His ever faithful friend Frank would then be able to tip the contents out into the empty wheelbarrow which had been patiently waiting there, and the process could be repeated several times until all the coal was recovered.

It was an exhausted Ron, however, who returned home later that afternoon and tried to creep into the house unseen.

"What on earth have you been doing Ron?" shouted his mum from the kitchen, having seen him creep in with those extra eyes which most mothers seem to have in the back of their heads. "You're blacker than the inside of your dad's coal sacks. Anyone would think it was you who'd been tipped down the grates into the cellars, not the coal. Go and clean yourself up before your dad sees you."

Little did his mum know how close she was to the truth!

However, despite setbacks such as this, the determined lad persevered in his endeavourer to earn the five shillings he needed to buy the air rifle. The work and money from his dad wasn't, unfortunately, as regular as he would have liked and his mum couldn't always guarantee his penny for cutlery cleaning. It was with great excitement and relief, therefore, that after about three months of saving, he was able to proudly present the money to his father.

"I've got the money, dad. I've got it. Don't forget, it's the Haenel air rifle in the window that I want. Can you go today, dad?"

As Ron stood there in the small kitchen of their two-up and two-down terrace in Mitchell Street, to which his parents had recently moved, time seemed to almost stand still for him. His younger brother Lewis stopped chatting, and for a moment or two his mother paused in the midst of doing her washing in the stone sink in the corner of the room. A small shiver ran down the cheeky faced youngster's spine, despite the afternoon sun trying to force its way though the kitchen's small street-facing window.

"What's up, dad. It's not been sold has it?"

A small, fearful tear had now welled up in one of the poor boy's eyes and was wondering whether or not to roll down the chubby cheek which sat invitingly below it.

"I'm afraid, son, that I'm going to have to spend this money on a good pair of corduroy trousers for you instead. Your present pair is almost worn right through, and me and your mum can't afford to buy you any more."

To Ron, those words from his dad represented the end of the world at that time. He had worked, toiled, hoped and waited for this one thing in life he wanted more than anything else, and now he was at the receiving end of a broken promise from his own father.

"But dad, you PROMISED," he blurted out amidst an explosion of tears and despair. "You promised I could have it if I earnt the money."

Unfortunately, the miners' strike, mass unemployment and living from hand to mouth over the last few years had hardened Ron's father who, whilst feeling sorry for his son, did not feel that he could say so.

"Now come on, Ron. It's not all that bad. Time's are 'ard me lad, and we've got to accept it."

To an eleven year old boy, however, a promise is a promise, particularly when it's made by the one person in the world a young lad looks-up to. He felt dreadfully let down, and ran out of the room with his mind in turmoil. Sadly, Ron was never able to totally forgive his father for what he did, although as a family they continued to work, laugh and cry together like everyone else. The incident did, however, teach the young boy a valuable lesson as Ron, now in his 93rd year, still upholds the vow he made to himself eighty years ago of never making a promise which he might not be able to keep, and of always keeping a promise once it has been made. As far as the corduroy trousers were concerned, he was duly presented with them and told to wear them on a daily basis. However, despite being of the hardest-wearing quality, they wore out in a very short time. Only you and I know that this was due to Ron deliberately engaging in a bum-shuffling vendetta whilst sitting on very rough surfaces and seats, thereby wearing out this part of the trousers in double quick time. As Ron says, it was a bit of revenge which made him feel better at the time.

Despite this never-to-be-forgotten incident in Ron Cowen's early school days, life carried on. Money was still short and his father's coal-delivery business still had to

survive to keep bread on the table. During weekends and school holidays the young lad accompanied his father to the Park Goods Yard near the Canal Wharf. This is where the coal trains arrived, huffing and puffing their way into the sidings with their string of clanking complaining wagons crawling along behind. Ron used to help to shovel the coal into sacks as it was thrown onto the back of their lorry by his dad using a much larger shovel. He also enjoyed breaking up the large lumps of coal which were also thrown into the lorry by his tough, strong father so that they could fit into the sacks . The coal Board Agent, Mr Cook, who supervised the loading-up and buying of coal at this central site, had a special name for Ron's dad.

"Na then, Lumpy. I see yer've got them strong arms of yours movin' well this mornin'. Yer've put more coal in the back of that wagon of yours in 'alf an hour than I could shift in a day. That young lad o' yours dunt do bad either, does he?"

It was in situations like this that Ron felt proud of his dad. Not only was he strong, he was also a hard worker. He was, unfortunately, also generous to a fault at times, and when he popped down to the pub at night to quench his parched throat, he would call out "Wot's everyone 'avin'?"

The grateful punters would respond with "good old Tommy," until his money ran out, and then didn't really want to know him afterwards. As Ron put it when recalling his father's actions eighty years later: "It's at times like this, when you're down and out, that you find out who your friends are, isn't it?"

It wasn't just coal deliveries that Tommy Cowen used his coal wagon for, however. Despite the sides of the wagon being emblazoned with the wording BEST HOUSE COAL – YOUR LOAD NEXT, he took local anglers on fishing trips at weekends to far and wide. It was Ron and his brother Lewis' job to clean out the coal dust from the back of the

wagon first and then fit seats along each side of the long wide vehicle which otherwise usually carried several tons of the black stuff. Their dad had built a clever wooden frame for such occasions which the brothers had to carefully cover with large tarpaulin sheets to keep out wind and rain when necessary. Tommy's wagon was well known as being the best rigged-out vehicle in the business and helped to bring in a bit of much needed money to supplement the family's meagre income. "Talk about child labour," Ron would often say during his reminiscences in later years.

You might just wonder, with Ron working most weekends, some evenings and most school holidays for his dad, if the poor lad had any time for proper holidays. Well, one of the odd jobs that Tommy Cowen undertook did involve some special recreation for his son. In between doing coal deliveries and fishing trips, the versatile coalman also had a contract with the GPO for taking their linesmen out into Derbyshire where telephone lines were being transferred underground instead of along the miles of telephone poles which supported them above ground level. Ron used to go with the men first thing in the morning and spend the rest of the day on the Derbyshire moors gleefully running uphill and down dale chasing grouse from one side to the other. With the warm sun beating down and a tasty picnic put together by his mam, he spent many a summer's day enjoying the freshness and freedom of the wonderful countryside amongst the wild life and shrubs which lived and grew there. He was, of course, tired by the time his dad picked him and the linesmen up about teatime, but he felt it was worth it.

HOLIDAYS

Ron did, nevertheless, have one proper holiday during his childhood when he actually saw the sea. His mum and dad took him and Lewis to Boston for a few days where he unsuccessfully tried his hand at fishing. He and Lewis also spent most of one day trying to find the 'Boston Stump', an old church which reputedly had 365 steps to climb up inside if you wanted to get to the top. From Ron's recollections, they were so tired by the time they found the well-known landmark, that they didn't bother checking if there were actually that number of steps inside. During this week-long holiday, the family of four also called at Skegness and other coastal resorts in their cleaned-out and covered coal wagon. I bet there weren't many families who could afford such luxurious transport in those days.

The highlight of the holiday was, as you might expect, the first of several visits to the beach.

"You'll never guess where we're going to tomorrow, Lewis," a very excited Ron whispered to his equally excited brother on the last day in Boston. "We're going to Skeggie beach which, I've been told, has about a hundred miles of soft warm sand to play on and has warm, bright blue water to swim in. It'll be great, won't it?"

It was Ron's friends back in Mitchell Street who'd given the young, excited holiday-maker these 'factual' details of Skegness, and they'd also asked him to check out just how blue the water really was.

Despite the exaggerations regarding the beach and the sea, the two lads were almost beside themselves with

excitement as they took their first tentative steps onto the soft warm sand which sifted playfully through their bare toes. The sight of the sea in the distance created a memory of a lifetime, and to these boys, they were in their own heaven.

"Let's run to the sea, Ron," shouted Lewis. "I'll beat yer."

As the two lads bounded down to the huge expanse of water which seemed to extend for ever into the distance, the soft golden grains under their feet gradually changed to a harder, almost ribbed surface of saturated sand which the receding waves had mischievously made as they scurried back to the sea. Shallow pools of water also appeared at irregular intervals as if to create obstacles for the two children to either avoid or splash through as they continued their mad race to the welcoming water's edge. It was a day they would always remember, although when Ron returned home and was asked by his friends about the colour of the sea, his answer wasn't what they expected to hear:

"Well, it were a mucky brown, really."

Ron and Lewis did have a few odd days out with their parents over the next year or two, usually with the Crookes

Working Men's Club of which their dad was a member. The five-penny, cheap-day returns to the coast on the good old charabang lasted about seven or eight hours, and enjoyable though they were, they couldn't really compare to their first and only real holiday in Skeggie.

As Ron got a little older, it was bike-riding which gave him a lot of pleasure and independence. Trips to locations such as Hathersage and Chatsworth with his thirteen year old pals from Mitchell Street were always looked forward to with excitement. It was on one such trip that one bright spark (as Ron later put it) suggested that they all cycle to Cleethorpes the following day without telling their parents, just in case they stopped them from going. Ron recalled this event quite clearly.

That next morning, the six young cyclists prepared to set off on their 90 mile journey with the early morning sun in their faces. It was Bank Holiday Tuesday and thirteen year old Ron's parents were having a bit of a lie-in.

"I'm off now, mam," their son shouted as he hurriedly scuttled out of the front door before any one could ask him exactly where he was going. "I'm just off on me bike for a while with me mates."

They had all agreed to meet at the end of the street armed with bottles of water and any food they could rustle up without arousing suspicion. It was to be an adventure of a lifetime, and they were all excited.

The journey to this popular coastal resort took longer than they had anticipated, and it was late afternoon by the time they got there.

"I'm jiggered," croaked Frank, the smallest of the group. "Who's idea was it to come all this way?"

No one was taking the blame for the rather ill-thought out idea, however, but all agreed that a few hours on the beach was now absolutely vital if they were to regain enough strength for their return journey. The sun had also been beating down on their uncovered heads all day, and they were suffering the consequences.

"I think me 'ead's on fire, Alf, complained Ron. Let's go and buy ourselves a hat."

Ten minutes later, the bunch of adventurous youngsters walked out of a sea-front hat-and-novelty shop, each proudly wearing a sixpenny, black and white checked baseball cap to protect them from the stifling sun. Sixpence was a lot of money in the late 1920s, and spending that amount each had been rather a rash thing to do. This was evidenced by the situation which arose a few hours later after they had finished sunbathing on the beach and swimming in the sea. The slightly cooler evening was now gradually drawing in, and six stomachs were rumbling in unison as the most appealing aroma on God's earth drifted tantalizing towards them: the smell of freshly cooked fish and chips.

"By the cringe. That smells good. I've got to have some of them."

"Me too. I'm absolutely famished."

"Anybody got any money? I'm skint."

"Well you shunta bought that 'at, should yer?"

And so it went on. The desperately hungry and thirsty friends could only muster a few coppers between them, and the thought of a tasty fish and chips supper crumbled before their eyes.

"It's not chuffin' fair, piped up Harry. Whose idea was it to by these stupid hats anyway?"

But, of course, bickering amongst themselves would do no good, and as daylight was now fading, they all decided to bite their tongues and begin their treck home. That, however, was just the beginning of their troubles. As darkness fell, Ron and two other of his friends realized that the batteries in their bicycle lamps were dead and that further travel would be impossible. They had only managed about fifteen of the ninety mile return journey by this time, so the now slightly frightened group decided to stop and sleep on a grass bank by the roadside.

"I don't like it here, Ron," squeaked Alf. "It's very cold and I've not brought anything warm with me."

As the lads huddled together for warmth, Ron was glad that he'd chosen to wear the new, fashionable red polo-neck shirt which his mother had bought him, but even this was of little benefit as the increasing coldness of the night crept into their bones. The puffy white clouds of the afternoon had now dissolved away into the blackness of the night to allow a full moon to kindly drench the surrounding countryside with its magical light, and this gave a little comfort to our unfortunate travellers who, nevertheless, were now shivering gently on their grassy beds.

"Bloody 'ell, what's that?" shouted young William as he suddenly shot bolt upright in fear. "The bloody sea's coming in right behind us. We'll be drowned."

As the boys were nowhere to near the sea by this time, William's outburst came as something of a shock.

"What are you on about, Will?" exclaimed Ron who had by now taken time to focus his eyes in the direction his friend was pointing. "That's a cornfield swaying in the breeze that you're looking at, although I must admit that it does look rather like a choppy sea."

Despite the initial shock, this incident created some prolonged and welcome laughter amongst the six reckless friends who were in need of some respite from their feelings of loneliness and fear.

It was many fitful hours later when the welcome sun rose over the horizon and allowed the tired youngsters to mount-up again and continue on their way home. Within a short time, they came upon an early-opening café where they managed to get a large pot of tea between them for fourpence. Never before had tea tasted so good, although now with no money left at all, breakfast was not on the agenda. Fortunately, some hours later the hungry cyclists came upon a field of turnips which, from the shouts of delight, you'd have thought was a field of bacon and egg sandwiches. With one pen-knife between them, they chopped up and devoured several of those hard, uncooked vegetables to satisfy their extreme hunger.

It was 2-o'clock in the afternoon by this time and the weary travellers were now just outside Doncaster. Eventually they saw the sign they had been waiting for, Sheffield – 18 miles, which they greeted with a loud cheer. They wouldn't have been so cheerful if they had known what was awaiting them!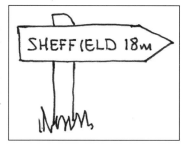

After what seemed to be an endless time taken to cover those last eighteen miles of their long tortuous adventure which had kept them away from home for a day and a half, Ron and the gang sailed down the hill leading to Mitchell Street, all shouting with delight at their triumphant return and eager to tell all and sundry of their exploits. A hero's welcome was what they naively expected, but it didn't turn out that way. As Ron turned the corner pedalling furiously towards his house, he saw his mother standing on the doorstep, 'gossiping as they used to in those days' as Ron so succinctly put it. She glanced up and spotted him just before he screeched to a halt in front of her with a big grin on his face.

"I'm home mum. I'm home."

Sadly, it was with total amazement and shock that the thirteen year old adventurer heard his mother's words of 'welcome home'.

"Where the bloody 'ell have you been. Get in that house and I'll deal with you later."

Accompanied by a sharp clip behind his head, he was propelled into the front room of their not so friendly home where he stayed until his mother returned to give him a proper roasting. His father's reaction later that day when he returned home from work was, as you might expect, no better, but we'll not go into that.

Ron did admit, at the age of 91, that upon reflection he realized that his mother must have been worried stiff when he didn't return home that Bank Holiday Tuesday night, and with no fancy gadgets like telephones available for them to use, all she could do was wait and hope as the hours of the following day also ticked away. I think he got the message following his parent's reaction to the whole episode, and I think he learnt from it.

OTHER INTERESTS

Although we've touched on several aspects of Ron's early life, we have yet to enlarge on another interest which threaded its way through his life from the age of five to fifteen. This was scouting. As a young cub, and then a fully-blown scout, Ron spent as much time as he could with this activity which encompassed evenings, weekends and school holidays whenever possible. He even managed to get out of helping his dad with the coal business on some occasions when special or important scouting events were planned, although to be fair his parents did encourage him in this aspect of his life which stood him in good stead to this very day.

Ron put a great emphasis on his scouting activities, and it is interesting to hear the views which he expressed in his 91st year:

"Thank God for my interest in the Scout Movement, for camping and for other interests. I could have finished up being a juvenile delinquent in those days."

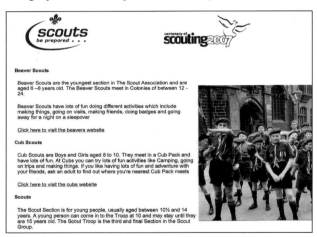

In fact, many young poor kids in those difficult days only managed to survive life with the help of the scouts, as they were taught to cook, cope with every-day problems, look after themselves and others, and manage their lives generally. It's strange that as I'm writing this, the Scout Movement is celebrating its 100th Anniversary. Although it is still very popular, to both boys and girls alike now, I suspect that it is sadly not the 'cool' thing to do in the eyes of many youngsters. What a pity it is that they don't give it a try. I suspect we'd have a much happier, more relaxed (and less bored) young society who wouldn't want to go around vandalizing things, taking drugs, or becoming young criminals. Perhaps we should introduce the Scout Movement into schools and give today's kids the opportunity of getting involved with it as a subject-option. Its food for thought, isn't it?

Before we move on to Ron's conversation from schooling to working boy at the age of fourteen, let's just have a quick look at a couple of rather humorous accidents which he was involved in as a young lad. Ron was well known for being accident prone, and had more falls off a bike that you or I have had hot dinners. However, these two incidents are a bit different.

The first one I'd like to mention took place when he was about six to eight years old. His dad had a horse and dray at the time and sometimes used to cart stacked bales of hay through the Wicker for a local farmer. Little Ron used to love to accompany him, and on this occasion had a special request to make.

"Daddy, can I ride on top of the hay-stack this time please. I won't fall off, honest."

Although his dad was slightly reluctant to agree to this request, he did give in under pressure from his cheerful, bright-eyed little son.

"Alright then, Ron. But you hold on tight, do you hear?"

It was about an hour later that Tommy Cowen's snorting horse clip-clopped up the Wicker pulling a dray packed high with bales of hay. Perched proudly on top was our Ron, looking as pleased as punch. It was about half-way along this famous street that things started to go wrong. The action of the dray's hard-tyred wheels on the cobbled road surface had caused the bales to shudder and vibrate. This in turn had caused the slightly-built lad on top to gradually slip down the stepped stack until he was precariously balanced on its lower edge.

"Daddy, daddy, help. I'm falling!"

Unfortunately, Ron's dad was a bit deaf and was unable to hear his son's cry for help. Little Ronald Cowen subsequently fell off the haystack and hit the hard road with a bump. The accident had, fortunately, been witnessed by an early morning pedestrian who had also been meandering up the wicker at that time. Waving his arms about and shouting as loud as he could, he stopped Tommy who was still as oblivious as ever as to what had happened.

"Excuse me, Mester. I fink sumfink's fell off 'n yer cart. It's still lying there in the road."

Tommy was at a loss to understand what could have fallen off his cart as he had made sure that the bales of hay had been tied on securely.

"I'll go and 'ave a look and see what it is," he responded, thanking the rather nervous looking witness for reporting the matter to him.

As he turned round and cast his eye over his still secure load, he noticed the small, huddled figure in the road several yards back.

"Chuffin 'eck," he gasped. "I think it's our Ron."

He rushed back and gathered the sobbing bundle up in his arms. Ron had unfortunately landed on his head, although despite sporting an egg-size bruise and being in a state of shock, the damage didn't appear to be too serious.

"Come on, me lad. We'll take you to the Children's Hospital for a check up."

Placing him carefully on the secure seat beside him, father and son made their way painstakingly slowly to the grand hospital building opposite Weston Park where the Accident and Emergency Department was always open. Fortunately Ron's injury was judged to be only superficial by the doctor, but I don't think he was allowed any more hay-stack rides in the future.

The second of his many accidents worthy of mention occurred when he was about ten years old when his dad had moved on from haystack-carting to coal deliveries. Both his parents had gone out for the evening and Ron had invited several of his young friends around to play Cowboys and Indians in the large back yard of his house. To make things more exiting and realistic, they chose to chase each other over the large roof of his dad's coal shed. It was during this game that Cowboy Ron decided to stay down below in the yard to try and 'shoot down' one of the Indians scuttling around on the roof above him. Unfortunately, the Indian slipped and dislodged a house-brick which landed on the poor lad's head (where else?) which necessitated yet another trip to the Children's Hospital (surprise-surprise!). Although the young cowboy had rather a bad gash and yet another egg-sized bruise on his head, he was, luckily, not seriously injured, although he still bears the scar of his accident today. Perhaps having a hard head is the secret of Ron's longevity of life, although I don't envy the tests he's had to endure to prove it.

WORKING DAYS

Anyway, let's move on to the daunting prospect of this young man finding a job now that his schooldays were over. He left school on January 7th, 1930, which was his birthday, and the bitterly cold weather did nothing to create any optimism of him finding a job in those still very difficult times.

By a stroke of good luck, however, a friend of Ron's told him that John Atkinson's Department store was looking for delivery boys to take advertising circulars around housing estates like Longley and Southey. This job, which unfortunately was only a one-off, involved the boys walking round these areas for hours on end with a bag of leaflets hung round their neck. Tedious and tiring though it was, it paid five shillings (25p) for the two days work, and the enthusiastic job-hunter jumped at the chance. Ron, with one or two other similar employees, were taken out to their designated areas in one of the company vans which was full of such leaflets and told to get rid of the lot, posting one only through each and every house letterbox. This, not

surprisingly, necessitated knowing where you were going. However, without the aid of a map, poor Ron got lost on both days and not only ended up walking round in circles trying to find a street he'd not already been on, he couldn't even find his way back to the van in the evenings to be taken back to town. Needless to say, the van driver was furious at having to spend half an hour at the end of each day touring the area trying to find him.

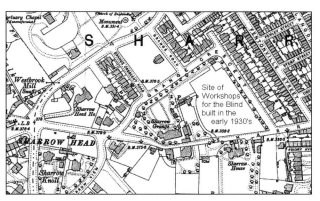

Not to be discouraged, however, the young school leaver religiously looked through the local newspapers every day in the jobs-vacant columns, and within six months had successfully applied for a job at the new workshops for the Welfare of the Blind which were being built on Sharrow Lane. The weekly wage, which included working Monday to Friday and Saturday mornings (8am to 12.30), was eight shillings (40p), but at least it was a start.

It was fortunate that the Workshops Superintendent at Sharrow Lane, a kind lady by the name of Miss Watts, was in charge at that time. Ron's parents had just split-up, and this very sympathetic lady fully understood how he was feeling at the time and took him under her wing. Ron stressed then, as he still does now, how lucky he was to start work at a place that saw to his welfare at a time when he felt so vulnerable and at a loss due to his family situation. Added to this, the fourteen year old had to report to the Magistrates Court in case he was called to give evidence relating to the unfortunate divorce of his parents. Ron remembers to this day that it was court number two. The significance of this will be clear later. This ordeal left a lasting impact on this sensitive young man, and even now, at the age of 92, Ron recalls the event with some feeling and relief: "I wasn't called, thank God."

It was during the first few years at Sharrow Lane that Ron also decided that he wanted to do keep-fit and weight training. By chance, he was taking a stroll along Gell Street just off Glossop Road one evening when he heard the sound of clanking metal coming from somewhere nearby, but below him. A small window just above pavement level seemed to be the source of the noise and, Ron being Ron, he just had to kneel down and peer through. To his utter amazement, he saw a weight-training class in progress, and his wish had somehow been granted. An old wooden door a few yards further down the street seemed to be the only probable access to the building, so Ron took the plunge and entered. Inside the entrance hall, a sign saying Sheffield Premier Athletic Club pointed to the lower floor rooms. He had found a new hobby which was to shape his future life for ever.

The gymnasium upon which the 16 year old had stumbled was run by a strong looking fellow called Tommy Lee, who had also formed the club. Training was given three nights a week at a cost of fourpence a night, with a shower at the end of each session thrown in. The shower was an absolute luxury in those days, as no one had a bathroom or shower at home except for the very rich. Tommy, who worked at the Edgar Allen Institute in Gell Street during the day, became a good friend of Ron's but was sadly killed in the Second World War.

Ron's interest in fitness and sport also stood him in good stead at the Workshop for the Blind where he worked. He was able to accompany the blind students in their Friday swimming sessions in the pool at King Edward VII School,

Ashopton Village about 1900

and on fine weekends on their tandem-bike rides into the country. These activities were given regularly in order that these disadvantaged people could access clean, fresh air and get varied exercise so necessary for their well-being. Of particular interest to Ron were the bicycle trips out into Derbyshire where in his earlier years he used to visit

Ashopton village about 1942

Ashopton village but now watched its demise as the huge Ladybower Reservoir was slowly constructed. I think there will only be a handful of readers who can claim to have witnessed these events as Ron has.

The work at the Sharrow Lane Workshops was both interesting and varied. When Ron first arrived there, he worked as a van-boy, accompanying the workshop's van driver, George Bostock, in delivering and collecting materials, equipment, tools and anything else that needed transporting. By the time he was 18, this growing young man was driving the van himself following his success at passing the newly introduced driving test in January of 1934. From this position he moved on to become Assistant Foreman in the Basket Department following which he became much more involved in guiding and developing the lives of the blind students who worked there by involving them in exercise and outings as already mentioned.

However, it was not just the work and exercise- related events that Ron liked at Sharrow Lane. He loved the social events, particularly the social evening and dance which was held there on Monday nights. It was at one such event that he first met his wife-to-be, Irene. Ron remembers it well, and I think he can describe the occasion in his own words far better than I can write about it:

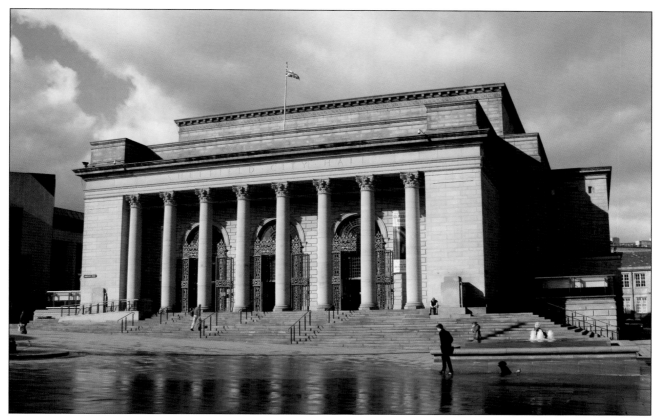

"I saw this lovely fair-haired person at the far end of the hall. She looked a bit of alright, I thought, so I strode up to ask her for a dance. She said 'Sorry, I can't dance', to which I replied 'You won't learn sitting there. Come on, let's try.' She accepted, even though she had come with a group of girls from Crookes who all worked at the Solvo laundry in Lydgate Lane."

It wasn't long before the two of them were dancing together at every Monday night social, and as they continued their courtship they tripped the light fantastic at locations such as the City Hall, the Abbeydale Cinema ballroom and the Glossop Road Baths dance-floor. They even had holidays at Butlins and Pontins where they successfully entered dancing competitions.

WORLD WAR II ARRIVES

Ron and Irene's courtship was one of happiness and fun and extended over a period of five or six years until World War II dramatically intervened.

It was April 1940 when the Ministry of Defence's buff-coloured envelope containing his call-up papers dropped though the letter box of Ron's home in Sutton Street where his mother and he had moved to following her divorce. Now 24 years old and with a powerful physique after all those years spent regularly training in the gymnasium, he accepted that he was about to move into a new phase of his life. Fighting for King and Country was something that most young men were proud to undertake in those days, and it was with his best foot forward that he reported a day or two later to the Cutlers Hall in Sheffield town centre for his compulsory medical examination.

Cutler's Hall

The medical, which was for fitness to join the Army, took place in groups of thirty, and as the men of all shapes and sizes stood there in their 'altogether' for about 20 minutes before moving on for an I.Q.test, many a fly-on-the wall would have been put-off its lunch at the sight of the recruits' 'belongings' displayed before them.

Following on from this, Ron went across to the RAF office as he had noticed a board outside stating that this area of the armed forces was experiencing a shortage of Physical Training Instructors (PTI's). Upon entering the office, he approached a very striking looking WAAF assistant (Women's Auxiliary Air Force) sitting behind a desk.

"Excuse me dear," said the would-be recruit as pleasantly as he could. "How do I go about getting a job as a PTI?"

The young lady in the smart blue uniform gave Ron a rueful smile which seemed to say "If you're joining the forces, mate, this will be the last time that you'll call a uniformed member 'dear'."

After explaining to the potential 24 year old raw recruit that priority for these posts went to existing fitness professionals, she handed him a list which identified such groups of people. In particular, sportsmen such as footballers, golfers, athletes and the like were listed, and Ron noticed that both of Sheffield's football teams appeared there.

"Well, Miss," continued Ron politely. "I've been involved in physical training for the last ten years, although not as a professional, and I do have a Central Council of Physical Recreation certificate. Will that count for something?"

At this point, an RAF officer came over to give his advice and told the enthusiastic, fit-looking young man standing before him that as he was so keen to join the RAF in this capacity, he would put his name down for general duties with a view to him registering as a PTI once the RAF had accepted him.

At last, Ron had got his wish (or so he thought), and he duly reported back to the Cutlers Hall the following Thursday for registration. From that day, everything seemed to move with a blur. He was given a list of about two dozen recruits of whom, he was told, he was now in charge. Armed also with a railway warrant, he and his new group took a train to the Padgate Receiving Centre near Manchester where they were all given their 'eating irons', a knife, fork and spoon, which they had to take care of personally for the duration of their stay in the RAF. The next day he and his comrades took the Oath of Allegiance and were duly sworn in and issued with their personal service numbers by which they would be known for the rest of their service life. Finally, number 995370 Cowen realized that he was in the RAF. It was April 26th 1940.

The 93 year old ex-serviceman and war veteran now relaxing in a pleasant Nursing Home in Sheffield could talk forever (as I found out) about his experiences during the war years. However, I think it would be more appropriate to make a whistle-stop tour of those six years, and just pick out some interesting events which took place. Let's start, therefore, where we left off.

Basic training for Ron and his colleagues meant whisking them off to Blackpool for an intense ten days instruction at the end of which they came out as 'fully trained airmen'.

It was there that they were also issued with their uniforms. A sign on the door as they entered the fitting room made it clear to the new servicemen that they shouldn't expect perfection:

"We have two different sizes: Too big and too small. If it doesn't fit, bring it back and we'll change it."

During this time of rapid expansion within the Royal Air Force due to the thousands of men and women being recruited to fight in the war, there was a significant shortage of Non-Commissioned Offices (NCOs) to lead them. Six likely candidates at Blackpool had been selected for consideration, one of whom being Ron. Fortunately, this 24 year old confident and fit young man was able to point to his experience gained as a Senior Patrol Leader in the Scout Movement when the question of leadership arose in his interview for the post. This was enough to satisfy the Commanding Officer at that time, and number 995370 Cowen was duty promoted to Corporal.

Immediately after this, Corporal Ron and eight hundred other 'fully trained' men were posted to No.9, Bombing and Gunnery

(B&G) School in North Wales. No sooner had they sat down for tea, than the school was attacked by three German Dornier fighting planes which first bombed the Mess, killing three officers, and then strafed the dispersing panic-stricken recruits on their subsequent runs. This, as Ron put it, was his "Baptism of Fire".

This incident proved to be a regular occurrence at dusk and dawn, although the location of this training school for air gunners and bomb aimers on the coast of North Wales was supposed to be a secret. Ron was designated to be a part of the ground-staff ear-marked to protect the school and its airdrome, and was given training by an old soldier from the Army on how to use machine guns. Unfortunately, he soon found out that the guns he and his men had been given were remnants from the First World War, which explained why his instructor was a World War I veteran. As Ron said when I asked him how they coped with such antiquated

weapons: "The guns hadn't even got any ring sights on them so I told my crew to spray the buggers like a hose pipe when the enemy attacked."

But, of course, it was the air-crew who were the most vulnerable. The training course at No. 9 B&G School was very limited, which often led to a short life for many of the young 18 and 19 year old lads who had to go into action after only a few weeks training. This, sadly, was war, and time was on nobody's side.

Whilst Ron was at this training camp, he got his first major disappointment when he tried to register as a Physical Training Instructor as he had originally been advised to do. The Flight Corporal in the Orderly Room (a higher rank than Ron's) decreed that no ground-defence personnel could change to any other trade or duty owing to the delicate war situation at that time. Ron did, nevertheless, undertake the physical training of his colleagues on defence duties to ensure that they kept in peak condition. Fortunately, word of this had got round, and when the Sergeant PTI attached to the school was off sick, the Station Warrant Officer asked Ron to step in and take over. Such was the success of his training session, that the Warrant Officer marched into the Orderly Room and instructed the Corporal to process Ron's application to become a Physical Training Instructor immediately. The young RAF officer had at last got his foot on the bottom rung of the ladder which would lead to his

chosen Service career.

Ron had been in the RAF for some months now, during which time his long-term sweetheart Irene had been patiently waiting for him. The outbreak of war had interrupted their original plans to marry in the summer of 1940, but by keeping mainly in touch by letters they had re-arranged the date to March 8th, 1941. Temporary leave for an occasion such as this would, he had been assured, present no real problem.

However, true love never runs smooth, they say. At the beginning of February of that year he was told not only to report to the RAF School of Physical Training at St. Athans in South Wales on the 28th of the month, one week before his planned wedding, but also that no provision for leave would be allowed during his training, regardless of circumstances. You can almost hear Ron chuntering, can't you?:

"Chuffin 'eck. I've waited all this time, and now my leave's stopped. I just don't believe it."

It certainly was a blow, although to some degree the budding PTI was better off than some of his colleagues who were sent abroad and never saw their loved ones for months, and sometimes years. He had managed the odd weekend on leave during that first year, although often by the time he'd made it to Sheffield, it was almost time to return to camp. Such was the price you had to pay for love.

However, we've seen through our story of this man that a disappointment was often followed by a bit of good fortune. Well, it happened again this time. By sheer coincidence, the Warrant Officer at the training school to which Corporal Cowen had been transferred had himself got married only a week or two earlier and, being able to empathise with Ron's dilemma, arranged for him to have a 48 hour weekend pass for the occasion. Ron and Irene were of course overjoyed, although it must have been one of the most rushed weddings on record as we shall see.

Overnight travelling down from Wales to Sheffield was

followed by a hastily arranged wash-and brush-up at his mother's house before making the short walk to St. George's Church where the wedding took place. It was a real grand affair, despite the rush, and Irene looked a dream in her white, flowing wedding dress and train, behind which four beautiful bridesmaids gracefully tip-toed.

The wedding reception itself was held at Irene's parents' house at 34 Stannington View Road in Crookes, but it was not until very late on that Saturday night that Ron and his bride were able to occupy their 'honeymoon suite' in the back bedroom of Irene's uncle's house a bit further up the road at number 110.

Although Ron had not slept since leaving his camp on the Friday evening, it's unlikely he got much sleep that night either, and with having to travel back to Wales on the Sunday evening, I think we can presume that this young man, fit though he was, would have been totally shattered. As Ron himself starkly put it, "It was one night of love and back to the camp!"

It was, in fact, early Monday morning when he staggered into camp just in time for a breakfast of bacon and beans and a full session of physical training lasting all day. He knew he couldn't complain, otherwise he'd have got much more of the nods, winks and ribbing which were already being thrown at him. I don't know how a mere mortal could have coped with what in affect was three days without sleep. Only super-fit Super-Ron could have managed such a feat.

Following his stint at the training school, Ron finally qualified as a Physical Training Instructor. He had got there at last. This was the beginning of an interesting and demanding time in the Royal Air force for him as, over the next few years, he was sent to camps all over the country. Physical fitness does, as we know, usually lead to mental fitness, and both were vital ingredients in the make-up of British airmen who were fighting for their country. Ron,

with his considerable skills, enthusiasm and determination transformed uncertain young recruits into confident and equally determined fighting men of whom the RAF was justifiably proud. This dedicated man, who during this time was promoted to Sergeant, had a way of dealing with people which earned him their respect. In return, he always showed respect for those he taught, and I have no doubt that due to his influence and skills, many brave airmen's lives were saved as they winged their way across the skies with discipline, determination and both physical and mental fitness as

their guiding strengths. He should feel proud of himself, just as we are proud of him now.

There were, of course, many more interesting events we have not covered which touched the life of Ron Cowen during his six years with the Royal Air Force, but these are far too numerous to mention in this brief story of his life. We must not, however, forget to mention a particularly important event which would influence and affect his life for ever. On the 29 January, 1944, he became the proud father of a baby son, Tony, who to this day is the shining light of his life. Ron's loving wife Irene had continued living with her mother in Crookes

during Ron's enforced absence, and it was to her house that he managed to hitch-hike a lift in a Navel Officer's Jeep from his camp in Oakham in County Rutland the next day to see his wife and son. For a few blissful hours only, Ron,

Irene and Tony were together as a new family, and for that time nothing else mattered.

Although Ron was only able to see his son a few times a year for the first four years of the little lad's life, the thought of eventually being able to come home permanently to his loved ones gave him the strength to keep going until the dreadful war at last came to an end on May 8, 1945.

It seemed as if the whole country was out in the streets to celebrate the declaration of peace on that eventful day. The news of Germany's unconditional surrender came in a broadcast by Prime Minister Winston Churchill at 3-O'clock in the afternoon, and was followed a short time later by a broadcast by King

Winston Churchill: He joined the King

George VI. This was relayed by loudspeakers to about 30,000 people who had gathered in Town Hall Square in the city centre.

"Today," said the King, "we give thanks to God for a great deliverance."

The Sheffield Star, reporting in its newspaper after the event, aptly captured the mood of the occasion:

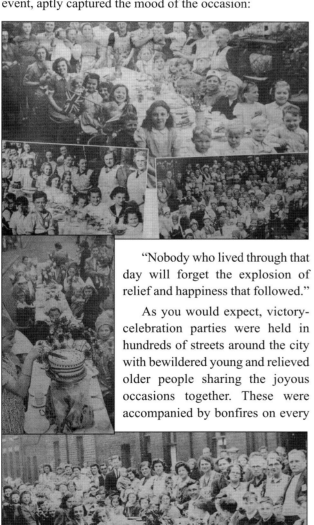

"Nobody who lived through that day will forget the explosion of relief and happiness that followed."

As you would expect, victory-celebration parties were held in hundreds of streets around the city with bewildered young and relieved older people sharing the joyous occasions together. These were accompanied by bonfires on every

bit of spare land available, a fact which was emphasized in the Star newspaper headline of May 10th which shouted out: CITY OF 1000 BONFIRES.

However, despite all the celebrations, Sergeant Ronald L Cowen, like all other servicemen and women, was still on duty. He was stationed at RAF Lindholme at the time and what followed was one of the proudest occasions in his life. An article in The Star newspaper's VE Day 50th

Victory parade headed by 12 bands

Open air service at Weston Park before the parade

The parade on Fargate

Anniversary Souvenir quotes Ron's own recollections of the occasion which was a once-in-a-lifetime honour of being asked to lead the Royal Air Force Contingent in a Victory Parade through Sheffield.

It must have been a magical feeling on that momentous day of May 12, 1945, when 5,000 members of the Armed Forces, Civil Defence and Voluntary Services together with 13 bands gathered in Weston Park prior to their rousing march into town. Amidst cheering, flag-waving crowds, the parade stretched out for about 2 miles as, to the accompaniment of drums, trumpets and bugles, it snaked its way noisily down Western Bank, Glossop Road and Division Street en-route to the Town Hall, Fargate and the Cathedral before completing its march outside the Sheffield Education Offices in Leopold Street.

It seems a little uncanny that it was in Gell Street outside the very building in which Ron began his physical training career that he formed up the servicemen and women to begin the parade, and then formally dismissed the contingent of comrades who had so gallantly fought for their country outside the very building in which he was destined to begin his new career a short time later. It's strange, isn't it, how life throws up these little events of coincidence which almost seem to have been pre-arranged?

BACK TO CIVVY STREET

But, of course, it was back to civvy-street after the war, and the reality of post-war Britain was a shock to most people. Towns and cities had to be re-built, jobs were hard to come by, and food and clothing was severely rationed. More importantly, thousands of families had lost husbands, wives, sons, daughters, fathers and even mothers. The joy of victory and the safe return of loved ones had to be sensitively balanced against the tragedy of loss for many others, and it was as if many were living in a dream world for a time. As we now know, the strength, resolve and determination which epitomizes British people in times of tragedy and hardship managed to pull the nation together as it rose above the difficult past into a new and better future.

Following Ron's return home from the RAF on March 8, 1946 (his Wedding Anniversary), he was not only anxious to find a job, but he also wanted to continue helping others as he had done during the war years. Being the man he was, he managed to do this by running two parallel careers, one as an Education Welfare Officer during the day, and another as a youth-club leader in the evenings. It might be useful to

Stothard Road

look at each of these two aspects of his life separately.

Let's start off with Ron's search for suitable

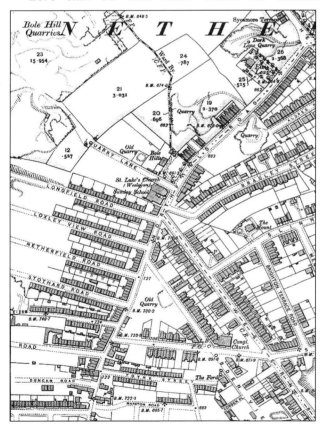

employment as it was necessary for him to urgently earn some money to pay the rent on a war-damaged house in Stothard Road in Crookes which had lost much of its roof in the blitz. Irene and her mum had managed to reserve this house a month or so earlier so that she, her husband and baby Tony could start life in a place of their own. There was, however, this little problem of it having a badly damaged roof which Ron was anxious to look at.

View from the Bolehills at the top of Stothard Road in 1900

View from Bolehills-2007

It was a cold and frosty March morning which saw Irene and Ron striding purposefully up this narrow street which was flanked on each side by rows of terraced houses which looked rather dishevelled and gloomy as they huddled together for comfort. The ravages of enemy air strikes had taken their toll on these homes which had previously stood proudly and defiantly in their lofty position overlooking much of the city. Their protective roofs had borne the brunt of the attacks, and number 15 was no exception.

Within a minute or two the happy couple arrived at their destination. Broken windows, missing tiles and a gaping hole in the roof told Ron in no uncertain terms that he'd arrived at their first home-to-be. A shiver of concern shook his body as he saw the property which was more badly damaged than he expected. His thoughts, however, were suddenly interrupted by Irene's excited voice.

"Come on, Ron love. Let's go inside and see what it's like. I've got the key."

The front door opened with some reluctance as it groaned its annoyance at being disturbed after its long winter sleep. Clouds of dust rose into the air and puffed their objection to the intruders who were stamping their cold, damp feet on the worn tufted doormat. A shriek from Irene told the two large brown spiders dangling from the light fitting that that she had broken their carefully constructed webs of silver thread with her flailing arms as she battled her way into the small entrance hall. It seemed to the present occupants of the house that the war was starting all over again, and they didn't like it.

"It could do with a good fettle, couldn't it love?" choked Ron as he was forced to breathe in a mixture of dust and cobwebs which attacked him with vigour.

"Now stop complaining, Ron. I'll soon have it looking spick and span. Let's have a look round."

Despite their initial problems entering the property, the couple seemed to be surprisingly pleased with their new little home. However, they had yet to go upstairs.

As they entered the front bedroom, which benefited from a glorious view of the sky through a sizeable hole in the sagging, damp ceiling, Ron had to stifle a gasp as he sucked in the icy-cold air which surrounded him.

"It's very nice, Irene love," he remarked as casually as his trembling voice would let him. "But don't you think it might be a bit cold and draughty in here for us?"

If the old, rusty, plaster-covered bed-stead standing mournfully in the centre of the room could have laughed out loud, it would have done so. "A bit cold and draughty?" it thought to itself. "It's like living on the top of Bradfield Moors in here. They must be mad, these young newly-weds."

Not surprisingly, Ron himself was thinking along the same lines although he, like the bedstead, managed to keep his thoughts to himself. Irene, however, was thinking differently.

"There's no point in being negative about things, Ron. My mam thinks the house is good value and it only needs a blob or two of plaster on the ceiling and a few tiles sticking on the roof, surely."

Irene's confidence and optimism was, of course, what was needed at this difficult time following the traumas of the devastating war. Ron understood this and, not wishing to destroy his wife's genuine enthusiasm, readily agreed with her whilst at the same time making sure he was crossing his fingers in hope.

Over the next few weeks, the happy couple worked long and hard together to make their new home as habitable and comfortable as they possibly could. The essential roof and ceiling repairs were carried out with the help of some savings Ron had managed to put away whilst in the RAF, while furnishings and home comforts were provided out of the small nest egg which Irene had managed to save from her modest wages she had earned at the laundry on Crookes. This was the beginning of their loving family life together, and the future looked rosy.

RON, THE SCHOOL BOBBY

About this time, the Sheffield Education Department was advertising for an Education Welfare Officer (EWO) to cover about six schools on the Wincobank, Shiregreen

Sheffield Education Offices in Leopold Street in early 1900s

The Leopold Hotel-2008 (Former Sheffield Education Offices)

and Flower Estates. This post, which Ron decided to apply for, was popularly known as the School Bobby in those days and was based at the Education Offices in Leopold Street. It involved ensuring that, as far as possible, all pupils attended school when they should do, although this was by no means an easy task.

As you can imagine, there were a large number of applicants for the job and Ron was delighted to find himself on the shortlist of six candidates who were to be interviewed by Education Committee councillors and senior staff.

These interviews took place on a beautiful spring day, and it was with nervous optimism that the ex-serviceman found himself climbing the steps to the magnificent stone building in Leopold Street which was basking in the late afternoon sun.

The interior of the building, which sixty years later has now been converted into a very smart hotel and restaurant, was as equally attractive as its imposing exterior. Oak-panelled walls in the conference room which was being used for the interviews created an immediate feeling of grandeur as the 30 year old applicant was ushered in by a smartly dressed clerk. A large highly polished table in the centre of the room tantalizingly reflected some of the sun's rays which poured in through large front windows, and somewhat contrasted with the stern, sombre appearance of the interviewing panel sitting behind it.

"Good afternoon, Mr. Cowen. Won't you please take a seat?"

The formal greeting from the Chairman of the panel, who had not yet managed to muster a smile, was representative of his stern-looking colleagues and, to a lesser mortal than Ron Cowen, might have been rather intimidating. However, after six years of active service in the RAF where strict formality was the norm, this setting was second nature to him.

"Good afternoon, Sir. Thank you, Sir."

Ron's response to the Chairman was followed by a long and thorough interview. Needless to say, the experienced RAF officer and physical education instructor who had built up a reputation in the RAF as a firm but understanding man who was able to empathise with young working-class recruits, was just what the doctor ordered. In addition, his own tough background as a young kid growing up in difficult times combined with his many years involved in the Scout Movement was another aspect of his experience which impressed the interviewing panel. All in all, he was probably a near-perfect candidate for the post.

As Ron was the last of the six candidates to be interviewed, he was advised to wait in an adjoining room after his grilling as the Chairman had decided to make a decision that afternoon. As he sat in the small but comfortable ante-room sipping a cup of Corporation tea (a rare luxury in those days), his mind was a whirl of activity as he tried to recall what he had said in response to the panel's searching questions, and where he might have gone wrong. It was with mixed feelings, therefore, that he was ushered back into the conference room about three quarters of an hour later to learn his fate.

"Come in Mr. Cowen. Take a seat."

This time, the bespectacled gentleman who greeted him looked different. He had a smile on his face, and his previous searching glare was now replaced by welcoming eyes which seemed to twinkle behind his rimless glasses.

Ron slowly sat down as this important person in his life continued.

"Well Mr. Cowen. Having regard to the considerable amount of experience you've had dealing with, guiding and leading children and young men, we think that you are just the man for the job. Congratulations."

As the somewhat larger than life figure in front of him stood up and offered his hand, the relieved candidate knew that this was a key moment in his life. Rising to his feet, Ron responded with a firm, grateful handshake knowing that he had secured a job which encompassed both his interest in education and his desire to help others. He was delighted.

"Thank you, sir. I'll do my best, and I won't let you down."

Those brief but meaningful words said it all to the man who was standing before him, now smiling broadly. No one can do better than their best, and the new School Bobby's confidence that he wouldn't let the Education Department down was very reassuring. I think that for the magnificent wage of about £1 a week, they were getting good value for money from our Ron, don't you?

There were many aspects of this job which proved to be interesting, and one or two that were not. The regular daily visits to each of his six schools involved an interview with the head teacher to discuss issues relating to the pupils, and to identify those which were proving to be particularly troublesome. Ron enjoyed these chats as it gave him the opportunity to build up a picture of those who needed more patience and understanding than others. In particular, the pupil's background and home life was always a major factor to consider.

When persistent absence occurred, playing truant as it was, and still is, called, it was the School-Bobby's job to visit the home of the offending schoolchild and discuss the situation with both the child and his or her parents. Ron had to admit that this could be both challenging and even unpleasant at times, with parents not being too co-operative in general. There were other times, however, when it was a pleasure.

Vew from Wincobank Hill overlooking Meadowhall-2002

Take the time when he had to visit Johnnie Smith's parents, for example. This little family lived in a mid-terrace house halfway up one of the steeply sloping streets which snaked up the hillside of Wincobank. Although most of the families there were poor, they were, in general, happy and hard-working, and Ron felt relaxed as he approached his destination. He had parked his car a little way down the street so as not to draw attention to his visit, but as he knocked firmly on the rather sombre front door which was now in front of him, he knew by the twitching of the grey net curtains in the adjacent front window that his visit had been expected.

"Oh, ello, luv. What a surprise. Won't you come in?"

Ron was no stranger to the friendly lady who opened the door, as Johnnie Smith made a habit of skipping school. As he followed the rather small, rounded figure into her neat, although rather dark front lounge (a room usually reserved for important visitors), she continued the conversation before Ron could draw a breath.

"I'm just about to make a cuppa', luv. Do you fancy one?"

"That's kind of you Mrs. Smith," replied Ron who was feeling a bit parched by this time. "I don't mind if I do."

The wise Welfare Officer knew that getting to know the children's parents in the relaxed atmosphere of a home brew and an arrowroot biscuit usually paid dividends, and this instance was no exception.

"Wot you come for this time, Mester Cowen? You 'avent come to see our Johnnie, 'ave you. 'E's at school."

"Well, I'm afraid, Mrs Smith, that he hasn't turned up again. It's the third time this week you know."

"'E's not turned up? Ooh, the little bugger. Just wait 'till he gets 'ome. I'll give 'im wot for."

Johnnie's mother had a round, cheerful face, and telling a 'porky' was not quite up her street.

"I tell you what, Mrs Smith," Ron patiently explained. "Why don't you pop upstairs and tell him to get out of bed and come down for a chat. It's the best thing, you know."

The kindly, middle-aged mum of local tear-away Johnnie Smith rose to her feet rather sheepishly and slowly made her way upstairs to fetch her son. She knew that if he persisted in playing truant, he could be taken to court and both of them would suffer the consequences. This was something that neither they nor Ron wanted to happen. Strangely enough, the first prosecution case that Ron had had to deal with as Education Welfare Officer had taken place at the same Magistrate's No2 court where he had been waiting to be called as a witness sixteen years earlier in his parents Divorce Hearing. It had brought back bad memories which he still remembers vividly today. As a consequence, in his capacity as School Bobby he only threatened the use of this action to wayward school children and their parents as a last resort.

By rights, it was the legal responsibility of the father in the family to ensure his child's continued attendance at school. Should the father not be at home, it was then incumbent upon the School Bobby to visit him at his place of work if necessary, rather than pursue the matter with the child's mother. Most mothers knew this of course, and Ron was never surprised to be told that their husbands were nearly always long-distance lorry drivers who never knew when they would be home. In this instance, Ron was aware that Johnnie's father had left him and his mother about a year earlier, and that it had been about that time that the angry and confused lad had started missing school.

A sudden creak of the room door brought Ron's thoughts back to the present as mum pushed her sullen-faced twelve year old son into the room to face him. As the two of them looked at each other, Ron pictured himself standing there as memories of his own youth came flooding back. He turned to the boy's mother who was standing there with an expression of despair on her face.

"I tell you what, Mrs Smith. Why don't me and Johnnie have a little chat together while you continue with your house-work. I'm sure you're very busy."

This opportunity of letting her son open-up to Ron in a relaxing and trusting atmosphere was appreciated by all concerned, and within an hour the young lad had decided to resume his education whilst Ron promised to sort things out at his school.

Although things didn't always turn out so well, in this instance a little understanding, care and patience worked wonders. Mother and son were smiling once again and Ron even got another arrowroot biscuit as he left the happy pair with Mrs. Smith's grateful words ringing in his ears:

"God Bless you, Mester Cowen."

Ron couldn't have expected a better result from his efforts, and it was successes such as this that gave him the real rewards for which he worked.

Sadly, despite this typical example of how this particular Education Welfare Officer carried out his duties, the holders of such posts were not always given the respect or recognition they deserved. In their ignorance, most schoolchildren and many parents in those days thought of them as the enemy, and I can still remember my schooldays when grownups and kids alike would shout: "You'd better do as yer told else the School Bobby'll get yer." Fortunately, Ron was able to shrug off this wrong perception and continue in his understanding and productive way.

Although Ron was to continue as an Education Welfare officer for the best part of his working life, he did try a spell in the Shiregreen Remand Home for Boys where he held quite a senior post. His skills of dealing with and understanding youths coupled with his RAF experience and Physical Training abilities were, once again, ideal for a job such as this. He was able to command respect from his charges who, for the most part, were able to accept his disciplined approach to their lives, particularly as it included many sporting activities led by this man of many talents himself.

Following a four year spell at the Remand Home, however, Ron still had a hankering to go back into the varied and rewarding job of Education Welfare Officer, and he successfully applied for such a post covering the Crookes and Walkley area of Sheffield where he stayed until his retirement at the age of 65. You could be forgiven for thinking that nearly thirty years in the same type of work might be a bit boring. However, you would be wrong, as no two days were ever the same. Ron was here, there and

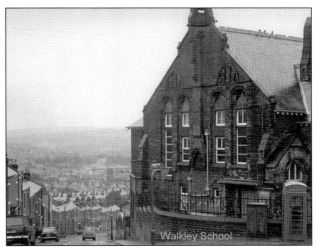
Walkley School

everywhere, and thousands of kids of all ages with problems of all types passed through his capable hands in that time. In addition, let's not forget that he had an evening job which I think we now ought to have a quick look at.

RON, THE YOUTH CLUB LEADER

You will recall that I mentioned earlier that Ron's other parallel life which he led was as a Youth Leader. His desire to help others led him to first join the Meynell Road Youth Club just above Wadsley Bridge. The meetings of this club were held in the school of the same name and Ron began working there in the summer of 1946. The club met three or four nights a week and also at weekends when outside activities such as football and cricket were played, depending on the season.

Ron's position at the club was that of assistant Youth Leader, and after catching a tram to the Wadsley Bridge terminus, he only had a short uphill walk to the school's club-room. He always made sure that he arrived early, as he was keen to ensure that cupboards and doors were unlocked and that the equipment was in its right place before the two hundred or so youths of both sex arrived. Activities such as badminton, table tennis, 5 a-side football and rounders were very popular in the evening sessions. They not only provided a wonderful and exciting few hours for all the members, they also provided a less-boring alternative to strolling round the streets in groups, causing mischief.

Contrary to the trend which is appearing in some schools today, competition was actively promoted. This ensured that not only did the boys and girls do their best and accept that it was normal to sometimes lose and sometimes win, it prepared them for the real world where competition in business as well as in sport is the plank upon which society walks.

After spending about twenty inspiring years at Meynell

Burgoyn Road School

Road, Ron moved on to the Pomona Street Youth Club for a couple of years before finally taking over as Youth Leader in charge of the well attended Burgoyne Youth Club which met at Burgoyne Road School in Walkley.

The Youth Club here used the large hall and rooms on the first floor for its many activities which, once again, were

enjoyed by nearly two hundred and fifty members. Opening times were from 7.00 to 10.00pm, and the club also held dances in the main School Hall once a month. It was Ron's idea to run these dances, although it usually took an hour or more for the two rows of opposite facing groups of boys and girls who lined the halls long walls to pluck up enough courage to ask each other to dance.

By and large, the behaviour at the club was exemplary. There was, however, one incident which Ron recalls which created quite a large police presence in the area. It was the occasion of the annual visit of an accountant from the Education Department whose duty it was to go through the youth club's books to ensure that the financial management of the club was carried out in accordance with City Council regulations. The youths, both boys and girls, were being exceptionally noisy that evening, and with Ron being downstairs providing the accountant with details he required, supervision was not at its best. Despite two warnings from the now exasperated Youth Leader to quieten things down, the noisy activities continued at full pace on the first floor, directly over the room in which Ron and the accountant were working.

Whether or not it was a bit of an over-reaction by the club's dedicated leader, I'm not sure, but after the members had disregarded the second warning, Ron promptly closed the club, leaving the boys and girls to spew out into the surrounding streets. Ten minutes later, an irate resident of Walkley phoned the police to report that about thirty rows of youths walking seven abreast were strolling noisily down South Road, Walkley's main shopping Street. It was a somewhat embarrassed Ron who had to explain to the police why all these kids, of whom he was still technically in charge so early in the evening, were behaving in this way. I don't think it ever happened again, mind you.

Ron's Retirement

200

RON, THE SPORTSMAN

Although Ron was 60 years old when he retired from his Youth Club activities which he had undertaken with great enthusiasm for 30 years, keeping fit was still foremost in his mind. On a daily basis, he either went running, cycling or swimming, and continued his regular weekly visits to King Edward VII School's swimming pool until he was 88. Even taking part in half marathons in Sheffield, Nottingham and Lincoln continued until his mid 70's, at which age he occasionally used his car where he had previously travelled on his trusty cycle.

GRANDAD RON, 70 GOES FOR GOLD

One significant activity in which this young-at-heart pensioner participated at the age of 70 was a national contest sponsored by the Legal and General Insurance Company to find the fittest OAP in Britain. With the title of Britain's Top Sporting Pensioner and a £3,500 cash prize up for grabs, Ron successfully worked through the rigorous

Golden Award Scheme selection contests which included sporting events such as swimming, cycling, weight-lifting and badminton. Although he didn't win the contest, he beat hundreds of similar and younger age contestants to make it

to the finals, an achievement of which he, his family and the city were very proud.

It is also important to remember that throughout his adult life, Ron had danced the nights away with his dear wife Irene on a regular basis, week in-week out, until the time came when osteoarthritis slowed her down in her 60's and very sadly took her life in 1997 at the age of 80. Ron was a regular visitor to her graveside in Crookes cemetery as he jogged around the surrounding area several times a week, and the adjacent photograph shows him pointing over Rivelin Valley at the breath-taking views which they both still shared.

Life does, however, catch up with everyone, even a super-fit person like Ron Cowen. He suffered three minor strokes during the latter few years of his eighties which curtailed his regular routine of swimming and jogging, although he did manage to successfully overcome these.

His 90th birthday celebration is also worth mentioning at this point. Ron was looking forward to it with particular enthusiasm as it included a visit around a 1940s Wartime Exhibition at Kelham Island Museum in Sheffield. About forty family members and friends had been invited, only to arrive at this special occasion after travelling from far and wide across the country to find that Ron was unable to attend as he had caught a virus the previous evening.

The sumptuous buffet and enlightening tour of the exhibition were enjoyed by everyone except the absent host, and was the one and only time that I had attended such an occasion to take photographs without the most important

person being there. Fortunately, I was able to take a group photograph of everyone present on which I superimposed a photograph of Ron clad in a tee-shirt and track-suit bottoms which I took a couple of days later. At least the birthday-boy can now pretend he was there.

The ever-young Peter Pan of Crookes did, nevertheless, manage to get to town with his grand-daughter Nicola in his 91st year to take part in the Battle of Britain parade

through the shopping centre. He was, not surprisingly, the oldest ex-serviceman there, and will probably be participating in such events as long as he has breath left in his body.

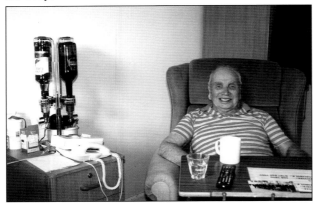

Now, as we come to the end of our story of this typical, yet remarkable, Sheffield man, he has vacated the flat in Brick Street in Crookes which he shared with Irene for about 25years, and is now earning a well-deserved rest at the Broomgrove Nursing Home, not far from Sheffield's Botanical Gardens. The walls of the room in which he now lives proudly display many large and small photographs of memories of his days in the Royal air Force, and you can't help but feel that you are entering a welcoming RAF

museum when you pop in to see him. His favourite photograph is a large signed image entitled The Last of the Few which shows members of the Battle of Britain Fighter Association standing in front of the famous Spitfire plane in which they collectively and successfully defended Britain.

Ron is cared for with love and respect by dedicated nursing and care staff at Broomgrove, and is able to enjoy living there at a pace which suits him. Today he has to make do with 'chasing' a dishy looking young nurse or care-assistant down the corridor which passes by his bedroom instead of taking part in a 13 mile half marathon, although his insatiable appetite for athletic success is still satisfied by his grand-daughter Nicola's continued activity in this area of the sport. Let's hope that young Ron reaches his hundredth birthday because I'd love to see if he could still make it to the end of the 100 foot long corridor in time to catch the nurse or carer of the day that he is probably still chasing!

God Bless you Ron, and thank you for the memories.

Schooldays

So far, we have looked at the lives of several individual Sheffield folk and have been amazed, amused and entertained by how they have lived or by what they have achieved.

However, perhaps most enlightening of all might be a look at the lives of young folk who, over the centuries, have been perceived by many people to be deserving of very little, a bit of a nuisance, often lacking in respect, often down-right rude and nearly always trouble-causers.

On the other side of the coin, many young folk over this period have considered themselves to be under-valued, bullied by adults, forced into unsuitable work, punished unreasonably, not respected enough and hardly ever understood.

In recognition of these conflicting opinions by adults and children, I think it would be worthwhile to try and be a fly on the wall in the schools of 100 years or so ago and compare their educational environment with that of schools of today. Perhaps we can all learn something from this comparison?

You may, of course, quite rightly feel that it should be the homes of children that we should be looking at, as it is there where they are moulded and shaped to prepare them for the task of integrating into and contributing to society. It follows, therefore, that it is the quality of the child's home-life and the quality of the environment in which the home is situated which influences the child's life and development. However, I feel that it is also in the schools, where children from the ages of four to sixteen spend most of their lives, that a significant influence on a child's life is made, and it is for this reason that our story about schooldays has been chosen.

Whilst I may have an opinion or two to express within this story, I will leave it to you, the reader, to make up your own mind as to whether schooldays are better or worse as a century or more has passed. You may also have a view of how things should possibly change to make the world go round a little smoother.

TEACHING IN VICTORIAN TIMES

Let's start by going back to Queen Victoria's reign in the 1800s.

We are told that during her 64 years on the throne of England, a sense of pride and respect was instilled into a population which had hitherto viewed Royalty as a regime of excesses and self-indulgence. With a new monarch who was determined to lead by example, the country had slowly but surely turned away from the concept of 'self' being the most important aspect of life, and had begun to respect more unselfish values.

It was, of course, no easy task to change the habits of a lifetime. However, during those first 40 years or so of her reign, new generations of families had been born and grown up. This was at a time when schooling was rapidly developing and the school teacher was identified as the instrument of change and the 'creator' of obedient and well-mannered children.

With this considerable burden of responsibility to carry, the teaching profession chose to apply the concept of strict obedience to their young charges in order that they could learn the important life-skill of self discipline as well as academic and domestic skills.

In order to look at how these skills were taught in Victorian times, I thought it would be helpful to visit two schools and sit-in on the daily events which were taking place there. Burgoyne Road School in Walkley and Springfield School on the outskirts of the town centre were the two I chose.

BURGOYNE ROAD BOARD SCHOOL

Let us begin by taking a stroll down Cundy Street in Walkley in the year 1881 to view the large, stone school-buildings which had recently been constructed there. It was cold and sunny on that morning of January 10th, although the sun's rays had kindly chased away some of the glistening white frost which was desperately trying to cling on to the steep, cobbled road surface.

Burgoyne Road School buildings, Walkley

The site of the school complex, which extended across to the adjacent Burgoyne Road where its goods and delivery entrance was located, encompassed a fall of 40 ft or so from top to bottom. This had a necessitated the construction of retaining walls to enable the sloping site to be divided into three terraces which formed the play grounds for boys, girls and infants.

Below these recreation areas, which linked into the three departments of the school at their different levels, the

Lower view of Burgoyne Road School buildings

front entrance to this very imposing, lofty building- block proudly displayed the sign 'Burgoyne Road Board School' to a small group of smartly dressed men who gathered there. Behind them, the two horses which had brought them in their sleek, black taxi-cab snorted impatiently, sending small clouds of condensed, hot breath spiralling upwards as though they were on fire.

Jimmy's Lads

Suddenly, the clunk of a large key disengaging levers and gears signalled the opening of the sturdy front door through which appeared three important-looking figures.

This interesting scene was, unbeknown to the gathering, being watched by two cheeky-looking young lads sitting on the low front wall of one of many terraced houses a little further up the street. The younger of the two boys was intrigued by the activity they were watching.

"Oo's that then, Jon?"

"They're the department 'eds, Jimmy."

Jon and his younger brother Jimmy had been given the day off lessons to celebrate the opening of their new school by Mr. Skelton Cole, the chairman of Sheffield's School Board (a bit like today's Education Committee). Along with an array of dignitaries which included Mr. J. Moss (the Clerk to the Board), Alderman Tozer (a member of the Board), the Board's Inspector of Schools, Mr Davies, the Superintendent of Officers, Mr. Gilley, and the Architect for the school's design, Mr. C. Innocent, he was to address the head teachers, parents and children in the girls department on this auspicious occasion.

"Wot's a department 'ed, Jon?"

"Don't you know anything, little brother? There's a headmistress for the Girls Department called Miss Corbett, a headmaster for the Boys Department called Mr. Drury, and another headmistress for the Infants Department called Miss Currie."

"I don't like the look of 'er Jon, that one with the black dress, funny looking glasses and bunched up white hair."

"Well, you'll 'ave to get used to 'er 'cos she'll be your headmistress when you start school tomorrow."

Poor Jimmy's face visibly paled and his almost permanent grin disappeared for a few moments.

"She looks too old to be a teacher, Jon. I like smiling ladies with long hair, don't you?"

"Now don't you worry Jimmy, she's just the head teacher. You won't see her very much unless you misbehave yourself."

"I don't think I'll bother going to school after all, Jon. Can you tell our mam that I've changed my mind?"

Jon put a reassuring hand on his little brother's shoulders and ushered him down to see the taxi-cab horses to take his mind off things.

The deputation headed by Mr. Cole had, by this time, disappeared into the building accompanied by the three head teachers. Arriving in the main schoolroom of the Girls Department, the party was received by polite applause from the large number of parents and children who had chosen to turn up for the event. Miss Corbett then formally opened the meeting.

"Thank you very much ladies, gentlemen and children. It is my pleasure to welcome Mr. Cole and his colleagues who have kindly come to officially open our wonderful new school. Before Mr. Cole speaks to us, let us sing one of our favourite songs, Land of Hope and Glory, and then all say the Lord's Prayer."

This initial welcome by the girls' headmistress was the signal for everyone to rise to their feet in this room designed to accommodate 130 children. The school itself could accommodate 933 pupils, of which 315 places were for boys, 315 for girls and 303 for infants. On this occasion, only the girls' main room was in use, but tomorrow would be a hive of activity everywhere.

"Wot's all them people standing up for, Jon," asked Jimmy in amazement. "They're not going already, are they?"

The tousled-haired, mischievous faces which peered over the bottom of the outer window ledge shouldn't really have been there, but 'Jimmy's lad's', as they were known locally, wanted to know what was going on without actually being part of the audience who'd arrived in their Sunday-best.

It wasn't likely that Jon and Jimmy had any Sunday-best clothes to wear. Like many others at the time, they came from a very poor family where laughter and mischief kept them going in the absence of good food. As far as clothes were concerned, the same ones had to make do day-in, day-out, week after week, whatever the occasion.

"They're going to sing a song, you daft ha'peth," Jon responded, "just like they do in assembly. They'll probably kneel down and say their prayers afterwards as well."

The brothers were suddenly aware of two steely eyes glaring at them from the stern face of Miss Corbett. She had a reputation for having eyes in the back of her head, so the fact that she'd spotted the two grinning, enquiring faces squashed against the newly polished glass was hardly surprising.

"Oh my gosh. Quick Jimmy, lets scarper or she'll 'ave us!"

As if by magic, the two boys vanished, and the proceedings in the schoolroom carried on. In fact, they carried on, and on and on, with Mr Cole giving a very comprehensive presentation on costs, pupil numbers, attendances in the city's schools, and just about everything else anyone could possibly wish to know about about education and improvements since School Boards were introduced just ten years earlier in 1870. I think he probably bored the pants off most of his audience but, as we all know, that's the risk you have to take when you ask a top politician to address a mixed meeting of teachers, parents and school children.

FIRST DAY AT SCHOOL - 1881

It was, however, now Tuesday, January 11th 1881, and little Jimmy's smile was missing as he stood in the assembly on his first day in school. Jon was also a little nervous but, being a tough, seasoned 7 year old, he had to appear confident and cheerful for his young brother's sake. The erect figure of Miss Currie, the Infants Department head teacher, dominated the area at the front of the large schoolroom which was also shared by several class teachers bedecked in long, grey or black dresses and rather pale, sombre faces.

"Welcome to Burngreave Road Infants Department, children."

The rather posh and sharply penetrating voice which cut through the nervous hubbub of children's chatter made Jimmy cringe, and all he felt like doing was bursting into tears and running away.

"The first thing I want you all to remember," the voice continued, "is that I expect TOTAL silence in assembly. Anyone caught talking in future will be punished."

"Chuffin' 'eck," the poor lad choked to himself. "I'm not comin' tomorrow. It's worse than I thought."

Little did Jimmy know that this 'welcome' was the precursor to a rather harrowing few years in the infants' classes of this modern, new school. No wonder his big brother, Jon, who had already experienced two years of Victorian teaching before moving here, had kept his views to himself so far. He hadn't wanted to scare his brother off.

After the stresses and strains of that first assembly, during which our new recruit took the opportunity during the saying of the Lord's prayer to ask Him if he 'could be allowed to go home', the one hundred and seventy or so five and six year olds were marched silently to their respective classrooms, whilst the remaining one hundred or so seven year olds stayed in the schoolroom in which they made up two classes.

Large class sizes were the norm in those days, with the six year olds also being split up into two classes of fifty four each, whilst the remaining sixty two five year olds were herded together into the Junior Infants or 'babies' room where a teacher and two trainee assistants awaited them.

The layout and structure of the schoolroom, the classrooms and the head teacher's room, with their varnished-pine panelled, half-glazed partitioned walling, had been designed to allow the head teacher to see every pupil and teacher under her control from her office. There was very little that went on in this department, therefore, that this eagle-eyed lady was likely to miss.

As Jimmy gazed around his posh, new surroundings in which rows of shiny, new desks stood proudly to attention awaiting the arrival of anxious little bums sitting on their hard, slippery seats, he wondered just what he had done to deserve being sent to such a place. After all, he thought to himself, he'd done all right up to now in life so why change it just because he'd had his 5th birthday?

"Come on children. Let's get you into your places."

One of the trainee teachers, with a hint of a smile on her fresh young face, gently directed the nervous children to their places and, for a few minutes, Jimmy's spirits rose a little. However, as he glanced towards Miss Smith, the teacher of the babies' class, he noticed that as she stood behind her tall desk with the morning light playing on her deep furrowed brow, she looked very stern, and he instinctively knew that life wasn't going to be easy from now on.

PUNISHMENT AT BURGOYNE ROAD SCHOOL
Miss Currie's Headship – 1881 to 1887

As Jimmy and Jon began their educational journey at Burgoyne Road Board School, let's move forward to see how the concept of strict obedience, which we mentioned earlier, was applied within the Infants Department by the head teachers.

Miss Currie, like all head teachers, had to follow the strict rules laid down by the School Board as they related to punishment. In particular, only she, and no-one else in the school, was able to administer it. There appeared, however, to be little, if any, guidance as to the degree of punishment which was appropriate for any given misdemeanour. It is interesting to note, therefore, that during her headship from January 1881 to may 1887, she administered 1,640 punishments to her children, which averaged out at one a day for every working day of the six and three-quarter years she ran the Infants Department.

During her first two years, misdemeanours such as disobedience, lateness, naughtiness, rudeness, talking, being dirty etc. were dealt with by giving the offending children 2 or 3 raps with a ruler or 1 or 2 strokes with the cane. Thereafter, Miss Currie introduced more taps with the cane than anything else, except when dealing with specific offences which upset her. Playing truant, for example, usually resulted in a whipping or a good whipping, as indeed did swearing. Strangely enough, being mischievous was also one of her dislikes, with a whipping also being given for this innocuous offence. Little Joe Sedall seemed to manage to commit just about every offence in the book whilst in the Infants Department and received punishments ranging from taps, raps, strokes and whippings during his stay there.

All in all, however, Miss Currie's punishment regime incorporating a philosophy of little and often, with a few whippings thrown in, seemed to work reasonably well in keeping modest order amongst the mainly six or seven year olds, and she rarely punished anyone younger.

Miss Derry's Headship – 1887 to 1896

Following Miss Currie's retirement in May 1887, however, her place was taken by a younger but even sterner head teacher by the name of Miss Derry. In order to make an impact on her young charges and establish her authority, she adopted a more severe punishment regime which appeared to be almost sadistic.

Take the time, for example, that little six year old Florence Clayton wasn't able to understand the questions that her class teacher put so abruptly to her. All the children in the first year were a bit scared, but Florence, being a very timid sort, was even more so.

"I don't know what you mean, Miss," whispered the distressed young girl as her exasperated teacher glared at her over the top of her thin-framed spectacles.

"I think you're being very stupid on purpose, my girl. We'll see what Miss Derry has to say about it. Come on."

Grasping the now sobbing Florence by her arm, she marched her victim into the head teacher's office to suffer the fate that many others had suffered before her. Sadly, for 'being very stupid', Miss Derry's standard punishment was a good whipping, even for a terrified, innocent six year old.

DATE 188_	NAME OF PUPIL	Age	Stand-ard	OFFENCE	PUNISHMENT, &c.	INITIALS of TEACHER
Nov 21	Alice Fellowes	7	I	Very troublesome	2 strokes	E.D.
" 28	Fred Honeley	7	I	Laziness	2 "	E.D.
" 30	Wilfred Hawley	7	I	Disobedience	2 "	E.D.
Dec 1	Annie Dawson	7	I		1 "	E.D.
" 14	Mabbott Fred	6		Dirty tricks	2 "	E.D.
" "	Matten Tom	7	I		"	E.D.
" 15	Henry Wilson	5		Disobedience	1 "	E.D.
" "	Eight boys	6		"	2 "	E.D.
1888						
Jan 12	John Coy	7	I	Disobedience	2 "	E.D.
" 13	Fred Baggaley	7	I		2 "	E.D.
" 16	John Turner	7	I	Cont.	2 "	E.D.
" 17	W. Etherington	6		Troublesome	2 "	E.F.
" "	W. Berrill	6			2 "	E.F.
" "	S. Smalley	6			2 "	E.F.
" 20	W. Baggaley	6		Crying	a good whipping	E.D.
" 26	Bertie Fowsaker	6		Disobedience	2 strokes	E.F.
" "	Arthur Bolton	7	I			E.F.
" 27	Florence Clayton	6		Very stupid	a good whipping	E.D.
Feb 14	Norah Nicholson	7	I	Bad behaviour	1 stroke	E.D.

Miss Derry could, of course, be a little more caring, as her punishment for being simply stupid (rather than very stupid) was only a slapping, as five year old Andrew Morton and six year old Florence Gillatt found out a short time afterwards.

Florence Clayton's friend William Baggaley, however, was quite a bright, albeit sensitive six year old lad and no-one could reasonably call him stupid. Unfortunately, he was prone to burst into tears when his teacher picked on his defenceless little friends. This had proved to be his undoing the previous week when he committed the unacceptable crime of showing his emotions by crying, for which he received the same terrible punishment as Florence, a good whipping.

We might all be forgiven for thinking that these unnecessary extremes of punishment were the limit of Miss Derry's repertoire. We would be wrong, for when seven year old Frank Sykes splashed water in his friends face whilst using the washing facilities, he received a shrashing for 'wetting another boy'.

Although Miss Derry was head teacher of the Infants Department for just over nine years, it was, however, only for the first 3 years that she pursued her 'reign of terror', with caning, slapping, whipping and thrashing being the order of the day. During these three years, she administered 347 punishments which, at an average rate of one every two days, must have struck terror into the 300 or so infants under her care and management.

Whether the intensity of her punishments had successfully stopped the children from misbehaving, or whether the parents or the School Board had taken action to prevent such abuse we don't really know. What we do know, however, is that the next six years were almost punishment-free according to the school records. It is of course quite possible that Miss Derrie simply chose not to enter the punishments she administered into the Punishment Book, contrary to School Board Rules, although it is most unlikely.

Lizzie Faberer's Headship 1896 to 1906

When Lizzie Faberer started as head teacher on August 25 1896 following Miss Derry's transfer to a nearby school, things appeared to take a turn for the better. Her outward-looking approach to school life was of significant benefit to the children who attended there.

But, was she also a strict disciplinarian who ruled with a rod of iron like Miss Derry, or was she more understanding? Let's have a look at her record.

During her ten and a bit years from August 25 1896 to November 21st 1906, she administered 440 punishments to her pupils, which averages out at about one punishment a week. This, in itself, represents a significant reduction in the frequency of punishment. However, Miss Faberer's policy appeared to be one of advocating firmness with tolerance amongst her teaching staff but, when incidents were reported to her by them, she dealt with the offenders extremely firmly.

Six years old Clarence Crowe was testimony to this approach as he was regularly punished, receiving a whipping for such offences as rough or disobedient behaviour, spoiling school materials and swearing. Whippings were also given for showing temper and being rude to a teacher. Of significance, however, was the fact that these and other punishments such as caning were now applied to five year olds, whereas pervious head teachers rarely if ever, punished anyone in the 'babies' class.

Of all the punishments which Lizzie Faberer administered, perhaps the most unreasonable was that given to five year old Ernest Robinson. Poor little Ernest had an uncontrollable habit of screaming which probably upset both his teacher and the headmistress. On Friday August 24th 1900, he began screaming in class and was given a whipping for his sins. He started screaming again on Monday 27 August following the weekend break and persisted in his habit on the Tuesday and Wednesday following, for which again he was similarly punished. Whether or not whippings on four consecutive schooldays stopped his habit is unknown. It is more than likely that his mother kept him at home to prevent further occurrences of this common method of Victorian discipline. I wonder how much real education people such as Ernest received in those days? Perhaps he grew up to be a well behaved pillar of society? You never know, do you?

PUNISHMENT TODAY

But, of course, we now live in the 21st century when, in some cases, the tables have turned. Physical punishment is absolutely forbidden in our schools and, sadly, in some of them, the children appear to rule the teachers. This problem appears to be more evident at junior and senior level as pupils become aware of their human rights and the legal protection that new legislation gives them. Some pupils appear to take advantage of the situation to the desperate disadvantage of the teacher. It is not unusual these days for articles to appear in the national press describing the desperate plight of a mature and respected teacher or head teacher who has been suspended for daring to confront and restrain an out-of control aggressive student.

Sadly, the Local Educational Authorities appear to automatically assume the teachers to be guilty until proven innocent if a pupil makes an accusation against them, even when that pupil has a history of proven trouble-making. An automatic suspension, sometimes lasting years rather than months, can and does destroy dedicated and otherwise unblemished careers, not to mention the personal grief and distress which is caused to the individuals and their families. It seems to me that the pendulum has swung to the other extreme in this now enlightened society where individuals rights are often more important than justice.

DATE 1900	NAME OF PUPIL	Age	Class Stand-ard	OFFENCE	PUNISHMENT, &c.	INITIALS of TEACHER
	Harold Hall	6	1	Disobedience in the	1 stroke	L.J.
	Frank Ratcliffe	6	1	Playground	1	L.J.
Aug 24	Ernest Robinson	5	3	Continual screaming	a whipping	L.J.
27th	Ernest Robinson	5	3	" "	a whipping	L.J.
28th	Ernest Robinson	5	3	" "	a whipping	L.J.
"	David Blewitt	5	3	Bad behaviour in	1 stroke	L.J
"	Harry Archer	6	3	the Playground	1	L.J.
"	Arthur Ibbotson	6	3		1	L.J.
"	Ben Deakin	6	1	Destroying reading book page 4	2	L.J.
29	Ben Deakin	6	1	Destroying blotting paper	2	L.J.
"	Ernest Robinson	5	3	Continual screaming	a whipping	L.J.
30	David Blewitt	5	3	Pulling hats off the pegs in	1 stroke	L.J.
"	Ralph Metcalf	6	2	the cloak room + throwing then on to the floor	1	L.J.

SCHOOL ACTIVITIES AND TEACHING METHODS - BURGOYNE SCHOOL 1896 TO 1926

But, of course, school life in Sheffield during Lizzie Feberer's headship, which spanned the passing of Queen Victoria in 1901 and the beginning of the new Edwardian era, was not all doom and gloom. Life for the schoolchildren was, indeed, as exciting as it was challenging. The challenges were mainly those of illness and poverty encompassed in a new learning environment, whilst the excitement manifested itself in exploring the wonders of knowledge and taking part in events such as parades and tea-parties to celebrate Royal visits and similar important occasions. In those days, bad weather was also a serious problem, as walking to school was the only method of transport for the vast majority of the children. A few horse-trams and buses were available to those who could afford them, but very inclement weather, particularly snow and ice, prevented even this from of transport from accessing the steeply sloping hillsides of Walkley and Burgoyne Road School.

To get a flavour of what things were like, let's have a whistle-stop tour of the Infants Department at this school over the 30 year period from 1896 to 1926. I'm sure you'll find it interesting.

It was August 17th 1896 and the three-week mid-summer holidays had just ended for the 320 children who somewhat reluctantly returned to school that sunny morning (little did they know that 50 years or so later they would have been getting a six or seven weeks break for their summer holiday). It was Lizzie Faberer's first day at school as head teacher and she was finding her feet and getting to know the staff and her pupils. Five teachers were employed to look after the children, these being Miss Fairclough, Miss Simpson, Miss Cuthbert, Miss Lenthall and Miss Barton, assisted from time to time by one or two pupil teachers. With only five classes for the 320 or so children now attending this department, class sizes of 60 or more were not unusual.

However, our new head teacher was a little unfortunate as, within a few days of arriving, the 'heavens opened' and each day for the next few weeks brought torrential rain. With the rain came greatly reduced attendances, with 50 or 60 children being unable to attend daily.

Teaching standards were, nevertheless, very high, and each of the five infant classes, including class 5, (the babies), were subject to monthly examinations overseen by the head teacher. Arising from these, adjustments were made to the teaching practices, and emphasis was put on those areas where standards of learning were noticeably low. By this method, significant improvements were able to be obtained and most pupils benefited considerably.

In addition to the monthly examinations, Her Majesty's Inspector of Schools made an annual official visit to the school together with several speculative visits during the year to make sure that standards were being maintained.

It is also interesting to note that the combination of those school examinations and the official inspections which took place appeared to be very successful in maintaining standards of education. They didn't appear to involve masses of paperwork, the production of league tables of results, the classification of 'good schools' and 'bad schools' or the creation of success-related stress that occurs these days. In fact, despite the inappropriately extreme methods of punishment which were used, perhaps we could learn something by taking a selective look at the 'old-fashioned' teaching practices which allowed teachers to teach, pupils to learn and a degree of respect to be instilled into the children which they could beneficially take with them into the future.

The school year was also different in those days, as it finished at the end of November. New children started school, therefore, in December of each year and existing children moved up to higher classes at the same time. I presume that the school year-end, which moved from November to July in 1899, did so when the length of the school's summer holidays was extended to five weeks. This change does appear to make sense, as after so many weeks away from school, it's like starting all over again for the children, isn't it.

It is also of interest to note how topical the teachers made some of the lessons for their young charges.

17 1897

February 8th The registers were checked this morning by Mr Quine.

List of Object Lessons (1897)

A Classes 1 & 2 (Six year old children)
I Natural History Lessons.
1. The cat	6. The Horse	11. The frog
2. The cat's cousins	7. The rabbit	12. The lark
3. The dog	8. The Mole	13. The swallow
4. The sheep	9. The butterfly	14. The robin
5. The cow	10. The bee	

II Lessons from Plants & flowers.
15. Parts of a plant	20. The daisy
16. The root	21. The buttercup
17. The stem	22. The primrose
18. Leaves	23. The wild rose
19. The bluebell	24. The poppy

III Objects & Subjects
25. Sponge	28. Haymaking
26. Coal	29. Harvest - a cornfield
27. Cotton	30. Sheep-washing & shearing.

A good example of this is given by the List of Object Lessons for each class produced by the head teacher to supplement the less exciting number, reading and writing lessons. A copy of her copper-plate entry made in the School Diary or Log-Book in 1897 clearly shows this.

If you compare these subjects with those taught in infant schools these days, there would probably be little difference, other than the fact they would now be taught in much smaller classes and in classrooms whose walls are covered in wonderful, brightly coloured posters, paintings and creative pictures. The recently taken photographs of happy infant children in schools across the city, shown below, are a good example of this:

Intake School

Woodthorpe School

Hucklow School

Springfield School

However, to continue our 30 year mini-tour around Burgoyne Road School Infants Department, let's drop in at certain interesting times to see what was happening and how people coped.

Tinsley School

Pye Bank School

Dealing with bad weather conditions

Let's have a look at how these Victorian five to seven year olds coped with going to school in the very bad winters which were common place in those days. The steep roads on the Walkley hillside upon which this large school was built were treacherous in icy or snowy conditions, and presented a daunting challenge to anyone, let alone very young children. Nowdays, Radio Sheffield or Hallam FM would simply announce on its early morning bulletins the list of schools which would be closed in periods of heavy (and not so heavy) snowfall. From the Log -book of this famous school, however, it is clear that every child was expected to try and get to school regardless of the intensity of the weather, and with Shanks' Pony being their only mode of transport, the effort was certainly considerable.

It is also clear from these records that regardless of the severity of the weather or the number of young children who battled through the elements, the school never closed. It is also unlikely that the quality of heating in the 1890s classrooms was as good as that of today, although this did not appear to be a deterrent and was never a reason to stay away from school.

Dealing with Illness

It wasn't, however, just bad weather which those hardy youngsters had to cope with. Illness was a major problem in those days, particularly that involving infectious diseases such as whooping cough and measles. During June of 1897, for example, a whooping cough epidemic was closely followed by a measles epidemic which jointly resulted in 226 infants out of a total of 379 on the school books going down with the diseases in that month. Epidemics of these two illnesses occurred on a regular basis in those days, and it is with great relief that modern day society is almost free from them thanks to the discovery and mass availability of vaccines which successfully combat their dreadful effects. Most of the children at Burgoyne Road School will not have been so lucky as those of today, and sadly, some will have died or suffered permanent health problems as a result.

Although whooping cough and measles seemed to be the most commonly occurring ailments, chicken pox, mumps and bronchitis also did their best to cause distress and disruption. Scarlet fever also reared its head on a regular basis, and isolation from this serious disease was always necessary to prevent it spreading.

However, it was the occurrence of the acute, infectious disease of diphtheria which created the greatest fear in those dark days when medical knowledge in this area of combating diseases was very limited. It was the November of 1898 when the dreaded disease hit Burgoyne Road School and the neighbourhood around it. The population as a whole was in a state of panic, and ninety infant children were off school in the first week, during which time two of them sadly died. By the end of the second week, the number of absentees had risen to one hundred and forty, and another two, young, innocent lives had been lost. On the 15th day of that dreadful month of November, Lizzie Faberer, the head teacher, sent all her infant children home and the whole school was closed until further notice. It was a month later, on December 12th, that the School Board decided that it was safe to re-open it, although with less than half the children turning up, many were obviously still sick or too afraid to return.

It is worthwhile reminding readers at this point that the sadness, grief and difficulties which were created by the unremitting advance of serious diseases which affected children during this period of time were quite common place. Teaching and learning had to continue within this environment, which was a far cry from the safe, health-conscious environment in which today's children are taught. Perhaps when we complain of having a sniffle, or throw a 'sickie' because we feel a bit off-colour, we should remember how lucky we are compared to those in times gone by.

Up to this stage in our mini-tour of time, we've looked at two of the major challenges (weather and illness) which faced school children during Lizzie Faberer's headship. Let's now have a look at some of the more exciting and rewarding activities which took place.

Going to the Circus

One rather special event which caused great excitement in the summers of 1898 and 1899 was the arrival in Sheffield of Barnum and Bailey's Circus. Although it was not a school event, it obviously held an enormous attraction to the 370 children in the Infants Department, 250 of whom took an unofficial day off on each occasion to watch the circus's spectacular Street Parade through town.

It was a beautiful sunny morning on the 13th day of June, 1898 when the parade began and slowly made its way along Fargate towards The Moor. Hundreds of children from all over the city had 'wagged' off school to gaze in awe at the long, colourful spectacle of horse-drawn caravans, wagons and cages which snaked up the street behind the huge lumbering elephant which led them. A galaxy of clowns in their outrageously coloured outfits and huge permanently wide smiles did their best to out-do the agile acrobats and trapeze artists who pranced and somersaulted their way alongside the glittering mobile show, whilst a drum-banging musician succeeded in making every stray dog in the area howl and bark in anger and dismay.

Little Lydia Jenkinson had come to watch the parade with her three friends Willie Challoner, Albert Rotherham and Minnie Robinson, although none of them had sought permission to do so from the school. Whether or not their parents were with them is uncertain, but even at five and six years old there appeared to be little danger presented to a group of such children in those days. Today, many children of that age are not even allowed out of their gardens, let alone nipping into town.

As the four chums gazed in almost disbelief at what they were seeing, a particularly large cage rumbled into view. It was five year old Albert who spotted the magnificent, powerful-looking beast inside first.

"Look, look, look! It's a giant, striped cat."

Eight little eyes opened wide with amazement and just a little fear as one of Barnum and Bailey's two magnificent tigers pushed its huge face up to the thick protective steel bars of the cage and glared at the children. For a few seconds, fear turned to terror as a gentle snarl displayed huge, white, pointed teeth in a mouth which looked capable of eating them all in one gulp. The four little truants held their breath and wished for a moment or two that they'd gone to school instead.

Suddenly, a white-painted face with smiling, bright red lips popped up in front of them and announced the circus' evening event

"Are you coming to the show tonight children? Tell your mams and dads it's the greatest show on earth. You mustn't miss it."

The shock of suddenly seeing the friendly clown, who then danced away as suddenly as he had arrived, brought the children back to reality. By this time the tiger cage had been replaced by one containing an assortment of yelping dogs, and Lydia, Willie, Albert and Minnie were happy once more.

A bit of circus history

It might be interesting at this point to tell you a little bit about this circus which, by this time, was acknowledged as one of the biggest and best in the world. P.T. Barnum was originally a famous American Showman and entertainer. In 1871 he lent his famous name and financial backing to an existing circus run by D. Castello and W. Coup which was subsequently transformed and renamed P.T. Barnum's Great Travelling Museum, Menagerie, Caravan, and Hippodrome. With a mouthful of a title like that, no-one was likely to try and repeat it, and within a short time, it was better known as Barnum's: The Greatest Show on Earth.

But what about James Anthony Bailey? He, in fact, had joined forces with a fellow American by the name of James Cooper to form the Cooper and Bailey Circus in the 1860s which, within a few years was Barnum's main competitor. By 1881, however, both Barnum and Bailey had recognised the value and attractiveness of each other's circus and decided to combine to form the Barnum and Bailey Circus.

However, let us not forget that these two showmen were playing to American audiences, and Burngoyne Road School in Sheffield was simply a pin-prick on time's horizon. It was the death of Phineas Taylor Barnum in 1891 at the age of 81 that changed this situation. Bailey bought his partner's share of the circus from his widow and began touring the United States for a few years. The show was so successful that Bailey decided to make a tour of Europe which began in England on December 27th, 1897 and lasted five years to the end of 1902. It was during this time that it came to Sheffield.

In case you want to know what happened to the circus after its tour of England, I've included a few extra facts, as follows, to complete its brief history.

Following the death of James Bailey in 1906, the circus was sold to the seven Ringling Brothers who, together with their own circus, created a giant show whose enormous success eventually made the surviving brother, John Ringling, one of the richest men in the world by the late 1920's. Although the combined Ringling Brothers and Barnum & Bailey Circus was bought in 1967 by the Feld brothers, Irvin and Israel, who had made a name for themselves in the rock 'n roll tour production industry, the circus still exists today under its original combined name giving shows across America in indoor Arenas rather than in tents.

Animal welfare has also been given very high profile in that country, with the circus opening the Centre for Elephant Conservation in Florida in 1995 which is used for breeding, research and the retirement of its Asian Elephant herd. The circus also participates in breeding programmes for endangered species used in the shows including the Bengal tiger and elephant. In addition, the tiger population is retired to Big Cat Rescue when their age so dictates and even the dogs in the shows are all rescued from animal shelters. Perhaps we in this country could take a leaf out of the American book?

Celebrating Royal Events

Queen Victoria

It was, however, Royal events which this school and its children looked forward to with great expectation. May 21st, 1897, was such an occasion when Queen Victoria honoured the town with a visit to officially open the new Town Hall and bestow the title of City on our ever growing town.

Morning lessons on May 20th in the brightly lit room of Miss Register's class of six year olds had concentrated on the life and times of the country's popular Queen who, within four days, would be 78 years old. It was with great interest that they had listened to their teacher telling them that Victoria had been a lively, cheerful girl who had always been fond of drawing and painting, just like themselves. Let's join them, shall we?

"Excuse me Miss," piped up little Ada Sanderson shooting her hand high up into the air."

"Yes, what is it, Ada."

"Well, Miss, I just wondered how she became a Queen. I'd like to be one when I get older, if that's all right."

Miss Register, who was still only a pupil teacher, was a little taken aback by this rather searching question which she did her best to answer without confusing the enquiring child. She explained that Victoria was, in fact, the granddaughter of King George III, and ascended the throne at the age of 18 when her uncles, King George IV, and King William IV, died without having any heirs, thus making her Queen in her own right. More difficult questions were, however, yet to come.

"My mam's got a husband, Miss. Has the Queen got one?"

Freckled-faced Augustus Platts had never been backward at coming forward, and the young lad's question was now moving into a more personal area of Victoria's life.

"Well, that's a very good question, Augustus," smiled the young teacher who hadn't yet learnt to adopt a forever stern approach to her young charges. "The Queen did in fact marry a young German Prince, children, when she was 21 years old. Do any of you know his name?"

The puzzled faces which peered out from behind rows of not quite so shiny desks, which were now sixteen years old, told Miss Register that at least she was teaching the children something new, and that her pupils were actually interested in the subject under discussion for once.

Suddenly, a little grubby hand popped up on the next to the back row, and a rather dishevelled looking Fred Milner was almost at bursting point waiting to have his say. It was the same little hand that only a few days before had suffered the pain of three hard strokes of the head-teacher's cane for indulging in dirty habits in the school yard. Whether this offence involved something like spitting, or even having a quick wee against the back wall, is uncertain. What we do know is that his punishment hurt.

"It's nice to see that one of you might know the answer," exclaimed the somewhat surprised Miss Register. "What do you think his name was, Fred?"

"I fink its Albert, Miss, 'cos that's the same name as me dad, and me mam told 'im to stop actin' like a bluddy prince and get some work done, and…"

"Yes, yes, that's enough Fred. You've explained things very well and you've got the name right. Well done."

A pink glow had replaced the somewhat pale, sallow complexion of the pupil- teacher who was beginning to wonder just what her class of six year olds would come out with next. She didn't have to wait long to find out. It was now little Willis Garside, who himself had suffered two strokes of Lizzie Faberer's cane for disobedience and rudeness recently, who decided to join in the debate.

"Excuse me, Miss. Is Prince Albert coming to Sheffield with the Queen? He ought to, didn't he, if they're married?"

"Well, Willis," explained Miss Register as gently as she could, "Queen Victoria's husband Albert died twenty one years after they were married. She was only 42 years old then, and that's very young to lose a husband isn't it?"

Despite an air of sadness descending on sixty or more concerned little faces, the discussion around Queen Victoria had generated a lot of interest, and the children felt better after they were told that the Royal couple had nine children before Albert died who would be able to keep their mother company. What they weren't told, however, was that Victoria was so devastated by Albert's death that she didn't appear in public for three years. This seclusion had created a lot of unrest and criticism amongst the public, and it wasn't until 1866, five years after her tragic loss, that she had properly resumed her official duties. As a sign of her decision to continue mourning her beloved prince, she had also resolved to wear black for the rest of her life, a resolution she kept to the very end.

However, let us get back to our little Sheffield folk in Miss Register's class as 12 Noon approached. It was at that time that their one and a half day holiday began, during which time many of them would, with their parents, pop into town to try and get a glimpse of the great lady. Let's see how they got on.

Queen Victoria's Visit

It was now the morning of May 21st, and activity and excitement in the town centre was beginning to peak. Although the Queen was not due to arrive until about five o'clock, people from far and wide had been arriving all morning to bathe in the glorious kaleidoscope of colour created by seemingly endless displays of flowers, gently waving flags, banners, drapes and freshly painted walls and frontages.

High Street and Fargate provided the route being taken to the new Town Hall by the Royal entourage, although High Street itself was, unfortunately, being widened on its south side at the time and somewhat resembled a large building site. It had been with great determination and dedication, therefore, that the Town Council had erected poles, hoardings and wooden frames in front of the half demolished buildings and decorated them with drapes, banners, flags and flowers in an effort to create a street-scene fit for the Queen.

At the top end of this street, which forms the junction with Fargate and Church Street, a magnificent, huge floral arch formed a colourful and imposing gateway to Fargate through which the Queen's coach would pass. The purple and blue velvet canopy to this arch also proudly displayed below it a large drape showing that Victoria's visit was taking place in her 60th year as Queen of England, a record only she herself was to surpass.

On this occasion, the children of Burgoyne Road School were amongst the ever-growing crowds with the consent of their head-teacher. In particular, Ernest Butcher, John Brown, Willie Turner and Gertie Lister were delighted to be able to be as disobedient as they wanted (within reason of course) without the fear of incurring a caning. As the small group of four young children huddled amongst the excited crowds of people jostling each other behind the protective rows of policemen who lined the route, a sudden cheer accompanied by a continuous wave of applause heralded the arrival of a detachment of the Household Cavalry. The uniformed officers in their glittering attire sitting astride their magnificent chestnut horses was quite a sight to behold.

"Wow, Gertie," piped up Ernest as he felt the hairs on the back of his neck stand up with excitement. "Just look at those soldiers on those big horses. Are they here to look after the queen?"

"I think so, Ernest. I wonder where she is?"

Suddenly, an open carriage pulled by four, black, snorting horses with their highly groomed coats glistening in the late afternoon sun came into view a few yards behind the cavalry. Three people were sitting in the carriage, one of whom being dressed in black and wearing a black veil. This small, but upright, figure was also holding a small parasol to protect her from the still quite powerful sun which heralded her arrival with its warm glow. The Queen of England was honouring our fair town, and her pleasure

Diamond Jubilee procession in 1897

Coronation of King Edward VII

at seeing the cheering Sheffield folk waving and shouting their welcome was acknowledged by her regular, responsive waves and polite nods of her head. This was a truly historic moment for the thousands of people who had only ever heard about the iconic Queen whose devotion to her county and its people is recalled in the annals of history for ever.

Little Willie Turner, however, had other things to say.

"I thought queens were supposed to wear crowns and that," he grumbled. "I can't see her proper with that black cloth over her face. What do you think John?"

His friend John Brown was, not surprisingly, equally concerned.

"I can't believe it, Willie. She's even got her umbrella up and it doesn't even look like rain."

Despite their understandable disappointment at the Queen's appearance, the children really enjoyed the occasion as yet another detachment of Household Cavalry followed Victoria's carriage. The evening which followed was also full of laughter, merriment and dancing which, together with the evening darkness being lit up by hundreds of coloured lights which adorned the streets, created a carnival atmosphere for all concerned.

This show of support for Queen and country was typical of that shown by schools and, indeed, most Sheffield folk in those days. In fact, until very recent times, our country as a whole has always been very loyal to its Royal Family, and despite some unpopularity arising following Princess Dianna's tragic death several years ago, it was obvious from Queen Elizabeth's very successful 80th birthday celebrations, that she still has the support of most of the country behind her.

Queen Victoria's visit to Sheffield in 1897, as we saw, prompted the School Board to allow its schools to close for the day, and this decision was replicated on many occasions in years to come. I have mentioned below for your general interest, a few similar royal events for which the grateful infants at Burgoyne Road School were granted a day or so's holiday.

Coronation of King Edward VII

The first event worthy of mention is the Coronation of Edward VII in the August of 1902 following the death of his mother Queen Victoria seven months earlier on 22nd January 1901. The great lady had at last, after a record

breaking 64 year reign, managed to rejoin her beloved husband Albert, something she had dreamt about for forty years since his premature death.

For the school children, perhaps the most exciting part of this event began on Friday, August 22nd. There were three days to go to the Coronation which had been planned for Monday, the 25th, and Miss Fairclough's class of six year olds had just returned to their desks after lunch.

"Now then children, you all know that our new King is being crowned on Monday, don't you? To celebrate this special occasion, you will all receive a free gift. I want you…"

Before Miss Fairclough could finish what she was saying, a multitude of cheers and gasps of delight rang out from the surprised pupils, a rare incident in this usually very quiet class.

"EXCUSE ME, CHILDREN," retorted their now rather stern-faced teacher. "Silence is ESSENTIAL in my class unless I say otherwise. Is that understood?"

Their teacher's sudden rebuke resulted in the children dropping their heads as their initial excitement evaporated into normality, and for a few seconds a hush hung over the classroom. However, the thought of being given a free gift was too much for young Connie Rose.

"Excuse me, Miss."

"Well, Connie. What is it?"

"Can we still have our presents…please?"

Connie was the smallest child in the class, and as she sat there with her blonde curls tumbling over her large, soulful eyes, even the tough, no-nonsense Miss Fairclough had to soften.

"Of course you can Connie. Now let us all settle down and see what we can find in these boxes on my table."

To the children's delight, the brown boxes which sat tantalizingly on the table in the corner of the room proved to be very exciting. The first one was full of medals showing an outline of Edward VII and the date of his Coronation. All the children were proud to be given and wear one of these. The other two boxes, however, proved to be the ones which created most excitement, particularly when Miss Fairclough lifted out several cakes and boxes of chocolates.

"Wow. Are those for us, Miss?" chimed little Colin Short as he eyed-up the goodies with obvious delight. "I'd love one of those chocolates."

"I'd like some of that cake, if you don't mind," continued his friend Harold Straw. "It looks really, really scrumptious."

"Now, now children. What have I told you. There's enough for a chocolate each AND a piece of cake each, but only if you settle down and behave. You can help me to pass them round Kate."

Kate Bell was more than pleased to help her teacher in this way. She was rather a nervous little girl, and her uncertainly in the past had led her to being caned for disorderly behaviour in the playground when all she thought she was doing was enjoying playing with her friends. Being chosen to share out chocolates and cake was a real boost to her confidence, as well as being one of the tastiest duties she had ever been given.

That Friday afternoon proved to be one of the most enjoyable that these young infant pupils had experienced at school, and was the beginning of three days of festivities and street parties which encompassed the weekend of Saturday and Sunday and a day's holiday from school on Monday which had been sanctioned to celebrate the day of the Coronation itself. Let's not forget that England had not crowned a monarch for over sixty years, which meant that to the vast majority of the population this was a unique and quite emotional experience. In fact, when you think about it, there would only be a handful of elderly people, particularly amongst the working class where life expectancy didn't actually reach 60 years of age, who would be able to turn to their children and grand-daughters and say: 'Eeh, lass, I remember when that 18 year old Victoria came to throne in 1837. It were a lovely do that were.'

Other visits by Royalty

There were, of course, many more occasions over the years which our ever-changing infants at Burgoyne Road

King George V and Queen Mary

School enjoyed. King Edward VII visited the city in 1905, and four years later his son George (later to become King) visited Sheffield with his wife Mary in their capacity of Price and Princess of Wales. Following the death of Edward VII, the Coronation of his son as King George V in 1911 was again met

Edward VIII-1936

with rejoicing and festivities. It was to be another nine years, however, before King George V and Queen Mary visited the city in 1919, this once again prompting a school holiday and a grand welcome in the city centre by flag-waving schoolchildren. Shortly after this event. George and Mary's only daughter Princess Mary gave the country a Royal Wedding in 1922, this being followed the year after by the marriage of their second son George to Elizabeth. Little did the Royal couple realize that they were destined to be England's future King and Queen about twelve years later upon the abdication of Edward VIII in 1936 after having been on the throne for only ten months.

However, this is not really a history lesson but a flavour of some of the main events which were celebrated by Burgoyne Road School infants during the thirty years we have been looking at. To complete this section, however, we should mention one other important event which was celebrated by the school during this period. On the 17th July 1919, the schoolchildren were asked to meet in the schoolroom at 1 o'clock to take tea to celebrate the signing of peace which ended the dreadful hostilities and loss of life incurred during the First World War. Furthermore, to the delight of our infants, they were given an extra week's holiday to commemorate what was probably the most significant day of their lives.

Well, we seem to have spent quite some time experiencing various aspects of school life within the Infants Department of Burgoyne Road Board School in Walkley. Now is the time to move over to Boomhall on the outskirts of the busy town centre where another interesting school awaits us.

SPRINGFIELD PRIMARY SCHOOL
Broomspring Lane, Broomhall

As we're looking at how young school children coped with life a hundred or more years or so ago, I thought it would be interesting to sit in on a typical 1880's school day at our next port of call, Springfield Primary School.

Springfield School

This school, whose four-storey designed building is probably the most impressive in the city, was opened in 1875 and now hosts children of all nationalities within its huge stone walls.

Miss Sharp was the headmistress of the infants' school in those Victorian times and was true to her name. She was a strict disciplinarian but felt genuinely that this was good for her pupils, not only now but also in later life when they would have to cope with a very difficult and challenging adult world.

You might wonder how it is that we are able to sit in on a typical Victorian school day. This has been made possible by the creation at Springfield School of a replica

Victorian Classroom in which lessons are given to infant children several times a week. Schools across Sheffield are invited to send their six and seven year olds to experience the harsh reality of school-life which befell their peers of yesteryear, and my presence at one such lesson as an 'invisible' observer and photographer was, I can assure you, an eye-opener of significant proportions. Everyone, including myself, was dressed in Victorian clothes, with Miss Sharp and the visiting school teachers looking rather prim and severe while the children looked almost cute in their flat caps, waistcoats, mop caps and smocks. The accompanying photographs will give you a very clear picture of how these Victorian school-folk looked.

It is worth mentioning here that the whole Victorian Classroom project is based on authentic, historical facts and information which have been carefully researched by the project manager Candice (Miss Sharp when dressed up for lesson-time). In addition, the school-room furniture, equipment, books, writing aids and everything else you might expect to see has, over the years, been painstakingly collected so that participants in the event genuinely take a step back in time. Unfortunately, as is often the case in these days of tight budgets, the project has to be self funding. From my experience, this is probably one of the most interesting and educationally stimulating experiences that young school children could participate in, and Local Education Authority funding would be invaluable in securing its future and making possible further improvements which, as yet, are not able to be implemented. If there is one thing I am sure about, it is that the experience will stay with each participating child for the rest of his or her life.

Lessons at Springfield School in 1883

Let's now join our 21st century Victorian pupils as they stand at the entrance to the school hall in 'May 1883', after having been addressed by Miss Sharp. Two rows of slightly nervous children, seven boys and seven girls, file silently into the room and stand to attention, holding out their hands for their usual cleanliness inspection. 'Cleanliness is next to Godliness' was one of the school's mottoes, and Miss Sharp was always very keen to enforce its message.

The boys hand inspection

"Right boys, it's you first," she instructed with a sharpness of voice which matched her name. "Let's hold those hands out."

To say that the children were a little nervous of the headmistress is probably a major understatement. Although not particularly tall, her erect figure clothed in a long black skirt and matching top gave her a rather severe appearance. It was, however, her eyes which said it all. Dark and piercing, they glared out from behind a pair of rimless spectacles which perched

Miss Sharp

defiantly on her small nose under the shadow of her black-rimmed, straw boater.

Miss Sharp's careful inspection of the first six pairs of slightly shaking hands went off without too much comment from the eagle-eyed lady. However, it was when she reached the rather cheeky-faced little boy at the end of the line that the situation changed.

"Herbert Williams! What is this?" she shrilled. "It looks as though you've had those DIRTY little hands down the back of a fire grate if you ask me. You stay there. I'll sort you out later."

As poor Herbert stood there awaiting his fate, Miss Sharp carried out her inspection of the seven young girls who looked quite angelic in their white mop-caps and smocks. To their great relief, their dainty little hands were adjudged to be 'satisfactorily clean', and

The girls hand inspection

the attention moved ominously back to Herbert Williams.

As the stern-looking headmistress approached her adversary, a faint smile hovered between her lips as Herbert, with a bit of superb acting, blurted out his explanation.

"I fell down on the way to school Miss. I couldn't help it, honest."

"Very well, Herbert. You're not going to be punished, but you cannot go into class with dirty hands. You'll have to wash them."

Relieved beyond belief, the flat-capped pupil followed the flowing black figure to a flower-patterned bowl and jug which were sitting patiently on a small table next to the classroom door. Relaxing next to the jug, which was half full of cold water, was an equally patient square of hard soap.

"Right, Herbert. There's the water and soap. Now get on with it."

Lifting the jug very carefully, the little seven year old poured some of the water into the waiting bowl with still slightly trembling hands.

"Is that enough Miss?"

"Enough, Herbert? Enough? You've splashed more water onto the table than you've poured into the bowl. Never mind, just get hold of that soap and give those dirty hands a good wash."

Miss Sharp's tolerance level was not, as we can see, particularly high, and the remaining girls and boys who had been made to stand round and watch the hand-washing event were certainly learning by example what their headmistress expected of them.

After poor little Herbert Williams had finished drying his hands on a small towel kindly given to him by Miss Sharp, the rather demanding lady did a smart about-turn to address the rest of the class.

"We can't spend all day here, children. Get back into line quickly and remember, no talking."

Unfortunately, amidst nervous shuffling and movement to re-form the two neat rows of boys and girls which their teacher demanded, Ernest Shortland did the unforgivable; he tripped over. Struggling quickly to his feet, his pale, freckled face peered out nervously from under the rim of his deep red, wide-rimmed cap. He had just- cause to be nervous as his watery eyes met the stern piercing glare of the one person he was trying too hard to please. As expected, Miss Sharp wasn't too pleased.

"Ernest Shortland. Come here this minute."

With heavy legs that would hardly carry him and a look of total dejection and apprehension written all over his face, the young lad slowly made his way towards the black figure in front of him.

"You know what you are, don't you my lad," retorted the exasperated headmistress.

"Er…no Miss. I'm not sure."

"You're clumsy, boy. CLUMSY!"

"Yes Miss. I'm sorry Miss. I won't do it again."

"Well, you'll wear this notice around your neck for the next hour or so to remind yourself and everyone else in here that clumsiness will not be tolerated."

At this point, Miss Sharp turned and produced from the desk behind her a rather well-used piece of card on which the word 'clumsy' was printed in large letters and hung it around Ernest's neck. Despite the embarrassment of having to wear such a notice, the young pupil was very relieved as no physical punishment had been threatened as he was half expecting.

It was, however, now time to go into the classroom and meet their class teacher, Miss Stockly. Clothed in a long black skirt and top over a white blouse, this silver haired

Compare this photograph taken about 70 years later.   1940s collection for the War Effort

teacher presented a similarly intimidating figure to that of Miss Sharp. She and her assistant also shared the stern facial expression as the headmistress, and as the boys and girls filed past the latter into the classroom, each one handing her their one penny tuition fee, they couldn't help but wonder what was in store for them.

It's just worth reassuring you, the reader, and in particular any mothers of young schoolchildren, that this school-day experience under the headship of Miss Sharp was only a very well orchestrated and convincing replica of school-life at Springfield School about 130 years ago, with the children and their accompanying teachers all playing an incredible acting part. As an observer, however, I can also say that both Candice's portrayal of Miss Sharp and Miss Stockley's portrayal of a Victorian class-teacher were so good that most of the schoolchildren actually felt that the whole experience was real for much of the time. Their reactions to the situations in which they found themselves were, therefore, both genuine and occasionally rather daunting. They did, nevertheless, finish off the whole day with smiles and a feeling of achievement.

However, let's continue where we left off with the children queuing up to go into class.

The Victorian Classroom itself was quite large and bright with its one outer wall being lined with large sash

windows. The rows of shiny but well-worn medium oak desks and chairs were positioned either side of a central walkway in order that the boys and girls could be properly segregated. Later on in their school life as they left the infants, they would all be taught in boys or girls-only classes, but for now some degree of mixing was allowed.

At the front of the class, the two most prominent features were the teacher's desk and a large blackboard on which the date and year, 1st May 1883, had been chalked in large letters. Of more significance, however, was the wall behind the desk which was adorned with a large clock, a photograph of Queen Victoria, a large, colourful Union Jack (now only called a Union Flag because Union Jack is a navy term.), and an assortment of punishment aids to focus the minds of the children. To the fourteen pairs of eyes which stared to the front of the classroom on that school-day morning, the bewildering display of authority set against a back-cloth of allegiance to Queen and country was more confusing than it was helpful.

Henry Merrill was the first of the pupils to put his foot in it.

"Excuse me Miss. Why is that huge flag on the wall, and who is that old lady in the picture underneath it?"

If Miss Stockley had really been able to burst, then I think this was the time she would have done so. As it is, her face went red to the point at which her blood pressure and pulse rate must have been at danger level, and the poor young lad who'd asked the innocent questions wasn't sure whether to laugh or cry.

"Did you say who's that lady?" she choked. "That's your QUEEN my lad. And that flag is on the wall because it represents YOUR COUNTRY! How can you possibly not know these things?"

"I don't know Miss. Thank you Miss. I'm sorry Miss."

Trying to calm down, the irate teacher turned to one of the two pupil teachers who had been assigned to help her that morning.

"Miss Brown. Get one of those dunce caps from that table in the corner and put it on this foolish boy's head and send him to the back of the room as far away from me as possible. I can see that I'm going to have a very difficult time with these children from what I've seen so far."

That incident did, in fact, set the scene for what was to follow. Take delicate little Martha Barlow, for example,

with her sweet, angelic face and appealing eyes. Miss Stockly chose her for monitor-duties a short time later

which involved her walking round the class handing out pens to all the children. Bertha Sorbit had already been given similar duties which entailed taking round a tray of inkwells which each child had to carefully place in the holes provided for them in their desk tops. Unfortunately, when it came to the task of writing, it was no easy matter dipping the long handled pens with their slotted nibs into the ink without occasionally causing a blot or two. Martha Barlow was the unfortunate pupil to find this out.

"What on earth are you doing, child?" retorted Miss Stockley who had been strolling around the class to see how well the children had been writing on their single sheet

of clean white paper. "Didn't I specifically tell you all to be careful when you used the ink wells? Just look at all the ink on your page. It's a disgrace."

The punishment for this demeanour was, unfortunately for Martha, not simply hanging a 'clumsy' or 'careless'

card round her neck. This time, a single stroke of a two foot bamboo cane on the little girl's outstretched fingers was deemed to be more appropriate, although by rights this should only have been executed by Miss Sharp as head teacher.

Needless to say, the rest of the class were allocated their share of the discipline regime during the morning with Arthur Knowles being sent to the headmistress for a caning for writing in an untidy fashion on his slate-board, and Eliza Jane Sheppard suffering the same fate for continually talking.

Little Nesbet Martin, who tended to slouch a little whilst sitting at his desk, suffered a more unusual

punishment, that of having to wear a wooden back-board around which his arms were wrapped in order to make him sit up straight, whilst Lottie Innocent found out what it was like to be called a fidget. As well as hanging a Fidget card around her neck, which told the rest of the class what she was, her hands were tied behind her back using a pair of fidget boards (a bit like knuckle-dusters) in each of which had been drilled four small holes to accommodate her fragile little fingers. This unusual gadget (demonstrated here by an assistant) certainly stopped the poor child from fidgeting with her pen or pencil while her teacher demanded her attention.

Another punishment aid which was used in Victorian times, although not at Springfield School, was the Naughty Basket. A photograph of this device which was hung on the back wall of Miss Stockley's classroom showed that it took the form of a small framed seat (similar to the younger children's swings in our parks today) which was suspended from the classroom ceiling at the front of the class. If a child was particularly naughty, he or she would be placed in this basket for all to see and kept hanging there for as long as the teacher chose. This extreme method of discipline and punishment by shame and ridicule must have been frightening to the young infant children, although as an alternative to canings or beatings I suspect that they actually preferred it. It was suggested to me that the expression 'he's a basket case' originated from the use of this particular punishment contraption. It sounds plausible, doesn't it?

However, to get back to Miss Stockley's class, it was not all doom and gloom for the children as a 'carrot and stick' approach to learning was used. For those who misbehaved or didn't do exactly as they were told, there was a punishment. For those who were helpful and well behaved in the eyes of the teacher, there was a reward in the form of a certificate and pendant presented to the best boy and girl at the end of the week. This occasion was a formal affair which involved the headmistress participating in the presentation and the children clapping the successful recipient who was usually glowing with pride.

Following the morning lessons, playtime in the school yard brought welcome relief and pleasure to the children. Despite having to be marched from the classroom to the yard like a regiment of soldiers and then having to line up in two rows (boys and girls) until the teacher said otherwise, the occasion was always eagerly looked forward to. The school provided a host of equipment for the children to use including such favourites as the stick and hoop, yo-yo's, skipping ropes, and chalk with which to draw and make patterns on the playground surface.

For those who were musically minded, wooden whistles, mouth organs and even an accordion were available under supervision, and to some degree all these activities helped these children to better accept their disciplined life during lesson time.

This period of playtime was the last activity in which the visiting schoolchildren had to participate as part of their Victorian experience, and they loved it. The tensions and uncertainties which they had endured in the Victorian class now melted away and were substituted by these exciting and unusual games and activities of yesteryear, and all in all, the whole day proved to be a great success.

A BRIEF OVERVIEW OF SCHOOLDAYS

As we look back at the schooling of yesteryear based on the experiences gained at both Burgoyne Road and Springfield schools, we can see a conflicting host of good and bad practices. Discipline and respect for others was most certainly taught, although the degree of punishment enforced to achieve these was most certainly excessive, and often downright cruel.

At the other end of the spectrum, we hear and read in the media that many of today's children have little or no respect for themselves or others, punishment is more-or-less forbidden, and children in many schools almost rule the teachers. These views, however, may be a rather wild generalisation, although by virtue of them being true in some cases, are very concerning.

To get a better appreciation of how things really are today, let us look at both sides of the coin.

If we pop down to Burgoyne Road School today, we find that it is now called St. Mary's Church of England

Primary School and is run by a relatively young, dynamic headmaster by the name of Mr. Rose. This forward-looking head teacher has introduced a Behaviour Policy for his school which not only defines good behaviour and bad behaviour, but also sets out sensible reward systems and fair misbehaviour consequences. He has also set down a process for dealing with bullying.

Mr. Rose's outlook is one of caring and mutual respect, which he knows will lead to a more rewarding educational experience in his school together with the benefit of acquiring real life-skills as they develop there.

If you were to visit Springfield School today, you would find children of all nationalities and cultures working happily together, all receiving the right start in life to make them better citizens. Indeed, as I've travelled around many primary schools all over the city in my capacity as a photographer over the last few years, I have found all such schools to be places where these young children are taught with caring and enthusiasm, resulting in the children being relaxed, happy and outgoing.

TODAY'S SCHOOL CULTURE
A FEW IMPRESSIONS AND CONCERNS

What, therefore, is the problem? Is the media always scare-mongering when it reports on problems relating to schools and schoolchildren? Let's have a look at a few news items which have hit the headlines over the last year or two and see how they fit into the jigsaw of educational discontent which appears to be growing in this country at the moment.

Patriotism and Religion

Let's start with two subjects we've already touched upon. We've looked at the importance attached to Queen and country by both Burgoyne Road School and Miss Sharp's Victorian Class at Springfield School in '1883'. In addition, we've also observed the latter school's successful integration of multi-national and multi-cultural young children into its classes more than a century later.

It was with surprise, therefore, that I read a recent newspaper article describing how a 14 year old pupil was ejected from class at a school in Wiltshire after he had written God Save the Queen on his notebook. His teacher is reported to have said that the young boy's action would offend Muslim children. In addition, the report also went on to say that Bibles are locked away during Religious Education lessons because they are 'not relevant'. Although these may be isolated incidents, it is actions such as these that can not only cause or aggravate tension in schools but also cause confusion in the minds of the young children being taught there.

Racism

On a similar theme, an article appearing in the press about a year later stated that a 14 year old schoolgirl from Manchester was actually arrested for alleged racism and spent three and a half hours in a police cell after asking her teacher if she could change the discussion group she had been put in. This request had been made because the other five participants in the group were Asian and were, it was claimed, only using their own language to discuss the subject in hand. The schoolgirl appeared to have been treated like a criminal by her teacher and the police who, it was reported, asked her to remove her shoe laces and jewellery before being fingerprinted and placed in the bare cell. Whilst there may be more background to this story than we are aware of, the action taken by both the teacher and the police appears to be completely over-the-top and does nothing to ensure a harmonious relationship in the classroom.

Disruption and Threatening Behaviour

On a different theme, a lot of footage seems to be given to the unruly and often vicious behaviour which purportedly exists in schools across the country. An article which exemplifies this and which appeared in a national newspaper recently relates to an ex-soldier who had taken up teaching. He had ended up in hospital with temporary blindness and severe concussion after being assaulted by a particularly difficult pupil. Although he wanted to press charges, the school opposed any such move and purportedly terminated his supply contract because he chose to go ahead with his action. It is interesting to quote just two statements made by this supply teacher, the first of which being: "Two generations ago it would have been unthinkable for staff to be kicked, punched, sworn at, shoved or threatened. Yet that now happens all the time in our schools, and the trouble-makers know they can get away with it." He then concluded his article with the following words: "No one could come from a tougher background than me, yet I have to say that I would not dream of sending any children of mine to an English state school. I would rather crawl through broken glass than inflict such a punishment on them. They- and the teaching profession – deserve better."

The report by this teacher goes on to be equally critical in other areas based on his personal experiences, and makes very interesting reading. However, perhaps such dramatic problems are mainly confined to poorer, inner-city areas where many children may be under-privileged and relative poverty and lack of social facilities may exacerbate their problems. On the other hand, perhaps not. Perhaps someone should find out?

If you were to ask a lady by the name of Angela Mason, an ex-teacher who returned to supply teaching in her mid to late 50's, she would tell you that classroom chaos, disruption and threatening behaviour was certainly alive and kicking as we move through the 21st century. Many readers may well recall seeing the channel 5 Television Documentary which she produced in April 2005 based on secret filming of classroom behaviour in schools in London and the North of England. Despite identifying and highlighting such undisciplined behaviour by this hard evidence, she was charged with unacceptable professional conduct by the General Teaching Council and barred from teaching for a year. Mrs Mason's reported view on her punishment is one which may very well be shared by many other people: "The General Teaching Council has done nothing to help pupils or teachers by sanctioning me in this way. They are out of touch with reality if they think my film gave the wrong impression of what's going on in schools today."

These two reports by supply teachers (the ex-soldier and Mrs Mason), are quite damming of today's classroom behaviour and lack of discipline. They are even more significant because, as supply teachers, these two educationalists who have chosen to speak out must have encountered many different environments as they moved from school to school, during which time their experiences appear to be consistently bad. For the millions of people who read these newspaper articles and watch television documentaries, their view of schooling in England today is probably at an all-time low. I cannot personally subscribe to this view because I live in a privileged area where local schools have good reputations and are well thought of. However, I am concerned that I may be in a minority. Regardless of my views, reported behaviour such as those described must, nevertheless, contribute significantly to the public's perception of today's schoolchildren.

National Curriculum

Another interesting issue relates to the subjects that the Government decides should be taught in schools (called the national curriculum). A recent study on British education by the independent think-tank Civitas (The Institute for the Study of Civil Society) is reported to be very critical of politicians hijacking the curriculum to promote fashionable causes. Traditional subjects such as history, geography and science are claimed to be being corrupted by political agendas, and pupils are claimed to be leaving school with huge gaps in their knowledge because lessons are being manipulated to promote trendy subjects such as gender-awareness, the environment and anti-racism. It is even claimed that teenagers pursuing GCSE history were invited to study the 9/11 attacks using Arab Media and Osama bin Laden's speeches as source material without balancing American input.

The Civitas study, which was presented as a subject by subject critique by seven teachers and academics, has been entitled The Corruption of the Curriculum and on the surface is both worrying and enlightening. Although it is reported that the government has dismissed the Civitas report, claiming it was 'based on a profound misunderstanding of the national curriculum and modern teaching methods', it is, nevertheless, of great concern for the millions of parents who genuinely want the best for their children in educational terms.

To the average member of the public like me, therefore, the whole situation is very confusing. Have these chosen teachers and academics completely lost the plot with their study and findings as suggested by the government, or has a gradual decline and rather unhealthy change in our teaching practices been allowed to proceed unchecked over the last decade or so? Regardless of which is the case, the uncertainty which exists only seems to add to the seemingly ever-growing jigsaw of educational discontent.

Political Correctness

The issue of political correctness appears to constantly throw up incidents which defy common sense these days. If we add health and safety with its inseparable link to the current claim-culture ravaging the country, we have a trio of issues which appear to have turned our lives upside down.

Kids can't play conkers at school in case they get blinded, sports-days at schools are reportedly cancelled in case some-one falls down or (heaven help us) in case someone actually loses a race. We've had swings banned in playgrounds and children made to wear crash helmets whilst riding donkeys on Bognor beach. Football in school playgrounds is taboo in some schools in case a child gets a grazed knee, and hopscotch on paving slabs is equally as dangerous in the mind of some safety- conscious officials. Some teachers are now reportedly being told not to apply sun cream to vulnerable pupils for fear they might be accused of abuse. Even a lifeguard instructor and her husband were prevented from taking their own three children into a toddlers' pool because safety rules now decree that there should be one adult per child, even if the children can swim.

It's a good job Health and Safety regulation together with its following of compensation lawyers wasn't around in those glorious Victorian days, as all the school kids would have been millionaires and most of the schools bankrupt.

An observation on these issues regarding school children which appeared in the national press probably sums up the situation nicely: "And they wonder why youngsters spend hours stuck in stuffy bedrooms playing computer games. The authorities wring their hands about childhood obesity, while at the same time outlawing just about every form of physical activity from French cricket to egg and spoon races."

Human Rights

The teaching profession, sadly, also has it rough when it comes to deciding what it can and cannot do. Physical punishment of any sort is absolutely taboo (remember even the Prime Minister's wife Cherie Blair was questioned by several police offices when she laughingly tapped a 17 year old youth on his back who was playing a prank on her at a fencing competition), and teachers may even risk breaching human rights laws if they confiscate drugs, mobile phones or even weapons according to one informed press report.

It would appear that even being a police officer is no protection from unreasonable accusation. This was highlighted in a newspaper article last year when a policeman chased and arrested a masked youth who had threatened to stab a schoolmaster. As the youth had banged his head during a struggle with the officer who was trying to arrest him, he had lodged a complaint to the police authority. This has reportedly led to the officer, who was only doing his duty, facing investigation and possible disciplinary action.

The message that incidents of this sort send out is that schoolchildren are automatically given the 'human right'

by law to do more or less what they want without fear of punishment or disciplinary action being taken against them. On the other hand, the real victim in such cases appears to have no 'human right' to do his or her job to the best of his or her ability, and certainly cannot expect the privilege of being assumed innocent of any accusation until proven guilty. It appears to me that the law has been turned on its head in many cases and, in the long term, does nothing to help children to become better members of society.

Well, I suppose I could go on for ever listing all the nonsense that seems to have filtered into our society, but there is no point. I have identified all the foregoing issues both as food for thought and also to highlight the different world our schoolchildren find themselves in compared to a century or so ago.

It is really up to you, the reader, to make up your own mind whether or not things are better or worse. In practice, it's probably a mixture of both. For my own part, I found my schooldays during the second half of the 1940's and most of the 1950's to be pretty much ideal. Discipline and respect was the order of the day, modest punishment was applied when necessary, and freedom was given which allowed children to be young, alive and adventurous during their exciting childhood. The quality of education was excellent, and for those who wanted to succeed, hard work and dedication was expected. In addition, correctly spoken and written English was of great importance in all schools where correct spelling, punctuation and use of grammar was the standard expected to be achieved by most pupils.

The education of the nation's schoolchildren is, without doubt, a very important and emotive topic. My experience of education today relates mainly to that of my grand-children who appear to have been (and still are being) pretty well taught. This has given me reasonable confidence in and reassurance about teaching, particularly at the younger end of the spectrum. Perhaps it is at the more senior level that things sometimes begin to go wrong, particularly in disadvantaged areas where poverty, unemployment and broken homes are at higher levels than elsewhere.

Problems during school holidays

It is worth just mentioning another issue at this stage which may be of interest to the reader. Firstly, despite the in-school problems we have identified, a recent (July 2007) survey which was carried out amongst thousands of school children is reported to have identified a significant problem existing for such children during the long summer holidays. It would appear that due to the trend these days for both parents to be working, the unsupervised children, now without the support of their teachers, are at considerable risk from anti-social behaviour and in particular, bullying. Seventy percent of those children interviewed considered this to be a problem for them and many would welcome the idea of schools providing supervised activities for them during this time. This provision is, in fact, available in many schools in Sheffield, although it sounds like many other areas of the country are not so fortunate.

Englishness, Working Wages and Role Models

Finally, an item of food-for-thought rather than real concern relates to the issue of schoolboy interests and role models. One of the main topics of conversation amongst schoolboys is, and always has been, football. An August 2007 report in a national newspaper highlighted the fact that within the twenty teams forming the English Premier League in the 2006 season, 280 of the players were foreign and 246 were English. The number of foreign players who had registered with English Premiership clubs by the beginning of the 2007 season had reportedly risen to 331. This compares with just 11 foreign players starting the first weekend of the Premiership fifteen years earlier in 1992. If we add to these statistics the fact that the Premiership now hosts five foreign managers, and nearly half the clubs have overseas owners, I get the impression that 'Englishness' is rapidly disappearing in this sport at the top level. In fact, the report mentions that one top Premiership club actually has players of 24 nationalities on its books.

Whilst I fully acknowledge that we are privileged to see these skilful and exciting players in our football grounds and on television every week, I sometimes wonder where it's all going to end. I can see in the not too distant future an English team being the champions of Europe with not one Englishman amongst them. That's life, I suppose, although I do think it's a bit sad, don't you?

However, on top of all this most schoolchildren are now aware that wages for some of the top footballers have gone past the £100,000 a week level (about £5 million a year), with many more having to settle for a mere £40,000, £60,000 or even £80,000 a week. It makes me wonder just how kids see the world these days. It must be a little confusing, and it must make it difficult for some to prepare themselves for the reality of life when they leave school which involves difficulties in finding work relating to their interests at a wage or salary which will be only a fraction of that earned by their sporting heroes. It's food for thought, at least.

So, there we have it; a snapshot of Victorian education, a personal view of 1950's education, two supply teachers' and other experts' views of 21st century education, a host of incidents and problems highlighted in the recent press and my own observations of today's teaching practices in Sheffield. Depending on which views, ideas and practices you accept, you will either be filled with hope or despair. I think it's about time that politicians, teachers, employers, parents and the children themselves began to work together to restore confidence in our nation's education system and learn from past mistakes and successes to give everyone

hope for the future. Perhaps a merging of the best of the old with the best of the new would do the trick. These photographs of today's happy children in a Victorian setting seems to support this view, don't you think?

However, let us not forget that during these school-day adventures spanning over a hundred years or more, we have encountered many young Sheffield children, all of whom have been wonderful characters in their own way. From a local view point, that is very rewarding and encouraging and bodes well for Sheffield folk. Perhaps this last photograph of a doting great grandad and great grand-daughter puts into perspective the need for the young girl's educational future to be as good as the elderly gentleman's

educational past. If we all work together and do our best, then I think it will be.

Sheffield Folk

A few final thoughts

Having now completed my story-telling about the lives and times of twenty or more characters who lived and worked in our fair city, I feel rather proud of the fact that I am also a Sheffielder. I have found it enriching to research the enormously varied yet surprisingly natural lives led by these Sheffield Folk. In particular, regardless of status or wealth, the core qualities running through all their lives were honesty, integrity and a genuine desire to do their best in all they undertake. I have long held the view that if you assume the best in people, it will nearly always bring out the best in them. In addition, I am also of the view that having belief in yourself will guide you through life with confidence. The characters in this book all appeared to share these ideals which they practiced as a matter of course. I am sure that if we look into our own lives, we will find that we are not so different. Let us all be proud of who we are.

Whilst the last Section in this book has primarily dealt with schoolchildren rather than individual characters, I thought it was important to highlight those who, after all, will be our future generation of Sheffield folk. I hope that you found it interesting.

APPENDIX 1

I have included a few definitions in this appendix to clarify some of the wording used in the Tommy Ward Story:

MILL: A building fitted with machinery for manufacturing purposes.

WATER MILLS: These include the buildings, the Water Wheel, the Grinding Wheels, Hammers and Forges.

NB. Many old Water Mills originally had a small hamlet of cottages located nearby where the workers, and sometimes the owners, lived.

A WHEEL refers to the building in which a grinder etc works.

A HULL refers to each separate workshop in the building. Eg. A grinding hull.

There are two main types of WATER WHEEL:

OVERSHOT: Water comes down on top of the wheel, fills the pockets and turns it. (This type is about 63% efficient)

UNDERSHOT: Water flows through the bottom of the wheel and pushes it forward. (This type is about 22% efficient)

The DOOMSDAY BOOK, produced between 1080 and 1086AD, identified the following types and numbers of Mills in England:

5624 Corn Mills, 1168 Fulling Mills (cloth making), 1217 Tanning Mills (leather making), 1361 Paper Mills, 1376 Saw Mills and Hammer and Stamping Mills. Other Mills in use include Steel and Iron Forging Mills (cutlery and tools etc), Mills for the manufacture of weapons (the earliest in use), Rolling Mills (later used for rolling copper and silver together to produce Sheffield Plate) and Wire Drawing Mills.

A few more definitions as follows may also be useful:

A Smith: A person who forges iron; a worker in metal (goldsmith, tinsmith etc).

A Blacksmith: A Smith who works in iron.

A Forge: A Blacksmith's workshop; a furnace or hearth for melting metal; a Smithy.

To Forge: To shape metal by heating in a fire and hammering.

A Smithy: A Blacksmith's workshop; a forge.

Smithery: A Smith's work.

It may also be of interest to know that the name Hull (as used in Grinding Hull where grinding was carried out using initially water, then steam, then electricity) was derived from the German word 'Hulle' meaning 'dirty building'.

APPENDIX 2

This appendix relates to the references to Norton Hall and Grounds in both the J. G. Graves Story and Edna's Story:

Norton Hall and Grounds was originally owned by the Offley and Shore families.

Following the failure of the Parker-Shore Bank in 1843, they were put up for sale in 1850.

The Hall and Grounds were bought by Charles Camell, the head of one of the world's largest steelworks, in the 1850s.

The grounds, named Norton Park in the late 1800s, were finally bought by J. G. Graves in the late 1920s and presented to the public of Sheffield as a gift. Thereafter it was named Graves Park.

APPENDIX 3

This appendix expands the reference to the Dale Dyke Dam disaster in the Henry Dixon Story. In particular, it presents an old original manuscript which it is believed was written at the time of the disaster. The content of the manuscript takes the form of a long poem which emotionally describes the dreadful events which took place. At that time, on March 12th, 1864, the collapse of this dam was acknowledged as the worst natural disaster that England had ever encountered. The photograph I have taken of the manuscript has been printed to a reasonably large scale to enable you to appreciate it, and the text has been typed out below to enable you to easily read it.

My sincere thanks go to my good friend Joe Castle for allowing me to photograph and reproduce this valuable historic document:

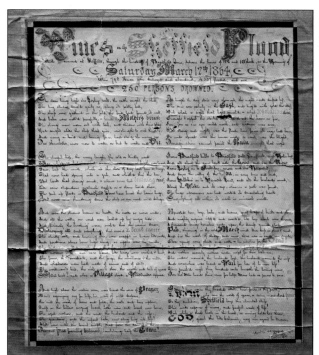

Lines on the Sheffield Flood

Which occurred at Sheffield, through the bursting of Bradfield Dam,
between the hours of 12 and 10 o'clock, on the morning of
Saturday, March 12th, 1864
When 798 homes were destroyed and abandoned, 4357 flooded, and
over
250 PERSONS DROWNED

The stars hung high o'er Loxley vale, the cattle sought the shed,
The tiny stream danc'd gaily on, along its pebbly beach,
The sheep were gather'd in the fold, the bird had found its nest,
And babes were nestl'd peacefully, beside the MOTHER'S breast.
The strong man worn out with his toil, and children with their play,
Had sought alike the sleep, that gives new strength to meet the Day,
And many a lov'd one and loving form had closed the weary eye,
In slumbers never more to wake, or but to wake and DIE.

The cheerful lisp, the merry laugh, the cold or kindly word,
Was whispered but in silent mien, and scarce a breath was heard,
Save but the wind, which at the close of day had been a breeze,
That now had sprung into a gale, and whistl'd through the trees,
But hark that strange sound, When comes that DEAF'NING roar,
Like some stupendous avalanche dash'd on a storm tossed shore,
The pent up floods in Bradfield Dam have burst the basin huge,
And now comes thundering down the steep in one mad deluge.

And soon the streams became as brookes, the brooks as rivers wide,
And allthe valley one vast sea, lash'd up by angry tide,
And furiously the bursting wave rushed through the ravine drear,
DESTROYING ALL and everything that cross'd its dread career.
The sturdy oak, the towering elm, were snapped in twain like reeds,
And ponderous stones borne high along, as ripples bear the reeds.
The bridges crumbled neath the …..., the ….. were torn and rent,
And massive oak and iron beams, like twigs were writh'd and bent.
The farm, the homestead and the forge, the wheelhouse and the mill,
And whatsoever man had made, of science and of skill,
The worman's hut, the rich man's stow, the wealth and toil of years,
Were lost! and where a VILLAGE stood, a WILDERNESS appears.

And high above the water's roar, was heard the voice of PRAYER,
Man's agonizing cry for help, his wail of wild despair,
For mid the wash of barn and field, the roots and trees uptorn,
Swift on the billows surging breast, both men and beast were borne.
The aged matron, and the maid, the husband and the wife,
The grandson and the infant babe, new struggling into life,
Alike were with the torrent swept, that from the dam now down,
In one vast foaming Cataract, overwhelming half the TOWN.

At length the day star's rays shone out, the night clouds drifted by,
The sun rose calmly in the EAST, and ting'd with gold the sky,
But what a sight that light reveal'd-what DESPOLATION dire,
Enough t'appal the stoutest heart, and set the brain on fire,
Far, far as e'er could reach, sad evidence was seen,
How strong and mighty was the flood, how fierce its rage had been,
So wide spread was the havoc, made, so vast was the blight,
Imagination cannot paint the RUIN wrought that night.

From Bradfield hills to Bradfield Dale, Damflask and Malin Bridge,
And all along the green bank side, the Gorge, and o'er the Ridge,
From Loxley on to Owlerton across and o'er Neepsend,
And down the valley of the DON, in every turn and bend,
From Hillsbro' on to Harvest Lane, and all the lowland round,
Along the Wicker and its ways, where e'er a path was found,
The huge uproarious sea had work'd its devastating track,
Engulphing all within its reach in universal wrack.

Uprooted trees, logs, bales and beams, great heaps of bricks and
stone,
And mighty engines ripp'd and crack'd, like toys about were thrown,
A thousand beings homeless made, upon the damp ground stood,
PALE shivering in the cold MARCH wind, knee deep in slime and
mud,
And o'er the waste of sludge and mire, stern men in bands were
spread,
Close eyeing every chink and nook-the searchers for the DEAD!
And children for their fathers wept, and fathers for their sons,
And mothers scarcely mothers made, wept for their little ones.
The widow mourned the husband lost, the husband mourned the wife,
And everywhere was heard a WAIL for loss of human life!
Thus perish'd nigh three hundred souls beneath the boiling wave,
For though men heard their cries for help, Man had no power to
save.

O Man! how vain thy boasted skills, how feeble is thy power,
To HIM who can the work of years- destroy in one short HOUR.
To thy ambition, Sheffield lays this elemental strife,
This wide expanse of misery, and fearful waste of life!
But while a throb beats in the heart, or mem'ry holds her throw,
GOD, grant the like Calamity, may ne'er again be known.

J. F. Shepherd
Attercliffe

APPENDIX 4

I thought that it would be interesting to schedule the offences committed by the Victorian schoolchildren at Burgoyne Road School over the period 1881 to 1910, and to then identify the type and severity of punishments which were handed out by the various Head Teachers (all Ladies) over this time. You will note that the severity is shown to vary significantly for the same offence on many occasions. This variation was sometimes due to the seriousness of the misdemeanour, but was more often due to the attitude to punishment taken by each of the five Head Teachers who worked at this school over this thirty year period:

1. DISORDERLY BEHAVIOUR: 1to 2 raps of the ruler or cane
2. SCABELLING A DESK: 2 raps with a cane
3. DISOBEDIENCE: 1 to 4 taps or strokes of cane; A Whipping or Good Whipping
4. INDECENT CONDUCT: 3 raps with a ruler
5: LATENESS: 1 or 2 raps or strokes of the cane
6. PLAYING TRUANT: 2 to 4 strokes of the cane; Whippings and Good Whippings; A Thrashing or a Good Thrashing
7. STEALING: 2 to 3 raps with a cane; 1 to 4 strokes of the cane
8. THROWING STONES: 2 raps with a cane; 1 or 2 strokes of the cane
9. NAUGHTINESS: 1 or 2 raps with a cane; 1 stroke of the cane
10. CARELESSNESS: 1 or 2 raps with ruler or cane; 1 or 2 strokes of the cane
11. SPITTING: 1 or 2 raps with a cane; 1 or 2 strokes with a cane
12. SHOWING TEMPER: Up to 4 raps with a cane
13. SCREAMING: A Slapping or a Whipping
14. UNTRUTHFULNESS: 2 or 3 raps of a cane; 1 to 3 strokes of the cane
15. SHOUTING: 1 to 3 strokes of the cane
16. RUDENESS: 1 or 2 taps or strokes of the cane; A Whipping
17. IDLENESS: A tap with a cane; Arm smacked; 1 or 2 strokes of the cane
18. TAKING HOME OTHER BOYS' CAPS: 2 strokes of a cane
19. TALKING IN CLASS: 1 or 2 taps or strokes with a cane
20. UNTIDY WORK: 1 or 2 taps or strokes with a cane
21. COMING TO SCHOOL AT 9.50am: 2taps or 2 strokes of the cane
22. IDLENESS AT KNITTING: 2 stokes of the cane
23. DIRTYNESS/BEING DIRTY: 1 or 2 strokes of the cane
24. BLOTTING A BOOK: 1 stroke of the cane
25. TRYING TO PLAY TRUANT: 1 stroke of the cane
26. UN-NEAT SOWING: 2 taps with a pointer
27. CARELESS DICTATION: 1 or 2 strokes of the cane
28. PLAYING OUT OF SCHOOL: 1 stroke of the cane
29. RUDENESS AND DENYING IT: 2 strokes of the cane
30. TEARING, DEFACING OR SPOILING A BOOK: 1 to 3 taps or strokes with a cane
31. DESTROYING BLOTTING PAPER: 2 strokes of the cane
32. CRUELTY TO OTHER CHILDREN:
    (a) Molesting little girls on way home after school: 1 or 2 strokes of the cane
    (b) Smacking a little girl on the face: 2 strokes of the cane
    (c) Hitting a girl on the nose: 4 strokes of the cane
    (d) Cruel treatment of a small boy: 1 or 2 strokes of the cane
    (e) Pushing boys: 1 stroke of the cane
    (f) Rough behaviour in the playground: 1 or 2 strokes of the cane
    (g) Being rough and cruel-fighting: 2 or 3 strokes of the cane
33. NOT ANSWERING NAME: 1 tap with the cane
34. TRIFLING IN SINGING LESSONS: 1 tap with the cane
35. BAD AND DISGRACEFUL WRITING: 1 or 2 taps with the cane
36. WHISTLING: 1 tap with the cane
37. WHISTLING IN SINGING LESSONS: 1 stroke of the cane
38. RUNNING HOME AND TELLING A STORY: 2 taps with the cane
39. SWEARING: 1 or 2 taps with a cane; A Whipping
40. INATTENTION: 1 or 2 taps with a cane; 1 stroke of the cane
41. RUNNING OUT OF SCHOOL OR RUNNING HOME: 1 to 4 taps with the cane; 1 or 2 strokes of the cane; A Good Whipping
42. CLIMBING A WALL: 1 tap with the cane
43. FIDGETTING: 2 taps with the cane; 1 to 3 strokes of the cane
44. RESTLESSNESS: 1 tap with the cane
45. WRONG SUMS: 1 tap with the cane
46. WHISPERING: 1 tap with the cane
47. BITING A BOOK: 1 tap with the cane
48. THROWING CAPS AND HATS IN WATER: 1 tap with a cane; 2 strokes of cane
49. TAKING A CAP HOME AND DESTROYING IT: 2 strokes of the cane
50. THROWING AWAY A BOY'S HAT: 2 strokes of the cane
51. TAKING A LITTLE GIRL'S HAT OFF HER HEADAND THROWING IT AWAY: 2 strokes of the cane

52. PULLING CAPS OFF PEGS IN CLOAKROOM AND THROWING ONTO FLOOR
1 stroke of the cane
53. COPYING: 1 tap of the cane
54. DECEIT: 1 tap of the cane
55. CUTTING ELASTIC OFF HAT:
2 taps of the cane
56. BAD BEHAVIOUR: 1 to 3 strokes of the cane
57. LAZYNESS: 1 or 2 strokes of the cane;
A Shaking; A Slapping
58. SHOUTING AFTER TEACHER:
2 strokes of the cane
59. TROUBLESOME: 1 or 2 strokes of the cane
60. VERY TROUBLESOME: A Slapping
61. BITING A GIRL: 2 strokes of the cane
62. DIRTY TRICKS: 2 to 4 strokes of the cane
63. UNTIDYNESS: 1 stroke of the cane
64. JUMPING: 2 strokes of the cane
65. CRYING: A Good Whipping
66. BEING STUPID: A Slapping
67. BEING VERY STUPID: A Good Whipping
68. WETTING ANOTHER BOY: A Thrashing
69. INKING A CHILD'S PINAFORE:
1 stroke of the cane
70. RUBBING PAINT ON BOY'S COLLAR:
3 strokes of the cane
71. BAD MARCHING: 1 stroke of the cane
72. DIRTY HABITS IN THE PLAYGROUND:
2 to 3 strokes of the cane
73. SPITTING IN THE SAUCERS OF PAINT:
Hand smacked
74. INSUBORDINATION:
2 strokes of the cane; A Whipping
75. KEEPING BACK SCHOOL MATERIALS:
3 strokes of the cane
76. DEFACING SCHOOL FURNITURE:
1 stroke of the cane
77. NOISY HABITS: 1 stroke of the cane
78. CHANGING PENCILS AND BREAKING THE POINTS: 1 stroke of the cane
79. BEARING FALSE WITNESS: A Slapping
80. CHALKING SCHOOL WALLS:
1 stroke of the cane
81. FRIGHTENING LITTLE GIRLS IN THE PLAYGROUND: 1 stroke of the cane
82. DISTURBING GIRLS PREMISES:
1 stroke of the cane
83. THROWING WATER OVER CHILD:
1 stroke of the cane
84. DEFIANCE: 1 or 2 strokes
85. DEFIANCE OF THE TEACHER: A Whipping
86. SCRIBBLING WITH PENCIL ON BOY'S CLEAN COLLAR: 2 strokes of cane
87. MAKING NOISES WITH THE MOUTH:
1 stroke of the cane
88. CONTINUALLY TAKING LUNCH FROM SMALLER BOY: 2 strokes of cane

89. SPENDING BANK MONEY:
2 strokes of the cane
90. ASSISTING TO SPEND BANK MONEY:
1 stroke of the cane
91. MAKING RUDE REMARKS ABOUT HIS TEACHER: 2 strokes of the cane
92. DISTURBING THE GIRLS SCHOOL:
1 stroke of the cane
93. RUNNING INTO THE GIRLS' SCHOOL YARD:
1 stroke of the cane
94. TURNING ON THE CARETAKER'S TAP IN THE OFFICE: 2 strokes of the cane
95. WILFULLY SPOILING HIS DRAWING:
1 stroke of the cane
96. BRINGING MATCHES TO SCHOOL:
1 stroke of the cane
97. PLAYING WITH OR STRIKING MATCHES:
1 or 2 strokes of the cane
98. PLAYING WITH MATCHES AND SETTING FIRE TO THE PAPER IN THE WASTE PAPER PIPE: 2 strokes of the cane
99. MAKING A SCENE WHEN SPOKEN TO:
2 strokes of the cane
100. KEEPING BACK CRAYONS:
2 strokes of the cane
101. KEEPING ANOTHER CHILD'S BALL:
2 strokes of the cane
102. KEEPING ANOTHER BOY'S HALFPENNY AND TELLING UNTRUTHS ABOUT IT:
2 strokes of the cane
103. PLAYING IN CLOAKROOM, THEN THROWING A HAT ON THE GAS:
2 Slight smacks on palm of his hands
104. THROWING HIS PENCIL ON THE FLOOR:
1 stroke of the cane
105. LAUGHING OR TALKING IN CLASS:
1 stroke of the cane
106. TALKING AND LAUGHING REPEATEDLY:
2 strokes of the cane

Well, that's the lot. I hope you found these entries taken from the school's Record of Punishments book to be interesting.

Limited Edition Book

The following list is of people who wanted to be part of our limited edition collectors copy of "Sheffield Folk".

Every publication of the special edition will be signed and personally numbered by Bob Horton and will also be recognised by its own limited edition cover.

James Larkin

Leonard Forrester

Christine Openshaw

Marian Barnsley

Dennis Turner

Micheal Tooley

Howard J Goodison

Margaret Joel

Gary Sherwin

Sarah Woodhead

June Greathead

Philip Anthony Outram

Stanley Barton

Stewart Leslie Boswell

The Tickhill Family

Big Ada

Brian Ward

David James Payton

Mary Highfield

Catherine Gibson

Terry Buxton

William Evison

W H Bushell

Alwyn Russell

Geoffrey Barton Moore

Mr Harvey Howe

Mrs Patricia Mills

Richard Hobson

Margaret Gladwin

Trevor

Tony Medlicott

Bob Swain

Pauline

Vi Levick

Lee Bunting

Mr Stanley Robinson

Darren Eyre

David L Helghington

June B Stancer

Percy G Moxon

Harry Sadler

Margaret Holland

John David North

Karl D Halliday

Eric Shipley

Roy Milner

Roy Young

Dorothy Robinson

Douglas

Margaret

Carol

Stephen Redfern

Jeremy H Crawshaw

Kevin James Murdock

Margaret and Eric

Martyn John Horton

Michael J Elam

Elsie Isaac

Darryl Graham Lomas

John Naylor

Lynda Hodgson

William Elliott

Sadie Turner

Derek Tingle

Janet

Eric Hollin

Keith Cowley

David Roger Wright

Alf Hird

Margaret

Joyce Lockley

Jean Foster

John Fletcher

Linda Pass

Ivan Edward Hayter

Roy Dimelow

Robert Michael Prestwood

Gordon Gregory

Wayne Smallwood

Terry (For his Birthday)

Jean Margaret Brown

Colin Morton

Norman Johnson

Marian Hodgson

Anthony Higgins

Nev Furness

Fred Bridgman

Mrs J Ward

John Mason

Mrs Ann E Barton

Sheila

Barrie Garton

Sam Leary

Jennifer Mary McDermott

Dorothy Sampson

Alan Whitehouse

C J Wells

Nellie Mitchell

Freda Williams

Anthony Wilson

A K Jennings

Michael Collier

Mr Thomas Harrison (Dad)

William Flint

Peter Webster

Lottie France

David Allsop

Steve Shaw

Jean Bland

Derek Barnett

Edward Bonsall

Henry Bestall

Colin Brown

Joan

Mary F Ashton

Mrs M J Bennett

Dave Furness

Mrs C Riches

I Ford

Ron and Irene Ives

James Mappin

Roger

Alan D Fisher

Michael Bladen

Timothy Hawnt

Don Law

Tim Aitken

George Jacklin

Aileen Ellis

Gerry Ancell

Aileen Ellis

Peter

Kenneth Clayton

John Ludlam

The Revill Family

Michael Taylor

Mrs Shirley Eddleston

Michael Keith

Bob Horton

Doug and Nellie Hinchcliffe

Damian Murray

Paul Adamson

Mark Pearson

Kenneth Parkin

Alan Dungworth

Mr Ernie Bland

Mrs J E Bramwell

Walter Saunderson

Brian W Tasker

Connie Richardson

Stephen Anthony Holmes

Frank West

Margaret Blockley

Jack Cotterill

James Brian Whitham

Stuart Gillott

Daniel R Flannagan

Tom Turner

John Janiszewski

Geoff Walker

Mr Douglas Mills

Allan Phillpots

To Maureen

Shirley from Mum and Dad

Sue Smith

Mary Winifrede Downs

David Higton

Mrs V Redfern

M J Morley

Roy Vincent Johnson

All the Oggy's

Anthony

Jack Birkinshaw

Michael Russell Hague

"Stanley Scriven ""Dad"""

Norman Heron

Alex Lavender

Malcolm Ward

Dave Peckett

Neil Flint

Roger Poxon

Jimmy Peaker

William Tyzack

Charles

Pank

Terry Gateley

David Boucher

June Harrison

Harry Swift

Lynda Crofts

Neil Haythorne

Paul Freer

Steve James

Kenneth James Doleman

Marjorie Ward

Frank Browse

Bryan Greenwood

The Warnes Family

Olive Herrett

Michael Melia

Josie Fiddler

To Renee

Paul Eastwood

Vincent Lawless

Brian Boulding love Tracey xx

Julie Skelton

Sylvia Unwin J.P

Colleen Wainman

Gary Cardwell

Ian

David Bartles

Pam Armstrong

Dot Brand

Janet E Jenkinson

David Alan Kennell

John Hopewell

Arthur Dixon

Grahame Anthony Smith

David Wayne Smith

Nelly Baines

Brian Fletcher

Eileen

Jack Lee

R.E Hughes

Alan Oliver

Jean Bradley

Winnifred Bacon

Andrew Lawson

Ray Brown

Audrey Commander

Paul Digby

Dennis Wilman

Jonathan Hague

Rodger Gordon

Leonard Burgin

Raymond Allwood

David Fletcher

Brian

Fred Wattam

Howard Jones

Merv Anwyl

Alan Walker

Brian Millward

Kath

Sandra

Doug Rhodes

George W Revill

Barbara

Benny Gibson

Andrew Moat

Lynne

E Redfern

A Redfern

Roger Butcher

The Flanagan Family

Brett Taylor

Stephen Fidment

Anna Wager

S E Herring

Janice B Walker

Hilda Legge

Brenda & Jim Swaby

Robert Fredrick Hallam

John Richard Goodinson

Olwen

Rod Dyer

Gordon Briggs

Barrie

Dennis Oxspring

Derrick Greaves

Fredrick Dalton

Frank Skinner

Betsy & Ernest

Eric Foster

Malcolm Andrews

Roger & Marlene

Malcolm Fellows

Stan Phillips

Clifford Merrill

Steven Brian Holmes

Jim Wilkinson

Brian Skinner

Hazel Hall

Brian Haythorne

Mary Haigh Glover

Timothy J Pickford

Ronnie Allen

Christopher Gibson

Josie. A Special Mum and Nan

Mr and Mrs J G Poulton

N A Lifford

Peter Halliday

Kevin Gregory

Ronald Marsden

Fredrick Micheal Ring

Grace Robinson

Oliver

Nellie Hall

Jo and Michael

Charles Butler

Keith Webster

Barry Joell

Graham Kirk

Glenyse Mary Furniss

James Armstrong

Kevin Arnold Briggs

Dennis Tobin

Paul Rawlings

A W Rider

Carol Hurst

Andrew

Ken Taylor

Roy and Carol Hellewell

Susan Sanderson

Russ Goddard

Mr Stuart Dawson

Vincent Ronald Gash

Dennis Kitchen

Frances Annie

Graham Knight

The Fieldhouse Family

Daryll Palmer

Alan Lowis

Wilfred James Peet

Derek Pickering (with love from your Daughter)

Michael Walker